The End of the Unrepentant

The End of the Unrepentant

A Study of the Biblical Themes of Fire and Being Consumed

J. WEBB MEALY

WIPF & STOCK · Eugene, Oregon

THE END OF THE UNREPENTANT
A Study of the Biblical Themes of Fire and Being Consumed

Copyright © 2013 J. Webb Mealy. All rights reserved. Except for brief quotations in critical publications or reviews, no part of this book may be reproduced in any manner without prior written permission from the publisher. Write: Permissions, Wipf and Stock Publishers, 199 W. 8th Ave., Suite 3, Eugene, OR 97401.

Wipf & Stock
An Imprint of Wipf and Stock Publishers
199 W. 8th Ave., Suite 3
Eugene, OR 97401

www.wipfandstock.com

ISBN 13: 978-1-62032-710-4

Manufactured in the U.S.A.

S.D.G.

Contents

  Introduction: What This Book Is and How to Read It · 1

1 Surveying OT Passages That Picture Fire and Being Consumed · 7

2 Surveying Passages from the NT Gospels and Epistles That Picture Fire and Being Consumed · 35

3 Surveying Passages in the Book of Revelation That Picture Fire and Being Consumed · 75

4 The Changing of the Ages in the Old Testament · 97

5 The Changing of the Ages in the New Testament · 139

6 Future Judgment and Resurrection in the New Testament · 150

7 Answering Unresolved Questions from Chapter 2 · 192

8 The End of the Unrepentant: Hermeneutical and Theological Conclusion · 205

  Appendix: Passages That Refer to Fire or Being Consumed, Organized by Recurring Themes · 251

  Scripture Index · 253

  Other Works Cited · 266

Introduction

What This Book Is and How to Read It

Don't be afraid of people who kill the body, but can't kill the soul.
Be more afraid of the One who can destroy both body and soul in Gehenna.
—Matthew 10:28

Who This Book is For

This book is for people who love God and love the Scriptures, but can't understand how a loving and just God could have a plan to torture human beings forever. If you believe that the Scriptures are trustworthy, but you have never felt at ease ethically with the doctrine of everlasting torment, then this book is for you.

What This Book Is

This book aims to be a rigorous and methodologically consistent examination of every passage in the Bible that employs the ideas of *fire* and *being consumed* in relation to the fate of the unrepentant. There are two specific reasons why I've defined the scope of the study in this way. The first is that the familiar word "hell," with its connotations of everlasting and fiery torment in some kind of underworld prison, does not come from any single word in the Bible—so I can't simply examine all the passages with the word "hell" in them. Hell is a conventional religious concept, not a biblical word.[1] The second

---

1. The King James translation renders four different biblical words or expressions with the English word "hell": (1) the Hebrew noun *she'ōl* (Strong's #H7585), which connotes the grave, or the dark, underworld repository of the spirits of the dead; (2) the Greek noun *geenna* (Strong's #G1067), a transliteration from Hebrew often rendered into English as "Gehenna," which pictures a ravine where the corpses of God's enemies are burned and completely disposed of (see Isa. 66:24; Mt. 5:29–30; 10:28); (3) the Greek noun *hadēs* (Strong's #G86), similar to *she'ōl*, and pictured as an underworld repository or prison for the spirits of the dead; and (4) the Greek verb *tartaroō* (Strong's #G5020), which means to confine a spirit entity (such as an angel) in the deepest, darkest parts of the underworld. Not one of these words

reason is that most people's ideas about the fate of the unrepentant are linked to a single statement by Jesus:

> It's better for you to go into the Kingdom of God with one eye, than to have two eyes, and get thrown into Gehenna—$_{48}$where "their worm doesn't die, and the fire doesn't get put out."[2]

In this one statement, we have images of fire and of being consumed as pictures of what will happen to the *bodies* of those are excluded from God's Kingdom. Jesus is quoting the 66th chapter of Isaiah in this saying, so understanding what Jesus means will require us to look closely at how Isaiah and the other prophets of the Old Testament (both before and after him) used this kind of imagery. In fact, every New Testament reference to a fiery final destiny for the unrepentant has deep roots in the thinking and imagery of the Old Testament. We are going to start at the beginning and look at it all.

This book, by nature, is not going to be an easy read. The reason for this is simple: the Bible has a lot to say on the subject we are going to be examining. Something like 170 biblical passages are relevant to the discussion. In addition, I'm going to have to be particularly methodical, because I'm going to be presenting an interpretive option that has been ferociously resisted by many in the Christian mainstream. The best way for me (or for you) to persuade people on this subject is to demonstrate that every relevant passage has been examined, and nothing has been swept under the carpet.

Many Bible teachers act as though they believe in the following logical argument:

> God wouldn't want us to be uncertain about anything.
> Bible teachings that were difficult to understand would make us uncertain.
> Therefore, every teaching in the Bible must be easy to understand.

In my view, people who are worried about being uncertain have no business teaching the Bible, because God's business always has been, and always will be, difficult for human beings to understand. As Peter says of the apostle Paul,

> There are certain things in his letters that are hard to understand—which ignorant and unstable people twist. They also do the same thing to the other scriptures—leading to their own destruction. (2 Pet. 3:16)

One of the most common ways of twisting the Scriptures is to oversimplify them for the sake of creating a nice, neat doctrine that can prop up a false sense of certainty. Some of the things I'm going to say are going to have some complexity, for the simple reason that the Scriptures themselves have some complexity. I don't need to apologize for that.

---

corresponds in any direct way with contemporary people's idea of an everlasting and fiery prison for the resurrected unrepentant.

2. Mk 9:43–48 || Mt. 18:8–9, quoting Isa. 66:24. Two parallel lines ("||") indicate that passages are parallel.

How I Came to Write This Book

I am a Christian, a believer in and follower of Jesus. God's grace enabled me to come to a personal and life-changing faith in Jesus Christ as a young man of 18. Since that moment, I have always loved reading the Bible, and over the course of the two years following my conversion, I read the Old Testament four times and the New Testament eight times. Since that time, I have probably read most passages within the covers of the Bible another twenty times, not including hearing the Scriptures read in worship. From the beginning, I have noticed that the overwhelming majority of Bible passages do not threaten the unrepentant with unending torment, but rather with the devastating tragedy of being refused entry to eternal life. I have found myself meditating on this fact, and wondering how to make theological sense of the handful of disturbing passages that seem to picture a fate of everlasting torment.

I had a breakthrough insight in my senior year of college, while I was writing a paper about the millennium in the book of Revelation. As I pondered John's words, I suddenly realized that the book of Revelation itself—the one and only book within the covers of the Bible that explicitly and unambiguously speaks of unending torment for the unrepentant—was offering an alternative vision of the ultimate fate of the unrepentant. Thanks to John's pointed repetition of the phrase "after the thousand years," I came to recognize in Rev. 20:7–10 a picture of the resurrection, judgment, and annihilation of the unrepentant. I then realized that his account of the end of the unrepentant had the same narrative structure (i.e. it shared the same story line) as the "Isaiah Apocalypse" of Isaiah 24–27. I continued meditating for many years upon Revelation's dual pictures of the end, and I ultimately presented my insights systematically in a book, *After the Thousand Years: Resurrection and Judgment in Revelation 20*.[3] This monograph currently stands as the single most thorough and methodologically rigorous exegesis of Revelation 20 ever published.

Over the years, I've always had the sense that my results in *After the Thousand Years* should and could be integrated with the teachings of the entire New Testament. As you will see, the results of this integration are going to be highly fruitful. Many passages in the New Testament are going to make sense for the first time, thanks to the illumination of Isaiah 24–27, which brought the millennium of Revelation 20 into focus for me. More than this, the Isaiah 24–27 paradigm will serve to clarify many relationships between passages. Passages that once seemed irreconcilable—or at best confusing in their relationship—will now make straightforward sense side by side.

The events that provided the immediate impetus for starting this long-contemplated project came last year in 2011, after the publication of Rob Bell's book, *Love Wins*.[4] In it, he dared to suggest that a contemporary Christian would be in good company among the luminaries of the Christian faith if they felt uneasy about the idea that God

---

3. JSNT Supplement Series, 70; Sheffield: Sheffield Academic Press, 1992. This was the published version of my PhD thesis of the same title, for which I received a doctorate in Biblical Studies from the University of Sheffield, Sheffield, England.

4. New York: HarperOne, 2011.

will torment people forever.[5] For his candor, he was subjected to a firestorm of criticism by conservative Christian teachers and preachers. He was the object of what can only be called a massive religious rage, and was branded as a dangerous heretic and false teacher. Bell is trained as a pastor and evangelist, not as a biblical scholar, but I'm convinced that his instincts are sound on this subject. I've decided that this is my opportunity to offer the insights I have gained over the years and to make the biblical case that he briefly sketched. This book is the fruition of my own biblical study.

How to Read This Book

The secret of reading this book is to get a sense of the method, and then read faster or slower, depending on your level of interest in each individual passage. The exhaustive nature of the study makes for a certain level of potential tedium (especially in Chapters 1 and 2) if you give equal attention to everything. So if you see a passage that is very much similar to another one that you have already seen explained in a way that you found satisfactory, and you're ready to move on, then feel free simply to skim, just to make sure that there's nothing of exceptional interest in the passage under discussion. If you have a concern to make sure that you don't miss anything, everything is here. But if you just want to get the highlights, then you can move along at a faster pace to suit yourself.

By all means use the original biblical language tools I have given you in the footnotes. You don't need to be a professional Bible scholar to evaluate my claims about what biblical words mean. All you need is a King James Bible and *Strong's Exhaustive Concordance* to examine every single biblical instance of a Greek or Hebrew word and decide for yourself. For this purpose, I highly recommend www.blueletterbible.org, an online resource that greatly streamlines this kind of Bible study. Just type an English word from the KJV in the *LexiConc*[6] search box, and you will see all the Hebrew and Greek words that are translated as that word in the KJV.

The Structure of the Argument

Chapters 1-3 contain a survey of every passage in the Bible that pictures fire or being consumed as a punishment for leading an unrepentant life.[7] The passages will be

---

5. *Love Wins*, pp. 107–11.

6. This is a combination of (1) dictionaries (lexicons) of original biblical languages and (2) a Bible concordance. The dictionaries are not the best currently available, being over a hundred years old, but they are serviceable.

7. For quotations of the Old Testament, unless otherwise noted, I have used the *New Revised Standard Version Bible*, copyright © 1989, by the Division of Christian Education of the National Council of the Churches of Christ in the United States of America. Used by permission. For quotations of the New Testament, I have used *The Spoken English New Testament: A New Translation from the Greek by J. Webb Mealy* (Preliminary Edition; Oakland, CA: SENT Press, 2008). This is my own scholarly translation of the New Testament. Its renderings are designed to be extremely close the Greek, while at the same time making the text as natural sounding and accessible as possible to non-Christians and new Christians. It is relatively free from Christian jargon, and completely free from archaic English. You can read it or purchase a copy online at www.sentpress.com.

examined in canonical order from Genesis 1 to Revelation 22. We will find that certain important questions arise that cannot be answered from the information available within this set of texts alone. In order to answer them, we will need to study what the Bible has to say about the future coming of God's Kingdom and the inauguration of a new age, and the relationship between that great transition and the expectation of future resurrection and judgment.

Chapters 4–5 take up this challenge. They survey all the passages in the Bible that look ahead to a great transition from the current age to an age of renewal, in which God's Kingdom is fully manifested throughout the world.

Chapter 6 examines all the passages in the Bible that contain the idea of resurrection. This chapter will also look carefully at the relationship between resurrection—both of the faithful and of the unfaithful—and the coming of a new age in which God's Kingdom rules on earth.

Chapter 7 finishes the exegetical work of the book by going back, with the knowledge gained in Chapters 4–6, to look for a second time at a small handful of passages from Chapter 2. These will be passages in which there was no immediate way to determine whether certain punishments pictured for the unrepentant were lengthy but limited in duration, on the one hand, or everlasting, on the other hand. By the end of Chapter 7, we will have demonstrated a biblically-based paradigm that results in a clear, consistent, and satisfying interpretation of all the passages that we have surveyed.

Chapter 8 is the conclusion of the book. It lays out the biblical theology and the understanding of the Christian Gospel that inform the view that I have presented. It also briefly critiques the theology that is often implicit in the belief that God torments people forever.

1

Surveying OT Passages That Picture Fire and Being Consumed

THE TASK OF THIS, our first chapter, is to undertake a careful survey of all the significant Bible passages in the Old Testament, from Genesis to Malachi, that refer to fire, burning, or being consumed as divine punishment of human beings. There are more than fifty of them, so we have our work cut out for us. We are going to discover that a number of recurring themes are associated with these images. I have identified nine of them as I have studied my way through the Scriptures, and I will be pointing them out for you as we go along. Let's discuss each of them briefly before we begin.

Theme 1. Instantness—In a number of passages, the role of fire in the text is going to make it clear that God's judgment has resulted or will result in a punishment that is *sudden* in its onset and *instant* in its destructive effects. The destruction of Sodom and Gomorrah in Genesis 19 is an example of this theme, as is Elijah's calling down of fire on the bands of soldiers sent to arrest him in 2 Kgs 1:10–14. A number of passages *predict* or *threaten*, as opposed to narrating, God's use of fire as a punishment, and a number of these predictions also presuppose an element of instantness (e.g. Ps. 11:6).

Theme 2. Completeness—Many of the passages are going to emphasize the idea that the fire of punishment results in *complete* destruction. One or both of two different kinds of completeness may be in view in a passage. There is the completeness of *breadth*, as when a prophecy predicts that the fire of destruction will sweep through a whole city or a whole country, destroying everything (e.g. Jer. 17:27; 21:10–14). There is also the completeness of *thoroughness*, as when the passage emphasizes the idea that the fire will *consume*, or *completely* burn something to ashes (e.g. 1 Kgs 14:10).

Theme 3. Irrevocability—The image of fire is often employed to express a divine *decision* to destroy someone or something. A number of our passages express the idea that the moment when God starts a fire (either metaphorically or literally) signals the point at which there is no going back on his decision to send destruction (e.g. 2 Kgs 22:16–17). In other words, the decision *cannot be revoked*. Irrevocability speaks of a kind of point of no return, beyond which there is no possibility of reversing the decision, and no possibility of undoing the effects of the destruction that has been decreed by the decision (e.g. Isa. 34:9–10).

Theme 4. Permanence—The image of fire and the idea of being consumed are often associated with the idea that the destruction being described or predicted is going to be *permanent*. In ancient times, before the advent of mechanized firefighting equipment, it was simply a fact of life that huge fires periodically burned down entire cities. Rebuilding typically began as soon as the ashes were cool. Sometimes, however, there are prophecies that a city will be burned down and never rebuilt. The figure of a fire that never stops smoldering is a prophetic way of expressing the assurance that the coming destruction is going to be permanent in its effects. For example, Isaiah 34 prophesies that the land of Edom will burn up, and will never stop smoldering (vv. 9–10). No one will ever replace or rebuild what has been destroyed.

Theme 5. Finality—The idea of *finality* is that of *completion* (as distinct from *completeness*). The *final* action is the action that completely resolves the situation that calls for the action, such that no further action will ever be required in relation to it. Some passages use the picture of fire to emphasize the idea that a problem or threat is going to be dealt with in such a way that it will never be a problem again (e.g. Isa. 66:22–24).

Theme 6. The Disposal of Trash—A number of passages associate fire and the idea of being consumed with the metaphorical idea that the guilty are going to be disposed of like trash. Sometimes the metaphor turns on the idea of household or urban waste (e.g. 1 Kgs 14:10), and sometimes it evokes agricultural or garden waste (e.g. Ezek. 15:1–8; Mt. 7:19).

Theme 7. The Unpreventable or Unstoppable Nature of the Destruction—Many passages associate fire or being consumed with the warning that a coming destruction is going to be impossible to resist, escape, or control (e.g. Deut. 28:26). The image of an "unquenchable" fire occurs many times, and in each case the force of the imagery is that the fire will be impossible to put out until it has succeeded in completely burning up and destroying whatever it is that God has sent it to destroy (e.g. 2 Kgs 22:16–17 || 2 Chron. 34:25).

Theme 8. The Impermanence of Human Life—Language about fire and being consumed is not infrequently accompanied by a reminder that the life of the unrepentant is corruptible and will not go on forever (e.g. Isa. 51:8; Jas 5:2–3).

Theme 9. Anguish—In a few passages, pictures of fire and burning are accompanied by descriptions of physical or emotional distress on the part of the fire's victims (e.g. Isa. 50:11; Mt. 13:50).

Book-by-Book Exposition of Old Testament Passages

Genesis 19:24–28

> ²⁴Then the Lord rained on Sodom and Gomorrah sulfur and fire from the Lord out of heaven; ²⁵and he overthrew those cities, and all the Plain, and all the inhabitants of the cities, and what grew on the ground . . . ²⁷Abraham went early in the morning to the place where he had stood before the Lord; ²⁸and he looked down towards Sodom and Gomorrah and towards all the land of the Plain, and saw the smoke of the land going up like the smoke of a furnace.

These verses are excerpted from the famous story of fire and brimstone (i.e. sulfur) raining down from the sky and destroying the cities of Sodom and Gomorrah (Gen. 19:12–29). From it readers learn that if you insist on living destructively, it's possible that God will destroy you, in a way that is **1** instant, **2** complete, **3** irrevocable, **4** permanent, and **5** final. The fate of these cities is the fate of being wiped out, annihilated, gone forever. Supposedly, no one lived in that location ever again.

Numbers 16:23–35

> [Context: in Num. 16:1–22, Korah, a Levite, joins with Dathan and Abiram, descendents of Reuben, to rebel against the leadership of Moses and Aaron. Their claim is that Moses and Aaron have fraudulently appointed themselves to be God's sole ministers. Everyone, they say, is equally worthy of performing priestly roles, and everyone should be allowed to minister to God (vv. 1–3). Moses calls their bluff, and invites them to present themselves to God the next morning for God's determination (vv. 16–17). Verses 23–35 narrate the showdown.]
>
> ²³ And the Lord spoke to Moses, saying: ²⁴ Say to the congregation: Get away from the dwellings of Korah, Dathan, and Abiram . . . ²⁸ And Moses said, "This is how you shall know that the Lord has sent me to do all these works; it has not been of my own accord: ²⁹ If these people die a natural death, or if a natural fate comes on them, then the Lord has not sent me. ³⁰ But if the Lord creates something new, and the ground opens its mouth and swallows them up, with all that belongs to them, and they go down alive into Sheol, then you shall know that these men have despised the Lord."
>
> ³¹ As soon as he finished speaking all these words, the ground under them was split apart. ³² The earth opened its mouth and swallowed them up, along with their households—everyone who belonged to Korah and all their goods. ³³ So they with all that belonged to them went down alive into Sheol; the earth closed over them, and they perished from the midst of the assembly. ³⁴ All Israel around them fled at their outcry, for they said, "The earth will swallow us too!" ³⁵ And fire came out from the Lord and consumed the two hundred and fifty men offering the incense.

The End of the Unrepentant

This graphic story suggests that high-handed rebellion against God, and attack on God's faithful and holy servants, puts you at risk of **1** instant, **2** complete, and **7** inescapable destruction by God. The earth instantly swallows up Korah and his people, and fire instantly consumes Dathan and Abiram and their supporters.

Deuteronomy 28:26 (including material from 28:15 for context)

> ¹⁵But if you will not obey the Lord your God . . . ²⁶Your corpses shall be food for every bird of the air and animal of the earth, and there shall be no one to frighten them away.

Verse 26 is a statement among the curses the Israelites agree to face if they break the covenant promises they have made with God at Sinai. The text threatens a **2** complete, **3** irrevocable, and **7** unpreventable judgment in which your corpse is entirely eaten on the open ground rather than being given an honorable burial. This theme of a cursed death and being eaten by wild animals—with no hope of anyone or anything stopping the process—is going to appear in relation to the figure of the accursed emperor king (popularly seen as the antichrist) in Isa. 14:18–20. It will also be seen in relation to the armies of the Beast (who is himself an evil emperor figure) in Rev. 19:17–21.

Deuteronomy 29:19–28

> ¹⁹ All who hear the words of this oath and bless themselves, thinking in their hearts, "We are safe even though we go our own stubborn ways" (thus bringing disaster on moist and dry alike)— ²⁰ the Lord will be unwilling to pardon them, for the Lord's anger and passion will smoke against them. All the curses written in this book will descend on them, and the Lord will blot out their names from under heaven. ²¹ The Lord will single them out from all the tribes of Israel for calamity, in accordance with all the curses of the covenant written in this book of the law. ²² The next generation, your children who rise up after you, as well as the foreigner who comes from a distant country, will see the devastation of that land and the afflictions with which the Lord has afflicted it— ²³ all its soil burned out by sulfur and salt, nothing planted, nothing sprouting, unable to support any vegetation, like the destruction of Sodom and Gomorrah, Admah and Zeboiim, which the Lord destroyed in his fierce anger— ²⁴ they and indeed all the nations will wonder, "Why has the Lord done thus to this land? What caused this great display of anger?" ²⁵ They will conclude, "It is because they abandoned the covenant of the Lord, the God of their ancestors, which he made with them when he brought them out of the land of Egypt. ²⁶ They turned and served other gods, worshipping them, gods whom they had not known and whom he had not allotted to them; ²⁷ so the anger of the Lord was kindled against that land, bringing on it every curse written in this book. ²⁸ The Lord uprooted them from their land in anger, fury, and great wrath, and cast them into another land, as is now the case."

Surveying OT Passages That Picture Fire and Being Consumed

This passage comes in the middle of a series of warnings that Moses gives to the Israelites after they have received the Sinai Covenant (Deut. 28:16–68).[1] Moses employs the metaphor of God's wrath as a fire that first smolders dangerously (v. 20), then bursts into flame (v. 27). Verse 23 compares the fate of the stubborn idolaters to that of Sodom and Gomorrah and the nearby towns, which suffered an inundation of fire and sulfur (sulfur was known in the ancient world as an exceptionally hot-burning substance). If certain Israelites, who are bound by oath under the Sinai Covenant, form an attitude of stubbornness and arrogance in flouting the covenant, then they should not expect any leniency from God. God is not going to look the other way, nor is he going to change his mind and forgive them (v. 20); nor is what happens going to be some sort of chastisement from which the insolent can hope to recover their previous position of grace and good standing under the covenant. On the contrary, their names are going to be "blotted out from under heaven" (v. 20), i.e., they are going to be put to death. The sense of the **2** completeness, **3** irrevocability, **4** permanence, and **7** unpreventability of the judgment are the main themes in evidence here. The comparison to Sodom and Gomorrah could perhaps suggest the theme of **1** instantness, but that is not emphasized.

1 Kings 14:10

> [10] I will bring evil upon the house of Jeroboam. I will cut off from Jeroboam every male, both bond and free, in Israel and will consume the house of Jeroboam, just as one burns up dung until it is all gone.

The prophet is saying that God is someday going to wipe out the family line of Jeroboam completely. He uses the simile of burning excrement until it is totally gone. The reference to fire here functions to emphasize that the destruction coming is one that is **2** complete and **5** final. Finality refers to a destructive process having a definite end at which point it is finished. Note how the words "consume" and "consumed" are being used here and in further references below. Use of the concept of "consume" is a way of bringing out the idea that the destruction being pictured is **2** complete. When you are eating something, less and less is left of it as you eat more and more. When you've consumed it, none of it is left. Another concept that comes in here is that the party being destroyed will be **6** treated as you treat trash. In the ancient world they didn't have skip-loaders or other large earth-moving machines to bury trash—they burned it.

2 Kings 1:9–15

> [9] Then the king sent to him [the prophet Elijah] a captain of fifty with his fifty men. He went up to Elijah, who was sitting on the top of a hill, and said to him, "O man of God, the king says, 'Come down.' " [10] But Elijah answered the captain of fifty, "If I am a man of God, let fire come down from heaven and

---

1. The warnings section follows and corresponds to a speech promising a full spectrum of blessings that the Israelites will experience if they obey the Sinai Covenant (Deut. 28:1–14).

The End of the Unrepentant

> consume you and your fifty." Then fire came down from heaven, and consumed him and his fifty.
>
> [11] Again the king sent to him another captain of fifty with his fifty. He went up and said to him, "O man of God, this is the king's order: Come down quickly!" [12] But Elijah answered them, "If I am a man of God, let fire come down from heaven and consume you and your fifty." Then the fire of God came down from heaven and consumed him and his fifty.
>
> [13] Again the king sent the captain of a third fifty with his fifty. So the third captain of fifty went up, and came and fell on his knees before Elijah, and entreated him, "O man of God, please let my life, and the life of these fifty servants of yours, be precious in your sight. [14] Look, fire came down from heaven and consumed the two former captains of fifty men with their fifties; but now let my life be precious in your sight." [15] Then the angel of the Lord said to Elijah, "Go down with him; do not be afraid of him." So he set out and went down with him to the king . . .

This story, of course, recalls the story of the destruction of Sodom and Gomorrah by fire from heaven in Genesis 19 as well as the fiery destruction of Dathan and Abiram in Numbers 16. All three stories share the themes of **1** instant, **2** complete, and **7** inescapable destruction. Beyond this, the three stories also demonstrate that it is gravely hazardous to assume you can attack the representatives of God with impunity simply because you are stronger and more numerous than they are. Later in this study, we're going to discover that such stories are surprisingly relevant to the question of what ultimately happens to the unrepentant.

2 Kings 22:16–17 ‖ 2 Chronicles 34:25

> [16] Thus says the Lord, Behold, I will bring disaster upon this place and upon its inhabitants, all the words of the book that the king of Judah has read. [17] Because they have abandoned me and have made offerings to other gods, so that they have provoked me to anger with all the work of their hands, therefore my wrath will be kindled against this place, and it will not be quenched.

These are the words of the prophetess Huldah to Josiah, king of Judah. In her prophecy, God's wrath—the destructive expression of his anger—is metaphorically described as a fire which, once it is set alight, will completely burn Jerusalem ("this place") down. The "book that the king of Judah has read" (v. 16) is almost certainly some version of the book that we know as Deuteronomy. The prophecy by Huldah makes contemporary for the time of Josiah the dire warnings of Deuteronomy 29, which we looked at above. The image of a fire that cannot be put out (v. 17) evokes the themes of **2** completeness, **3** irrevocability, and **7** unpreventability.

Psalm 11:5–6

> ⁵ The Lord tests the righteous and wicked,
>   and his soul hates the lover of violence.
> ⁶ On the wicked he will rain coals of fire and sulfur;
>   a scorching wind shall be the portion of their cup.

The picture of God raining down fire and sulfur recalls the destruction of Sodom and Gomorrah in Genesis 19, and brings the theme of **1** instant and **2** complete destruction. The "scorching wind" may possibly be underlining this by developing a metaphor based on an agricultural disaster. The life of the wicked will be instantly destroyed, just as one's crops can suddenly be scorched and killed by a disastrous hot windstorm. It is more likely, however, that the scorching wind refers to the ferocious torrent of fire (v. 6a) that comes down on the lover of violence.

Psalm 21:8–11

> ⁸ Your hand will find out all your enemies;
>   your right hand will find out those who hate you.
> ⁹ You will make them like a fiery furnace
>   when you appear.
> The Lord will swallow them up in his wrath,
>   and fire will consume them.
> ¹⁰ You will destroy their offspring from the earth,
>   and their children from among humankind.
> ¹¹ If they plan evil against you,
>   if they devise mischief, they will not succeed.

It's hard to tell here whether it is the Lord or Israel's king who is being addressed in v. 8. If we read this as a messianic psalm, however, the outcome is equivalent. As Paul says, Christ is God's agent for destroying all the forces of rebellion and death (1 Cor. 15:21–28).

Fire here is associated with the themes of **2** complete and **3** irrevocable destruction. Once you're *swallowed up* by fire, you're gone for good (v. 9). The next verse (v. 10) underlines this by assuring the readers that this generation of enemies will not simply be replaced by a new generation that rises up: the threat from enemies will be **4** permanently removed.

Isaiah 1:28

> ²⁸ But rebels and sinners shall be destroyed together, and those who forsake the Lord shall be consumed.

This passage, by using the metaphor of a "consuming" destruction, states the general principle that sinful people are going to be **2** completely destroyed.

The End of the Unrepentant

Isaiah 26:10–11

> [10] If favor is shown to the wicked,
>   they do not learn righteousness;
> in the land of uprightness they deal perversely
>   and do not see the majesty of the LORD.
> [11] O LORD, your hand is lifted up,
>   but they do not see it.
> Let them see your zeal for your people, and be ashamed.
>   Let the fire for your adversaries consume them.

This picture of destruction brings out its **1** instantness and **2** completeness. The invaders think that they are going to attack and defeat God's people without resistance, and they don't have a clue what is just about to happen. Isaiah prays that God will strike them with breathtaking swiftness, and that fire will inundate them and devour them completely. Note the strong similarities between this passage and Ps. 21:8–11, above. Both focus on the treachery of the enemies, and both speak of fire "consuming" them.[2]

Isaiah 33:11–12

> [11] You conceive chaff, you bring forth stubble;
>   your breath is a fire that will consume you.
> [12] And the peoples will be as if burned to lime,
>   like thorns cut down, that are burned in the fire.

This passage emphasizes the idea of the people being **6** disposed of like trash. Chaff and stubble are the parts of the grain-bearing plant that are separated from the edible part. They are typically burned. Thorns are annoying weeds, useless "trash" plants that are no good for anything except burning. The word "consume" points to **2** completeness, as does the phrase "burned to lime," which means burned completely to ashes (ashes + water = lime). Significantly, Isaiah here and elsewhere (see Isa. 50:11, below) prophesies that people's own destructiveness will be the thing that ultimately destroys them: *"your breath is a fire that will consume you."*

Isaiah 33:14

> [14] The sinners in Zion are afraid;
>   trembling has seized the godless:
> "Who among us can live with the devouring fire?
>   Who among us can live with everlasting flames?"

The word "devour" here points to **2** completeness. What are "everlasting flames"? Since they "consume" people, it appears that they are flames that can threaten generation after generation. That is, the flames of destruction never seem to go away from the sinful

---

2. In both passages, the Hebrew verb translated "consume" is *'akal* (Strong's #H398), and the Greek word in the LXX translation is *katesthiō* (Strong's #G2719).

people as a group— they are always burning someone up. The Hebrew word translated as "everlasting" here is *'olam*,[3] which has a number of possible connotations, including "age-old," "perpetual," "long-lasting," and "lifelong." Unlike the word "everlasting" in English, the Hebrew word *'olam* does not necessarily imply unendingness at all. There are dozens of places in the Hebrew Bible where *'olam* simply means "long-lasting," and an explicit temporal end-point of the process being described as *'olam* can be found in the context.

It's useful to read this Isaiah 33 passage in context of the events that it is discussing. The circumstance behind the text is that the king of Assyria was marauding around with his army and burning down one city after another; hence Isaiah was prophesying that unless Judah repented, all its cities, even including Jerusalem, would be burnt to the ground. It may well be that the typical resident of Jerusalem being quoted in Isa. 33:14 is saying that everyone is finding it intolerable living with the continuous threat of having their city burned down.

Isaiah 34:2–3

> [2] For the LORD is enraged against all the nations,
>   and furious against all their hordes;
>   he has doomed them, has given them over for slaughter.
> [3] Their slain shall be cast out,
>   and the stench of their corpses shall rise;
>   the mountains shall flow with their blood.

This passage concentrates on the idea that those being destroyed are **6** going to be thrown out like trash. Dead people were supposed to be buried properly, whereas trash was simply thrown into a ravine outside the city and burned. (For the theme of burning, see the next passage, just a few verses further on in Isaiah.) Ancient garbage dumps stank just like modern ones, especially from the smell of decomposing scraps of meat—in this case, the meat of human flesh.

Isaiah 34:9–10

> [9] And the streams of Edom shall be turned into pitch,
>   and her soil into sulfur;
>   her land shall become burning pitch.
> [10] Night and day it shall not be quenched;
>   its smoke shall go up forever.
> From generation to generation it shall lie waste;
>   no one shall pass through it forever and ever.

Pitch (i.e. tar) and sulfur are both absolutely toxic to plant life, and they are known to burn extremely hot together. The idea is that Edom's land is going to be made **4** permanently uninhabitable because there will be no way to grow food, and no water to drink.

---

3. See Strong's #H5769.

The End of the Unrepentant

When an ancient army defeated a nation they were invading, and burned down their croplands, that was a very serious setback for the defeated country, but it wasn't permanent. They could grow new crops starting the next growing season. From the perspective of the Judahites, the problem with sworn enemies such as the Edomites was that even if God defeated them, they were presumably going to bounce back. Ancient peoples' experience was that all cities (including those of their enemies) periodically burnt to the ground—whether by accidental fires or by war—and that they were simply rebuilt again. This prophecy is picturing a situation in which the Israelites will never have to worry about their Edomite enemies rebuilding again, because the Edomites will never again be able to inhabit their land at all. Edom will be a permanent toxic wasteland. Paradoxically, it may well be that the only thoroughly effective way of conveying the concept of a **2** complete, **3** irrevocable, and above all **5** final, defeat of enemies to the imagination of the ancient Israelites was to picture a scenario that did not on its literal level have the nature of "finality"—since it was pictured as going on and on indefinitely. What is being pictured here in prophetic imagery is truly a "final" defeat of the Edomites.

Isaiah 47:14–15

> ¹⁴ See, they are like stubble,
>   the fire consumes them;
> they cannot deliver themselves
>   from the power of the flame.
> No coal for warming oneself is this,
>   no fire to sit before!
> ¹⁵ Such to you are those with whom you have labored,
>   who have trafficked with you from your youth;
> they all wander about in their own paths;
>   there is no one to save you.

Reference to stubble brings in the idea of **6** trash, together with the idea of **1** instantness, because stubble takes fire and burns up in a flash, with a big "whoosh." "Consume" brings in **2** completeness. The phrases "this is no coal for warming yourself" and "there is no one to save you" bring in the idea that the destruction is **3** irrevocable and **7** unpreventable. This is not a fire that can be managed, extinguished, or domesticated in any way by human effort. Once it touches you, you are rapidly consumed like stubble.

Isaiah 50:9 || Isa. 51:8

> ⁹ It is the Lord God who helps me;
>   who will declare me guilty?
> All of them will wear out like a garment;
>   the moth will eat them up.

This passage and its parallel bring in the theme of the **8** impermanence of God's enemies—the fact that they are by nature mortal and subject to decay and destruction. God's enemies are going to be destroyed because they have nothing permanent in themselves. Despite the idea of the guilty being eaten up, theme **2** (completeness) is not strongly present, since moths make a lot of holes, but don't generally eat something up entirely. Closer is the theme of **6** being disposed of like trash, because moth-ruined garments become "worn out," and worn-out garments are thrown away (Ps. 102:26).

Isaiah 50:11

> [11] But all of you are kindlers of fire,
>   lighters of firebrands.[4]
> Walk in the flame of your fire,
>   and among the brands that you have kindled!
> This is what you shall have from my hand:
>   you shall lie down in torment.

This passage is speaking to those who are highly destructive, and don't realize that their destructiveness is going to end up destroying *them*. Isaiah seems to be saying that eventually they're going to set *themselves* on fire.[5] Isa. 50:11 is the first passage in the Old Testament to introduce the theme of **9** anguish or pain. If this passage intends to evoke physical, as distinct from emotional, pain, then it seems to be saying that those who are destructive will not be able to put their own fire out, when they suddenly realize that it is now burning them. From time immemorial, the wise thing to do if your clothing catches on fire has always been to roll on the ground to put out the flames. But these people will simply lie there in agony. Their self-inflicted destruction is being pictured as **7** unpreventable, once it starts. If, on the other hand, the pain characterized here is *not* intended to be understood as physical pain,[6] then it probably is to be understood as the pain of regret and remorse that in destroying others, one has destroyed oneself as well. The passage would then foreshadow Isa. 65:11–15 (see below).

---

4. According to the NRSV footnotes, the rendering "you lighters of firebrands" follows the Syriac (an ancient translation from the original Hebrew). The Hebrew text of Isaiah says, "you clothe yourselves with firebrands."

5. Or, if we follow the Hebrew (see previous note), they don't realize that they are currently on fire with the destructiveness with which they have clothed themselves.

6. The exact meaning of the Hebrew word *ma'atsebah* (Strong's #H4620), which NRSV translates here as "torment," is difficult to determine, because it only occurs in this one verse in the entire Hebrew Bible. The LXX, the earliest translation of the OT, renders it as *lupē* (Strong's #G3077), which most often refers to sorrow, grief, and emotional distress, rather than physical pain. The Vulgate similarly renders it as *dolor*, which is also a word most often referring to sorrow and grief, rather than physical pain.

The End of the Unrepentant

Isaiah 51:6–8

> ⁶ Lift up your eyes to the heavens,
>   and look at the earth beneath;
> for the heavens will vanish like smoke,
>   the earth will wear out like a garment,
>   and those who live on it will die like gnats;
> but my salvation will be forever,
>   and my deliverance will never be ended . . .
> ⁷ Do not fear the reproach of others,
>   and do not be dismayed when they revile you.
> ⁸ For the moth will eat them up like a garment,
>   and the worm will eat them like wool;
> but my deliverance will be forever,
>   and my salvation to all generations.

Again the theme of **8** impermanence is being brought in. The heavens will "vanish like smoke"—the proverbial impermanent substance. Those who are against God will "die like gnats"—creatures proverbial for having a fleeting lifespan. "The moth will eat them up like a garment, and the worm will eat them like wool" repeats the idea that the wicked are utterly impermanent, and subject to decay and destruction, but God's salvation extends on into the infinite future, "to all generations." The disappearance of the earth itself signals the **2** complete, **3** irrevocable, and **7** unpreventable character of the destruction that faces the enemies of God. You can't run away from destruction when the entire earth is destroyed under you, and the heavens are destroyed above you. The earth "wearing out like a garment" also brings in the theme of **6** trash—the worn out garment becomes something to throw away.

Isaiah 51:12

> ¹² I, I am he who comforts you;
>   why then are you afraid of a mere mortal who must die,
>   a human being who fades like grass?

This passage, only a few verses down from our previous passage, Isa. 51:6–8, is a reference to the theme of **8** the impermanence of the wicked. Whether Isaiah prophesies fire, or worm, or moth, or death, or fading like grass, to picture their end, it's always in support of one idea: The wicked *don't last forever*.

Isaiah 65:13–15

> ¹³ Therefore thus says the Lord God:
> My servants shall eat,
>   but you shall be hungry;
> my servants shall drink,
>   but you shall be thirsty;
> my servants shall rejoice,
>   but you shall be put to shame;
> ¹⁴ my servants shall sing for gladness of heart,
>   but you shall cry out for pain of heart,
>   and shall wail for anguish of spirit.
> ¹⁵ You shall leave your name to my chosen to use as a curse,
>   and the Lord God will put you to death . . .

This passage develops the theme of **9** intense anguish or pain that forms the clear OT background of Jesus' language of "weeping and gnashing of teeth" (see Lk. 13:28). The anguish pictured in this Isaiah passage, as in the Lk. 13 passage that will allude to it, is that of *frustrated desire*. It is the anguish of those who are cast outside the realm of blessing and are looking in with an intense yearning that has no power to fulfill itself. And what is the ultimate destiny of these miserable and frustrated outcasts? "You shall leave your name to my chosen to use as a curse, and the Lord God will put you to death" (v. 15; cf. Isa. 66:24, discussed below). The last thing these judged ones do before they are executed is to see—and to fully recognize—the goodness and beauty that they, by their own choice, have irrevocably thrown away by refusing to listen when God called out to them: "I will destine you to the sword, and all of you shall bow down to the slaughter; because when I called, you did not answer, and when I spoke, you did not listen, but you did what was evil in my sight" (65:12).

Isaiah 66:14–16

> ¹⁴ You shall see, and your heart shall rejoice;
> ¹⁵ For the Lord will come in fire,
>   and his chariots like the whirlwind,
> to pay back his anger in fury,
>   and his rebuke in flames of fire.
> ¹⁶ For by fire will the Lord execute judgment,
>   and by his sword, on all flesh;
>   and those slain by the Lord shall be many.

This passage pictures a radical world-judgment that will spell the vindication and rescue of those faithful to God (v. 15), and the putting to death of everyone else ("all flesh," v. 16). The only one of our recurring themes that is clearly visible here is that of **2** completeness. All of God's enemies are going to be slain, and the repeated mention of fire cannot help but connote the thoroughness of the judgment that is being pictured.

The End of the Unrepentant

Isaiah 66:22–24

> [22] For as the new heavens and the new earth,
>   which I will make,
> shall remain before me, says the LORD,
>   so shall your descendants and your name remain.
> [23] From new moon to new moon,
>   and from Sabbath to Sabbath,
> all flesh shall come to worship before me,
> says the LORD.
>
> [24] And they shall go out and look at the dead bodies of the people who have rebelled against me; for their worm shall not die, their fire shall not be quenched, and they shall be an abhorrence to all flesh.

There are some important things to notice about this, the very last passage in the book of Isaiah. First, it sets up the contrast between the permanence of the New Heavens and the New Earth and of the faithful who live there, on the one hand, and the **8** impermanence of those who have rebelled, on the other hand. Secondly, the book ends with a comment on what is going to happen to the *dead bodies* of those slain in the judgment of the "rebels." People will be able to go out and look at the dead bodies of the rebellious by going out the gates of the New Jerusalem. Isaiah knows of the impermanence of the old heavens and earth, and he recognizes the human mortality of even those who love God. But he also knows of a new heavens and a new earth, created by God (Isa. 65:17–25; 66:22), and he looks forward to new bodies for those who have died for living in their integrity for God: "You shall see, and your heart shall rejoice; your bodies shall flourish like the grass" (66:14). So death is not **5** the final disposition of *all* human beings. After death there is either resurrection to life and participation in the renewal, or execution and exclusion from that renewal, which results having your dead body being **6** treated like trash. In the trash dump, your prospects for life in the new creation are extinguished totally, as the corpse that is all that is left of you is **2** completely, **3** irrevocably, **4** permanently, **5** finally, **7** unpreventably *destroyed* ("their worm shall not die, and their fire shall not be quenched," v. 24).

There is no necessity of imagining a kind of Promethean punishment here, as if God were pictured as miraculously causing the flesh to regenerate as the fire burns and as the worms eat.[7] If you take the description literally,[8] or at least at face value, then such a concept will not even begin to arise—because these have been described as corpses: as dead, inert bodies that no longer feel anything. The implication is that they are being burned up so that their rotting state does not cause any health hazard for those who live

---

7. In the Prometheus myth of ancient Greece, Prometheus steals fire from the great god Zeus and gives it to human beings, and Zeus is so enraged that he ties Prometheus to a rock and ordains an eagle to come every day to eat his liver while Prometheus is still alive. Every day his liver regenerates so that he must face the agonizing pain without end (see Hesiod, *Theogony*, 507–616; Aeschylus, *Prometheus Bound*).

8. Those who advocate for an endless state of conscious torment invariably claim to be "taking the Bible literally." They are not taking *this* passage literally.

in the New Jerusalem. The scene of anguish, the terrible despair and frustration of being excluded from what is good, comes *before* the slaying that produces this field of corpses (see again Isa. 65:11–15).

But for the sake of argument, let's experiment here with the idea that Isaiah intends us to imagine a kind of endless burning of the corpses of "the people who have rebelled against me" (v. 24). Let's first consider what groups comprise the rebel corpses. Reading v. 24 in context makes it clear that the subjects of this punishment are *all* of God's enemies, both from within and from outside of the community of faith in God. When God brings a new heavens and a new earth and a new Jerusalem, two classes of people will be gathered together and permanently destroyed by fire: those within the walls of Jerusalem who pretend to be worshipers of God, but who secretly serve idols by sacrificing to them, and all of the enemy nations that gather to attack Jerusalem when the moment of renewal comes (65:11–15; 66:1–6, 14–18).

Isaiah has already prophesied that the land of Edom (the archetype of a perennial enemy threat) would burn continuously without end (Isa. 34:9–10, discussed above). This imagery in Isaiah 34 has never been fulfilled literally (otherwise the southern portion of the contemporary nation of Jordon would be continuously on fire with burning sulfur). Nor was it ever intended to be taken completely literally. The characterization of endlessly burning pitch and sulfur is recognizable as a kind of temporal hyperbole whose point applies equally here in Isaiah 66: the enemies of God's people are not going to be defeated, simply to regroup at some later time and pose an even greater threat. If we assume (strictly for the sake of argument) that continuous, everlasting burning and consumption by worms is being *pictured* here in Isaiah 66, then we have clear precedent in Isaiah 34 (see the treatment of that passage above) for interpreting the imagery. Perpetual burning conveys the themes of the **4** permanence and **5** finality of the cessation of danger from perennial enemies.

Jeremiah 4:4

> [4] Circumcise yourselves to the LORD,
>   remove the foreskin of your hearts,
>   O people of Judah and inhabitants of Jerusalem,
>   or else my wrath will go forth like fire,
>   and burn with no one to quench it,
>   because of the evil of your doings.

This prophecy poses a simile, in that it likens God's anger to a fire that can't be put out. I suggest that the key concepts brought forward by the simile are the **2** complete, **3** irrevocable, and **7** unpreventable nature of the destruction that the people will encounter unless they repent. There will come a point, prophesies Jeremiah, when it will be too late to reverse the decision and stop the process of destruction decreed by God's anger. The decision to punish will be **5** final, and no one will any longer be able to turn it back by prayer or repentance. In a manner of speaking, no one is going to be there to pour water on the fire of God's anger and stop it from fully accomplishing its effects. The implication is that if no one can quench it, it will burn Judah down completely.

The End of the Unrepentant

Jeremiah 7:20

> [20] Therefore thus says the Lord God: My anger and my wrath shall be poured out on this place, on human beings and animals, on the trees of the field and the fruit of the ground; it will burn and not be quenched.

This passage asserts the **2** completeness, and **7** the unpreventable nature, of the outworking of God's wrath.

Jeremiah 15:14

> [14] I will make you serve your enemies in a land that you do not know, for in my anger a fire is kindled that shall burn forever.

Neither the Hebrew nor the Greek (LXX) version of Jeremiah contains the word "forever." NASB, JPS, New Jerusalem, and many other translations have "A fire has started in my wrath, and it's going to burn you." The only thing the Hebrew indicates is that God's wrath has destructive potential like fire. In his insistence that the fire has started, and that it *will* burn, Jeremiah evokes theme **7**, that the judgment coming is unpreventable.

Jeremiah 17:4

> [4] By your own act you shall lose the heritage that I gave you, and I will make you serve your enemies in a land that you do not know, for in my anger a fire is kindled that shall burn forever.

The Hebrew here for "forever" is *'ad 'olam*.[9] This could be rendered "for all time" and "permanently." Positively speaking, the metaphor of fire here clearly means that the people are going to go into exile—that is how the saying begins. Given the larger context of the statement within Jeremiah's prophecies and the historical outcome, there are two things that this prophecy does not mean: 1. that God would stay angry with the people of Judah forever, and 2. that the land of Israel would literally be burning without end. Not only did the people in fact come back from the Babylonian exile after 70 years, but Jeremiah himself prophesied that the return from exile would happen. So in a certain way, the warning of a coming fire that would burn *'ad 'olam* describes a destructive process that was conceived of by the prophet not only as eventually coming to an end, but even as eventually being healed. So maybe *'ad 'olam* is a metaphorical way of threatening the **3** irrevocable nature of God's decision to send them into exile. But looking at it from another vantage point, all but a small handful of those who went into exile *never came back*. The nation came back in the generation of their children or grandchildren, but the generation that went into exile faced an **3** irrevocable and **5** final punishment. In their case, the metaphorical fire of separation from their homeland never stopped burning.

---

9. See Strong's #H5704 and #H5769.

Jeremiah 17:27

> [27] But if you do not listen to me, to keep the Sabbath day holy, and to carry in no burden through the gates of Jerusalem on the Sabbath day, then I will kindle a fire in its gates; it shall devour the palaces of Jerusalem and shall not be quenched.

God is here warning the Israelites through Jeremiah that unless they repent the Babylonians are going to come and completely burn Jerusalem down (which they actually did, during Jeremiah's lifetime). The main themes are the **2** completeness, **3** the irrevocability, and the **7** unpreventability of the destruction that is coming unless they repent.

Jeremiah 21:10, 12–14

> [10] For I have set my face against this city for evil and not for good, says the Lord: it shall be given into the hands of the king of Babylon, and he shall burn it with fire . . . [12] O house of David! Thus says the Lord:
>
> Execute justice in the morning,
>   and deliver from the hand of the oppressor
>   anyone who has been robbed,
> [13] or else my wrath will go forth like fire,
>   and burn, with no one to quench it,
>   because of your evil doings.
> . . .
> [14] I will punish you according to the fruit of your doings, says the Lord;
>   I will kindle a fire in its forest,
>   and it shall devour all that is around it.

The same themes are at play here as in Jer. 17:27 above; refer to that passage for comments.

Jeremiah 32:29

> [29] The Chaldeans who are fighting against this city shall come, set it on fire, and burn it, with the houses on whose roofs offerings have been made to Baal and libations have been poured out to other gods, to provoke me to anger.

Here Jeremiah voices a specific and historical prediction that makes explicit the significance of the recurring metaphor of a fire of God's anger that no one can extinguish.

Jeremiah 34:2

> [2] Thus says the Lord, the God of Israel: Go and speak to King Zedekiah of Judah and say to him: Thus says the Lord: I am going to give this city into the hand of the king of Babylon, and he shall burn it with fire.

See the comment on Jer. 32:29.

The End of the Unrepentant

Jeremiah 34:22

> [22] I am going to command, says the Lord, and will bring them back to this city; and they will fight against it, and take it, and burn it with fire. The towns of Judah I will make a desolation without inhabitant.

In Jer. 32:29; 34:2, 22 Jeremiah ultimately spells out the completely real and practical force of the previous prophetic language that threatens a fire that cannot, or will not, be quenched. The Babylonians are really and truly going to burn down all the cities of Judah, including Jerusalem. There is going to come a time when it's **3** too late to change God's mind, and there is **7** no way to stop it. Theme **2**, the completeness of judgment, is also at play here.

Jeremiah 37:8, 10

> [8] And the Chaldeans shall return and fight against this city; they shall take it and burn it with fire . . . . [10] Even if you defeated the whole army of Chaldeans who are fighting against you, and there remained of them only wounded men in their tents, they would rise up and burn this city with fire.

Verse 10 here emphasizes the **3** irrevocable and **7** unpreventable nature of God's decision. Whatever temporary twists and turns there may be in the historical process, whatever hopeful moments might appear, this destruction by fire has been decreed by God, and it is *going* to happen. Even if things looked terrible for them and great for you, it would still happen.

Jeremiah 38:17–18, 23

> [17] Then Jeremiah said to Zedekiah, "Thus says the Lord, the God of hosts, the God of Israel, If you will only surrender to the officials of the king of Babylon, then your life shall be spared, and this city shall not be burned with fire, and you and your house shall live. [18] But if you do not surrender to the officials of the king of Babylon, then this city shall be handed over to the Chaldeans, and they shall burn it with fire, and you yourself shall not escape from their hand." . . . [23] All your wives and your children shall be led out to the Chaldeans, and you yourself shall not escape from their hand, but shall be seized by the king of Babylon; and this city shall be burned with fire."

Jeremiah is once again talking about the practical, historical, physical outworking of the prophecies about the "fire" of God's anger.

Jeremiah 39:8 || 52:13

> [8] The Chaldeans burned the king's house and the houses of the people, and broke down the walls of Jerusalem. . . . He burned the house of the Lord, the

king's house, and all the houses of Jerusalem; every great house he burned down.

This statement comes in the midst of a narrative describing king Nebuchadnezzar's army defeating Judah. (Jeremiah's spelling for the name is Nebuchadrezzar.) Jeremiah's prophecies about a fire that could not be quenched had a literal and historical fulfillment.

Jeremiah 43:12–13

> ^{12} He [the king of Babylon] shall kindle a fire in the temples of the gods of Egypt; and he shall burn them and carry them away captive; and he shall pick clean the land of Egypt, as a shepherd picks his cloak clean of vermin; and he shall depart from there safely. ^{13} He shall break the obelisks of Heliopolis, which is in the land of Egypt; and the temples of the gods of Egypt he shall burn with fire.

When some of the Judeans escaped to Egypt, taking Jeremiah with them as a prisoner, Jeremiah prophesied that Nebuchadrezzar would defeat Egypt also, so that the Judeans' flight to Egypt would not save them from what they feared.

Jeremiah 48:45; 49:2, 27

> ^{45} In the shadow of Heshbon
>   fugitives stop exhausted;
> for a fire has gone out from Heshbon,
>   a flame from the house of Sihon;
> it has destroyed the forehead of Moab,
>   the scalp of the people of tumult.
> . . .
> $^{49:2}$ Therefore, the time is surely coming,
>   says the LORD,
> when I will sound the battle alarm
>   against Rabbah of the Ammonites;
> it shall become a desolate mound,
>   and its villages shall be burned with fire;
> then Israel shall dispossess those who dispossessed him,
>   says the LORD.
> . . .
> ^{27} And I will kindle a fire at the wall of Damascus,
>   and it shall devour the strongholds of Ben-hadad.

These three passages prophesy literal destruction by fire (equivalent to what happened to Judah when the Babylonians came) for three of Judah's neighbor countries: Moab, Ammon, and Syria.

The End of the Unrepentant

Jeremiah 50:32; 51:58

> [32] The arrogant one shall stumble and fall,
>   with no one to raise him up,
> and I will kindle a fire in his cities,
>   and it will devour everything around him.
> . . .
> [58] Thus says the LORD of hosts:
> The broad wall of Babylon
>   shall be leveled to the ground,
> and her high gates
>   shall be burned with fire.
> The peoples exhaust themselves for nothing,
>   and the nations weary themselves only for fire.

The weight of these two prophecies is that Babylon too is going to get its share of (literal) fire, in due time. Sooner or later, all the nations that destroy and take over other nations end up getting destroyed and taken over themselves.

Jeremiah 52:12–13

> [12] In the fifth month, on the tenth day of the month—which was the nineteenth year of King Nebuchadrezzar, king of Babylon—Nebuzaradan the captain of the bodyguard who served the king of Babylon, entered Jerusalem. [13] He burned the house of the LORD, the king's house, and all the houses of Jerusalem; every great house he burned down.

This passage, which comes at the end of the book of Jeremiah, simply narrates the destruction of Jerusalem that Jeremiah's prophecies had predicted.

Lamentations 4:11

> [11] The LORD gave full vent to his wrath;
>   he poured out his hot anger,
>   and kindled a fire in Zion
>   that consumed its foundations.

Here we have a poetic lamentation that looks back on the fiery destruction of Jerusalem. Theme **2** is at play here—a fire that consumes the foundations themselves accomplishes a very thorough and complete destruction.

Ezekiel 15:1–8

> [1] The word of the LORD came to me:
> [2] O mortal, how does the wood of the vine surpass all other wood—
> the vine branch that is among the trees of the forest?

>³ Is wood taken from it to make anything?
> Does one take a peg from it on which to hang any object?
> ⁴ It is put in the fire for fuel;
> > when the fire has consumed both ends of it
> > and the middle of it is charred,
> > is it useful for anything?
> ⁵ When it was whole it was used for nothing;
> > how much less—when the fire has consumed it,
> > and it is charred—can it ever be used for anything!
>
> ⁶ Therefore thus says the Lord God: Like the wood of the vine among the trees of the forest, which I have given to the fire for fuel, so I will give up the inhabitants of Jerusalem. ⁷ I will set my face against them; although they escape from the fire, the fire shall still consume them; and you shall know that I am the Lord, when I set my face against them. ⁸ And I will make the land desolate, because they have acted faithlessly, says the Lord God.

Ezekiel's warning is that the coming judgment of the inhabitants of Jerusalem will be **2** complete, **3** irrevocable, and **7** unpreventable, and **6** will result in their being disposed of like (agricultural) trash.

Ezekiel 20:47

> ⁴⁷ [S]ay to the forest of the Negev, Hear the word of the Lord: thus says the Lord God, Behold, I am about to kindle a fire in you, and it will consume every green tree in you, as well as every dry tree; the blazing flame will not be quenched and the whole surface from south to north will be burned by it.

If you look at the following verses (21:1–5), you'll realize that Ezekiel is conveying virtually the same prophecy as Jeremiah against the city of Jerusalem. I suspect that the term "Forest of the Negeb" might be hinting at the great quantity of expensive lumber that wealthy people have imported from the great forests of Northern Israel and Lebanon in order to build the fine houses and other buildings of Jerusalem. The word "Negeb" refers to the desert region in the south of Palestine, which is hot and dry, and not at all known for forests. All the fine houses, however, are simply more fuel for the coming fire. The image is of a forest fire that burns totally out of control. The destruction of Jerusalem by fire will be **2** complete, **3** irrevocable, and **7** unpreventable.

Ezekiel 21:28, 31–32

> ²⁸ As for you, mortal, prophesy, and say, Thus says the Lord God concerning the Ammonites, and concerning their reproach; say:
>
> A sword, a sword! Drawn for slaughter,
> > polished to consume, to flash like lightning.
>
> . . .

The End of the Unrepentant

> ³¹ I will pour out my indignation upon you,
>   with the fire of my wrath
>   I will blow upon you.
> I will deliver you into brutish hands,
>   those skillful to destroy.
> ³² You shall be fuel for the fire,
>   your blood shall enter the earth;
> you shall be remembered no more,
>   for I the Lord have spoken.

Verse 28 here qualifies for inclusion in our survey because of a fact that is hidden in the English translation. The usual Hebrew word for "edge" in the phrase "edge of the sword" is *peh*, which literally means "mouth."[10] So v. 28, when it speaks of a sword being "polished to consume," is staying close to the metaphor according to which a sword's edge "eats" what it cuts. The experience of judgment and destruction by the sword is here being portrayed as **7** unpreventable, because a sword that moves as fast as lightning cannot be dodged or parried.

The picture of a stream of fire coming at the Ammonites from God's mouth, together with the words "you shall be remembered no more" (vv. 31, 32), suggests a destruction that is **1** instant (or at least rapid), **2** complete, **3** irrevocable, and **4** permanent.

Ezekiel 28:18–19

> ¹⁸ By the multitude of your iniquities,
>   in the unrighteousness of your trade,
>   you profaned your sanctuaries.
> So I brought out fire from within you;
>   it consumed you,
> and I turned you to ashes on the earth
>   in the sight of all who saw you.
> ¹⁹ All who know you among the peoples
>   are appalled at you;
> you have come to a dreadful end
>   and shall be no more forever.

This is a prophecy against the king of the wealthy trade city of Tyre. John's prophecy against Babylon the Great in Revelation 18 uses a lot of language from this passage. Interestingly, there is some way in which the king's destruction comes "from within." The reference in v. 18 to reducing him to ashes conveys the idea of **2** complete destruction; the words "you have come to a dreadful end and shall be no more forever" (v. 19) convey the ideas of **3** irrevocability, **4** permanence, and **5** finality.

---

10. See Strong's #H6310. This is true in NT Greek as well, which you can see illustrated in Lk 21:24 and Heb. 11:34. In both these verses, the word *stoma* (Strong's #G4750), normally "mouth," is the word translated as "edge" in the phrase "edge of the sword."

Ezekiel 30:14–16

> ¹⁴ I will make Pathros a desolation,
>   and will set fire to Zoan,
>   and will execute acts of judgment on Thebes.
> ¹⁵ I will pour my wrath upon Pelusium,
>   the stronghold of Egypt,
>   and cut off the hordes of Thebes.
> ¹⁶ I will set fire to Egypt;
>   Pelusium shall be in great agony;
> Thebes shall be breached,
>   and Memphis face adversaries by day.

This passage, which prophesies that the Babylonian army is going to come and do great damage to Egypt, fails to display most of our recurring themes. The only theme explicitly present is **9**, that the judgment results in some form of anguish. Many of the prophecies of the OT seem to be designed with the potential to apply not simply to matters going on historically in the prophets' lifetimes, but also to matters concerning the ultimate transition between the current age and age to come. Given that this particular prophecy does not include any universalizing or absolutizing language, its references to fire and its effects on the Egyptian cities are probably to be understood historically and realistically.

Ezekiel 38:21–22; 39:3–6

> ²¹ I will summon the sword against Gog in all my mountains, says the Lord GOD; the swords of all will be against their comrades. ²² With pestilence and bloodshed I will enter into judgment with him; and I will pour down torrential rains and hailstones, fire and sulfur, upon him and his troops and the many peoples that are with him.
> . . .
> ³ I will strike your bow from your left hand, and will make your arrows drop out of your right hand. ⁴ You shall fall in the mountains of Israel, you and all your troops and the peoples that are with you; I will give you to birds of prey of every kind and to the wild animals to be devoured. ⁵ You shall fall in the open field; for I have spoken, says the Lord GOD. ⁶ I will send fire on Magog and on those who live securely in the coastlands; and they shall know that I am the LORD.

This passage is presented as a kind of ultimate confrontation between God and the human forces of evil. Ezekiel prophesies that the attack of Gog and his hosts will take place during the peaceful age that is to be inaugurated with the coming of the Davidic Messiah. Comparing Ezek. 37:21–28 and 38:8 makes it clear that the raining down of fire on Gog and all his hosts is *not* to be pictured in the context of the crisis that results in the transition to the new age of righteousness and peace under the Messiah. It is instead characterized as occurring long after that age has been established ("after many days," 38:8):

The End of the Unrepentant

Ezekiel 37:21–28, 38:8

> [21] Thus says the Lord God: I will take the people of Israel from the nations among which they have gone, and will gather them from every quarter, and bring them to their own land. [22] I will make them one nation in the land, on the mountains of Israel; and one king shall be king over them all . . .
>
> [24] My servant David shall be king over them; and they shall all have one shepherd. They shall follow my ordinances and be careful to observe my statutes. [25] They shall live in the land that I gave to my servant Jacob, in which your ancestors lived; they and their children and their children's children shall live there forever; and my servant David shall be their prince forever. [26] I will make a covenant of peace with them; it shall be an everlasting covenant with them; and I will bless them and multiply them, and will set my sanctuary among them forevermore. [27] My dwelling-place shall be with them; and I will be their God, and they shall be my people. [28] Then the nations shall know that I the Lord sanctify Israel, when my sanctuary is among them forevermore.
>
> . . .
>
> [38:8] After many days you shall be mustered; in the latter years you shall go against a land restored from war, a land where people were gathered from many nations on the mountains of Israel, which had long lain waste; its people were brought out from the nations and now are living in safety, all of them.

The mention of fire and sulfur raining down on Gog's hosts (38:22) recalls the fate of Sodom and Gomorrah (Gen. 19:12–29), and through that allusion brings in the threat that this confrontation is going to result in the **2** complete, **3** irrevocable, **4** permanent, **5** final, and **7** unpreventable destruction of these enemy forces. The reference to birds and wild animals that will come and eat up the corpses of the armies (39:4) adds emphasis to the theme of **2** completeness and **5** finality. There is no mention of any soldiers who either escape or survive to bury their comrades: without exception, all of the attackers are slain.

Daniel 7:9–14

> [9] As I watched,
> thrones were set in place,
>   and an Ancient One took his throne;
> his clothing was white as snow,
>   and the hair of his head like pure wool;
> his throne was fiery flames,
>   and its wheels were burning fire.
> [10] A stream of fire issued
>   and flowed out from his presence.
> A thousand thousand served him,
>   and ten thousand times ten thousand stood attending him.
> The court sat in judgment,
>   and the books were opened.

> ¹¹ I watched then because of the noise of the arrogant words that the horn was speaking. And as I watched, the beast was put to death, and its body destroyed and given over to be burned with fire. ¹² As for the rest of the beasts, their dominion was taken away, but their lives were prolonged for a season and a time. ¹³ As I watched in the night visions,
>
>> I saw one like a human being
>>> coming with the clouds of heaven.
>> And he came to the Ancient One
>>> and was presented before him.
>> ¹⁴ To him was given dominion
>>> and glory and kingship,
>> that all peoples, nations, and languages
>>> should serve him.
>> His dominion is an everlasting dominion
>>> that shall not pass away,
>> and his kingship is one
>>> that shall never be destroyed.

I have quoted this rather long passage in order to indicate a context for the fire that destroys the beast in v. 11. It's clear that the setting is a world-judgment that stands as the transition point between the current age of history and "the world/age to come." The scale is global and social, rather than personal and individual. The beast that is slain and burned is interpreted as a great kingdom or empire—the last empire in history (vv. 17, 23). Many of the themes we've been identifying are clearly at play here: the beast's judgment is **1** instant, **2** complete, **4** permanent, and **5** final. It also **6** results in the beast's body being disposed of like trash (by burning, v. 11).

Amos 5:6

> ⁶ Seek the Lord and live,
> or he will break out against the house of Joseph like fire,
>> and it will devour Bethel, with no one to quench it.

When Amos talks about the Lord's judgment "breaking out," that's a reference to the suddenness of judgment, comparing it to the suddenness of a fire breaking out. That's theme **1**, instantness. Themes **2**, **3**, and **7** are also here. Once the fire begins to burn, it will complete its work, and no one will be able to put it out until it is done. It will carry on burning until it "devours" (i.e. totally eats up and destroys) Bethel.

Obadiah 18

> ¹⁸ The house of Jacob shall be a fire,
>> the house of Joseph a flame,
>> and the house of Esau stubble;

The End of the Unrepentant

> they shall burn them and consume them,
>> and there shall be no survivor of the house of Esau;
> for the LORD has spoken.

Stubble is what is left in the field after the grain harvest. It's the leafy part of the wheat or barley plant and the lower stalk, and a field full of stubble burns like a summer grass fire. Farmers often burn their fields after the harvest, which kills weeds and pests and fertilizes the ground in preparation for the following season's planting. In this case the illustration of burning up the stubble-field serves to convey theme **6**, being disposed of like trash, and **2**, referring to the completeness of the destruction, since there will be "no survivor."

Zephaniah 1:18

> [18] Neither their silver nor their gold
>> will be able to save them
>> on the day of the LORD's wrath;
> in the fire of his passion
>> the whole earth shall be consumed;
> for a full, a terrible end
>> he will make of all the inhabitants of the earth.

The main themes here seem to be **2** the completeness of the destruction ("*all* the inhabitants"), and **5** the finality of the destruction ("a full, terrible end").

Zephaniah 3:8

> [8] Therefore wait for me, says the LORD,
>> for the day when I arise as a witness.
> For my decision is to gather nations,
>> to assemble kingdoms,
> to pour out upon them my indignation,
>> all the heat of my anger;
> for in the fire of my passion
>> all the earth shall be consumed.

Judgment on the earth is being expressed through the metaphor of a raging forest fire that burns a huge area. Anyone who has been in the vicinity of a wildfire understands the reference to intense "heat." The passage also conveys theme **2**, completeness ("all the earth shall be consumed").

Malachi 4:1–3

> [1] See, the day is coming, burning like an oven, when all the arrogant and all evildoers will be stubble; the day that comes shall burn them up, says the LORD

of hosts, so that it will leave them neither root nor branch. ²But for you who revere my name the sun of righteousness shall rise, with healing in its wings. You shall go out leaping like calves from the stall. ³And you shall tread down the wicked, for they will be ashes under the soles of your feet, on the day when I act, says the LORD of hosts.

In the simile of the burning oven and the metaphor of the burning of stubble fields, we again see the familiar combination between theme **2**, the theme of complete destruction, and theme **6**, the theme of being disposed of like trash. The combination of the burning oven and stubble is not coincidental, since ancient people used dry grass and stubble as kindling to light their wood-burning or charcoal burning ovens (see Mt. 6:30). The words "it will leave them neither root nor branch" convey the idea of a forest fire that leaves absolutely nothing alive in its wake, emphasizing theme **2**, completeness; and the words "ashes under the soles of your feet" re-emphasize both themes, and perhaps also convey theme **8**, the theme of the impermanence of the wicked.

SUMMARY REMARKS ON THE THEMES OF FIRE AND BEING CONSUMED IN THE OT

We have now looked at every significant OT passage that refers to fire or being consumed as expressions of God's judgment. There are about fifty-seven of them, from Genesis through Malachi. Why are they relevant for Christians who want to answer the question of what ultimately happens to the unrepentant?

In the first place, they are relevant because they are authoritative, canonical revelation in their own right. The typical Christian attitude—according to which OT prophecies only become of interest when they are quoted in the NT—stands very far from the attitude of Jesus and of Peter, Paul, the author of Hebrews, and all of the other NT writers. To them, the OT is *the revealed Word of God*. It is all fresh, relevant, and important ("living and active, and sharper than any two-edged sword," Heb. 4:12). In their eyes, none of it stands as second-tier revelation. If you asked any of the NT authors, they would tell you that these passages are important to study and listen to for their own sake (e.g. 2 Pet. 1:19).

Of course, many of these passages are also relevant individually and specifically, because Jesus and the NT writers unmistakably quote and allude to them in their teachings. If you want to understand their teachings, you must seek to understand the scriptures they directly appeal to as authoritative revelation. Otherwise you will miss an entire, and oftentimes crucial, level of meaning in their words. But beyond this, these passages are relevant *as a whole collection*, because they form the *overall* scriptural background and context for nearly all the important teachings of Jesus and the authors of the NT on this subject. Together, they create a kind of shared world of authoritative stories and teachings about how God acts. They create a conceptual world that Jesus held in common with his audiences and with the authors of the New Testament. Making sense of what Jesus and the writers of the NT mean when they speak about the ultimate fate of the unrepentant thus requires sensitivity to the fact that their teachings are delivered with this entire set of passages as the backdrop. Take away this backdrop, this extensive interpretive network within Scripture itself, and you will automatically supply another one of your own devising. Will you get it from Mediaeval superstitions? From Dante or Milton? From biblically challenged contemporary preachers? From inherited contemporary conceptions about time and eternity? The truth is that each person's interpretive grid is inevitably going to be influenced by some combination of these and other conceptions extraneous to the world out of which Jesus and his apostles spoke and wrote. But if you give due attention to the significance of these OT Scriptures when you read the NT, you will give yourself the best chance of getting to the heart of what is being taught.

2

Surveying Passages from the NT Gospels and Epistles That Picture Fire and Being Consumed

Matthew 3:8–12 || Luke 3:7–9 (the preaching of John the Baptizer)

₈Bear fruit worthy of a change of heart.[1] ₉And don't think you can say to yourselves, "We have Abraham as our father." Because I'm telling you: God can raise up children for Abraham out of these stones! ₁₀The ax is already laid to the root of the trees, and every tree that doesn't bear good fruit is going to be chopped down and thrown in the fire. ₁₁I'm baptizing you with water for a change of heart.[2] But the one who is coming after me is more powerful than I am. I'm not even worthy to carry his sandals! He is the one who will baptize you with the Holy Spirit and with fire. ₁₂His winnowing fan is in his hand, and he'll clean his threshing floor well, and he'll collect his wheat for storage.[3] But the chaff he'll burn with fire that can't be put out.

JOHN THE BAPTIZER IS steeped in the imagery of the prophets, and he expects the predicted great day of God's judgment to come very soon.

His first metaphor is of the fruitless tree that is chopped down and burned. This image recalls the prophecy of Jeremiah, who prophesied of the olive tree that once bore fruit, but now is going to be burned by a raging fire (Jer. 11:16). Jesus is going to use the very same metaphor: see Mt. 7:15–19 below. John's speech brings forward quite a few of the themes we've observed in the prophets. Being chopped down and thrown in the fire suggests a destruction that is **3** irrevocable, **4** permanent, **5** final, and which **6** results in being treated as waste to be disposed of. John's warning that people had better not depend on having Abraham as their ancestor (as though simply being a Jew guaranteed

---

1. Traditionally: "worthy of repentance."
2. Traditionally: "repentance."
3. The ancient mss have slight variations here. It could also be "the wheat for his stores," or "the wheat into storage."

The End of the Unrepentant

one's entrance into the age to come) evokes both theme **7**, that judgment is unpreventable, and theme **8**, that the life of the unjust is impermanent.

His second metaphor is that of the farmer who winnows wheat and then burns the chaff (the inedible parts of the wheat plant). The most familiar method for winnowing is to toss the crushed wheat tops in the air in a breeze, so that the outer husks and other (relatively light) inedible materials go sideways, and the denser wheat kernels go nearly straight down. You use a winnowing fan when the breeze isn't strong enough to separate the wheat kernels from the chaff. When he uses the metaphor of the winnowing fan, John is thinking of the Messiah as the King who, as supreme judge, separates the wheat (righteous people) from the chaff (wicked people). As in v. 10, we have the wicked pictured as being thrown in the fire, which suggests a judgment that is **3** irrevocable, **4** permanent, **5** final, and which **6** results in being treated like trash. In this case the "trash" is agricultural waste that is disposed of by burning.

Luke 3:7–9 is almost word-for-word identical with this passage, so we will not treat it separately.

Matthew 5:21–22 (partial parallel in Mark 9:42–48)

$_{21}$You've heard that it was said to people in olden times, "Don't murder,"[4] and that whoever murders will face[5] judgment. $_{22}$But I say to you that anyone who's furious at a fellow human being will face judgment. Also, anyone that says "Fool!" will face the High Court.[6] And anyone who says, "Stupid!" will face the fire of Gehenna.[7]

Gehenna (also known as the Valley of the Son of Hinnom) is a ravine that lies right outside the walls of Jerusalem.[8] I strongly suspect that Jesus sees the scene depicted in the final verses of Isaiah 66 (see above in our survey) as having Gehenna as its setting. The reason for this is that in another saying (Mk 9:47b–48), Jesus refers to "Gehenna, where 'their worm doesn't die, and the fire doesn't get put out,' " a clear quotation from Isa. 66:24. Note here Jesus' use of a three-tiered escalating parallelism, in which the consequences go from bad, to worse, to worst possible: judgment (v. 21), the High Court (v. 22a), fire of Gehenna (v. 22b). Jesus doesn't make explicit links here between judgment, on the one hand, and Gehenna, on the other hand. But by associating the two, he implies that consignment to the fire of Gehenna is going to be the ultimate consequence of being found guilty in the judgment.

---

4. Exod. 20:13; Deut. 5:17.
5. Lit. "will be liable to," and similarly below.
6. Lit. "Sanhedrin." This was the native law-making body and high court of the land under the Roman occupation.
7. Prn. ge-***henn***-a.
8. Another place-name associated with this ravine is Topheth (2 Kgs 23:10; Isa. 30:33; Jer. 7:31–32; 19:6, 11–14).

Surveying Passages from the NT Gospels and Epistles That Picture Fire and Being Consumed

Matthew 7:19 (no parallel in Mark or Luke)

> $_{19}$Every tree that doesn't bear good fruit is chopped down and thrown in the fire.

The preaching of Jesus here parallels that of John. We can see theme **6** yet again. A fruit tree that turns out not to bear any fruit is removed and disposed of along with the garden waste. The words "thrown in the fire" evoke theme **2**, the theme of completeness, and themes **3** and **4**, concerning the irrevocability and permanence of the judgment.

Matthew 10:28 || Luke 12:4–5 (no parallel in Mark)

> $_{28}$Don't be afraid of people who kill the body, but can't kill the soul. Be more afraid of the One who can destroy both body and soul in Gehenna.

Behind this saying is Jesus' belief that bodily death does not result in the final end of the person. Jesus teaches that God holds in existence the life (or *soul*) of all human beings who have died.[9] Thus, the mention of the destruction of *body and soul* suggests the **2** completeness of the destruction, and its **3** irrevocable nature.

Luke 12:4–5 || Matthew 10:28

> $_{4}$And I'm saying to you friends of mine, don't be afraid of those that can kill your body, but after that there's nothing more they can do. $_{5}$I'll show you who you should be afraid of—be afraid of the One who, after killing you, has the authority to throw you in Gehenna.

Luke's version of this saying has a number of verbal differences from Matthew's, but the content is close. One thing that is made explicit here is that there are two phases of divine punishment: God can remove you from bodily life (i.e. God kill you), and then, at a later time, consign you to Gehenna. One can certainly get the impression that Gehenna is worse than death, but in Luke's version of this saying, just what it is that is worse about Gehenna is not spelled out. We can at least note the expression "who has the authority to throw you in Gehenna," which (1) adds theme **7**, that the destruction is unpreventable, and (2) implies that Gehenna is a kind of garbage dump where God *throws* trash. So theme **6** may well be implicit in this version of the saying.

Matthew 13:24–30, 36–43 (no parallel in Mark or Luke)

> $_{24}$Jesus gave them[10] another parable and said, "Heaven's Reign is like a man who planted good-quality seed in his field. $_{25}$But while people were sleeping, his enemy came, scattered darnel weeds[11] in amongst the wheat, and went

---

9. See Mt. 22:23–33; Mk 12:18–27; Lk. 20:27–40.
10. Lit. "set before them."
11. Darnel looks like wheat until it is full grown.

The End of the Unrepentant

away. ₂₆When the plants grew up and bore fruit, then the darnel weeds showed up. ₂₇And the servants of the head of the house came up and said to him, 'Sir, didn't you plant good-quality seed in your field? So how come it has darnel weeds?' ₂₈He said to them, 'Some enemy of mine[12] did this.' And the servants said to him, 'So, do you want us to go out and gather up the darnel weeds?' ₂₉But he said, 'No, otherwise in gathering up the darnel weeds, you'll uproot the wheat with them. ₃₀Leave both to grow together until the harvest. At harvest time I'll say to the harvesters, "First gather up the darnel weeds and tie them in bundles to be burnt. Then[13] gather up the wheat into my bins." ' "

. . .

₃₆Then Jesus left the crowds and went back to the house. His followers came up to him and said, "Explain the parable of the darnel weeds in the field to us." ₃₇He answered:

The one who plants the good-quality seed is the Human One, ₃₈and the field is the world. The good-quality seed is those who belong to God's Reign.[14] The darnel weeds are those who belong to the Evil One.[15] ₃₉The enemy that scattered them is the devil. The harvest is the wrapping up of the age, and the harvesters are angels. ₄₀So, just as darnel weeds are gathered up and burned, the same will happen at the wrapping up of the age. ₄₁The Human One will send out his angels, and they'll separate out of his Realm all the people who trip people up, and those who go around acting lawless. ₄₂They'll throw them in the burning furnace. In there there's going to be people crying and grinding their teeth. ₄₃Then the people of integrity[16] are going to shine like the sun in the kingdom of their Father. If anyone has ears, let 'em hear!

The main theme evoked by the image of useless darnel weeds being bundled up to be burned is theme **6**, the theme of judgment pictured as the disposal of trash (in this case agricultural waste). The parable of the darnel weeds functions much like the parable of the fruit tree that bears no fruit. Young darnel plants appear similar to wheat plants, and of course wheat bears edible fruit (the wheat berries, from which bread flour is made). But when the darnels grow to maturity it becomes clear that they are not going to produce anything edible. In fact, their seeds are toxic. So they are gathered up and disposed of. Themes **3** (the irrevocable nature of the destruction), **4** (the permanence of the destruction), and **5** (the finality of the destruction) are present. Theme **8** (the impermanence of rebellious humanity) is also present: darnel is an example of a seasonal grass that grows up and dies in one summer, and is then only useful for lighting fires in cooking ovens; see Mt. 6:30. Seasonal grass is proverbial in the Bible for the impermanence of human life.[17]

Jesus talks in Mt. 13:42 about people being thrown in "the burning furnace" (traditionally, "the fiery furnace"), as though his hearers should recognize exactly what that

12. Lit. "An enemy person."
13. Lit. "But."
14. Lit. "the children of the kingdom." It's a figure of speech.
15. Lit. "the children of the Evil One."
16. Traditionally: "the righteous."
17. E.g., 2 Kgs 19:26; Pss. 37:2; 90:5–6; 92:7; 103:15; 129:6; Isa. 37:27; 40:6–8; 51:12.

Surveying Passages from the NT Gospels and Epistles That Picture Fire and Being Consumed

is. Where in the Hebrew Scriptures do we find reference to a "burning furnace," and what does it represent there? Only in one place: Daniel 3, the famous story of Shadrach, Meshach, and Abednego. The fiery furnace in that story is the means that the emperor Nebuchadnezzar uses to threaten everyone who will not bow down to his statue. In that story, the furnace is employed as a method of execution that results in instant and fearsome death. Gruesome as all this is, it is so far totally consistent with the various pictures associated with the theme of fire in the Old Testament—including the one in Isaiah that speaks of people being horribly burnt to death by their own devices (Isa. 50:11). Those who live destructively (metaphorically expressed in the image of them going around lighting fires), says Isaiah, will at some point be burnt up by their own destructiveness. They won't just quietly wink out like a light, but they will experience for themselves the painful destruction that they have been causing around them. The harm that they have inflicted on others will encounter them in their turn, and they will find themselves in agony. Jesus follows Isaiah closely in this theme. He warns that all those who pretend to be subjects of God's Reign, but go around harming others—that is, "all those who trip people up,[18] and those who go around acting lawless" (v. 41)—will be cast into the furnace of destruction, in which they themselves will face anguish.

But here is where it gets intriguing. If it can be forgiven even to contemplate the horrifying imagery of this saying for a moment, surely if there were such a thing as a giant furnace into which people were being dumped alive, the sounds coming out of it would be the wrenching and abbreviated screams of death—not the disconsolate whimpers of "crying[19] and teeth-grinding." I'm persuaded that Jesus is alluding here to Isa. 65:11–15, which we encountered above:

Isaiah 65:11–15

> $_{13}$Thus says the Lord God: My servants shall eat, but you shall be hungry; my servants shall drink, but you shall be thirsty; my servants shall rejoice, but you shall be put to shame; $_{14}$my servants shall sing for gladness of heart, but *you shall cry out for pain of heart, and shall wail for anguish of spirit.* $_{15}$You shall leave your name to my chosen to use as a curse, and the Lord God will put you to death.

Internal to this (Isaiah) context, it appears that those who have forsaken the Lord (65:11) are crying, wailing, and in anguish because they realize that they are summarily and irrevocably excluded from the good things of the renewal that God is going to accomplish for the faithful (see Isa. 65:9–10). They realize that the latest moment to repent and change their minds has now passed. They see exactly what others have to look forward to, but they themselves are never going to be able to enjoy; the only prospect ahead of

---

18. Traditionally: "stumbling blocks"; Jesus clearly uses this term to refer to people who do real harm to others, and particularly to the most vulnerable, in the worshipping community (see Mt. 18:7; Lk. 17:1).

19. Traditionally: "weeping," but the Greek word here suggests at least some amount of vocal expression in addition to the shedding of tears.

The End of the Unrepentant

them is the death sentence. Their pain is emotional, not physical. *It is the pain of envy, despair, and frustrated longing for an unending life that they cannot have.*

Jesus' reference to people who grind their teeth also alludes to Ps. 112:9–10, which underlines this same idea with the greatest possible clarity:

Psalm 112:9–10

> [9] [The righteous] have distributed freely, they have given to the poor;
> their righteousness endures forever; their horn is exalted in honor.
> [10] The wicked see it and are angry; they gnash their teeth and melt away;
> the desire of the wicked comes to nothing.

When we bring this idea to Jesus' words, it coheres closely with his description of the lost: they cry bitterly and grind their teeth, which fits much better with an experience of envy, despair, and frustrated desire than with the physical agony of dying (or being tormented) in a fire. Can we find a saying of Jesus himself that makes this meaning of the words "crying and grinding teeth"—i.e., emotional anguish at being excluded from life—completely explicit? We can indeed. Jesus says:

Luke 13:28

> [24] Try your hardest to go in through the narrow doorway. Because I'm telling you, a lot of people are going to try to go in, and they're not going to be able to. [25] After the owner of the house gets up and locks the door, then you'll start showing up outside to knock on the door. You'll be saying, "Sir, open up for us!" And he'll say back to you, "I don't know where you're from." [26] Then you'll start saying, "We used to eat and drink right there with you![20] You taught in our public places!"[21] [27] And he's going to be saying to you, "I don't know you, or where you're from. Stay away from me, all you who keep doing wrong!"[22]
> [28] *There's going to be crying and teeth-grinding out there, when you see Abraham, Isaac and Jacob, and all the prophets in God's Reign—and yourselves excluded outside.*[23]

Mt. 8:11–12 is slightly less explicit, but appears to be making the same point:

Matthew 8:11–12

> [11] I'm telling you, lots of people are going to come from the East and from the West and eat the banquet dinner[24] with Abraham, Isaac, and Jacob in Heaven's

---

20. Lit. "right in front of you."
21. Lit. "marketplaces" or "main streets."
22. Lit. "all you perpetrators of injustice."
23. Lit. "kicked out outside."
24. Lit. "come and lie down with Abraham . . . " Moderns sit to eat at a banquet; people of Jesus' day reclined. "The banquet" is supplied to help bring forward the reference to Isa. 25. See also Isa. 24:14–15.

Reign. ₁₂But some of the children of God's Reign²⁵ are going to be thrown outside in the darkness. Out there, there's going to be people crying and grinding their teeth.

Note that in neither of these passages is there any mention of a fire that can be interpreted as the cause of the excluded people's crying and teeth-grinding. In Mt. 8:11–12 they are *outside in the dark*, whereas the celebration, symbolic of the joyous and full life of community and belonging in the renewal, is *inside*, where there is *light*. In the absence of anything physical being mentioned that might draw our attention as a possible cause their discomfort, the entirely natural interpretation here is that those outside are in anguish over what has just happened to them: they have been thrown out into the darkness.

Since we're taking a close look at this topic, let's pause now to examine all the rest of the passages in the New Testament (all of them are in the teaching of Jesus) that include the phrase "crying and teeth-grinding." We'll quickly discover that, far from being associated with notions of endless torment, they all have one theme in common: *the pain of being rejected and excluded.*

On "Crying and Teeth-Grinding": Matthew 22:1–14 (partial || Luke 14:15–24)

₂Heaven's Reign is like this: a certain king²⁶ held a wedding for his son. ₃He sent his slaves out to invite the guests to the wedding celebration. But they didn't want to come. ₄Again he sent out other slaves. He told them, "Say to the invited guests, 'Look, I've prepared the dinner! My bulls and calves have been sacrificed, and everything is ready. Come to the wedding celebration!'" ₅But they didn't pay any attention. One went off to the field that he owned, and one went off to his business. ₆The rest grabbed his slaves and abused them and killed them. ₇The king was furious. He sent his armies and killed those murderers and burnt their city. ₈Then he said to his slaves, "My wedding is ready, but the ones who were chosen weren't worthy. ₉Go over to the city gates, and invite whoever you find to the wedding." ₁₀So those slaves went out on the streets and were gathering everyone they found—whether they were evil or good. And the wedding hall was full of dinner guests.²⁷ ₁₁But when the king came in to look over the dinner guests, he saw a man there who wasn't dressed in wedding clothes. ₁₂He said to him, "Friend, how did you come in here without wedding clothes?" But he couldn't say a word.²⁸ ₁₃Then the king said to the servers, "Tie his feet and hands, and throw him out there in the darkness. There are going to be people crying and grinding their teeth out there." ₁₄Because lots of people are invited, but few are chosen.²⁹

---

25. Lit. "the children of the kingdom," but it means "some of those who are children of the kingdom," not "all the children of the kingdom."
26. Lit. "there was a man who was a king who."
27. Lit. "full of those who were reclining."
28. Or "he had no excuse"; lit. "he was silenced."
29. Lk. 14:15–24 has a version of this parable, but it does not contain the expulsion of the improperly dressed guest. It does, however, end with the theme of exclusion: "I'm telling you, none of those people [I] invited are going to taste my banquet!" (v. 24).

The End of the Unrepentant

On "Crying and Teeth-Grinding": Matthew 24:45–51 || Luke 12:41–46

$_{45}$So who is the reliable slave, the smart one? Suppose the owner has put the slave in charge of his household, to give out food to everyone at the right times. $_{46}$The blessed slave is the one the owner finds doing that when he comes. $_{47}$I'm telling you seriously: he'll put that one in charge of all his possessions. $_{48}$But suppose the slave is bad, and says inwardly,[30] "My master is taking a long time." $_{49}$And the person begins to beat the other slaves, and eat and drink with drunks. $_{50}$That slave's master will come on a day they don't predict, and at a time they don't expect.[31] $_{51}$He'll cut that slave in two with the whip, and he'll put the person over with the play-actors. Over there, people are going to be crying and grinding their teeth.[32]

On "Crying and Teeth-Grinding": Matthew 25:14–30 || Luke 19:11–27

$_{14}$It's just like a man who is going out of town. He calls his slaves over and gives them responsibility for his properties. $_{15}$He gives five talents to one, he gives two talents to another, and he gives one talent to another.[33] Each one gets an amount in line with their own ability. And he leaves town. $_{16}$Right away, the person with five talents goes and does business with them and makes another five. $_{17}$In the same way, the person with two makes two more. $_{18}$But the person with one talent takes it and goes off and hides it in the master's field. $_{19}$After a long time their master[34] comes and settles accounts with them. $_{20}$The person with five talents comes up to him and presents five more, and says, "Master, you gave me five talents. See, I've made five more talents." $_{21}$The master says, "Well done! You're a good and trustworthy slave. You've been trustworthy in charge of a few things; I'm going to put you in charge of a lot of things! Come in and celebrate with your master!"[35] $_{22}$Then the one with the two talents comes up and says, "Master, you gave me two talents. See, I've made two more talents." $_{23}$The master says, "Well done! You're a good and trustworthy slave. You've been trustworthy in charge of a few things; I'm going to put you in charge of a lot of things! Come in and celebrate with your master!"[36] $_{24}$Finally the slave that received one talent comes up and says, "Master, I know you—you're a tough businessman. You harvest where you didn't plant, and you gather in places where you didn't scatter seed. $_{25}$I was afraid, so I went off and hid your talent in the ground. See, you have your money back."[37] $_{26}$But the master says

---

30. Lit. "But if that bad slave says in his heart."

31. Lit. "know."

32. Luke's version doesn't mention crying and teeth-grinding, but only that the slave is severely whipped and put "with the unreliable ones" (v. 46).

33. A talent was unit of money that could be considered worth many thousands of dollars.

34. Lit. "the master of those slaves."

35. Or "Come, enjoy your master's approval!" Lit. "Come into your master's joy!"

36. See the nt. on v. 21.

37. Lit. "See—you have what is yours."

> back to him, "You bad, cowardly slave! You already knew that I harvest where I haven't planted, and gather in places where I haven't scattered seed! ₂₇So you should have put my money in the bank. That way,³⁸ when I came I would have gotten my money back with interest. ₂₈So take the talent away from him, and give it to the one who has ten talents. ₂₉As the saying goes,³⁹ 'Everyone who has will get more,⁴⁰ and they'll have more than enough. But the one who doesn't have will even get what they have taken away from them.' ₃₀Now⁴¹ throw that useless slave out there in the darkness! There are going to be people crying and grinding their teeth out there."⁴²

We see, from this survey of passages that refer to crying and teeth-grinding, that Jesus uses a variety of parables to illustrate the idea that the transition to the age of renewal is not going to be pleasant for some people who have been assuming that they are his followers. Many are going to experience anguish when, after complacently assuming that they were "in" with Jesus and/or God's Reign, they suddenly find out that Jesus actually expected his followers to *act* in a manner consistent with their expectation of taking part in God's reign. Repeatedly Jesus uses this same figure—of crying and teeth-grinding, traditionally known as "weeping and gnashing of teeth"—to characterize the experience of utter and horrible despair that *faithless disciples* will experience when the transition to the age of renewal comes. Their pain will not arise because they are being subjected to exquisite torments by God or by angels. It will be because they are confronted with the knowledge that their past actions prove that they have consistently ignored Christ's invitation to participate in the heralding of the blessed age to come—and now it is too late to change their minds.

There is a fair amount of potential irony in the fact that so many Christians have been led to assume that the threat of "weeping and gnashing of teeth" hangs exclusively over non-Christians—when the function of this theme *in each and every instance in Jesus' teaching* is to warn *his own followers* and would-be followers against complacency and hypocrisy in following him.

Having finished this excursion, we now resume our sequential survey of passages that deal with fire and being consumed as images of divine punishment.

Matthew 13:47–50 (no parallel in Mark or Luke)

> ₄₇Again, Heaven's Reign is like a fishing net that's thrown in the lake. It scoops up all kinds of fish. ₄₈When it's ready, it's dragged up on the beach, and they sit down and collect the good ones and put them in baskets. And they throw out the bad ones. ₄₉That's what it will be like at the wrapping up of the age. The

---

38. Lit. "You should therefore have put it with the bankers, and."
39. Lit. "For." The master in the story appears to be quoting a proverb.
40. Lit. "to everyone who has will be given."
41. Lit. "And."
42. Luke's version differs significantly from Matthew's, and does not mention any punishment that happens to the slave who buries the money given him (cf. Mt. 25:28–30; Lk. 19:24–26). It's not at all impossible that Jesus told his parables with different variations and elaborations from time to time.

The End of the Unrepentant

> angels will go out and separate out the evil people from among the people of integrity.[43] ₅₀They'll throw them in a burning furnace. In there there's going to be people crying and grinding their teeth.

Once again we see the theme of judgment as **6** the disposal of trash—in this case, we have a parable about the disposal of undesirable fish. It's important to note that Jesus is not saying that rejected fish get burnt up in a furnace—after all, a first-century fisherman would never *burn up* useless fish, because that would be a pointless waste of wood. What happens to the fish is that they get *thrown out*. He says that angels will be involved in separating good people from evil people at the end of the age—just like one sorts the various kinds of fish that one catches in a fishing net. The parable of the net is a *simile* ("Heaven's Reign is like . . . ," v. 47), whereas what immediately follows appears to be a *metaphor*, the metaphor of the "burning furnace." If we take the figure as a metaphor, the most obvious force is that of complete destruction. Furnaces that are used for heating burn up their fuel completely, and incinerator furnaces burn their trash up completely. If, on the other hand, we try taking this part of the saying literally, then it seems to be saying that at the end of this age, some human beings will be captured by angels, who will incinerate them alive in some kind of enormous furnace (once again, see Dan. 3 for the biblical background to this idea). Unpleasant as this idea may be, the general force of it seems equivalent regardless of whether the furnace is understood as metaphorical or literal. *In either case* the saying would seem to indicate that the destruction that is coming for evil people at the end of the age will be **1** instant, **2** complete, **3** irrevocable, **4** permanent, and **5** final, **6** resulting in the guilty being disposed of like trash. Given that angels are presumably far stronger than human beings, this judgment looks to be **7** unpreventable, and it is pictured as **9** resulting in intense anguish—the anguish of knowing that you have been excluded from the life of the age to come.

Matthew 18:8–9 || Mark 9:43–48[44] || Matthew 5:29–30

> ₈And if your hand or your foot trips you up, cut it off and throw it away from you. It's better for you to come into life maimed or with a disability, rather than having two hands or two feet to be thrown into the age-long fire. ₉And if your eye trips you up, take it out, and throw it away from you. It's better for you to come into life one-eyed, rather than to get thrown with two eyes into the fire of Gehenna.

As we have seen, this saying's concluding image of a burning Gehenna (v. 9) appeals to the most starkly **5** *final* of all the images of destruction in the Old Testament, namely Isaiah 66 (esp. vv. 14–16, 24). In that passage, fire cleanses the land from the unclean corpses of God's enemies. It is as though God has a **6** trash dump for those found unworthy of participation in the New Jerusalem and the age of universal renewal (Isa.

---

43. Traditionally: "the righteous."

44. Mark's version of this saying closely parallels Matthew's, but with a couple of significant differences, which will be considered immediately after the Matthew version.

Surveying Passages from the NT Gospels and Epistles That Picture Fire and Being Consumed

65:17—66:24, esp. 66:22-24). Gehenna is clearly no interim state;[45] neither Isaiah nor Jesus presents it as anything like a temporary and remedial punishment. On the contrary, Gehenna is put forward as a picture of the 5 final, 4 permanent, and 3 irrevocable removal from the new creation of those human beings who have proved themselves unworthy to be participants in it.

But what about being "thrown into the age-long fire" (Mt. 18:8)? Is that being put forward as parallel to, and therefore as equivalent to, the fate of being "thrown . . . into Gehenna" (v. 9)? Or do we perhaps have a twofold *escalating* parallelism—in which case "the age-long fire" could be understood as a state preliminary to the final and extinguishing punishment of Gehenna? It does seem entirely possible that we are seeing here, as in Mt. 5:21-22 and a number of other sayings of Jesus, a pair of escalating unpleasant outcomes.[46] First we are confronted with the dreadful prospect of being thrown into "the age-long fire" (v. 8), then that of being thrown into "the fire of Gehenna" (v. 9).

Nothing we have read so far offers enough of an interpretive foothold to confirm (or to rule out) either one of these possibilities: age-long fire *equals* Gehenna, or age-long fire *points to a condition that may be imagined as prior to* Gehenna. We will therefore put a bookmark here and return when we find other passages that can shed light on the ambiguity.

Notwithstanding this puzzle, the punch line of Jesus' saying here in Mt. 18:6-9 is clear: better to lose a part of you in this age and to gain the life of the age to come than to keep all of you in this age and find yourself in the trash dump when that age comes. Better, indeed, to *throw away* part of you than to find that 6 you as a whole person are *thrown away* in the ultimate trash dump (Mt. 18:8, 9). It is common for Christians to unconsciously read culturally acquired concepts of an everlasting hell into this saying, with the result that they assume Jesus is talking in metaphorical terms about being temporarily maimed (in this mortal life) versus being everlastingly tormented (in the life to come). But this is a misreading. The terms of his comparison are obviously *not temporal*. When Jesus says "it's better for you to come into life maimed . . . ,"[47] he is posing the idea that it would be better, if you had to choose, to throw away a body part and enter upon the life of the renewed world as a maimed person, than to remain an able-bodied person, and to be thrown out from the renewed world and end up as one of the burning corpses of Isa. 66:24. This saying, as Jesus has posed it, in no way implies that he actually thought that there would be maimed people in the resurrection. His point is that *even if* the choice were as stark as he was posing it, it would still be obvious which choice to make. It does violence to this saying to read a "correct" view of the resurrected existence

---

45. Contrary to the indomitable optimism of the Jewish oral tradition, which hopes that people burned in Gehenna will only stay there for 11 months, and afterwards be resurrected to eternal life.

46. Jesus seems to favor using escalating parallelism with two or three elements. Compare Mt. 5:21-22; 5:25-26; 5:29-30; 11:21-24; 18:6-9 (par. Mk 9:42-50); 23:20-22. Similar forms appear in teachings on topics other than the fate of the unrighteous: Mt. 5:38-41 (?); 7:9-10; 10:37-38; 11:41-42 (descending rather than escalating); 23:20-22; Lk. 6:27-29.

47. Note that this version of the saying is stronger than the one that occurs in the Sermon on the Mount (Mt. 5:29-30), which does not put forward the idea of entering *the resurrection life* as a maimed person. Mt. 5:29-30 also does not contain the word "fire," so it has not been given an independent treatment.

The End of the Unrepentant

(that people will have whole, restored bodies) into your interpretation of it, so that the contrast appears to be between *temporary* impairment and *endless* destruction. We will take the opportunity to examine the expression "the age-long fire" when we encounter it again in Mt. 25:41 below.

Themes operating here are **2** the destruction is complete, **3** the destruction is irrevocable, **4** the destruction is permanent, **5** the destruction is final, **6** the destruction results in the guilty being disposed of like trash, and **8** the impermanence of human life.

Mark's version of this saying (Mk 9:43–48) is very close to Matthew's, but it has two differences, which we will now examine.

Mark 9:43–48 || Matthew 18:8–9

$_{43}$And if your hand trips you up, cut it off. It's better for you to go into life with a disability[48] than to have two hands, and go into Gehenna—**into the fire that can't be put out.**[49] $_{45}$And if your foot trips you up, cut it off. It's better for you to go into life with a disability than to have two feet, and get thrown into Gehenna. $_{47}$And if your eye trips you up, tear it out. It's better for you to go into the Reign of God with one eye, than to have two eyes, and get thrown into Gehenna—$_{48}$**where "their worm doesn't die, and the fire doesn't get put out."**[50]

Whereas Matthew's version of this saying has two parallel elements, Mark's has three. And whereas in Matthew's version the first element speaks of the risk of being "thrown into the age-long fire," in Mark's version the first element has "go off into Gehenna—into the fire that can't be put out." Mark's version also contains (in v. 48) the only explicit NT quotation from Isa. 66:24, the last verse in Isaiah.

In Mark's version, all three elements refer to the risk of ending up in Gehenna. In Matthew's version, on the other hand, the second and third of Mark's three elements are combined in a single element, resulting in a two-element structure. As I mentioned above, the structure of Mathew's version raises the question of whether the parallelism of the two elements suggests an escalation from age-long fire to Gehenna.

There are a number of ways of understanding the differences between these two versions. One way is to suppose that Jesus probably used this saying in his teaching on various occasions, and it is only natural that he would have allowed himself variations on his own teaching material from time to time and from place to place. In illustration of this, we could point to Mt. 5:29–30, which contains yet another variation, which is unique to Matthew. Another possible way of understanding the differences is to note the likelihood that the sayings of Jesus circulated in the Christian communities for many years before being written down, so that slight variations and paraphrases would naturally have arisen over time in the process of oral repetition and transmission within the various communities. In that case, Matthew's and Mark's versions could simply be two

---

48. Or "maimed."
49. The oldest mss do not contain vv. 44 and 46, each of which repeats v. 48.
50. Isa. 66:24.

Surveying Passages from the NT Gospels and Epistles That Picture Fire and Being Consumed

traditional variations of one original saying. A third way of understanding the difference would be to assume that all the evangelists, including Matthew and Mark, understood that they had the authority in the Holy Spirit to paraphrase the traditional words of Jesus, just as contemporary preachers readily paraphrase and loosely quote sayings of Jesus from the Gospels in their preaching material. Whatever mechanism ultimately lies behind the differences, Matthew's and Mark's versions of this saying now have different literary structures. Each has to be interpreted on its own terms, and may not simply be squashed into reassuring conformity with the other. As they stand, each version is equally canonical, and therefore each one deserves to be treated as an inspired saying in its own right.

Mark's version, in addition to sharing all the themes present in Matthew's version (**2** the destruction is complete, **3** the destruction is irrevocable, **4** the destruction is permanent, **5** the destruction is final, **6** the destruction results in the guilty being disposed of like trash, and **8** the impermanence of human life), contains an added theme: **7** the destruction is unpreventable. This theme is present in both of the portions that Mark has that are not paralleled in Matthew (formatted in **bold** above). You can't stop an "unquenchable fire" from burning you up completely, nor can you be saved from being eaten completely by worms that refuse to die off (vv. 44, 48).

Matthew 25:31–46, esp. 41 (no parallel in Mark or Luke)

> $_{31}$When the Human One comes in his glory, all his angels will be with him too. Then he's going to sit on his glorious throne. $_{32}$All the nations are going to be assembled there in front of him. He'll sort them out from one another, just like a shepherd sorts the sheep out from the goats. $_{33}$He'll put the sheep on his right and the goats on his left. $_{34}$Then the King will say to the ones on his right, "Come, all of you who have my Father's blessing! Come inherit the Reign that has been prepared for you ever since the creation[51] of the world! $_{35}$Because I was hungry, and you gave me something to eat; I was thirsty, and you gave me a drink; I was a foreigner,[52] and you welcomed me in; $_{36}$I was naked, and you clothed me; I was sick, and you looked after me; I was in prison, and you came to visit me." $_{37}$Then the people of integrity[53] will say back to him, "Lord, when did we see you hungry and feed you, or thirsty and give you a drink? $_{38}$When did we see you as a foreigner and welcome you in, or naked and clothe you? $_{39}$And when did we see you sick or in prison, and come and visit you?" $_{40}$And the King will answer them, "I'm telling you seriously: whatever you did for the most insignificant one of my brothers and sisters here, you did it for me."
>
> $_{41}$Then he will say to the ones on his left, "Get away from me, all of you cursed ones! Go away into the age-long[54] fire prepared for the devil and his angels. $_{42}$Because I was hungry, and you didn't give me anything to eat; I was

---

51. Lit. "foundation."
52. Or "a stranger," and so throughout this parable.
53. Traditionally: "the righteous," here and in v. 46.
54. Traditionally: "eternal," here and in v. 46.

The End of the Unrepentant

thirsty, and you didn't give me anything to drink; ₄₃I was a foreigner, and you didn't welcome me in; I was naked, and you didn't clothe me; I was sick and in prison, and you didn't look after me." Then those ones will also say back to him, ₄₄ "Lord, when did we see you hungry, or thirsty, or as a foreigner, or naked, or sick, or in prison, and not serve you?" ₄₅Then he will say to them, "I'm telling you seriously: whatever you didn't do for the most insignificant one of my brothers and sisters here, you didn't do it for me either." ₄₆And that group will go off into age-long punishment. But the people of integrity will go off into age-long life.

This passage used to be known as the Parable of the Sheep and the Goats, but it is more commonly known now as the Judgment of the Nations. Its interpretation appears to break the consistent pattern that we have seen developing as we've surveyed more than 60 passages from the OT and the Gospel of Matthew. For the first time, we find an image of fire that appears to point to *a long period of imprisonment and punishment* (Mt. 25:46), as distinct from a fate of destruction that is more or less instant, complete, and annihilating. In addition, we find in this passage yet another idea that we have not seen previously in our book-by-book survey of biblical passages that picture God's judgment as followed by fire or being consumed: the idea that angelic beings and human beings will be consigned to the *same* fire (v. 41). Let's examine these new elements in the order in which we encounter them in the text.

We begin with the idea that the transition to the age of renewal will be attended by a judgment with a negative outcome that will be *the same for unrighteous angelic beings and for unrighteous human beings* (v. 41). Where, in the books of Scripture that we have already gone through (from Genesis 1 to Matthew 25), and can we find this idea? I can think of at least three relevant passages; let's look at them in canonical order.

Psalm 82

¹ God has taken his place in the divine council;
    in the midst of the gods he holds judgment:
² "How long will you judge unjustly
    and show partiality to the wicked?
    Selah
³ Give justice to the weak and the orphan;
    maintain the right of the lowly and the destitute.
⁴ Rescue the weak and the needy;
    deliver them from the hand of the wicked."
⁵ They have neither knowledge nor understanding,
    they walk around in darkness;
    all the foundations of the earth are shaken.
⁶ I say, "You are gods,
    children of the Most High, all of you;
⁷ nevertheless, you shall die like mortals,
    and fall like any prince."

Surveying Passages from the NT Gospels and Epistles That Picture Fire and Being Consumed

> ⁸ Rise up, O God, judge the earth;
> for all the nations belong to you!

This psalm appears to describe a vision (vv. 1–7), followed by a prayer for God to come to the earth as judge of all the nations (v. 8). My understanding is that the scene narrates a confrontation that happens in the heavenly angelic council, over which God presides. God is convicting, and sentencing to death, some of the angelic beings of the council, who are here referred to as *'elohīm*,[55] "gods" (v. 1), and as "sons/children of God" (v. 6). The charge they are guilty of is that of subverting justice in human affairs on the earth. This connects with the biblical theme of angelic beings having a divinely sanctioned role in human affairs—a role that many of them misuse, with heavy consequences for humanity. There is, of course, a familiar NT idea of demons as rebellious angelic beings that plague human individuals and interfere in people's lives in various ways. But in addition to this, we can also discern a well-developed biblical theme of large-scale destructive angelic involvement or interference in the affairs of humanity.[56] In other words, angels don't just plague individuals; a number of biblical writers see them being involved on a social structure level, a national level, and even on an international level.

Psalm 82 is more evocative than explicit, but it is my understanding that it refers to these kinds of angelic influence on a social level, and that v. 5 pictures the fate of the unjust *'elohīm* when they are judged and punished by God at the transition point between the current age of human history and the coming age of renewal and recreation of the world.

> They have neither knowledge nor understanding; they walk around in darkness; all the foundations of the earth are shaken (v. 5).

At the critical moment of the dissolution of the present creation, the disobedient and destructive *'elohīm* find themselves disempowered and consigned to the prison of the formless underworld, with the result that their former ability to influence the course of human affairs is completely taken away (cf. Isa. 24:22; Rev. 20:1–3). For the psalmist, it is common knowledge that human princes (and all human beings) go to Sheol, the dark and formless underworld, when they die (see esp. Isa. 14:3–21; Ezek. 32:17–32). But in the psalmist's vision, God sends the unjust *'elohīm* into the same state of total powerlessness and lifelessness, into the same formless underworld. Thus it says, "you shall die like mortals, and fall like any prince" (v. 7).

---

55. Strong's #H430.

56. See Gen. 6:1–4; Job 1:6—2:8; Daniel 10:1–11:1; many places in *1 Enoch* (a non-canonical book that was familiar to, and regarded as prophetic by, some NT writers such as Jude); and many places in the NT such as Mt. 4:1–11; Lk. 4:1–15; Rom. 8:38; 1 Cor. 6:3; Eph. 6:12; Col. 2:15; 2 Pet. 2:4; Jude 6 (referring to Gen. 6:1–4); Rev. 9:14–15; 12:7–17; 20:1–3, 7–10. We can gather the following principles from reading passages such as the ones just cited: (1) that God treats angels as being worthy and capable of receiving delegated authority; (2) that angels, no less than human beings, are not only capable of making moral choices, but of making *destructive* moral choices; (3) that angels, no less than human beings, have been created into the identity of children of God, with all that implies about their worth and their full accountability to God; and (4) that angels, no less than human beings, stand under the threat of having their powers of life and agency removed if God judges them to have persisted in misusing these gifts.

The End of the Unrepentant

Isaiah 14

Isaiah 14 *may* be understood as containing a parallel to the picture we saw in Psalm 82, but perhaps the appearance of a significant parallel only arises when one reads Isaiah 14 concordantly (1) with Isa. 24:21-23, (2) with a saying of Jesus in Lk. 10:18, and (3) with chapters 12 and 19 of the Book of Revelation. When Isaiah 14 is read strictly on its own terms, it appears to be speaking about the king of Babylon, and ironically pretending that he sees himself as an angel who belongs to God's heavenly judicial assembly (cf. Isa. 14:13-14; Ps. 82). On the surface, this passage, in close similarity with the vision in Ezekiel 28, appears to be speaking metaphorically when it pictures the great king as an angelic being who competes with the other heavenly angels and eventually even with God himself. Thus we are presented with the image of a glorious angel who, as a result of his unlimited pride, finds himself thrown down from heaven to earth and even to Sheol, the underworld. There he will discover that he is every bit as mortal and vulnerable to destruction as any human being (see Isa. 14:14-20; Ezek. 28:1-19). The exalted king, who had previously been arrogant enough to assume that he deserved a seat in God's heavenly assembly (see Ps. 82), now rubs shoulders in the underworld with dead human beings (Isa. 14:16-19; Ezek. 28:8-10, 16-18).

Regardless of the fact that Isaiah 14 and Ezekiel 28 seem to make good sense when read on the assumption that they originally were ironic and non-literal in their references to a great and glorious angelic being cast from heaven and joining the human dead, Jesus may well have read the two passages literally. He says to his followers, "I saw Satan falling from heaven like lightning" (Lk. 10:18), which is certainly reminiscent of both passages. Jesus, in other words, appears to have in his imagination a scene in which Satan, a powerful senior angel, is thrown out of heaven.

The famous Christian poet and theologian John Milton has done a great deal to muddy the waters when it comes to the interpretation of Isaiah 14 in popular Christianity. Milton seems to have crafted his epic narrative poem *Paradise Lost* on the assumption that Jesus' statement described an event that had already occurred before the world was created.[57] Milton thus reads the statement of Jesus together with Isaiah 14 and Ezekiel 28, and from them creates a fantasy narrative according to which the fall of Satan occurs in the prehistoric past, while Jesus is still in a pre-incarnate state. Milton's reading, despite the profound influence it has exerted on English-speaking Christianity, introduces a great knot of incoherence into the shared NT picture of the present and future relationship between Satan and the world of humanity. The apostle Paul talks about Jesus having subjected (presumably rebellious) principalities and powers in the heavenly realms to himself through his work on the cross (Eph. 6:12; Col. 2:15); Paul also talks about Satan as the current "ruler of the powers of the air" (Eph. 1:1-2). Peter talks about Satan being actively out on the prowl for someone to eat (1 Pet. 5:8-9); and the Book of Revelation speaks of Satan as the one who is only expelled from heaven together with "his angels" a scant three and a half years before the end of the present age (Rev. 12:1-14). Up until that future moment, he is considered to have full access to heaven, and stands as the one who "accuses our brothers and sisters day and night in front of God" (Rev. 12:10). Even the

---

57. See *Paradise Lost*, ch. 1.

Surveying Passages from the NT Gospels and Epistles That Picture Fire and Being Consumed

OT book of Job pictures Satan as having at-will access both to God's presence in heaven and to the human realm on earth during the current age (Job 1:6—2:8).

In view of all this, it appears that Milton is simply mistaken when he jumps, from the fact that Jesus says he *saw* Satan fall from heaven, to the conclusion that the Son of God claims to have witnessed Satan's expulsion from heaven and confinement in the underworld at some point in the distant and pre-creation past. It's entirely possible—and entirely consistent with all the passages just cited—to take Jesus' words as indicating that he has witnessed, in a vision, the destined *future* expulsion of Satan from heaven. In a similar way, Jesus clearly foresaw both the eventual fall of Jerusalem and the various labor pains of the world to come. He lived on earth as a fully human person, and, as a genuine human being, he was certainly capable of having prophetic visions and dreams about the future. Alternatively, one can posit that Jesus saw the future downfall of Satan because as Son of God he was able to gaze into the future at will. In either case, Satan's "fall" needn't be interpreted as an event in the pre-creation past.

Isaiah 24:21–23

> [21] On that day the LORD will punish
> > the host of heaven in heaven,
> > and on earth the kings of the earth.
>
> [22] They will be gathered together
> > like prisoners in a pit;
>
> they will be shut up in a prison,
> > and after many days they will be punished.
>
> [23] Then the moon will be abashed,
> > and the sun ashamed;
>
> for the LORD of hosts will reign
> > on Mount Zion and in Jerusalem,
> > and before his elders he will manifest his glory.

These verses (vv. 21–23) form the climax of Isaiah 24. This chapter itself forms the first movement of a self-contained apocalyptic section that runs from 24:1—27:5. There will be a lot more to say about this broader passage later, but what concerns us here is the fact that the "heavenly host on high" and "the kings of the earth on the earth" (24:21–22) are sent *together* to the prison of the "pit" (a familiar way of talking about the underworld of Sheol).[58] Both the Isaiah 24 passage and the Matthew 25 passage that we started with are set in the context of a description of a cataclysmic divine intervention and world judgment that brings the current age of human history to a dramatic close (Isa. 24:1–6, 17–20; Mt. 24:29–31; cf. also Dan. 7). Each of these descriptions suggests that only a fraction of humanity will be spared to participate in the age of renewal that follows the crisis (Isa. 24:6; Mt. 24:21–22). Each puts forth the idea that angelic beings (Mt. 25 has "the devil and his angels," v. 41; Isa. 24 has "the hosts of heaven on high," v. 21; cf. Rev. 20:1–3) and human beings (Mt. 25 has "the nations," v. 32; Isa. 24 has "the kings of the

---

58. See, e.g., Ps. 28:1; 30:3; 88:4–6; 143:7; Prov. 1:12; Isa. 14:15, 19; 38:18; Ezek. 26:20; 31:16; 32:18, 23–30.

earth on the earth," v. 21; cf. Rev. 19:19–21) will be excluded from the coming reign of God (Isa. 24:23; 25:6–10; Mt. 25:31, 34), and will instead be thrown *together* into a place of imprisonment (Isa. 24:22; Mt. 25:41).

"Fire" in Matthew has already been established as a stable symbol that points to the complete destruction of one's bodily life that follows on a divine verdict of condemnation in the coming great judgment of humanity. Nonetheless, it is impossible to miss in Mt. 25:46 the fact that the statement that certain people will go away "into age-long punishment" (Gr. *eis kolasin aiōnion*) interprets the previous description of them being sent "into the age-long fire" (Gr. *eis to pur to aiōnion*) in v. 41. Taken together, these two verses (vv. 41, 46) evoke something beyond the instant and annihilating destruction that is evoked by passages such as Mt. 13:42, with its "burning furnace"—namely, the fate of being consigned by Jesus to an extended period of imprisonment in a state of conscious but bodiless (and therefore totally powerless and frustrated) existence.

It turns out, then, that the teachings of Jesus can be seen to put forward two contrasting pictures of the future fate of the unrighteous. According to the first picture (which dominates the large majority of his characterizations), the prospect ahead for the unrepentant is **1** instant, **2** complete, and **3** irrevocable destruction. According to the second picture, the unrighteous face the annihilation of their bodily life, but this is not the end of the story. Instead, destruction of their bodily life results in a lengthy sentence of "punishment" (Gr. *kolasis*[59]) in a condition of imprisonment that is pictured as fiery. Interestingly enough, we are going to encounter just such a picture of intensely miserable (and presumably bodiless) imprisonment in the fiery underworld of Hades in the parable of Lazarus and the Rich Man (Lk. 16:19–31, which we will treat in detail in its turn later on). I say "bodiless," because the rich man in the story, finding himself dead and languishing in the flames of Hades, pleads with Father Abraham to send Lazarus (who has also died) to the rich man's brothers, who are still living ordinary mortal lives on earth in the current age of history (16:27–28). In the general Jewish world-view out of which this parable comes, death sends one's body to the grave and one's spirit to the underworld (Sheol/Hades), where one must wait with all the dead for a future resurrection and judgment at "the end."[60] So it would be hazardous to assume that the rich man's miserable imprisonment in Hades is to be understood as his permanent and everlasting state. The far more natural assumption is that this fiery imprisonment only holds him for a future day of final judgment, on which he will be summoned to a trial that will

---

59. Strong's #G2851; Mt. 25:46; 1 Jn 4:18. See also the related verbs *kolazō* (Strong's #G2849; Acts 4:21; 1 Pet. 2:20 some mss; 2 Pet. 2:9) and *kolafizō* (Strong's #G2852; Mt. 19:5; Mk 14:65; Lk. 10:11; 15:15; Acts 5:13; 8:29; 9:26; 10:28; 17:34; Rom. 12:9; 1 Cor. 6:16; Rev. 18:5).

60. It's not possible to determine, from the information in the Synoptic Gospels alone, whether Jesus taught the future resurrection of the unrighteous as well as that of the righteous. However, Acts credits Paul, Luke's mentor and close associate, with belief in the resurrection of both the just and the unjust (Acts 24:15); likewise, Jesus in John's Gospel (Jn 5:29) and the Book of Revelation (Rev. 20:13–15) both teach that the unrighteous will be called forth from the realms of death to face judgment in a resurrected state. I think it's safe to infer from these three pieces of information that Jesus and his Jewish hearers would have pictured the Rich Man's condition as a kind of pre-trial custody, in which he awaited resurrection and judgment.

determine his ultimate disposition as a resurrected person. We'll have the opportunity to discuss this issue at some length later.

Focusing once again on our discussion of Matthew 25, it seems clear enough from the wording of Mt. 25:46 that, as a direct consequence of a world judgment that occurs "when the Son of Man comes," some people are to be consigned to an extended period of fiery imprisonment and punishment. This punishment will be based their conduct in mortal life. The crucial question for our entire inquiry, however, is whether this period of punishment is to be understood as having an endpoint. Trying to put this question to rest at this stage would require a lengthy departure from our sequential survey, so suffice it here to note that there are sayings of Jesus in the synoptic Gospels that picture what happens to the unrighteous at the transition to the age to come as *refusal of resurrection and consignment to the underworld of Hades*—rather than *resurrection from Hades for final judgment and punishment*.[61]

Thanks to the poor translation of the Greek word *aiōnios*,[62] readers of English Bibles since Wycliffe's time have been given the consistent impression that the punishment in view in Matthew 25 is "everlasting." But the Greek word *aiōnios* by no means always means "everlasting."[63] Young's Literal Translation renders this word as "age-during." That's actually a pretty good rendering, at least in the current context. But *aiōnios* can also be demonstrated to have a number of very different meanings in the Greek Bible, such as "ancient" or "age-old." One could thus attempt to make a case that when Jesus refers to "the age-long fire that has been prepared for the devil and his angels" (Gr. *to pur to aiōnion to ētoimasmenon* . . .) in Mt. 25:41, he's actually talking about an "age-old" fire, since it is already "prepared for the devil and his angels," just as the kingdom that the righteous receive is an age-old kingdom in the sense that it has been "prepared for you since the creation of the world" (Mt. 25:34). But reading the word *aiōnios* in this

---

61. For example, in Mt. 11:23 || Lk. 10:15, Jesus warns the people of Capernaum that in (the day of) judgment, "you're going to fall down to Hades" (quoting Isa. 14:15). As we will discuss in detail later, Hades is never pictured in the NT as the abode of resurrected people, but rather as the abode of the spirits of those who have died or have been killed. Human beings who are in Hades await resurrection and final judgment (see Lk. 16:19–31, which we will discuss below).

62. Strong's #G166, most often translated in English Bibles as "eternal."

63. Liddell, Scott, Stuart Jones, and McKenzie's *Greek-English Lexicon* (hereafter LSJ) is the standard and authoritative general dictionary of ancient Greek. It defines *aiōnios* as "lasting for an age . . . , perpetual, eternal." Bauer, Arndt, Gingrich and Danker's *Greek-English Lexicon of the New Testament and Other Early Christian Literature* (hereafter BAGD) is the standard and authoritative dictionary of the Greek of the NT. It defines *aiōnios* as (1) pertaining to a long period of time . . . (2) pertaining to a period of time without beginning or end . . . (3) pertaining to a period of unending duration . . . ." The idea of "everlasting" is not the first definition in either of these dictionaries. Moreover, *'olam* (Strong's #H5769), the OT Hebrew word most often translated by *aiōnios* in the Septuagint (also known as the LXX), does not usually connote "everlasting" either. Brown, Driver, and Briggs's *Old Testament Hebrew Lexicon* (hereafter BDB) defines *'olam* as "long duration, antiquity, futurity, for ever, ever, everlasting, evermore, perpetual, old, ancient, world, ancient time, long time (of past) (of future), for ever, always, continuous existence, perpetual, everlasting, indefinite or unending future, eternity." The biblical uses and connotations of the Hebrew word *'olam* must be understood to have a major influence on the connotations of *aiōnios* for NT authors—not only in their reading of the Greek OT, but in their use of the word. The LXX was the first major translation of the Hebrew Scriptures into any other language, and first-generation Christians (including the apostles) generally looked on the LXX as their Bible.

way would be a stretch, given the later expressions "age-long punishment" and "age-long life." It's not conceptually difficult to imagine that these latter two expressions could mean a punishment that has been predestined since the creation of the world and a resurrection to life that has been predestined since the creation of the world. The thing that makes that understanding of the term *aiōnios* difficult to sustain here is the overall sense that emerges from the context of the story as a whole. The temporal setting of the Judgment of the Nations is the great transition point between the current age and the age to come. The word *aiōnios* in this context almost has to mean "characteristic of, or lasting for, the age/world to come." There is, in other words, a life that is full of the Spirit and of the power of God, which is characteristic of the resurrected existence enjoyed by the faithful in the age to come. That life is properly described as *aiōnios*. In the absence of information in the context to the contrary, the natural assumption would be that that life endures for the entire age. In the same way, in contrast to the various forms of punishment familiar in this mortal life, there is a kind of punishment specifically proper to the age to come. It is the punishment of having one's bodily life taken away and being imprisoned for that age in the underworld, where the combination of agonizing remorse and frustration over the loss of one's bodily life burn like fire.

What would be helpful, in order for us to be confident that *aiōnios* carries this latter meaning in Mt. 25:41, 46, and that it does not simply mean "everlasting," is a similar example in which it specifically and clearly means "for the age." We're blessed to have precisely such an example in *4 Maccabees*, a book roughly contemporary with the lifetime of Jesus—a work that Jesus even appears to quote.[64] We not only have *aiōnios* in *4 Maccabees*, but also the added bonus of a reference to *punishment* described as *aiōnios*. In the story that the author is telling, all of a young boy's older brothers have just been tortured and burned to death because they wouldn't give up their Jewish faith. The boy fearlessly addresses the king, who is threatening him with the same horrible fiery death as his brothers:

> Because of these [crimes], justice is going serve you up to a more concentrated and age-long (*aiōnios*) fire, and to tortures that will not release you for the whole age.[65]

The author of *4 Maccabees* has just given us a highly illuminating parallel to Mt. 25:41, 46. What is an "eternal fire" (Mt. 25:41 has the same two Greek words, *pur*[66] and *aiōnios*)? It's a fire that's going to torture the evil king without letting up "for the whole age." What age is Jesus referring to in Mt. 25:46? The age to come, the first great age of the Reign of God, which he inaugurates with this very judgment. How long does that age last? Jesus

---

64. Compare: "But that the dead rise—Moses revealed that in the passage about the burning bush, when he says, 'the Lord, the God of Abraham and the God of Isaac and the God of Jacob.' Now, God is certainly not the God of the dead, but of the living. Because everyone lives to God" (Lk 20:37-38); ". . . believing that to God, they [those being martyred for their faith] aren't dying, but just like our patriarchs Abraham, Isaac, and Jacob, they live to God" (*4 Macc.* 7:19).

65. *4 Macc.* 12:12. Gr. *anth' hōn tamieusetai se hē dikē puknoterō kai aiōniō puri kai basanois hai eis holon ton aiōna ouk anēsousin se.*

66. Strong's #G4442.

doesn't tell us that during his earthly ministry. But in Revelation 20, he reveals that it lasts a thousand years. We'll have a close look at that passage in its turn.

In conclusion, Jesus doesn't tell us in Mt. 25:31-46 that the goats are going to be punished without end—he tells us that they're going to be punished for the whole of the coming age. This raises the question of what happens *after* the age to come. If the whole idea that the age to come might not last forever seems strange, that is in no small part because the translators of the King James Version have muddied the waters by both under-translating and over-translating the word *aiōnios* in Mt. 25:46.[67] It is common among English-speaking Bible readers to assume that one endless and undifferentiated age of "eternity" follows the current age of history. But that is not how the biblical writers typically conceptualize the age schemes of the world.

Let me illustrate. Jesus' teaching of the Judgment of the Nations in Matthew 25 is clearly modeled on the great fiery judgment scene in Daniel 7 (see above in our survey). In that passage, "one like a Son of Man" is presented before God's throne, and receives kingly authority (Dan. 7:13-14). In that scene, just as in Matthew 25, the great decision concerns what people(s) and what nations are going to receive the authority to rule the earth in the age to come. God has intervened as judge of the world and has taken away—by instant and annihilating fire—the kingdom of the last empire in the current run of human history. A decision is now made to hand over the kingdom to "the people of the saints of the Most High" (Dan. 7:26-28). Their kingdom lasts for an entire age, and, beyond that, extends through an indefinite succession of following ages:

> And the saints of the most high will receive the kingdom, and they will possess
> the kingdom for the age, and for the age of ages.

There is, according to the prophecy of Daniel, a coming age of renewal that will be brought in by the sovereign intervention of God. The holy ones are going to be given divine authority to rule the world for that age, *and for all subsequent ages*. In view of Daniel's division of the world to come into a sequence of ages, a pair of questions arises that we must answer in order to interpret the "age-long punishment" of the goats in Mt. 25:46. The questions are these: (1) Does Jesus show signs that he views the age of renewal that follows the current age of history as a single, endless age that contains, so to speak, no further eschatological calendar items such as resurrections and judgments and fundamental changes of disposition for groups of human beings? Or is there evidence that Jesus, in agreement with Isaiah, sees the transition to the coming age of renewal as one that signals the lengthy co-imprisonment of unrighteous angelic and human beings—an imprisonment that presumably leads after a long delay ("after many days," Isa. 24:23) to a trial, followed by a final punishment (Isa. 24:21-23)? (2) If we find evidence that Jesus *did not* regard the coming transition to an age of renewal as the moment at which the unrighteous would be resurrected and consigned to their final disposition, can we detect his understanding of the difference between their condition in the extended state of imprisonment, on the one hand, and their condition following the subsequent trial that would determine their ultimate fate, on the other hand? I suspect that we will not able to

---

67. KJV of Mt. 25:46 renders *aiōnios* with two different words in the very same sentence: "and these will go away into everlasting (*aiōnios*) punishment, but the righteous into eternal (*aiōnios*) life."

The End of the Unrepentant

answer the second of these questions with total confidence.[68] We can, however, demonstrate that Jesus repeatedly used the idea of a lengthy prison term in his teaching about the fate of those who refuse to relate in a charitable and merciful way to their fellow human beings. Let's devote some attention to his "eschatological imprisonment" sayings.

The Theme of Eschatological Imprisonment: Matthew 5:23–26

> 23Suppose you are just bringing your offering[69] to the altar, and right there you remember that your fellow human being has something against you. 24Leave your gift there in front of the altar! Go, get reconciled with the person! Then, come back and offer your gift. 25Be quick, make amends with the person who has a complaint against you,[70] while you are both on the way to court. Otherwise the person will turn you over to the judge. The judge will then turn you over to the guard,[71] and you'll be thrown in prison. 26I'm telling you seriously: you are *not* going to get out of there until you've paid back the last cent!

Jesus here uses the idea of serving time in a debtor's prison to picture the fate of a person who sins against his or her fellow human being(s) and does not take steps to make amends in this life. Jesus begins this saying from the Sermon on the Mount (Mt. 5:21–26) by warning people not to despise others. He says that calling someone a fool could land you in Gehenna. His essential point is that if you think there is a class of people that you are not required to treat with respect and fairness, then you can expect to pay the full consequences of your behavior towards them in the life to come. Even if they have no power to hold you accountable for treating them unjustly and with disdain in this life, God will hold you accountable in the age to come. If you treat others mercilessly (even if only by despising them in your mind), then be warned: God is not going to treat you as leniently as you may think you deserve to be treated, but will be just as hard-nosed with you as you have been with your fellow human beings. All of that said, Jesus does not suggest that you will pay for your finite wrongdoing with an infinite prison term. He simply says, "You are *not* going to get out of there until you've paid back the last cent!" If you show zero mercy to your fellow human beings in your mortal life, God will show you zero mercy in the age to come. God is no respecter of persons, and clemency is a two-way street.

The Theme of Eschatological Imprisonment: Luke 12:57–59

> 57Also, how is it that on your own you don't judge what's right? 58For example, as you're on your way to court[72] with someone who has a lawsuit against you,

---

68. A third question also arises: are we entitled to form our views on the basis of other apostolic and prophetic scriptures, if Jesus never explicitly and specifically explains this presumed difference?
69. Or "gift."
70. Lit. "your opponent at law."
71. Or "bailiff"; lit. "attendant."
72. Lit. "to the magistrate."

make an effort to be reconciled with them. Otherwise, they might drag you off to the judge, and the judge will hand you over to the bailiff, and the bailiff will throw you in prison. $_{59}$I'm telling you, you're never going to get out of there until you've paid back every last penny.

In Luke's version of this saying, there is no reference to the importance of having a respectful attitude towards others. It's strictly about the necessity of making it right if you have done harm to another person in this life. Notice, however, how thoroughly Jesus ties together the concepts of respect, mercy, and forgiveness in the following saying:

The Theme of Eschatological Imprisonment: Matthew 18:21–35

$_{21}$Then Peter came up and said to Jesus, "Teacher, how many times can my friend[73] sin against me and I forgive them? Up to seven times?" $_{22}$Jesus said to him:

I'm not going to tell you up to seven times—no, up to seventy-times-seven.

$_{23}$As a result, Heaven's Reign is like a king who wanted to sort out the accounts with his servants. $_{24}$But at the beginning of the accounting one man was brought to him who owed ten thousand talents.[74] $_{25}$And since the man couldn't pay, the king commanded for him to be sold—along with his wife and children and everything he owned—to pay back the debt. $_{26}$So the servant falls down in front of him and says, "Be patient with me, and I'll pay it all back to you!" $_{27}$The king felt sorry for that servant, and let him off and forgave the loan.

$_{28}$But when that servant left, and he found one of his fellow servants who owed him a hundred denarii,[75] he grabbed him and started to choke him. "Pay back all of what you owe me!" he said. $_{29}$So the fellow servant fell down and begged him: "Be patient with me, and I'll pay you back!" $_{30}$But he wouldn't. Instead, he went off and had the man thrown into jail until he paid back the debt.

$_{31}$So when his fellow servants saw the things that had happened, they felt terrible. They went to their king and laid out[76] all the facts. $_{32}$Then the king called him in and said to him, "You evil servant! I forgave you that entire debt when you begged me to. $_{33}$Shouldn't you have been merciful to your fellow servant, just as I was merciful to you?" $_{34}$His king was furious. He turned him over to the torturers until he paid back everything he owed.

$_{35}$That's just how my heavenly Father is going to treat you, if each of you doesn't forgive your fellow human beings[77] from the heart.

73. Lit. "brother."
74. This is in the realm of tens of millions of dollars.
75. Prn. *din*-nahr-*ee*. A denarius was a standard day's wage. So we're talking about the equivalent of a few hundred dollars.
76. Lit. "clarified."
77. Lit. "your brother."

The End of the Unrepentant

We can either take this parable as hyperbolic—exaggerating in order to make a point—or we can take it as a hint that we owe a far greater debt of sin to God than we're accustomed to think. The unmerciful servant in this parable owes the king a truly hideous amount of money. A sum of 10,000 talents,[78] on today's silver market, might be worth about 400 million dollars; in very general comparative terms, the same amount of silver might suggest to the imagination of a first-century hearer something on the order of thirty or forty million dollars—an amount of money that only an exceptionally rich person would ever have, and which an average person would have literally no hope of acquiring. Nonetheless, the amount owed is finite, and the resolution of the parable assumes that the king will eventually get back what he owes, after an extremely long and unpleasant imprisonment on the part of the unmerciful servant.

In context of the whole discussion (Mt. 18:21–35), the people that Jesus addresses with this parable are his own followers, and his admonition is clear: those of you who have received God's grace must forgive people when they offend you, otherwise God will treat you as you treat others, and make you pay in full for your sins in this mortal life. What Jesus conveys here with a parable, he teaches directly and explicitly on a number of other occasions (Mt. 6:14–15; 7:1–2; Mk 11:25; Lk. 6:37). The Good News that Jesus brings is that God's mercy is radical and free, and it is capable of forgiving the most heinous of offenses. But God's grace does come with one absolutely non-negotiable condition attached: you *must* extend to others the grace that is given to you.

Let's pause now for a moment and take stock of what we've achieved. We have surveyed in turn every scriptural passage, from Genesis through Matthew's Gospel (including in our discussion those passages in Mark and Luke that contain direct parallels to the relevant passages in Matthew), that describes a future fate of fire or being consumed for those with whom God is displeased. We have discovered a pattern of common themes that have played themselves out with a great deal of consistency up until the 25th chapter of Matthew. Up to that point, the future prospect pictured for those who have rejected and turned away from God has been typified by **1** instant, **2** total, **7** unavoidable, **3** irrevocable, and **5** final destruction. Our examination of Matthew 25 has opened up a whole line of inquiry: what are we to make of the biblical theme of a coming lengthy and miserable imprisonment in a fiery underworld for the rebellious, an imprisonment that is more than once pictured in Scripture as the *common* fate of rebellious humanity and rebellious angelic beings? Are we perhaps to understand the repeated pictures of a lengthy future prison term as metaphorical ("non-literal") expressions of a doctrine of unending and tormented imprisonment? Is this interpretive choice strongly enough founded to require the setting aside of everything that we learned in our careful survey of every passage from Genesis 1 to Matthew 24? Is there, indeed, any way of reconciling the two biblical pictures that we now have of the future for the unrepentant: the picture of instant, total, and permanent destruction (i.e. annihilation), versus the picture of lengthy—or conceivably endless—imprisonment? I propose that the solution to this puzzle lies in considering that Jesus may well be following Isa. 24:22 when he puts forward the idea of a temporally limited eschatological imprisonment for human beings and angels (Mt. 5:23; 18:21–35; 25:41, 46; Lk. 12:57–59). Can a relatively

---

78. A talent in this context represents about 70 pounds of silver.

Surveying Passages from the NT Gospels and Epistles That Picture Fire and Being Consumed

"literal" approach to his teachings of long, but finite, eschatological imprisonment lead us to a coherent and theologically meaningful interpretation of the end of the unrepentant? I'm confident that it can, and later chapters of this book will carefully develop such an interpretation through a systematic examination of all the relevant scripture passages about "the end." The present order of business, however, is to complete our Genesis-to-Revelation survey of passages that use imagery of fire and being consumed. To this task we now return, picking up after Mt. 25:31–46. Note that because we have treated parallel passages in Mark and Luke as we went along in Matthew, there are no Mark passages to survey. That is because Mark contains no sayings of Jesus about fire and being consumed that are unparalleled in Matthew. Luke, however, does have two independent passages.

Luke 16:19–31 (The Parable of Lazarus and the Rich Man)

$_{19}$There was once a rich man. He used to wear clothes with expensive dyes and fine material,[79] and he'd eat glorious meals every day. $_{20}$And there was a poor man called Lazarus, who used to flop down[80] outside[81] his door, all covered with open sores. $_{21}$And he'd be desperate to fill his stomach with the things that were tossed out from the rich man's kitchen.[82] But instead, the dogs would come and lick his open sores. $_{22}$Now it happened that the poor man died, and he was carried off by the angels into the arms of Abraham. The rich man died too, and was buried. $_{23}$And in Hades he was in torture. He looked up and saw Abraham from a long ways away, and Lazarus in his arms. $_{24}$He shouted out, "Father Abraham! Have mercy on me, and send Lazarus, so he can dip the tip of his finger in water and cool my tongue! I'm in terrible pain in this fire!"[83] $_{25}$But Abraham said, "Child, remember, you got the good things[84] in your life, and likewise, Lazarus got the bad things. But now he's here being comforted, and you're in terrible pain. $_{26}$However,[85] a deep canyon has been put in place between us and all of you. So people that want to go across to you can't do it, and people can't cross from there to us either." $_{27}$And the rich man said, "Then I want to ask you something, Father. Send Lazarus to my father's house. $_{28}$Because I have five brothers. That way he can warn them, so that they don't come to this place of torture." $_{29}$But Abraham said, "They have Moses and the prophets. They should listen to them." $_{30}$But he said, "Please, no, father Abraham! But if somebody goes to them from among the dead, then they'll change their hearts."[86] $_{31}$But he said to him, "If they don't listen to Moses and the prophets, they won't pay attention even if somebody rises from among the dead."

79. Lit. "and he was clothed with purple and fine linen," i.e., fine, high quality clothes.
80. Or "get put down."
81. Lit. "in front of."
82. Lit. "the things that fell from his table." I think it refers to the food that got thrown away, not what literally fell off the table by accident.
83. Lit. "flame."
84. Lit. "your good things."
85. Or "And in any case," or, "But be that as it may."
86. Traditionally: "repent."

The End of the Unrepentant

Within the covers of the Bible, this parable is unique in its characterization of Hades as a place of fiery torment. In some ways it doesn't really fit well into our survey. It does not depict a coming judgment on the historical and earthly plane, as do, for example, many passages in our survey from Isaiah and Jeremiah that look ahead to the coming of invading armies. Nor does it depict an eschatological world-judgment of the type that we have seen in Daniel 7 and Matthew 25. It's a third kind of thing: an extraordinary tale of what happens to two individuals immediately after they die. This story certainly suggests that a person who lives unjustly in their mortal life should fear that they will face an intensely miserable afterlife in Hades, which is the underworld in which the spirits of the dead dwell. But for our purposes, it can be taken as uncontroversial that the eventual destiny of both the righteous and the unrighteous dead is that of being resurrected for judgment, after which each person either experiences eternal life or some form of destruction.[87] There is, of course, the whole fascinating discussion in this parable about the notion of sending a resurrected person from the realm of the dead to warn those who are living on the ordinary historical plane in this age. This indicates with complete clarity that the current fate of the rich man is not his final condition, but some kind of intermediate and temporary state that will be brought to an end when he is called forth to resurrection and judgment. In this parable, therefore, is Jesus perhaps evoking the same state of lengthy, miserable, and even tormented imprisonment that he elsewhere warns his followers to avoid, by making amends with those whom they have offended, and by extending grace to those who have offended them?[88] Clearly, whatever else may be true, the rich man's imprisonment in Hades has to be pictured as having an endpoint. We are not given so much as a hint as to whether the outcome for him in the eventual moment of resurrection will be better, equivalent, or worse. Nor does anything in this parable tell us whether the rich man will find his subjective experience of the "embodiedness" of existence in the future resurrection to be qualitatively similar to or entirely different from his subjective experience of "bodilessness" in Hades. In Hades, after all, the rich man still acts as though he, a person currently without a body, believes that he is experiencing bodily sensations such as being thirsty and agonizingly hot. Might we be intended to imagine that he, in relation to his entire body, is having something like the distressing experience of the amputee who feels painful sensations in the limb that is no longer there? Of course, as soon as we begin thinking like this, it begins to be obvious that this story is not given to us to teach us about the intricacies of disembodied existence in Hades. It's a *story*, whose point is simple enough to grasp: there are very serious consequences to our actions in mortal life—consequences that are by no means the less real for the fact that they only come into play after we are dead. But whatever we choose to take from this story, it seems a highly strange and even grotesque idea to imagine that one would be exquisitely punished for one's deeds in mortal life for an indefinite period in Hades while human history wrapped itself up on the earthly plane, only to be resurrected, judged for

---

87. E.g., Jn 5:29; Acts 24:15; Rev. 20:1–15. One can imagine a consistent eschatology in which the unrighteous would be abandoned to languish in the underworld (which is to say, their punishment would be that they would remain dead), and the righteous would be rewarded by being rescued from death and being given eternal life. But that option is never put forward in the NT.

88. Cf. Mt. 5:21–26; 18:21–35; Lk. 12:57–59.

the very same misdeeds in mortal life that had already landed one in the lengthy torments of Hades, and then consigned to yet more torment as a resurrected person.

Ironically, this story probably has more influence on most people's concept of hell than any other single passage of Scripture—and yet it doesn't talk about the prospect of resurrection, judgment, and final punishment, nor does it even refer to the final state of the unrighteous at all. In a word, it tells us *nothing* about hell per se. Not one of our themes is explicitly in play here, because even the rarely encountered theme **9**, that God's judgment results in some form of anguish, would only be in play if some reference to God's judgment were on the surface of the story. As the story reads, the reversal of fortunes experienced by the rich man is simply a brute fact: we are not told whether it results from some impersonal principle, like fate, or whether it results from some divine judgment that occurrs immediately upon the man's death.

Luke 17:28–30

> ₂₈It'll also be just like what happened in Lot's day.[89] They were eating and drinking, buying and selling, planting their fields, and building their houses. ₂₉But on the day that Lot left Sodom, fire and sulfur rained down from heaven and destroyed them all. ₃₀It'll be like that on the day that the Human One is revealed.[90]

As we've seen before, reference to the fate of Sodom immediately suggests a punishment that is **1** instant, **2** complete, **3** irrevocable, **4** permanent, **5** final, and **7** unpreventable. Everything in society and civilization as we know it, says Jesus, is going to be burned up in an instant on the day that signals the transition from this age to the age to come. By mentioning the revealing of "the Human One,"[91] Jesus recalls the great age-transition pictured in Daniel 7, and invites us to recall its "river of fire" (Dan. 7:9–10), and the **1** instant and **2** complete fiery destruction of the fourth beast, which is interpreted as the last great world empire of this age (Dan. 7:11, 23–26).

---

89. Lit. "days." Gen. 18:20–21; 19:1–29.
90. Dan. 7:1–27.
91. The Greek expression *ho huios tou anthrōpou* (traditionally translated as "the Son of Man") is more accurately and understandably translated into contemporary English as "the Human One." The traditional phrase "the Son of Man" does not convey to English speakers what the Greek words behind it mean, nor what the Hebrew (or Aramaic) words behind the Greek mean. In OT Hebrew, which is one source of the expression, the expression "a son/child of humanity" commonly means no more or less than "a human being" (e.g. Ps. 8:3–4). The same goes for Aramaic, a sister language of Hebrew that was probably the everyday language spoken by Jesus. For example, when Daniel says that he saw "something like *a son of man/humanity*" in Dan. 7:13, the Aramaic phrase *bar enash* lies behind the English, and means he saw what looked like *a human being*.

The End of the Unrepentant

John 15:6

> ₆If a person doesn't stay connected to[92] me, they get thrown away as a branch and dry up. And the workers gather up the dead branches[93] and throw them into the fire, and they get burned up.

Jesus here uses a parable from agriculture (specifically the cultivation of grapevines) to express a crucial warning to his followers: that failure to stay connected to him will ultimately result in your destruction. The picture of workers burning up dead trimmings from grapevines brings us back to many of the themes that we've been seeing over and over again in our survey. The destruction about which he warns is **2** complete, **3** irrevocable, **4** permanent, and **5** final, and **6** it results in the person being disposed of like trash.

2 Thessalonians 1:7–8

> ₅Your faithful endurance is proof of God's just judgment, and it's making you truly worthy of God's Reign. That's what you're suffering for. ₆And it's only fair[94] for God to pay back distress to those who are distressing you, ₇and to give relief to you and to us, the ones who are being distressed. Our relief is going to come at the revelation of the Lord Jesus from heaven with his mighty angels.[95] ₈In flaming fire, he's going to deal out retribution to those who don't know God,[96] who don't respond to[97] the good news of our Lord Jesus Christ. ₉They're the ones who're going to experience the sentence of eternal destruction when he comes, "from the presence of the Lord and from his powerful glory,"[98] ₁₀when he comes to be glorified with his holy ones.

Paul is alluding to a number of things at once in this passage, and unless they are recognized, the mention of retribution by "flaming fire" in v. 8 will not make any particular sense.

The first allusion is to the great judgment scene of Dan. 7:9–14, in which the final evil empire of this age is destroyed by fire, and the holy ones (who have been persecuted under that empire, Dan. 7:21) are given the authority to rule with God for the age to come. All of this happens when the "Human One" appears on the clouds of heaven (Dan. 7:13–14 || 2 Thess. 1:6–7), is presented in front of God, and is given authority to rule. In Daniel's vision, there is a river of fire flowing out from the throne of God (Dan. 7:10), and immediately Daniel sees the fourth beast of his vision, which represents the final evil empire of this age, destroyed by fire (Dan. 7:11). There is a subtle difference between Daniel and Paul here. Whereas Daniel sees the removal and destruction of the

---

92. Lit. "stay in."
93. Lit. "And they gather them."
94. Lit. "... suffering for, if indeed it is just."
95. Lit. "with the angels of his might."
96. See Isa. 66:15; Jer. 10:25.
97. Or "obey."
98. Lit. "from the glory of his power." See Isa. 2:10, 19, 21.

Surveying Passages from the NT Gospels and Epistles That Picture Fire and Being Consumed

world's final empire, followed by the establishment of the never-ending kingdom of the holy ones, Paul understands that Jesus, as the coming Human One, will be centrally involved, as God's co-regent, in the judgment and removal of the powers of this age, and the transformation leading to the age to come. The myriad of angels that attend upon God in Daniel's vision become "his [Jesus'] mighty angels" in Paul's statement (v. 7). The theme of the dramatic rescue of the persecuted holy ones (Dan. 7:21–22, 25–27 || 2 Thess. 1:5–10) closely unites the two passages. The differences in perspective between Paul's and Daniel's characterizations make perfect sense when we realize the second allusion that Paul is making.

The second allusion is to a saying of Jesus that we know from Mk 13:26–27 || Mt. 24:30–31 || Lk. 21:27–28.[99] In this saying, Jesus, himself making reference to Dan. 7:13–14, promises that his followers will see him, the Human One, coming on the clouds of the sky/of heaven with power and intense glory, accompanied by his angels, to rescue his chosen ones. Jesus clearly sees more in Daniel's vision than God rescuing, vindicating, and authorizing the holy ones. As many have noted, it is relatively natural to interpret the figure that "appears to be a human being" (7:13) in the vision of Daniel 7 as a symbol for the holy ones as a community. Taking it that way, the scene of judgment in front of God's fiery throne would illustrate the removal of ruling authority from the inhuman "beast," the symbol of the irrational and dangerous final civilization of this age, and the giving of ruling authority to a rational, peaceful, "human" entity, namely "the people of the holy ones of the Most High" (Dan. 7:26–27). But in the Olivet Discourse, the figure of "the Human One" is Jesus, who will be seen coming as the Savior of the holy ones. That figure does not simply symbolize the holy ones.

Paul's third allusion is to Isaiah 66:

Isaiah 66:14–16

$_{14}$You shall see, and your heart shall rejoice;
    your bodies shall flourish like the grass;
and it shall be known that the hand of the LORD is with his servants,
    and his indignation is against his enemies.
$_{15}$For the LORD will come in fire,
    and his chariots like the whirlwind,
to pay back his anger in fury,
    and his rebuke in flames of fire.
$_{16}$For by fire will the LORD execute judgment,
    and by his sword, on all flesh;
    and those slain by the LORD shall be many.

In this passage, the faithful are assured that they will be rescued and vindicated. As I mentioned in the sequential treatment of this passage above, it is even possible to see in

---

99. I say "we know [it] from Mk 13 . . . " because when Paul wrote 2 Thessalonians, the teachings recorded in Mk 13 and Mt. 24, later published in Mark's and Matthew's Gospels, may or may not have been available to Paul in writing. It may be that he learned them as oral traditions that needed to be memorized.

The End of the Unrepentant

v. 14 a hint of the promise of resurrection. The world-changing moment of rescue for the faithful will also, according to Isaiah, be a moment of fiery judgment and punishment of *all* enemies (v. 16). Paul's allusion to this passage does not particularly emphasize the theme of **2** completeness that characterizes the original.

Paul's fourth allusion is to Isa. 2:10–22, with its refrain, "from the terror of the LORD, and from the glory of his majesty" (vv. 10, 19, 21; cf. 2 Thess. 1:9). This passage, by repeating the idea that people will wish they could hide from God's presence when he comes as the judge of the whole world, conveys the theme that God's judgment and the attendant punishment is **7** unpreventable. It may reasonably be said that Paul's allusion brings the theme forward. Isa. 2:22, the final verse in the passage, explicitly draws in theme **8**, the impermanence of human life: "Turn away from mortals, who have only breath in their nostrils, for of what account are they?" Paul does not, however, explicitly bring this theme forward with the allusion.

Having examined these four allusions, what can we conclude as to the weight of Paul's language about "fire" in this passage?

In the first place, we can firmly conclude that Paul is thinking here in terms of the great future world-transition that is promised (or threatened, as the case may be) by Jesus and all the prophets. God is going to come and judge the entire earth and all of humanity: the unjust systems and empires of this evil age will be completely destroyed and removed, those who love and serve God will be rescued and vindicated, and a new world, founded upon God's righteousness and peace, will begin. The "fire" that very often accompanies pictures of this transition symbolizes the first, radically destructive, phase of a universal transformation from the present creation to the new creation, from the present heavens and earth to the "new heavens and earth."[100] The picture is that of a great confrontation between God and all of godless humanity—a terrifying confrontation that suddenly occurs when the unrighteous are going about their ordinary business in this age (e.g. Mt. 24:36–44 and parallels; 1 Thess. 5:1–3; 2 Pet. 3:1–7). This confrontation signals the **2** complete expulsion of unrighteous mortals (along with unrighteousness and mortality *per se*) from the present creation, in preparation for the re-creation of the world as a place in which immortal life rules in righteousness.

Paul's phrase "eternal destruction" (Gr. *olethros aiōnios*, v. 9) is noteworthy on two counts.

First, the adjective *aiōnios* (eternal),[101] in modifying the word *olethros* (destruction),[102] makes it clear that the destruction being described is **3** irrevocable, **4** permanent (or at least age-long), and **5** final. It's not as though these unrighteous mortals who are to be wiped off the face of the earth will then shortly be invited to take part in the new age of eternal life that will then be inaugurated. No, their destruction is **2** total, and it signals their complete exclusion from the age to come.

Secondly, the fact that Paul can put the two words *olethros aiōnios* together illustrates again[103] the fact that the word *aiōnios* does not connote "everlasting." Paul is pictur-

---

100. E.g., Isa. 64:1–2; 65:17; 66:15–16, 22; 2 Pet. 3:8–13; Rev. 6:12–17; 21:1–5.
101. Strong's #G166.
102. Strong's #G3639; 1 Cor. 5:5; 1 Thess. 5:3; 2 Thess. 1:9; 1 Tim. 6:9.
103. See the comments on Mt. 25:41, 46 above.

Surveying Passages from the NT Gospels and Epistles That Picture Fire and Being Consumed

ing their destruction as coming about decisively at a particular point in time—the end of this age. We are certainly not being invited to imagine it lasting a long time to complete (as though they were going to be destroyed *slowly*). Thus, in this kind of formulation, *aiōnios* seems to indicate that it is the *effect of* the destruction, or the *condition that results from* the destruction, that is permanent, or that lasts for the whole age to come, rather than *the process of* destruction that somehow requires the whole age to complete. Of course not: the long-prophesied destruction of the unrighteous that Paul refers to is more or less **1** instant. Another angle on this is to say that *aiōnios* indicates that the destruction being described is a destruction which is proper to or characteristic of the age to come, rather than being that which is familiar to, proper to, or characteristic of this age. These unrighteous people are not simply being subjected to ordinary death, but to a death that involves their summary exclusion from participation in the age to come.

Hebrews 6:4–8

> ₄Suppose people have already been enlightened: they've tasted the heavenly gift; they've shared in the Holy Spirit; ₅and they've tasted God's good word, and the powers of the coming age. ₆If they fall away after that, it's impossible to bring them back to a change of heart again.[104] Because they're hanging the Son of God on a cross all over again for themselves, and they're publicly disgracing him. ₇After all, when the ground drinks up the rain that often falls on it, and it grows plants acceptable to the people it's farmed for, then it gets a blessing[105] from God. ₈But if it produces thorns and thistles, then it's worthless, and it's close to being cursed.[106] It's destined to be burned.[107]

This passage resonates with a number of gospel passages that we've discussed in our survey, including Mt. 3:8–12 || Lk. 3:7–9; Mt. 7:19; 13:24–30, 36–43. The warning here, as in the great majority of these similar passages, is directed to those who consider themselves to be followers of Jesus and insiders to the Kingdom of God. The author of Hebrews is saying to those who have received the good things of the Kingdom of God through Jesus: *if Christian disciples do not follow through* in their discipleship, but go back to living in the same destructive ways as they once did, and as those around them in the world continue to live, then they must not hope to be protected by some kind of believer's fire insurance policy. To the contrary, they risk facing a destruction that is **2** complete, **3** irrevocable, **4** permanent, and **5** final, and **6** results in their being disposed of like trash.

---

104. Lit. (vv. 4–6 are one long sentence): "For it's impossible to restore again to a change of heart [traditionally: "to repentance"] those who've once been enlightened, who've tasted the heavenly gift, who've shared in the Holy Spirit and have tasted God's good word and the powers of the coming age, when they fall away."

105. Lit. "it gets a share of blessing."

106. See Gen. 3:17–18.

107. Lit. "Its end is for burning."

The End of the Unrepentant

Hebrews 10:27

₂₃We should hold fast to the public profession of our hope—because the One who has promised us is faithful. ₂₄And let's be thinking about how we can stir each other up into love and into doing good things.[108] ₂₅Let's not stop meeting with each other, as some have.[109] Just the opposite—let's encourage each other all the more as you see the Day[110] getting near.

₂₆Because if we sin deliberately after we've received the knowledge of the truth, there's no sacrifice for sins left anymore. ₂₇There's only *the terrible expectation of judgment, and a furious fire that's going to consume the enemies.*[111] ₂₈If somebody defies the Law of Moses, they die without mercy on the testimony of two or three witnesses. ₂₉But suppose there's somebody who tramples on the Son of God. Suppose they treat as unclean the blood of the covenant—the blood that made them holy. Suppose they insult the Spirit of grace. How much worse punishment do you think such a person will deserve? ₃₀After all, we know the One who said,

Revenge is for me alone. I will pay people back.[112]

And again:

The Lord is going to judge his people.[113]

₃₁It's a terrible thing to fall into the hands of the Living God.

Verse 27 above (formatted in italics) is the key verse for our study; I have included the rest of the passage as context. The context once again follows the pattern which, although not without exceptions in the NT, characterizes a strong majority of passages that warn of fiery judgment. The teaching, with its threat of punishment, primarily targets Christian disciples who do not act like disciples, rather than discussing punishment as the appropriate fate of outsiders and nonbelievers.

An alternative rendering of v. 27 might be, "There is only the fearful prospect of judgment and of a raging fire that is about to consume the opponents."

This verse is clearly an allusion to (the LXX Greek version of) Isa. 26:11, which we discussed above in our sequential survey. The shared words fire (*pur*), rage/zeal (*zēlos*), consume (*esthiō*), and enemies/opponents (*hupenantios*) tie the two passages together. Just as in Isaiah 26, the themes of **1** instantness and **2** completeness both stand out here. The **1** instantness is conveyed by the words "that is about to." The author of Hebrews doesn't quote the previous sentence in Isaiah, which says that "your hand is raised, but they don't know it," but his own phraseology makes it rather obvious that he knows that sentence, and that he has in mind the picture of a punishment that is poised to strike at

---

108. Lit. "And let's be thinking about each other for the purpose of stirring up love and good deeds."

109. Lit. "as is the custom of some." Going to meetings in a time of persecution greatly heightened the risk of being exposed and denounced as a Christian.

110. That is, the day of Christ's return as their savior (Heb. 9:28).

111. See Isa. 26:11.

112. Deut. 32:35.

113. Traditionally: "The Lord will judge his people." See Deut. 32:36; Ps. 135:14.

Surveying Passages from the NT Gospels and Epistles That Picture Fire and Being Consumed

once without warning. The **2** completeness of the destruction is conveyed both by the "raging fire" and by the statement that it will "consume the enemies/ opponents."

Hebrews 12:25–29

₂₅Make sure you don't ignore[114] the One who is speaking. After all, those others[115] didn't get away with it when they ignored[116] the One who warned them on earth. So how much less will we get away with it, if we're turning away from the One who is warning us from heaven? ₂₆That time, God's voice shook the earth, but now God has given this promise:

> I'm going to shake things one more time, and it won't just be the earth, but heaven too.[117]

₂₇And when it says, "one more time," it's clearly about the removal of the things that are shaken—which are created things.[118] That way, what remains will be what can't be shaken. ₂₈So since we're receiving a royal realm that can't be shaken, let's be grateful. Let's serve God with appropriate gratitude, reverence, and awe. ₂₉Because "our God is a consuming fire."[119]

Yet again our author characterizes the prospect of future judgment and punishment as a risk that his believing readers need to confront in relationship to themselves, rather than simply assuming that it has to do with outsiders. The words "God is a consuming fire" are a quotation from Deut. 4:24; 9:3; Isa. 33:14; see also the similar Zeph. 1:18; 3:8 (which we treated above in our sequential survey), which envision God's zeal burning up the entire (unrighteous) world. The author of Hebrews is on the same page as Zephaniah, since he looks ahead to a moment when God's fiery passion will remove everything in the present creation that does not have the inner quality of permanence (Heb. 12:26–28). We can see here the themes of **2** completeness, **5** finality (since there will only be *one* more crisis for the world, v. 27), and **8** the impermanence of human life (and, for that matter, of nearly everything in the current creation, v. 27).

James 3:5–6

If somebody doesn't trip up in what they say, that's a mature person.[120] They're also capable of keeping their whole body in line.[121] ₃Now, if we put bits in horses' mouths to make them obedient to us, we can steer their whole bodies.

114. Lit. "decline" or, more colloquially, "shine on."
115. Lit. "speaking, for if they." Verse 25 is one long sentence in Greek.
116. Lit. "declined."
117. Hag. 2:6.
118. Lit. "the removal of the things that are shaken, as of things made."
119. Deut. 4:24; Isa. 33:14.
120. Lit. "man."
121. Lit. "bridling the whole body."

The End of the Unrepentant

> ₄And think of[122] ships, too. They're so big, and they're driven by strong winds. They're steered by a tiny rudder in whatever direction[123] the pilot wants to go. ₅That's also how it is with the tongue. It's a small organ, but[124] it makes big claims. Look what a small fire it takes to start a big forest burning! ₆And the tongue *is* a fire! It's a world of bad behavior. It sits there among the parts of our body, polluting the whole thing. It sets one's whole life[125] on fire—and *it's* set afire by Gehenna.

This is a fascinating passage for our study. At first blush, it could appear that the presence of the words "fire," "burning," and "Gehenna" have created the mere illusion of relevance to our inquiry—a false positive in the concordance search. But there's more to it than that.

In the first place, James's reference to the proverbial forest fire that is set alight by a small flame (v. 5) helps illustrate and confirm our observation that the metaphor of a fire out of control naturally conveys the theme of the 7 unpreventable nature of upcoming divine judgment.[126] The tongue, says James, is uncontrollable, and so at times are the destructive consequences of its indiscretions.

Secondly, James's statement that the tongue is set afire by Gehenna reveals a lot about what he understands Gehenna to be. It would be very strange, after all, if James understood Gehenna to be a kind of prison in which God endlessly torments the damned, for him to say that Gehenna sets the tongue on fire (v. 6). If, on the other hand, Gehenna connotes for him an apt metaphor for utter destruction, then his reference makes perfect sense.

James 5:1–5

> Come on, now, you rich people: cry and wail over the miseries that are ahead for you![127] ₂Your wealth has rotted, and your clothes are moth-eaten. ₃Your gold and silver have turned to rust, and the rust that's left of them will be a testimony against you. And it's going to eat away your flesh like fire! You've hoarded things in the last days![128] ₄Look! The money[129] that you dishonestly withheld from your workers, who mowed your fields! It's shouting against you! And the cries of the harvest workers have come to the ears of the Lord

---

122. Lit. "And behold."
123. Lit. "where."
124. Lit. "and."
125. Or "It sets the cycle of nature."
126. See, e.g., Isa. 47:14–15; 50:11; Jer. 4:4; 7:20; 15:14; 17:27; Ezek. 20:47–68; Amos 5:6 above in the survey.
127. Lit. "that are coming upon you."
128. This expression "the last days" indicates the time of the transition between this current "age" and the glorious age to come (see Acts 2:17).
129. Lit. "pay." This is the unjust wealth that turns to flesh-eating rust in the day of judgment.

Surveying Passages from the NT Gospels and Epistles That Picture Fire and Being Consumed

of Hosts. ₅You've lived in luxury on the earth, and you've completely indulged yourselves.[130] You've fattened yourselves on the day of slaughter.

The main theme of this paragraph is the theme of *impermanence*. Money and things acquired with money will all eventually perish; James invites the rich to see this as so inevitable that it may as well already have happened (v. 2). All that remains when the fleeting luxuries of this world are gone is the record of how well or badly we have treated our fellow human beings. Wealth acquired at the expense of others will disappear, and yet it will remain—as irrefutable evidence against the wealthy in the judgment. That evidence, metaphorically speaking, will burn them alive (v. 3), which appears to mean that it will result in their **2** total destruction. James paints the day of judgment as "the day of slaughter" (v. 5), which invites his readers to see the sentence that follows upon a negative verdict against them as a death sentence that is **1** instant and **7** unpreventable.[131] Verse 5, read as a whole, re-emphasizes the theme of **8** impermanence, applying it specifically to human life. The very luxury that wealthy people live for, and which they unconsciously assume makes them more important, more permanent, than others, will ultimately result in their unceremonious removal from eternal life like so many cattle for slaughter.

2 Peter 3:3–12

₃The first thing to understand is this: in the last days,[132] scoffers are going to be living in mockery of the faith. They'll be living according to their own obsessions.[133] ₄And they'll be saying, "What happened to[134] the promise of his coming? Because from the time that our ancestors passed away, everything's been the same[135] as it has been since the beginning of creation." ₅They say that because they're deliberately ignoring something:[136] long ago the heavens and the earth were put together—out of water, and through water—by God's word. ₆Through those waters, the world of that time was destroyed by flooding. ₇And, by the same word, the present heavens and earth have been reserved for fire. They're being kept for the Day of Judgment, for the destruction of godless people.

---

130. Or "you've overindulged yourselves."
131. The biblical expression "led like a lamb to the slaughter" (e.g. Isa. 53:7; Jer. 11:19; 51:40) illustrates the popular concept of animals being completely helpless to resist their own slaughter. The standard Jewish method of slaughter since antiquity, cutting the animal's throat, brings instant unconsciousness and conveys the idea of instantness.
132. The expression "the last days" indicates the time of the transition between this current "age" and the glorious age to come (see Isa. 2:2ff; Acts 2:17).
133. Or "lusts."
134. Lit. "Where is."
135. Lit. "everything remains the same way."
136. Lit. "it escapes their attention willingly that."

The End of the Unrepentant

₈And here's one thing you shouldn't ignore,[137] dear friends: with the Lord, one day is like a thousand years, and a thousand years is like one day.[138] ₉The Lord isn't slow about the promise—in the way that certain people count slowness.[139] Far from it—the Lord is being patient with you.[140] God doesn't want people to be lost[141]—but wants everyone to find room for a change of heart.[142] ₁₀But the Day of the Lord is going to come like a thief.[143] On that day,[144] the heavens are going to disappear with a roar,[145] and the elements are going to burn up and fall apart.[146] And the earth, and what's done in it, is going to be discovered.[147] ₁₁Since everything is going to be destroyed like that,[148] what should you[149] be like? You should live holy and reverent lives, ₁₂as you look forward to, and work towards,[150] the arrival of God's day. That day will set off the fiery disintegration of the heavens, and the elements are going to melt as they burn.[151] ₁₃But in line with God's promise, we're waiting for "a new heavens and a new earth,"[152] where justice[153] lives.

When Peter refers in v. 3 to "the last days," he clearly means the coming final days of this current age. By "his coming" (Gr. *parousia*,[154] v. 4), Peter means the return of Jesus Christ ("his" in v. 4 refers back to "the Lord and Savior," v. 2). Peter says that Christ's coming will bring this age and this current creation to an end and bring in a new age and a new creation (v. 13). When Peter refers to "a new heavens and a new earth," he is quoting from Isa. 65:17; 66:22. But his words here recall not only the prophecies of Isaiah, but also those of Jesus himself. In Lk. 17:28–30 (treated above in our survey), Jesus looks ahead to the revelation of the Human One (i.e. Jesus himself, when he comes in glory) as a day

---

137. Lit. "And this one thing shouldn't escape your attention."
138. Ps. 90:4.
139. Lit. "—as some reckon slowness."
140. Some mss have, "he's being patient because of you."
141. Lit. "... you, not wanting some to perish."
142. Traditionally: "for repentance." See Ezek. 18:23; 33:11.
143. See Mt. 24:43–44; Lk. 12:39–40; see also 1 Thess. 5:2, 4; Rev. 3:3; 16:15.
144. Lit. "in which."
145. Or "a whoosh."
146. Or "disintegrate."
147. See Isa. 26:21. The mss are very divided about how this puzzling sentence should end: The oldest mss have "is going to be discovered"; other mss say "is going to be burned up completely"; some ancient translations have the word "not," producing "is *not* going to be discovered," i.e., "is not going to be found"; one has "is not going to appear"; one says "is going to be found disintegrated"; and a number of Greek mss and ancient translations simply leave all or part of the clause out altogether.
148. Some mss lack the words "like that," and make the word "since" explicit.
149. Some mss have "we," and some just leave it ambiguous between "you" and "we."
150. Lit. "looking forward to and hastening."
151. Lit. "... God's day, because of which the heavens, burning, will disintegrate, and the elements, burning up, will melt."
152. Isa. 65:17; 66:22.
153. Traditionally: "righteousness."
154. Strong's #G3952.

Surveying Passages from the NT Gospels and Epistles That Picture Fire and Being Consumed

when the entirety of human civilization will perish in fire. But he also looks forward to the "renewal of the creation" (Gr. *paliggenesia*[155]), at his future coming in glory (Mt. 19:28–29). It also is possible that Peter is consciously echoing the words of Jesus when he compares the future day of Christ's coming both to Noah's flood and to the destruction of Sodom and Gomorrah (cf. Lk. 17:26–28; 2 Pet. 3:6–7; 2:6, 9).

Peter describes the moment of transition between this age and the age to come as "the Day of Judgment" (v. 7), and he sees it as a moment of **1** instant (or at least sudden and totally unanticipated, v. 10), **2** complete, **3** irrevocable, **4** permanent, **5** final, and **7** unpreventable destruction of the godless by fire (v. 7). It is not, however, just the unrepentant human race living on the earth that he expects to be completely burned up in the transition from the old creation to the new, but the entire creation as we know it. "The heavens" (vv. 10, 12), "the elements" (vv. 10, 12), and "everything" (v. 11) are destined for fiery dissolution. The totality of this cosmic destruction testifies to the fundamental **8** impermanence of human life, and makes it urgent that Christians live in holiness and invest their hope and their action in God's promise of the new creation (vv. 11–13).

Given that Peter looks ahead to the complete and total removal of unrepentant mortal humanity from the earth at the coming of Christ, can we determine what he thinks lies ahead for those unrepentant human beings who have already died, or those who are destined to live and die after his time but before the end of the age comes? From his point of view, what is the condition of these dead in the intermediate period, and what prospect lies ahead for them when the "Day of Judgment" comes?

Reading a little earlier in 2 Peter, we find that he says this:

2 Peter 2:3b–12

> 3bJudgment has been ready for them [i.e., false prophets and false teachers, see vv. 1–3a] for a long time, and their destruction is waiting attentively.[156]
>
> 4After all, God didn't spare angels when they sinned—far from it. God threw them in dark caves[157] in the deepest part of the underworld,[158] and handed them over to be kept there until the judgment. 5And God certainly didn't spare the ancient world, but brought a flood on the world[159] of the godless.[160] He only protected Noah, a preacher of justice,[161] and seven others. 6And God condemned the cities of Sodom and Gomorrah to destruction[162]

---

155. Strong's #G3824.

156. Lit. "Judgment hasn't been idle for them from long ago, and their destruction is not falling asleep." Judgment and destruction are personified here, and the double negatives, as in 2 Pet. 1:8, are for emphasis.

157. Many mss have, "in bonds of darkness," the Greek words for "bonds" and "caves" being very close in spelling.

158. Lit. "assigned them to Tartarus." In popular mythology, Tartarus was known as the deepest part of the underworld.

159. Or "civilization."

160. Gen. 6–7.

161. Or "right living"; traditionally: "righteousness."

162. Many mss lack the words "to destruction"; they are implied in any case.

The End of the Unrepentant

by reducing them to ashes. God made them an example to people who'd be godless in the future.[163] ₇And God rescued Lot, a person of integrity, when he was being oppressed by the behavior of lawless, promiscuous people.[164] ₈(As he lived among them, that man of integrity felt tormented[165] day after day, as he saw and heard[166] lawless things being done.)

₉If that's all true, then[167] the Lord knows how to save people who have reverence for God from temptation. And he knows how to keep unjust people under punishment for a day of judgment—₁₀and especially those who follow their flesh in a lust for filthiness, and despise authority. People like that are daring and self-centered. They insult glorious angelic beings without fear.[168] ₁₁Yet angels, though they're greater in strength and power, don't bring insulting accusations against them.[169] ₁₂But these people are like irrational animals in nature—bred to be hunted down and killed.[170] They insult things they know nothing about, and they're going to be killed just like those animals.[171]

Peter writes allusively rather than precisely here, but it appears that he conceives of the unrighteous dead as being in a state of imprisonment in the underworld along with rebellious angels. They are all being held in custody until a great trial that is coming (2 Pet. 2:4–9). Peter also appears to regard the **1** instant, **2** complete, **3** irrevocable, **4** permanent, and **5** final destruction of Sodom and Gomorrah by fire ("to ashes," v. 6) as an appropriate analogy for what will happen to these imprisoned ones (angelic and human equally) on a future "day of judgment" (v. 9, cf. v. 12).

Jude 5–7

₅But I want to remind you of something—although you've known all this since the beginning. Jesus[172] saved a nation out of Egypt, but later destroyed the people that didn't believe. ₆And consider the angels that didn't keep to their own realm of authority, but left their own domain. He has kept them in permanent chains, deep in the darkness, for the great day of judgment.

---

163. Lit. "... ashes, having made them an example to coming godless people," or, following other mss, "to those who were about to live godlessly."

164. Gen. 19:1–29.

165. Lit. "tormented his soul."

166. Lit. "... day after day, by seeing and hearing."

167. This is the conclusion of an extended "if–then" argument form that starts in v. 4. I've removed the "ifs" and created sentences that stand on their own; otherwise vv. 4–10 would be all one long sentence.

168. Lit. "They don't tremble when insulting glories."

169. Some mss add the words, "in front of the Lord," or "from the Lord." Any of these three wordings may be original.

170. Lit. "born for capture and destruction."

171. Lit. "in their destruction [i.e., in the destruction of the animals captured through human hunting], they also are going to be destroyed."

172. Many mss have "the Lord." But although a copyist might well think that "Jesus" had to be some kind of mistake, and try to correct it by turning it into "the Lord," there's no reason for "the Lord" to be changed to "Jesus."

Surveying Passages from the NT Gospels and Epistles That Picture Fire and Being Consumed

₇And think of [173] Sodom and Gomorrah, and the surrounding towns. They did the same thing. They were committing sexual immorality and going off into perversion.[174] They provide an example of [175] the penalty of age-long fire.

Jude feels an urgency to write his letter because he believes that dangerous false teachers have infiltrated the Christian community (vv. 3–4). He puts forward three examples from OT scripture as warnings and illustrations of the fate that these false teachers can expect. First, they can look forward to being executed by God before ever reaching the promised land (v. 5). In the present context, Jude's words imply that these people will be refused a part in the eternal life that Jesus will mercifully grant to the holy ones in the age to come (vv. 20–22). Secondly, they can expect to be sent to the prison of the underworld to await a (presumably negative) great day of judgment (v. 6). Thirdly, like Sodom and Gomorrah, they can expect to be **1** instantly, **2** completely, **3** irrevocably, **4** permanently, **5** finally, and **7** unpreventably wiped out by "age-long fire" (v. 7).

As we've seen, Jude's expression "age-long fire" (Gr. *pur aiōnion*) occurs twice in the teachings of Jesus (Mt. 18:8; 25:41, both above in our survey). Intriguingly, Jesus speaks in one of these passages, Mt. 25:41, about humans being sent into "the age-long fire prepared for the devil and his angels," and Jude also seems to hint that he similarly foresees a common fate for rebellious angels and human beings. Of the angels who disobeyed God in the ancient world, he says, "He has kept them in permanent chains, deep in the darkness, for the great day of judgment" (Gr. *hupo zofon tetērēken*, v. 6b), and of the false teachers, he says, "The deepest darkness has been kept for them for the [coming] age"[176] (Gr. *zofos tou skotous eis aiōna tetērētai*, v. 13).

Having conducted our survey through the NT gospels and epistles, we now turn to the Book of Revelation, the final book of the Bible. It is in the visions of Revelation

---

173. "And think of": lit. "Similarly."
174. Lit. "going off after strange flesh." See Gen. 19:4–25.
175. Lit. "by experiencing."

176. The Greek expression *eis aiōna* is typically translated "forever," but it does not necessarily or always imply "forever without end." It seems to mean for the rest of *this* age and into the next, because it literally means "for/throughout the age," or "into/for the age [to come]." I don't think the vocabulary of the Koine Greek of the NT contains a single word that means precisely the same as the English word "forever." To get the idea of everlastingness across, writers use the expressions like *eis pasas tas geneas tou aiōnos tōn aiōnōn*, "for all the generations of the age of the ages" (Eph. 3:21), *eis pantas tous aiōnas*, "for all the ages" (Jude 1:25), *eis tous aiōnas*, "for the ages" (Lk. 1:33; Rom. 1:25; 9:5; 11:36; 16:27; 2 Cor. 11:31; Heb. 13:8, 21; 1 Pet. 5:11; Rev. 1:6), *eis tous aiōnas tōn aiōnōn*, "for the ages of the ages" (Gal. 1:5; Phil. 4:20; 1 Tim. 1:17; 2 Tim. 4:18; Heb. 13:21 some mss; 1 Pet. 4:11; Rev. 1:6 some mss; 1:18; 4:9, 10; 5:13; 7:12; 10:6; 11:15; 15:7; 19:3; 20:10; 22:5), *eis aiōnas aiōnōn*, "for ages of ages" (Rev. 14:11), and *ouk estin to telos*, "there will be no end" (Lk. 1:33). Recall that in Dan. 7:18 (discussed above in our survey) the angel tells Daniel that the holy ones of the Most High will receive the kingdom and possess it "for the age, and for the age of ages" (*heōs tou aiōnos kai heōs tous aiōnas tōn aiōnōn*, LXX, following the Aramaic original closely). *The second portion of this statement would not be necessary if the first contained the idea of everlastingness in itself.* Even the expression *eis aiōnas aiōnōn*, because it is such a rare formulation (only once in the NT), may not be intended to connote absolute everlastingness, but rather an extremely long time—on the order of some millions of years. For example, if a standard age is imagined to be 1,000 years, as in Rev. 20:1–10, then multiplying an age times an age ("an age of ages") would suggest a million years, and "ages of ages" would suggest some millions of years.

The End of the Unrepentant

that we will encounter the only two passages in the entire Bible that explicitly picture everlasting torment for any created being.

3

Surveying Passages in the Book of Revelation That Picture Fire and Being Consumed

At the Gateway to the Book of Revelation: A Look Back and Forward

We are now very close to finishing up our Bible-wide survey. At the same time, the last book ahead of us, the Book of Revelation, contains some exceptionally challenging passages. Before looking at them, I need to make some general observations about the nature of the Book of Revelation.

First, John understands that he is a prophet, and that he is giving a prophecy (Rev. 19:10; 22:8–9, 18). He also believes that all prophecy of Scripture is revealed by God, and that it all ultimately creates a single interwoven tapestry of meaning that tells the faithful what they need to know about the "end." It is many times observed by scholars that there are more allusions to OT scriptures in Revelation than there are verses. This means that you can't take any of his statements at "face value," because in general they will be composed so as to depend for their meaning on their relationship with a whole network of OT prophetic Scriptures. Try to read them without taking this background into account, and you can be guaranteed to misinterpret them. John also constantly cross-refers within his own composition, so you can't understand any statement he makes in isolation. You have to interpret every passage by understanding how it functions in the context of the entire document. That is why it is undisputed that Revelation is the single most complex piece of writing within the covers of the Bible.

Because this is the way that Revelation is designed, we are now going to need to slow down and spend more time talking about the relationships between each passage and other passages, both within the Book of Revelation and elsewhere in Scripture. Now, it's true that there is such a thing as becoming verbose in one's attempts to "explain away the plain sense of the text." As a reader, your way of checking to see if that dynamic is at play is to keep in mind the following questions at each stage of my exposition: Is this relevant? Does this make sense and ring true? Does it add clarity to the relationship between this passage and other passages to which it refers? If the answer to these questions is yes at each stage, then you can be assured that the length of the exposition is only indicative of the unusual density of meaning that John has packed into his text. I will not be leading you on a wild goose chase in order to distract you from the obvious meaning of the text.

Secondly, John has a purpose, and unless we take into account this purpose, we are very likely to come away with a weakened and distorted sense of what he means. His purpose, or the Spirit's purpose, if you like, is to strengthen followers of Jesus who will be facing extreme and even deadly persecution for their faith. The Book of Revelation is not simply a fascinating compendium of information offered for the spiritual entertainment of people who will never have to experience the things revealed. It is far wiser to look on it as a crucial roadmap for people who are going to have to travel the territory. Therefore, one aspect of the meaning of any text in the Book of Revelation that must be taken into account is its *force*: what is this statement designed to motivate Christians to do—or avoid doing—in their quest to remain faithful followers of Jesus?

Thirdly, everything that we encounter from here to the end of our survey will be things that an angel showed to John while he was in a visionary state (see Rev. 1:1, 10-19). There is no escaping the fact that virtually everything in his vision is revealed by means of symbolism. John makes it clear that he understands this. For example, in Rev. 5:6 the angel gives John a vision of "a lamb standing as though slain" in front of God's throne in heaven. The Lamb symbolizes Jesus, who, by dying on the cross, "purchased for God people from every tribe, tongue, people and nation" (v. 9). The Lamb that John sees has seven eyes, which John understands to represent "the seven spirits of God . . . " Two verses later (Rev. 5:8) he describes seeing "golden bowls full of incense, which is[1] the prayers of the holy ones." Towards the end of the book, the angel shows him a vision of the community of the redeemed in the symbol of a vast metropolis that is made of pure gold, whose light source is like a costly diamond, and whose dimensions are those of the cube 1400 miles on a side (21:11, 15-16, 18). No understanding is gained by taking this description literally. It takes some work to realize what is being revealed here, but everything falls into place when we realize that (1) the holy of holies in Solomon's Temple, the symbol of God's personal presence on earth, had the dimensions of a cube, (2) its walls were completely overlaid with gold, (3) John has previously compared "the One who sits on the throne" to a diamond (4:3), (4) John says that the city "has the glory of God" (21:11), and that "God's glory illuminates it, and its lamp is the Lamb" (21:23), but also that John "didn't see a temple in the City, because the Lord God, the All Powerful, and the Lamb, are its temple" (21:22). The conclusion: the community of the resurrected holy ones in the new creation will be the seat of God's full and glorious presence, the eternal holy of holies. What is revealed simply in an auditory form in Rev. 21:3 ("God's home is with humanity!") is shortly thereafter elaborated by means of rich visionary and inter-textual symbolism.[2] Just as Jesus tells parables that require the hearer to work, so

---

1. Literally, "are," but he's referring to the incense, which is plural in Greek, rather than to the bowls.

2. Why can't it be both literal *and* symbolic? Because John has already let us know in unambiguous fashion that he understands the things he sees in his visions as purely symbolic. There is no physical incense burning above the blue dome of the sky. Jesus is not literally a lion, nor a lamb (5:5-6), nor

Surveying Passages in the Book of Revelation That Picture Fire and Being Consumed

the book of Revelation requires its readers to work. That said, let's get down to the work of discussing our survey passages in the Book of Revelation.

The initial passage is from Revelation 14, and contains the *first example*, after more than 80 scriptures that we have examined so far, of a statement that clearly and unambiguously characterizes the future state of certain human beings as one of everlasting torment. This affirmation requires some clarification.

It is true that we have encountered a small handful of other passages above, such as Mt. 25:31–46 and Jude 5–7, which contain statements that have the *potential* to convey the idea of everlasting torment. But the final decision about their interpretation cannot be made without first making some careful observations about the way or ways in which Jesus and the NT authors view the relationship between four things: (1) the death of mortal human beings during (or at the close of) this age, (2) the so-called "intermediate state" (between death and resurrection), (3) the second coming of Christ, and (4) the resurrection and/or judgment of those who are "lost"—i.e., those angelic and human beings who are found unworthy of participating in the age to come.

As I will demonstrate later in this study, there is a significant class of statements in the Bible that allude to a very long period of imprisonment (presumably in the underworld of Hades) for unrighteous human and/or angelic beings. Some such statements seem to picture a dark dungeon, sometimes with chains (e.g. Isa. 24:21–23; Mt. 22:13;[3] Jude 6; Rev. 20:1–3); others picture those imprisoned as facing torment by torturers or by fire (e.g. Mt. 18:34; Mt. 25:41, 46; Lk. 16:22–26). Whatever else may be conveyed in such characterizations, all seem to agree in imagining a state that is (1) miserable, (2) helpless, (3) frustrated, (4) excluded from life, and often (5) chillingly long in duration. We are not free to form the conclusion that this common picture of lengthy imprisonment is to be imagined (non-literally!) as lasting forever, until we first settle the question of whether the NT contains a pattern of expectation that such a period of imprisonment will have an endpoint, beyond which presumably lies some kind of new condition for those formerly imprisoned. Still ahead of us in our sequential survey section lies Revelation 20, which pictures the imprisonment of Satan in "the abyss," followed *a thousand-year age later* by his release and ultimate punishment. Revelation 20 also pictures a judgment of human beings (vv. 4–6) whose outcome is that some rise to reign with Christ, whereas others are presumably consigned to, or are left incarcerated in, the underworld prison of Hades, *also for a thousand long years*, to await a later resurrection. We will thereafter see these unworthy ones being drawn out of Hades for resurrection, judgment, and their final disposition in Rev. 20:13–15. How do passages such as Matthew 25 and Revelation

---

is he a sword-swallower (1:16; 19:15). Everywhere you look in the Book of Revelation it's the same. It's not fair to John to insist on taking his descriptions literally because we would rather have straight, one-dimensional information than multi-dimensional revelation that we might have to work for, and that we might never completely understand. Yet that is exactly the point. John is giving us glimpses of *ultimate reality*: glimpses of God and of the destiny of ourselves and our entire planet. We human beings are frightened when we are confronted by things that we cannot fully understand, and therefore control. You do not control the Book of Revelation by attempting to take it literally; you indulge in denial of your own fear of not-knowing.

3. In this parable, the prospect of imprisonment is implied by the fact that the person is being arrested and bound on the orders of the king, but "what happens next" is not spelled out.

The End of the Unrepentant

20 mesh with each other?[4] In Matthew 25, are we to understand the "age-long fire" that befalls "the devil and his angels" and the "goats," otherwise described as the "age-long punishment" that befalls the "goats," as belonging to the period *before*, or to the period *after*, the resurrection and judgment of those counted unworthy to live and reign with Christ at his coming in glory? These questions are important, but they cannot be answered apart from a wide-ranging examination of the Scriptures to determine the relationship between this age and the age or ages to come, and between (1) Jesus' second coming, (2) the judgment of the living and the dead, and (3) the resurrection of the dead—both the faithful and the unrepentant. The following three chapters will examine these relationships in detail. For the present, however, we will properly leave these issues in suspense and continue our survey.

Revelation 14:6–12

[6] And I saw another angel flying in the middle of the sky. He had eternal good news to preach to those who live on the earth: to every nation, tribe, language, and people. [7] He was saying in a loud voice, "Revere God and give him glory![5] Because the moment[6] of God's judgment has come. So[7] worship the One who made heaven and earth, and the ocean[8] and the springs of water."

[8] A second angel followed him. He was saying, "She has fallen! Babylon the Great has fallen! From her cup, all the nations have drunk the wine of her furious craving for immorality."[9]

[9] A third angel followed them. He was saying in a loud voice, "If somebody worships the beast and his image, and accepts his stamp on their forehead or on their hand, [10] then they're going to drink the wine of God's fury, mixed full strength in the cup of God's anger! They're going to be tormented with fire and sulfur in front of the holy angels and in front of the Lamb. [11] The smoke from their torment goes up forever and ever. And those who worship the beast and his image get no rest day and night—and it's the same for the person that

---

4. In the world of academic biblical scholarship, it is never simply *assumed* that two texts from different biblical authors of Scripture will somehow mesh with each other. This book, however, is offered as a canonical study, in which the "Holy" quality of the "Holy Scriptures" is an agreed starting point between author and readers. Its intention is to engage author and reader in a mutual quest for religious and spiritual meaning, and it posits, as a point of faith, the assumption that the ultimate authorial presence behind Scripture as a whole is the Holy Spirit, and that all the Scriptures are revelatory. Under these assumptions, it is both allowed and expected to assume that rightly interpreted texts of Scripture will agree with one another, resulting in a coherent and edifying pattern of meaning.

5. The expression "give glory to God" probably means admitting that you have been in the wrong (see Josh. 7:19; Jn 9:24).

6. Lit. "hour."

7. Lit. "And."

8. Lit. "the sea."

9. Or, possibly, ". . . fallen—she who, drunk from the wine of the fury of her sexual immorality, drank up all the nations." Cities are always symbolized as feminine in the Bible and ancient Mediterranean literature. In Revelation, Empress Babylon's drunken sexual promiscuity becomes a metaphor for a suicidal addiction to wealth and luxury with which the Great City infects the whole world. See Rev. 18, below.

Surveying Passages in the Book of Revelation That Picture Fire and Being Consumed

accepts[10] the mark[11] of his name." ₁₂Here's where the endurance of the holy ones comes in: they're the ones who hold to God's commands and to the faith of Jesus.[12]

Let's begin by looking at vv. 6–8 to establish some context.

Verses 6–7 above start our passage off with a paradox. It's presented as "good news" that God is now coming to judge the world and everyone in it. Why might that be good news? It's good news because, as a sequential reader would have learned in ch. 13, the entire human world has been hijacked by "the beast," and murderous falsehood now appears to reign throughout the earth. For the moment, it appears that only in heaven, in the Jerusalem/Zion above (14:1–5 || 15:1–4; cf. Rev. 21:1–3), do God's truth and God's justice receive public acknowledgment. But now all of that is going to change. The true state of matters is going to be revealed on earth as in heaven, and the beast and his followers are going to be decisively overthrown. And that is good news.

Verse 8 introduces "Babylon" to the readers for the first time in the book, with an immediate announcement of its destruction. We won't discover this specifically until later, but Babylon is the capital city (and possibly, by extension, the home country) of the world-emperor "beast," and it (Babylon) is going to be suddenly destroyed by fire (17:1–18; 18:8–10; 19:1–3).

Verses 9–11 refer back to ch. 13, which first introduced the "beast," who appears to be looked upon as the world's last evil emperor. He is positioned as Satan's right-hand man, the blasphemous counterfeit of the slain and resurrected Jesus Christ (13:1–2). Everyone on earth—except those faithful to God and Jesus—will worship both him and Satan, who stands behind him (vv. 8–10). The beast and his mysterious assistant[13] will attain deadly power to force everyone on earth to acknowledge his (and Satan's) claims to divinity by putting a symbol of his name on their body (vv. 15–17).

Now the angel mentioned in v. 9 issues the gravest of all conceivable warnings to those who are thinking about submitting to the beast, which they will have to do in order to save their lives (see 13:7, 15) and to preserve their ability to buy things and participate in commerce (see 13:17). Those who give in to the beast's demands, he says, are "going to be tormented with fire and sulfur in front of the holy angels and in front of the Lamb. The smoke from their torment goes up forever and ever" (vv. 10–11). There are so many possible resonances in these words that it's hard to know where to start. We can mention the destruction of Sodom and Gomorrah by fire and sulfur in Gen. 19:24–28, the fiery destruction of the fourth beast/empire in Dan. 7:11, 26, the words of Jesus in the Parable of the Sheep and the Goats in Mt. 25:41, 46, and Paul's words in 2 Thess. 1:7–10. But the strongest resonance is probably with Isaiah 34, which we examined in our survey above. Let's look at it again:

---

10. Lit. "and if someone accepts."
11. This could refer to a stamp (with ink or dye), or a brand mark, or a tattoo.
12. That is, the faith to which Jesus calls them.
13. He is assisted by a second beast who will later be named "the false prophet" (Rev. 16:13; 19:20; 20:10).

The End of the Unrepentant

Isaiah 34:9–10

> ⁹ And the streams of Edom shall be turned into pitch, and her soil into sulfur; her land shall become burning pitch. ¹⁰ Night and day it shall not be quenched; its smoke shall go up forever. From generation to generation it shall lie waste; no one shall pass through it forever and ever.

On first glance, this passage may seem only coincidentally connected to Rev. 14:6–12, but there is nothing the slightest bit coincidental about the relationship. In addition to the fact that this is the only passage outside of the Book of Revelation (see Rev. 19:3) that talks about smoke going up continuously without end, the two passages also have in common a warning call to all the nations (Isa. 34:1 || Rev. 14:6), fire/burning and sulfur, "night and day," and "forever and ever." That's five separate connections. John clearly intends us to understand that these two passages are talking about the same thing. So let's explore what they have in common.

The first thing they have in common is the fact that each of them is looking ahead to God's radical judgment on the entire world. Despite the fact that the angel's warning message in Rev. 14:6 is called "good news" (putting, as we would say, a "positive spin" on it), the basic content of his message is clear: the game is over, and God is coming to judge the entire world. Isa. 34:1–5 is just as radical, if not more so: it puts out an announcement to all the nations that all of humanity is going to be killed and the present creation wrapped up (see Isa. 34:4 || Rev. 6:12–14).

Given that common worldwide scope of judgment, what are we to make of the specific focus on "Edom" in Isaiah 34? This focus, far from being a point of poor correspondence between the two passages, indicates a deep and significant linkage. First, as I observed when talking about Isaiah 34 in the sequential survey, Edom symbolizes the neighbor/brother nation that is a perennial threat and deadly enemy to Israel. Similarly, Christians are called to live cheek by jowl with their opponents, detractors, and persecutors for as long as the church exists in this age. There is no better analog in the OT for this relationship than Israel and Judah's relationship with Edom. The sense of deadly danger from one's very own close neighbors is right there in the near background of Revelation 14. Imagine not being able to go out and do *any* of the normal activities of life in society without risk of denunciation, imprisonment, and death. This is what John is talking about when he says that the beast's assistant arranges it so that no one can "buy or sell" without the mark of the beast, and also arranges it so that everyone who does not have the mark of the beast is killed (Rev. 13:15–17). You can't go buy food or anything else. You can't draw money from the bank. You can't have employment or engage in commerce of any kind. Like the Jews of Nazi Germany, you're thrown on the mercy of strangers, who may denounce you at any time in order to save their own lives. Horrifying as it is, John's characterization stands clear and unambiguous: the beast is going to be given permission by God "to go to war against the holy ones, and to defeat them" (Rev. 13:7 || Dan. 7:21, 25).

During the beast's regime, every individual Christian is going to feel their own personal Edom breathing down their neck. And the temptation that every single one will face at that time is the temptation of Esau, father of the nation of Edom. Even as Esau

Surveying Passages in the Book of Revelation That Picture Fire and Being Consumed

gave up his birthright when, in a moment of weakness, he felt fear for his own life (Gen. 25:29–34, esp. 32), so Christians under the regime of the beast will be tempted to capitulate and give worship to the beast and his sponsor, the devil, and so to throw away their priceless inheritance of eternal life. Give way to temptation like Esau, *and you become Esau, you become Edom* (see Heb. 12:16–17). John makes it very clear that those who collaborate with the beast are the end-times analog of Edom in OT times. And, once again like the situation in Nazi Germany, saving your own life will not simply require a passive acceptance of the beast's claims; it will require you to inform on your friends *and collaborate in the beast's program of exterminating Christians*. If you capitulate to the beast, you will truly have turned in your citizenship in the true Israel, and will have become an Edomite, the nearby deadly enemy of your Christian brothers and sisters.

How does all of this explain the function of the language of everlasting torment in Rev. 14:9–11? Understand that John is writing for people who will have to take their life in their hands in order to walk out the door every single day. They will face a constant choice: either (1) risk their mortal life for Jesus, or (2) trade away their eternal life. How can a person endure such intolerable stress without breaking? If you're desperate for rest from the strain of enduring under persecution, John has two-edged advice.

First, imagine that the effect of capitulating to the beast will be intense misery and torment without end *and without the rest you have been yearning for* (14:11). No human being can imagine the infinity of good things that lie ahead in eternal life (1 Cor. 2:9). Think of a consequence infinitely worse than dying, and you will scratch the surface of the tragedy that you would face in throwing away the gift of infinite life. If, in the intense stress of persecution, the glories of the age to come shrink far away, then use the fear that is totally present to you against itself. Remind yourself that capitulating will not give you rest at all, and that you will never, for all eternity, be able to change your mind, never be able to regain what you've thrown away in order to gain a brief reprieve from the physical death that you are going to have to face at some point anyway. Imagine an excruciating remorse that torments you forever and ever without reprieve, and you will have a glimpse of the cost making the wrong decision.

Secondly, concentrate on the fact that if you do hold out, you *will* receive rest:

> $_{14:13}$And I heard a voice from heaven, saying, "Write this down: Those who die in the Lord from now on are blessed. Yes, says the Spirit! They're going to be able to rest from their hard work.[14]

Can this really be the function of the language of everlasting torment? Can it really be for the purpose of giving Christians under the threat of deadly persecution the resolve to avoid giving up their faith? Let's let John answer for himself in v. 12:

> $_{12}$This is the endurance of the holy ones, the ones who hold to God's commands and to the faith of Jesus.

The Greek word translated "endurance" in v. 12 is *hupomonē*,[15] which in this kind of context means holding on to your Christian profession and to your faith under threat of

---

14. Lit. "from their hard labors."
15. Strong's #G5381; see Lk. 21:19; Heb. 10:36; 12:1; Rev. 1:9; 2:2; 3:10.

The End of the Unrepentant

persecution.[16] The angel has just painted a horrifying negative picture of failure in order to motivate people to hold out (vv. 9–11); now (v. 13) John hears another voice that offers a positive motivation for holding out: the promise of blessing, rest, and recognition in heaven for those who endure to the point of martyrdom. If anyone has any uncertainty as to whether the word "this" in v. 12 ("this is the endurance of the holy ones") refers backwards to vv. 9–11 or points ahead to what follows, a passage from the previous chapter (Rev. 13:9–10) seals the matter:

> If someone is destined for captivity, they'll go to into captivity.
> If someone is destined to be killed with a sword, they'll be killed with a sword.
> This is the endurance and the faith of the holy ones.

These verses, which quote from Jer. 15:2 and 43:11, warn the faithful Christian reader that there is no point in hoping you will be able to avoid the situation that is destined to develop under the regime of the beast. Just as the army of the Babylonian empire overran Judah (capturing the faithful and the unfaithful alike), and later caught up with the Judahites who fled to Egypt, so the enforcement power of the beast will prove itself to have worldwide reach (13:7–8). This, says John, is what you are dealing with. If you face up to it and steel yourself to maintain your profession of faith, you'll make it through. If you expend your energy in wishing for and fantasizing about finding some way of escape, you will only weaken yourself and put yourself in danger of failing the test when it comes. The words "This is the endurance and the faith of the holy ones" (13:10) thus refer to the immediately preceding quotation from Jeremiah and to the advice implicit within it. John is saying that the Jeremiah quotation is *for the purpose of strengthening the resolve of Christians facing persecution under the beast*. In Rev. 14:9–12 precisely the same pattern reveals itself. The angel issues a dire warning that contains multiple allusions to the prophecy of Isa. 34:9–10, and then John explains that the purpose of the reference is to strengthen the resolve of Christians facing persecution under the beast.

Rev. 14:11–12, in addition to being the first and only passage so far in our biblical survey to picture unending torment, also displays an unusual combination of the themes we have been watching. The themes of instantness, completeness, and permanence are not strongly present, nor are the themes of finality, the disposal of trash, the unpreventable or unstoppable nature of destruction, and the impermanence of human life. The only two themes clearly on display here are theme **3**, irrevocability, and theme **9**, anguish. Paradoxically, here the idea of irrevocability focuses on the person's decision, rather than God's. If *you* make the choice to capitulate to the beast, says John, you will find that *your* choice has become irrevocable. You will not be able to worship the beast, the counterfeit christ, and then turn around and say "Changed my mind!" when the true Christ appears. John invites his readers to imagine cooperation with the beast as

---

16. The King James Version unfortunately translates this word as "patience," which completely obscures what John is trying to say. The Greek noun *makrothumia* (Strong's #G3115; see Rom. 2:4; 9:22; 2 Cor. 6:6; Gal. 5:22; Eph. 4:2; Col. 1:11; 3:12; 1 Tim. 1:16; 2 Tim. 3:10; 4:2; Heb. 6:12; Jas 5:10; 1 Pet. 3:20; 2 Pet. 3:15) and the related verb *makrothumeō* (Strong's #G3114; see Mt. 18:26; Lk. 18:7; 1 Cor. 13:4; 1 Thess. 5:14; Heb. 6:15; Jas 5:7; 2 Pet. 3:9) are the appropriate words to convey the idea that we would think of when we hear the word "patience."

Surveying Passages in the Book of Revelation That Picture Fire and Being Consumed

resulting in intense anguish and torment without end, just as Isaiah invited his readers to imagine the enemy land of Edom smoldering without end.

Revelation 17:16

> $_{16}$And remember the ten horns you saw, and the beast? They're going to hate the prostitute, and they're going to make her desolate and strip her naked. They're going to eat her flesh and burn her up with fire.

The angel who is accompanying John on his visionary journey explains that "the prostitute" that he sees is "the great city that rules over the kings of the earth" (17:18). This great city is later named "Babylon the Great" (see 14:8; 16:19; 17:5; 18:2, 10, 21), which serves to solidify the sense that the beast's home country[17] is destined to become the final manifestation of that spirit of world domination which was once manifested by the Babylonian Empire. John's previous quotation from Jeremiah, we are invited to understand, has not simply been a snippet of Scripture yanked out of context and pressed into service in an entirely different setting. On the contrary, its function is to challenge us to recognize that Babylon the Great is destined to embody the ultimate earthly expression of the will to total domination, in relation to which the Babylonian Empire of Mesopotamia appears as a shadow cast backwards in time.

Some of our familiar themes appear to be in play here: being "eaten" and "burnt up with fire" suggests a punishment that is **2** complete and **3** irrevocable, and amounts to annihilation. Being burnt is one thing; being "burnt up" is quite another. Similarly, being eaten suggests not simply trauma, but death and disappearance. We'll find a number of our other themes coming out in the following passage, which also deals with the demise of Babylon the Great.

Revelation 18:8–21

> $_7$She has glorified herself so much!
> She has lived in so much luxury!
> Give her the same amount of torment and sorrow.
> Because she says in her heart,
> "I sit enthroned as Queen!
> I'm no widow!
> I'm never going to face[18] sorrow."

---

17. This makes sense whether or not we opt for the idea that John was expecting the beast to be the Emperor Nero coming back from the dead (a popular idea at the time). In that case, Babylon would be a code-word for Rome (see 1 Pet. 5:13), so obviously Babylon equals the capital city of the beast's empire. Independent of that whole idea, it's clear (1) that Babylon rules the whole world (17:8), (2) that the beast also rules the whole world (13:3–4, 7, 11–17), and (3) that Babylon "rides" the beast (17:3, 7), implying that he is her leader. Is the beast an unaccountable despot, who takes the drunken prostitute wherever he wishes, or is he a compliant "public servant," who takes the prostitute where she wishes to go, or a little of each? The relationship is highly ambiguous.

18. Lit. "see."

The End of the Unrepentant

₈Because of that, her plagues are going to arrive all on one day:
Death, sorrow, and famine,
And she's going to destroyed[19] by fire,
Because the Lord God, her judge, is powerful.

₉And the earth's rulers—the ones who visited her and joined in her luxury—
cry and hit themselves in grief over her, when they see the smoke from her fire.
₁₀They stand a long ways away, for fear of her torment, and they say,

How horrible, how horrible for you, O great city, Babylon,
The powerful city!
Because your judgment has come all in one moment![20]
₁₁And the earth's businesspeople[21] cry and grieve over her, because nobody
   buys their shipments anymore:[22]
₁₂Shipments of gold, silver, gems, and pearls;
Shipments of fine linen, expensive purple fabrics, silk, expensive scarlet
   fabrics;
Shipments of every kind of hardwood,[23] every kind of article made out of
   ivory, and every kind of article made out of expensive wood;
Shipments of copper, iron, and marble;
₁₃Shipments of cinnamon and spice;
Shipments of incense, perfume, and frankincense;
Shipments of wine, olive oil, pastry flour, and grain;
Shipments of beef and lamb;
Shipments of horses, carriages, and human bodies[24]—in other words, people's
   lives.[25]
₁₄Now all the fruit that you're so addicted to has disappeared,[26]
And all your luxuries and your shiny things have been lost;[27]
People will never find them any more.

₁₅The people who sell all these things, who got rich from selling them to her,
are going to stand a long ways away, for fear of her torment, ₁₆and they'll say,

How horrible, how horrible for you, O great city!
You wore fine linen, purple and scarlet!
You sparkled with gold, and jewels, and pearls!
₁₇In a single moment,[28] all that wealth has been ruined!

19. Lit. "burned down."
20. Lit. "hour."
21. Lit. "merchants."
22. For a similar list of products, see Ezek. 27.
23. Or "aromatic wood"; lit. citron wood.
24. The context is modes of transportation. I think it's about slaves to carry you around in a litter.
25. Or "and bodies—and human lives."
26. Lit. "And the fruit of the craving of your soul has gone away from you." It may be referring to literal delicious fruit, it may be symbolizing all the luxuries just named as delicious fruit, or both.
27. Lit. "And all the luxuries and the shiny things have been destroyed/lost from you."
28. Lit. "In one hour."

Surveying Passages in the Book of Revelation That Picture Fire and Being Consumed

And all the ships' captains, and navigators, and sailors, and everybody that made their living on the ocean,[29] stood a long ways away. ₁₈They cried when they saw the smoke from her fire.[30] They were saying, "Who's like the great city?" ₁₉They threw dust on their heads, and screamed, and cried, and grieved. They were saying,

How horrible, how horrible for the great city!
Everybody who had a ship on the ocean[31] got rich off of her—
Off of her wealth!
In a single moment,[32] she's been ruined!

₂₀Let heaven celebrate over her,
Together with[33] the holy ones, apostles, and prophets!
Because God has convicted her of her crimes against you.[34]
₂₁And a powerful angel lifted up a stone like a huge millstone, and threw it
    into the ocean.[35] He said,
That's how quickly[36] Babylon, the great city, is going to be overthrown.
She'll never be found again.

This passage prophesies the **1** instant (vv. 8, 10, 17, 19, 21), **2** complete (vv. 8, 14, 19, 21), **3** irrevocable (vv. 7–8, 20–21), **4** permanent (vv. 14, 21), and **5** final (v. 21) destruction of Babylon the Great. The world's rulers (vv. 9–10), merchants (vv. 11–17a), and ship owners (vv. 17b-19) are all seen bitterly lamenting her sudden destruction. Her downfall **9** results in anguish, not only for her (vv. 7–8), but for all those who have gotten wealthy by servicing her insatiable desire for luxury (vv. 9, 11, 18).

Revelation 19:3

Hallelujah! Her smoke goes up forever and ever!

This verse refers back to the just-narrated instant and total destruction of Babylon the Great by fire. It's also a reference back to Rev. 14:8–11 and to Isa. 34:10, both of which we examined above in our survey. As I commented on the Isaiah 34 passage, it seems clear that the thrust of the imagery of endless smoking/smoldering is hyperbolic, having the effect of double-underlining the promise that Babylon will never rise again. What is cast in dramatic watery imagery in Rev. 18:21 above is recast in dramatic fire-related imagery here. The force of this imagery, which is projected forward into temporal infinity, is that

---

29. Lit. "the sea."
30. Lit. "burning."
31. Lit. "the sea."
32. Lit. "In one hour."
33. Lit. "And."
34. Lit. "God has decided your case against her."
35. Lit. "the sea."
36. Or "how violently," or "how suddenly."

The End of the Unrepentant

Babylon's annihilation will be **3** irrevocable, **4** permanent, and **5** final. Ruins that smolder forever are, by force of logic, forever left un-rebuilt.

Let's pause for a moment and consider the effect of attempting to interpret this imagery literally. Let's agree, for the sake of this exercise, that Babylon the Great symbolizes a great human civilization that achieves the status of world empire on the earth at the end of this age. Let us then dare to imagine something like a great nuclear conflagration, which is to be instigated by the beast and the "kings of the east" (see Rev. 16:12–14; 17:12–13, 15–16). Let us imagine that the firestorm incinerates a large portion of humanity and destroys every living thing that it touches, along with every architectural and technological accomplishment of humankind within the borders of Babylon the Great. Now let us remind ourselves that God's plans for this earth (according to the Book of Revelation) include the radical dissolution of the current heavens and earth (6:12–14; 16:19–21; 21:1b) followed by their radical re-creation (21:1–4).[37] Consequently, if we are to interpret Rev. 19:3 literally, we will be required to imagine that God, in the process of renewing the entire creation, plans to miraculously lift the smoldering wreck of Babylon the Great from the skin of the present earth, and hold it in suspense while re-creating the world. We must believe that God will then transplant it into the new creation—rather like a dead and putrefying scab that God chooses to transplant onto the pristine resurrected body of the new earth and leave unhealed for all eternity. An immolated Babylon that miraculously persists in the new creation, and which literally never stops smoldering into the skies of the new creation, must surely present a radical affront to the Christian imagination. Ergo it cannot be, and is certainly not to be, taken literally as regards its temporal force. Just as we saw when we looked at Isaiah 34, the temporally-loaded imagery here in Rev. 19:3 serves to underline as strongly as possible to the human imagination the **3** irrevocable, **4** permanent, and **5** final nature of the destruction that is being prophesied for Babylon the Great.

Revelation 19:19–21 (esp. 20)

> [19]And I saw the beast, together with the earth's rulers and their armies. They'd gotten together to make war against the One who sat on the horse, and against his armies. [20]The beast was captured, along with the false prophet. He was the one who'd done those miracles[38] with the beast's approval. He'd used them to deceive[39] those who accepted the beast's stamp, and those who worshiped his image. Those two were thrown alive into the lake that's on fire with burning sulfur.[40] [21]All the rest were killed by the sword of the One who sat on the horse—the sword that came out of his mouth. And all the birds ate their fill of their flesh.

---

37. Cf. Isa. 24:1–20; 64:1–2; 65:17–19; 66:15, 22; 1 Pet. 3:7–13.
38. Traditionally: "signs."
39. Lit. "... who'd done the signs in front of him, by which he deceived."
40. Lit. "the lake of fire burning with sulfur." Sulfur was proverbial for burning extremely hot.

Surveying Passages in the Book of Revelation That Picture Fire and Being Consumed

By this point in the Book of Revelation, we've gotten enough information to believe that the beast and the false prophet—to the extent that they represent human beings, as distinct from institutions—are the two most pernicious characters ever to appear on the human scene. Between them, they have treacherously conspired in the destruction of the great civilization of Babylon the Great, and they have led the rest of the world over the cliff of Armageddon like so many lemmings (see 16:12–16; 19:19). Working in the employ of Satan, they have brought about the demise of all of humanity—Christians and others faithful to God first, and then everyone else. It's not surprising, therefore, to find that they suffer a particularly horrifying punishment. John sees them thrown alive into something like a volcanic caldera, whose molten lava glows bright red and throws up blue wisps of sulfurous flame far hotter than any ordinary fire. The beast in particular has been presented as a person of seeming indestructibility earlier in the text. He had been attacked with a sword, and yet had come back to life (13:3). His seeming invulnerability to death, indeed, had supplied the principal reason for all the people on earth to believe in him and to worship him (13:4, 14–15). In the presence of the One who truly has conquered death (19:19), the beast and his sidekick suffer the fate of **1** instant and **2** complete incineration.[41] It is hard to resist likening the beast's demise to that of the seemingly indestructible T-1000 humanoid robot in the 1994 film *Terminator 2: Judgment Day*, who finally meets his end in a fiery pool of molten steel. More in keeping with our method is to note the possible allusion here to Isaiah 30:

Isaiah 30:33

> The Assyrian will be terror-stricken at the voice of the LORD, when he strikes with his rod. And every stroke of the staff of punishment that the LORD lays upon him will be to the sound of timbrels and lyres; battling with brandished arm he will fight with him. For his burning-place has long been prepared; truly it is made ready for the king, its pyre made deep and wide, with fire and wood in abundance; the breath of the LORD, like a stream of sulfur, kindles it.

There are a number of connections here. In the first place, the king of Assyria was feared throughout the ancient world in Isaiah's time, and his armies were regarded as virtually invincible. The king of Assyria thus makes a natural typological precursor or symbol for the beast, who has been held in awe throughout the world (Rev. 13:4). Secondly, of course, we have the common reference to fire and sulfur. Thirdly, Isaiah's picture of a confrontation between God, who makes war from heaven, and the arrogant human king on earth, finds a strong echo in the confrontation between Christ[42] and the beast in Revelation 19—including the common theme of confident praise for God's victory that

---

41. We will shortly (Rev. 20:10) be reading that the beast, the false prophet, and the devil are to be tormented day and night forever and ever in that lake of fire. We will deal with that passage in its turn. But for the person who is reading the Book of Revelation from beginning to end, this first exposure to "the lake of fire" will strongly suggest the idea of instant incineration.

42. Christ, who confronts the beast and his armies from heaven (19:11), acts as God's representative: he is called "the Word of God" (19:13), and "he's going to stomp the grapes in the winepress of the furious anger of God, the All Powerful" (19:15).

The End of the Unrepentant

springs up in the midst of the battle (see Isa. 24:14–23; 30:33; Rev. 19:1–8). Fourthly, and less directly, the definite article that appears in the phrase "*the* lake of fire" (Rev. 19:20) probably implies that the lake of fire is something that already exists, since "the lake of fire" is not an obvious literary reference to anything we have already read about in Revelation or elsewhere in Scripture.[43] It thus potentially connects our passage with the statement in Isa. 30:33a that "his burning-place has long been prepared."

To the extent that we are encouraged to understand Isa. 30:33 as background for Rev.19:20, the connection between the two passages underlines the **2** complete, **3** irrevocable, **4** permanent, **5** final, and **7** unpreventable incineration to which the beast is destined.

It's tempting to pursue a possible relationship between our passage and Daniel 7, based on the facts that (1) Daniel sees "a stream of fire" coming from God's throne (Dan. 7:10), and (2) he watches as "the beast was put to death, and its body destroyed and given over to be burned with fire" (v. 11). The match-up, however, is not particularly good. For example, one is forced to imagine rather arbitrarily that the "stream of fire" flows into a "lake of fire," without any support from Daniel or any other known ancient text in Scripture or elsewhere. In addition, the beast of Daniel 7 explicitly represents an evil world empire, and not an individual king/emperor (v. 23). Since we have already encountered the total fiery destruction of the empire of Babylon the Great in Revelation (Rev. 17:16; 18:8; 19:3), the application in Revelation of the symbolism of the beast being slain and burnt in Dan. 7:11 would seem already to have been exhausted. The resonances are intriguing, but they don't rise to the level that would give us confidence that John wishes us to interpret Rev. 19:20 by reference to Daniel 7.

Revelation 20:1–10

> 20:1 And I saw another angel coming down from heaven. He had the key to the bottomless pit in his hand, and a huge chain. 2 He grabbed the dragon, the ancient serpent, who is the devil and Satan, and he chained him up for a thousand years. 3 He threw him in the bottomless pit, and closed it and sealed it over him. That way, he couldn't deceive the nations anymore, until the thousand years were over. After that, he has to be set free for a little while.
>
> 4 And I saw the souls of the people who'd been executed[44] because of the testimony of Jesus, and because of the word of God—whoever[45] hadn't worshiped the beast and his image, and hadn't taken his stamp on their forehead and their hand. They came alive[46] and ruled with Christ for a thousand years. 5 The rest of the dead didn't come to life[47] until the thousand years were over. This is the first resurrection. 6 The person who gets to take part[48] in the first

---

43. The phrase doesn't appear anywhere in apocalyptic literature either.
44. Or "beheaded": lit. "given the ax."
45. Or "and whoever."
46. Or "And they lived."
47. Lit. "didn't live."
48. Lit. "has a portion."

Surveying Passages in the Book of Revelation That Picture Fire and Being Consumed

resurrection is blessed and holy. The second death doesn't have any power at all over them. They're going to be priests of God and of Christ, and they're going to rule with him for the thousand years.[49]

₇And when the thousand years are over, Satan's going to be let out of his prison. ₈He's going to go out to deceive the nations that are at the four corners of the earth: Gog and Magog.[50] He's going to gather them together for battle.[51] They're as numerous as the sands of the ocean.[52] ₉And they came up, covering the breadth of the earth.[53] They surrounded the camp of the holy ones, the Beloved City.[54] And fire came down out of heaven[55] and burned them up.[56] ₁₀And the devil, who was deceiving them, was thrown into the lake of fire and sulfur—where both the beast and the false prophet are. They're going to be tormented day and night, forever and ever.

Let's spend a moment looking at the temporal setting and context of the fiery happenings of vv. 9-10. According to a common-sense reading, it would seem clear that this picture of an abortive attempt to attack "the camp of the holy ones, the Beloved City" (v. 9) is set a thousand years after the victorious second coming of Jesus Christ (see 19:11—20:10). Many influential interpreters, however, work hard to interpret the millennium (the "thousand years" of vv. 2-3, 4-6, 7) as an alternative viewpoint on the current age. That way, they can interpret this passage and the one that follows it (Rev. 20:1-10, 11-15) so that they finish up temporally at the second coming of Christ. Their motivation stems from two facts: (1) they fail to discover any reference to a future age that intervenes between the second coming of Christ and the last judgment anywhere else in the NT, and (2) they don't like the idea that Scripture might contain incompatible versions of the story of "the end." Interpreters of this persuasion are known as *amillennialists*. Interpreters such as myself, who think the thousand year reign of Rev. 20:1-10 makes the best sense when understood to commence at the second coming, are known as *premillennialists*. We will examine this issue in a fair amount of detail in the following chapters,[57] but the following comments will suffice for the moment.

In Revelation 12, John saw that Satan, whom he called "the dragon" (12:3, 7-9, 13, 17-18; cf. 20:2) and "the ancient serpent" (12:9; cf. 20:2), was forced out of heaven, and in his rage struck out to persecute the faithful on earth "for a time, times, and half a time" (12:7-9, 12-17). According to a voice that spoke from heaven, Satan now knew that he only had "a little more time" (v. 12).

---

49. Some mss have, "a thousand years."

50. Prn. **gog** and **may-gog**. These are encountered in Scripture as vaguely known enemy nations that live far, far away from Israel. See Ezek. 38.

51. Or "for the war."

52. Lit. "the sea."

53. Lit. "And they came up upon the breadth [or the plain] of the earth." See Hab. 1:6 for this imagery.

54. Lit. "and the Beloved City." "And" here means "that is."

55. Some mss add, "from God."

56. Lit. "ate them up." See 2 Kgs 1:10; Isa. 26:11.

57. See Chapters 4, 5, and 6 below.

The End of the Unrepentant

Immediately following the vision of ch. 12, John saw Satan making an association with the "beast," whose career was to last—not coincidentally— forty-two months, which equals three and a half years, otherwise expressed as 1,260 days, or one year (time) plus two years (times) plus half a year (half a time). See Rev. 13:5; 12:6, 14. Satan's "little more time" on earth thus corresponds precisely with the career of the beast.

The glorious coming of Christ as judge and "King of Kings, Lord of Lords" brings the beast's career to an abrupt end in Rev. 19:11-21. The very next verses (Rev. 20:1-3) show Satan's "little more time" on earth being brought to an equally abrupt end. After being expelled from heaven, and spending three and a half years active on earth in association with the beast, he is now captured and imprisoned in the underworld. The sequence: heaven ⇨ earth ⇨ abyss is unmistakable.

This sequence makes good and coherent sense within the overall narrative of the Book of Revelation. As we will see in detail in the following chapters, it also (1) corresponds very closely with the sequence of events pictured in Isaiah 24-27, one of John's favorite sections in Isaiah, John's most favored prophetic book,[58] and (2) coheres well with that which can be discerned in the teachings of Jesus, Paul, and the rest of the NT, to the extent that such teachings address the sequence of end-time events at all. We will therefore proceed on the assumption that the happenings of Rev. 20:7-10 are intended to be pictured as occurring long after the second coming of Christ.

Let's begin our exposition of the themes connected with fire and being eaten in this passage. In Rev. 20:8-10 John sees an overwhelming army surrounding the "camp of the holy ones," and as he watches, fire comes down from heaven and consumes[59] them. On the surface of the text, the destruction of Gog and Magog and their hordes appears to be **1** instant, **2** complete, and **7** unpreventable. When we look at the OT passages that John alludes to in his narration of this part of his vision, we'll find that his allusions strengthen the sense that these themes are at play.

In the first place, John's description recalls 2 Kgs 1:10-14, in which Elijah twice calls for fire to "come down from heaven and consume"[60] the king's soldiers who have come to arrest him. The allusion to that story lends weight to the sense of **1** instantness. See also Rev. 11:5, in which Christ's "two witnesses" call forth fire that "consumes their enemies" just as Elijah did.

In addition to its allusion to Elijah and the "two witnesses," Rev. 20:9 also contains a very clear allusion to Ezekiel 38, which we examined above in our survey. In addition to the connection created by John's reference to "*Gog* of the land of *Magog*" (see Ezek. 38:2; Rev. 20:8), there is an intriguing connection in the fact that Satan's hordes attack because they succumb to *temptation* (see Ezek. 38:10; Rev. 20:8). Finally,[61] the totally

---

58. The UBS *Greek New Testament* (2nd edn; New York: American Bible Society, 1968) lists well over a hundred quotations from Isaiah in the Book of Revelation.

59. The verb that John uses this to express the action of the fire that comes down from heaven is *katesthiō* (Strong's #G2719), which literally means to hungrily or aggressively eat, to devour, to gobble up. It's often used metaphorically in Greek to describe fire that completely burns things up.

60. The Hebrew verb that Elijah uses this to express the annihilating action of the fire is *'akal* (Strong's #H398), literally "to eat." As in Greek, this Hebrew word is used for the action of fire that burns things up completely.

61. I.e., this is the final connection that I will discuss here, which is not to deny that there are other

peaceful and blessed kingdom of Messiah David pictured in Ezek. 37:24 sets the scene for a much later ("after many days," Ezek. 38:8) attack by far-flung enemies, just as the millennial kingdom of Rev. 20:4–6 sets the scene for the much later ("when the thousand years are over," 20:7) attack by Satan and his hordes who come from "the four corners of the earth."

Perhaps the most striking connections are to be seen between our passage and Isa. 26:10–11, which we also examined above in our survey. In that passage, the wicked are "shown favor," i.e., grace, but they do not, from that experience, "learn righteousness" (26:10). Fatefully and fatally self-deluded, the wicked misinterpret God's grace as weakness or inattentiveness. They come into the "land of uprightness" expecting to gain an easy victory by treachery ("they deal perversely," v. 10). They have no idea that they are about to be "consumed"[62] by fire from God (vv. 10–11 || Rev. 20:9). A foreshadowing of the imprisonment of Satan in the underworld (together with rebellious human beings) at the transition to the reign of the holy ones with Christ can be seen in Isa. 24:21–23; 25:6–10 || Rev. 19:21–20:6. A clear precursor of the final demise of Satan along with the wicked can also be seen in Isa. 26:20—27:1 || Rev. 20:7–10. The fate of Satan, that ancient serpent, is the same in each passage: his destruction is **1** instant, **2** complete, **3** irrevocable, **4** permanent, **5** final, and **7** unpreventable.

John's readers could be forgiven for entertaining doubts as to whether Satan's destruction in v. 9 is absolutely **4** permanent and **5** final. After all, they have seen Satan succeed in convincing vast numbers of human beings to fight against Christ and the holy ones in Revelation 19. He and his hordes were thwarted, and he was completely disempowered, but he was later released. Now, having been exterminated in Rev. 20:9, will Satan perhaps spring up yet again sometime in the future? Or, for that matter, is it certain that the fire of v. 9 consumed *Satan*, or only the human beings that he had deceived? Verse 10 answers both of these questions. Satan, thrown into the same state of endless imprisonment and punishment as the beast and the false prophet, is never again going to be a threat to the holy ones.

John is here, as in Rev. 19:3, alluding to Isa. 34:10, which we discussed above in our survey. That passage is the one single text in the OT that refers to endless sulfur-hot burning.[63] It is common knowledge that the Book of Revelation was written for Christians under the pressure of persecution. The anxiety with which the persecuted faithful look upon Satan and their persecutors must surely mirror exactly the anxiety with which the Israelites looked upon the Edomites, their perennially hostile and exceedingly dangerous neighbor to the southeast. John's prophetic imagery here gives the same assurance to the faithful of the Christian era as Isa. 34:10 gave to the faithful of Isaiah's day: the promised cessation of danger from those who hate you and wish you harm is absolutely **4** permanent and **5** final.

I suppose that, when confronted with this unmistakable parallelism of imagery and theme, we have the option of engaging one of two possible tactics in order to salvage the idea that the lake of fire, with its endless torment, is to be taken literally in its temporal

---

and subtler connections between these two passages that can be explored.

62. Once again the verb here is *'akal*, literally "to devour."

63. Cf. "night and day ... forever and ever," Isa. 34:10; "day and night forever and ever," Rev. 20:10.

aspect. First, we could claim that Isaiah's prophecy reveals that Edom really will literally be burning and throwing up toxic smoke forever and ever. We could reason that since that passage is to be taken literally, it is only consistent that Rev. 20:10 should also be taken literally. Taken consistently, of course, this position would require us to embrace the multiple obscenity of imagining that Edom, Babylon the Great, and Gehenna (right outside the walls of the New Jerusalem according to Isa. 66:24) will belch their literal toxic smoke into the skies of the new creation for all eternity. Obscene though it may be, this option is available to us if we wish to embrace it. Secondly, we could choose to interpret Isa. 34:10 metaphorically and Rev. 20:10 literally. It may, indeed, be possible to find a precedent in Scripture for imagery that is presented metaphorically in the OT and is reinterpreted literally in the NT. The Human Being/Son of Man figure in Daniel 7 immediately comes to mind, for example.[64] Fertile minds could probably come up with other possible examples to add to this one. But the question that presses itself on us here is this: *Why would anyone who believed in a loving and just God wish to work so hard to hold on to the idea of literally infinite torment as punishment for finite wrongdoing, if they were shown a clear, reasonable, consistent, and even relatively compelling basis in Scripture for taking it non-literally?*

Revelation 20:11–15

> [11]And I saw a huge white throne, and the One who sat on it. From the presence of that One, earth and heaven had fled away, and there'd been no room found for them. [12]And I saw the dead, the powerful and the weak,[65] standing in front of the throne. And books were opened. And another book was opened: the Book of Life. The dead were judged on the basis of the things written in the books—on the basis of their actions.[66]
> [13]And the ocean[67] gave up the dead that were in *it*, and Death and Hades gave up the dead that were in *them*, and they were judged on the basis of their actions. [14]And Death and Hades[68] were thrown in the lake of fire. That's the second death, the lake of fire. [15]If somebody wasn't found recorded[69] in the Book of Life, they were thrown in the lake of fire.

Let me begin with some general exegetical remarks.

---

64. In Daniel 7, Daniel sees "one like a human being" being presented in front of God's throne, and being given "dominion and glory and kingship, that all peoples, nations, and languages should serve him" (vv. 13–14). Later in the chapter, an angel explains this part of Daniel's vision in these words: "The court shall sit in judgment, and . . . the kingship and dominion and the greatness of the kingdoms under the whole heaven shall be given to the people of the holy ones of the Most High . . ." (vv. 26–27). In other words, the Human One (traditionally "the Son of Man"), appears to be a metaphor for the community of the holy ones. In the NT Gospels and Book of Revelation, we are given to understand that this figure is a literal person, namely Jesus.

65. Lit. "the great and the small."
66. Traditionally: "their works."
67. Lit. "the sea."
68. Prn. ***hay-deez***.
69. Lit. "written."

John watches as record books are opened, which contain a complete accounting of everything that people have done in their mortal lives, and God the Judge determines the future destiny of all the dead on the explicit basis of what they have done in their mortal lives (v. 12). The "book of life" also stands open. We are not told why it is open. Is it in order to record the names of those who will, on the basis of this great judgment, be "considered worthy to take part in that age, and in the resurrection from among the dead" (Lk. 20:34), or is it perhaps open to reveal the already-recorded names of those selected for eternal life "from the creation of the world" (Rev. 13:8)? Or both? At least this much is clear: the fact of foreordination exists alongside, and does not contradict, the fact of judgment on the basis of what human beings actually do.

Whatever the answer to the above question, the result of the judgment is that all the inhabitants are drawn out from the traditional realms of the dead: from the primeval ocean, also known as "the deep" (see Gen. 1:2; Job 41:31–32; Ps. 104:6; Ezek. 26:19), from Death, and from Hades. In reading v. 13, it is easy to form the image of two great wastebaskets being emptied into the lake of fire. But imagining v. 13 in that way will not work. Death and Hades contain unresurrected souls, and imagining them being emptied out into the lake of fire leaves out both the (implicit) resurrection and the (explicit) judgment of those who have been contained in them. There is a second interpretation of John's words in v. 13 that makes better sense in the context. Death and Hades, as symbols of human mortality, are themselves thrown into the lake of fire (v. 14). If "the first death" is presumably the death that happens at the end of a mortal human life, and presumably results (for the unrepentant) in a period of incarceration, beyond which lies judgment, then "the second death" must refer to the death of the subsequently resurrected, tried, and condemned person—a death that is **2** complete, **3** irrevocable, **4** permanent, and **5** final. There will come a time, God says to John, when "death will no longer exist" (Rev. 21:4; cf. Isa. 25:6–10). "The second death," in other words, when applied to Death and Hades, appears to mean that they will no longer exist. Thus consistency suggests that "the second death," when applied to human and angelic beings, will mean that they too will no longer exist.

Death, after all, is one of the deepest symbols that we human beings have. The appearance to us is that death represents a kind of cessation, a kind of extinction of the person: the one who has died is no longer there. It is a matter of Christian revelation and hope that the death we subjectively observe to be final is not in fact final, but potentially leads to an infinitely greater life. Even the death of those destined never to be selected for eternal life is not, in the Book of Revelation and the NT generally, represented as the final extinction of the person. But the picture of a fiery lake, into which mortal created beings are dumped, and which is explained as "the second death," must press on the human imagination the idea of an extinction that is **2** complete, **3** irrevocable, **4** permanent, and above all **5** final. It must also, in the strongest possible terms, proclaim **8** the impermanence of human life, or, more accurately, the impermanence of any created being that obstinately chooses to live in breach of the purpose for which it was created.

It is noteworthy that John does not refer to endless torment in Rev. 20:13–15. The only two places in which he does so are 14:9–11, where the express purpose is to strengthen the resolve of those tempted to capitulate to the beast, and 20:10, where

The End of the Unrepentant

the apparent purpose is to reassure the faithful that Satan (and the beast and the false prophet) will never again be a threat to humanity. Indeed, these (Rev. 14:9–11; 20:10) are the only two verses in the entire Bible that explicitly picture endless torment for any sentient being, human or angelic.

Revelation 21:6–8

$_6$The Enthroned One said to me,
It's done!
I'm the Alpha and the Omega,[70]
The Beginning and the End.[71]
To the person who's thirsty,
I'm going to give free permission to drink from the spring of the water of life.[72]
$_7$The person that wins the battle is going to inherit all this.[73]
I'm going to be their God,
and they're going to be my child.[74]

$_8$But as for the cowards, and the untrustworthy,[75] and the filthy,[76] and the murderers, and the sexually immoral, and the sorcerers, and the idolaters, and all the liars, their inheritance is going to be in the lake that burns with fire and sulfur—which is the second death.

I have already said what I have to say about the expressions "the lake of fire" and "the second death" above, and there's nothing in this passage that is new in terms of its nature or its place in John's narrative of the end. One thing calls for our attention, however. In the list of the sorts of people who will be found deserving of destruction in the lake of fire, the first two items refer pointedly to Christians who give up their profession of faith in order to have their lives spared during the reign of the beast. Our passage closely echoes the words that conclude Christ's letter to Smyrna, in which Jesus promises,

---

70. These are the first and last letters of the Greek alphabet.
71. Isa. 44:6; 48:12.
72. Isa. 55:1; Jer. 2:13; Ps. 36:9; see Jn 7:37.
73. Lit. "these things."
74. See 2 Sam. 7:14, now extended to all the faithful.
75. Or "the faithless," or "the unbelievers." In John's world, all these amount to the same thing. Those who don't trust God and Christ will eventually prove themselves unwilling to risk their lives for the hope of resurrection, and so they will prove themselves untrustworthy by abandoning their faith under persecution and worshiping the beast.
76. Lit. "vile." By implication, they are filthy and disgusting because of practices to do with idolatry.

Surveying Passages in the Book of Revelation That Picture Fire and Being Consumed

Revelation 2:10–11

> ₁₀Be faithful right up to death, and I'll give you the crown of life ₁₁Whoever has ears, let them hear what the Spirit says to the communities. The person who wins this battle won't ever be hurt by the second death.

The eternal life that Jesus promises in positive terms in Rev. 2:10–11, God's voice from the throne promises again in Rev. 21:6–7. Similarly, what Jesus promises positively in Rev. 2:11 to the person who wins the battle (i.e. invulnerability to the second death) becomes a warning in negative terms in Rev. 21:8. Just as we have repeatedly seen in the teachings of Jesus, we see here in Rev. 21:8 that the most terrifying threats are not directed in the first instance towards those who are outsiders in relation to the Christian community, but to those hearers and readers who aspire to be, and believe themselves to be, faithful followers of Jesus. Whoever our "outsiders" may be—whether it be those non-Christians over there whom we never expect to meet, or these non-Christians here, whom we have invited to an evangelistic service, Scripture gives us scant encouragement to preach to non-believers, or to indulge the fantasy about non-believers, that endless fiery torment hangs over them. Almost without exception, the most fearsome warnings of fiery destruction (as in this case) are directed at Christians, and they are clearly intended to spur the would-be faithful to imagine, and be repulsed by, the possibility of *their own* perdition.

CONCLUDING REMARKS ON CHAPTERS 1–3

We have now looked squarely at every passage in the Bible, from Genesis to Revelation, that pictures the fate of the unrepentant in terms of fire or being consumed. Of those eighty-eight or so passages, the overwhelming majority—in the New Testament as well as in the Old Testament—clearly use this imagery to convey the idea of a complete, final, and irrevocable destruction.[77] Only four passages (Isa. 34:11–12; Rev. 14:11; 19:3; 20:10) explicitly picture a fire that keeps burning forever and ever, and of these four, two (Isa. 34:11–12 and Rev. 19:3, which alludes to it) are obviously not intended to be taken literally in their temporal aspect. In these passages, the picture of everlasting burning or smoldering has the function of conveying the strongest possible assurance that the deadliest enemy of the faithful will never rise again. The other two passages, Rev. 14:11 and Rev. 20:10, also show a very close literary relationship with Isa. 34:11–12. But whereas the everlasting fate pictured for the devil, the beast, and the false prophet in Rev. 20:10 makes excellent sense in terms of the assurance function that characterizes Isa. 34:11–12, the picture of everlasting fiery torment in Rev. 14:11 clearly has a separate

---

77. Passages such as Jude 1:5–23 and 2 Pet. 2:6 illustrate this statement, rather than undermining it. Granted, looked upon from the viewpoint of Christian eschatology, the destruction of the cities of Sodom and Gomorrah does not represent the final end *of the individual inhabitants* of those cities. Those people would typically be viewed as incarcerated in Hades awaiting judgment. But it is Peter and Jude's *use* of the story of the cities of Sodom and Gomorrah—along with the stories such as Korah's rebellion (Jude 1:11; Num. 16:1–35) and Noah's flood (2 Pet. 3:1–13; Gen. 6:1—7:24)—that must be noted. Peter and Jude employ these stories to illustrate the idea of a sudden, complete, and permanent destruction.

function. In that passage, the horror of everlasting torment is presented to the imagination of Christians for the purpose of strengthening their resolve to resist cooperating with the beast, even at the risk of their mortal lives.

When we recognize the *function* of the picture of everlasting burning in Isa. 34:11–12, this naturally frees us to draw the conclusion that this picture is not to be understood literally in its temporal aspect. Nonetheless, whatever it is that makes us feel free to use this biblically sanctioned interpretive move in relation to a geographical place, such as Babylon the Great in Rev. 19:3, does not necessarily make it equally easy to do so relation to personal beings in Rev. 14:11 and 20:10.

There are a number of possible reasons why this might be so. First, it's undeniable that repetition of an idea, in and of itself, has an effect on our thinking. Many people will have been exposed to repeated messages by authority figures insisting upon the literalness of everlasting torment. Such people may well find it difficult to switch tracks and begin viewing things in a different way. Secondly, human beings naturally find it difficult to conceive of their own extinction (Eccl. 3:11). Consequently, they may automatically find the notion that they are either headed for everlasting bliss or for everlasting torment more plausible than the notion that they might be headed for extinction. Thirdly, there is a certain amount of material in the teachings of Jesus that looks as though it might be talking about everlasting—or at least very lengthy—torment for human beings. The ambiguity around this is going to have to be straightened out in order to make headway with passages like Rev. 14:11-12 and 20:10.

Most Christian readers will rightly try to give first place to the teachings of Jesus when it comes to the interpretation of biblical materials. Such people are entitled not to be satisfied with an interpretation of a passage like Rev. 14:11-12 until they feel some confidence as to the relationship between that passage and teachings of Jesus such as Mt. 25:31–46, the Judgment of the Nations. However, an understanding of that passage (and ones like it, such as Mt. 5:23–26 and 18:8–9) cannot be gained by simply concentrating on what can be learned from passages that employ the imagery of fire and being consumed. A solid grasp of what is going on in Matthew 25 will require the acquisition of a much broader understanding of biblical eschatology. That's the role of the following chapters, Chapters 4–6. They will serve to fill in some very important biblical background to the teachings of Jesus and the NT that we surveyed in Chapters 2 and 3. Starting with the Psalms and the Prophets of the OT, and ending with the teachings of Jesus and the NT writers, we are going to study the biblical ideas of the coming of a new age of God's Reign, the idea of a world judgment, and the idea of resurrection, along with the relationship between these things and the idea of future rewards and punishments. With this broader knowledge, we will stand well equipped to interpret the more difficult-to-understand passages in our survey above.

4

The Changing of the Ages in the Old Testament

THE GENERAL TOPIC OF beliefs about the future in the Old Testament is a huge one. Nonetheless, our discussion won't have to be overly long, because we are going to be focusing in on one single idea: the expectation that this age is going to come to an end and be replaced by a new age of renewal, in which God's Kingdom will extend throughout the Earth.

Now, one qualification has to be made before we get about this task. That is to point out that none of the OT passages that we will be looking will use the specific terminology of "this age" and "the age/ages to come." What makes each of the included passages eligible for discussion in our survey is the fact that they all picture a future coming of God as judge and king to humanity as a whole, and they all seem to picture this coming, this arrival, as the inaugural moment of a worldwide reign of God in justice and peace. Conceptually, the era that follows upon the establishment of God's global reign is a "new age," whether it is described in those particular words or not.

One thing that makes our review of passages manageable is the fact you can read all the way from Genesis to Job—and even add in Proverbs, Ecclesiastes, and the Song of Solomon—without ever once encountering the expectation of a future transition from this age to an age in which God's Kingdom reigns throughout the world. The appearance is that the authors of the Pentateuch and all of the historical books operated under two common assumptions: (1) world history begins at the creation, and (2) certain major judgment and salvation events (such as the Flood, the Exodus, the Entry into the Promised Land, the Exile, and the Return) stand as the milestones of human history. Occasionally these events are viewed as being in the future, as when God tells Noah that he's going to bring a flood on the earth in Gen. 6:7, or as when Solomon prays in 2 Chron. 6:36–39 for the Israelites to be restored to their land after being sent into exile. They are much more commonly viewed from a contemporary perspective, or as having happened in the past. In all this material, there is never a single prediction that God is going to interrupt history and establish his kingdom as a completely new start for the entire world. The current age is all that comes into view.

For example, when Moses pronounces promises and warnings to the tribes of Israel in Deuteronomy 27–30, he prophesies that God will bless the Israelites in the Promised

The End of the Unrepentant

Land whenever they obey his commands and keep his covenant. He also prophesies that they will be cursed, and even risk going into exile from the land, whenever they turn away from God and break the covenant. Moses, unlike many of the later literary prophets[1] from Isaiah to Malachi, does not look ahead to a final radical transition, beyond which lies a new time or age in which God's reign will come in fullness and Israel will no longer face the risk of falling out of God's favor. He appears to view the current age, with its promise of blessing and risk of trouble, as stretching out indefinitely into the future.

The same viewpoint can be seen throughout the historical books, from Joshua right through Ezra and Nehemiah. These books constantly offer theological commentary on the successes and failures within the national histories of Israel and Judah. But they never express themselves in terms of a coming end to the current flow of human history as a whole. Even the occasional prophetic messages that we find reported in them do not look forward beyond contemporary events to predict anything like a decisive and transformative intervention by God in human history.

The same goes for the wisdom books of Job, Proverbs, and Ecclesiastes, and Song of Songs, which share insights of a more individualistic and philosophical nature, rather than contributing narratives of the history of the world and of the nation of Israel. They frequently speak about individual accountability to God, and they assert that God will eventually reward those who live justly and punish those who live unjustly. However, they do not express the idea that God will someday in the future intervene in the world to bring human history to a decisive end and judge humanity as a whole. To find this kind of expectation, we must turn to the Psalms and to the Prophets. To these we now turn, surveying relevant passages in canonical order.

Psalm 2

> [1] Why do the nations conspire,
>   and the peoples plot in vain?
> [2] The kings of the earth set themselves,
>   and the rulers take counsel together,
>   against the Lord and his anointed, saying,
> [3] "Let us burst their bonds asunder,
>   and cast their cords from us."
> [4] He who sits in the heavens laughs;
>   the Lord has them in derision.
> [5] Then he will speak to them in his wrath,
>   and terrify them in his fury, saying,
> [6] "I have set my king on Zion, my holy hill."
> [7] I will tell of the decree of the Lord:
> He said to me, "You are my son;
>   today I have begotten you.

---

1. The term "literary prophets" refers to those whose *writings* appear in our OT. It excludes figures such as Elijah, who figure in the narratives of the historical books of the OT, but who have not left a literary corpus for us.

> ⁸ Ask of me, and I will make the nations your heritage,
>   and the ends of the earth your possession.
> ⁹ You shall break them with a rod of iron,
>   and dash them in pieces like a potter's vessel."²

In this psalm, we see God installing his chosen king (called the "Messiah," the LORD's anointed one, v. 2) on Mount Zion, and announcing to the leaders of all the nations of the world that they are required to obey him. The psalm presents the picture of a violent and decisive confrontation that will result in God's victory over all who resist the establishment of God's global reign through the Messiah. The idea of a new age, a "messianic" age, is present, but no hint of resurrection appears in this passage.

Psalm 22

In this famous psalm, we hear the prayer of the one who is on the verge of death. Beset by a violent mob and without anyone to help him, he despairs of life. But God rescues him and saves his life: "From the horns of the wild oxen you have rescued me" (v. 21b).³ Full of joy at being restored to life, he prays,

> ²⁵ From you comes my praise in the great congregation;
>   my vows I will pay before those who fear him.
> ²⁶ The poor shall eat and be satisfied;
>   those who seek him shall praise the LORD.
>   May your hearts live forever!
> ²⁷ All the ends of the earth shall remember
>   and turn to the LORD;
>   and all the families of the nations
>   shall worship before him.
> ²⁸ For dominion belongs to the LORD,
>   and he rules over the nations.
> ²⁹ To him, indeed, shall all who sleep in the earth bow down;
>   before him shall bow all who go down to the dust,
>   and I shall live for him.
> ³⁰ Posterity will serve him;
>   future generations will be told about the LORD,
> ³¹ and proclaim his deliverance to a people yet unborn,
>   saying that he has done it.

The exultant conclusion to this psalm contains hints of both a new age of justice and universal reconciliation to God (vv. 26–28) and the promise of resurrection for those who, like the psalmist, have experienced oppression (vv. 26, 29). Verse 29 does not, in fact, go

---

2. Psalm 110 is very similar in this regard. But unlike Psalm 2, its picture of violent conflict with enemies is not explicitly global in scope. The defeated kings in Ps. 110:2, 5–6 may simply be interpreted as the leaders of neighboring enemy nations.

3. All four NT evangelists quote more than once from this psalm, which they regard as prophetic of the sufferings of Jesus. E.g., see Mt. 27:35, 46; Mk 15:24, 34; Lk. 23:34, 35; Jn 19:24, 28.

so far as to say that all the dead will be raised to life at the time when "all the ends of the earth shall remember and turn to the LORD." It affirms that even the dead will all bow down in respect to the LORD (Isa. 45:23, cf. Phil. 2:9–11),[4] and it expresses the confident hope that *the psalmist* will live. In addition, he prays that the hearts *of those who seek God* will live forever (v. 26). The contextual association between the idea of the dead acknowledging God and the hope of the psalmist himself "living" for God (v. 29) certainly creates a tantalizing *suggestion* of resurrection for the faithful, but it remains a hint.

Psalm 46

This psalm imagines God saving the people of Zion from huge cataclysms in the physical world ("the mountains shaking in the heart of the sea . . . its waters roar and foam . . . the mountains tremble with its tumult . . . the earth melts," vv. 2–3, 6–7), and from the onslaught of many enemy nations (vv. 6–7). The hint of a transition to a new age may be discerned in the promise that God will help Zion "when the morning dawns" (v. 5), and in the verses that end the psalm:

> [8] Come, behold the works of the LORD;
>   see what desolations he has brought on the earth.
> [9] He makes wars cease to the end of the earth;
>   he breaks the bow, and shatters the spear;
>   he burns the shields with fire.
> [10] "Be still, and know that I am God!
>   I am exalted among the nations,
>   I am exalted in the earth."
> [11] The LORD of hosts is with us;
>   the God of Jacob is our refuge.

The psalmist looks forward to the dawning of a new day for the world: a day in which God resides in Zion, and in which he is known and acknowledged ("exalted," v. 10) among *all* the nations. It is a day in which God puts an end to all war, and to all weapons of war. The psalmist hints that the forces that stand against God will be utterly wiped out: "See what desolations he has brought on the earth" (v. 8). Taken together, the elements of this psalm add up to a relatively clear picture of the coming of a new age: (1) massive cataclysms in the natural world, (2) a decisive confrontation in which God defeats all the enemy nations—and even removes them from the world, (3) salvation and protection for the faithful, (4) the establishment of global peace through God's personal agency, and (5) the promise of God's intimate presence among the faithful.

---

4. I belong to the school of thought that does not draw from these words the concept of universal salvation or reconciliation to God. As we just saw evidenced in Ps. 2, the belief that human beings will someday find themselves under compulsion to acknowledge God's sovereignty does not imply the belief that those who are forced to bow down will do so out of a spirit of reconciliation or right relationship with him. It simply implies the belief that all human beings, whether willingly or unwillingly, will someday have to acknowledge the presence, power, and authority of their Creator.

Psalm 47

This psalm invites all the peoples of the world to join in the worship of God, the "great King over all the earth," who "subdued peoples under us, and nations under our feet" (v. 3). It almost seems to be composed as a song that could be sung by the nations that "exalt" God (46:10) and who willingly participate in the international peace described in Psalm 46. Verses 8 and 9 contain a nigh on astounding vision of the inclusion of the Gentiles:

> [8] God is king over the nations;
>   God sits on his holy throne.
> [9] The princes of the peoples gather
>   as the people of the God of Abraham.
> For the shields of the earth belong to God;
>   he is highly exalted.

The acknowledgment of all the princes of the peoples as "the people of the God of Abraham" implies that in this psalmist's vision of the future, all nations are destined to be partakers of the Abrahamic covenant. In addition, the word "exalted" in v. 10 carries an undeniably positive connotation, removing any uncertainty as to whether that word implied the reconciliation (as distinct from the mere submission) of the nations in Ps. 46:10. This psalm, in summary, dares to envision a new age in which God takes up kingship over the whole world, and in which God is freely and eagerly welcomed with praises by all the nations.

Psalm 96

> [10] Say among the nations, "The LORD is king!
>   The world is firmly established; it shall never be moved.
>   He will judge the peoples with equity."
> [11] Let the heavens be glad, and let the earth rejoice;
>   let the sea roar, and all that fills it;
> [12] let the field exult, and everything in it.
> Then shall all the trees of the forest sing for joy
>   [13] before the LORD; for he is coming,
>   for he is coming to judge the earth.
> He will judge the world with righteousness,
>   and the peoples with his truth.

This psalm looks forward with great hope and expectation to the coming of God as king of the whole world. The psalmist imagines the whole created order joining in the celebration of God's enthronement as King and Judge. In contrast to the picture in Psalms 2 and 46, the focus here is completely positive. There is no mention of a destructive cataclysm in the natural world; neither is there any hint of a violent confrontation with nations that resist the rule of God. The atmosphere that it creates is entirely one of celebration.

The End of the Unrepentant

Nonetheless, this psalm creates the sense of a total transformation that affects all of humanity and all of creation.

Psalm 97

> [1] The LORD is king! Let the earth rejoice;
> let the many coastlands be glad!
> [2] Clouds and thick darkness are all around him;
> righteousness and justice are the foundation of his throne.
> [3] Fire goes before him,
> and consumes his adversaries on every side.
> [4] His lightnings light up the world;
> the earth sees and trembles.
> [5] The mountains melt like wax before the LORD,
> before the LORD of all the earth.

This psalm, yet another enthronement psalm, contains all the major themes that we have seen associated with the idea of a new age:

- the announcement of God's kingship over the entire world (v. 1),
- the hope that far-off Gentile nations will gladly join in the celebration that welcomes God's enthronement (v. 1),
- the conviction that God is coming as judge of all of humanity (vv. 2, 10–12),
- the picture of a large-scale and violent confrontation in which God's enemies will be decisively defeated (v. 3), and
- the expectation that a global natural cataclysm will accompany the transition to God's reign (vv. 4–5).

The slightest hint of resurrection for the righteous may be detected in vv. 10–11:

> [10] The LORD loves those who hate evil;
> he guards the lives of his faithful;
> he rescues them from the hand of the wicked.
> [11] Light dawns for the righteous,[5]
> and joy for the upright in heart.

Psalm 98

> [1] O sing to the LORD a new song,
> for he has done marvelous things.
> His right hand and his holy arm
> have gained him victory.
> [2] The LORD has made known his victory;
> he has revealed his vindication in the sight of the nations.

---

5. This is following the LXX and the Syriac; Masoretic Text has "Light is sown for the righteous," which has equal potential to be read as a hint of resurrection.

> ^{3} He has remembered his steadfast love and faithfulness
> > to the house of Israel.
> All the ends of the earth have seen
> > the victory of our God.
> ^{4} Make a joyful noise to the LORD, all the earth;
> > break forth into joyous song and sing praises.
> ^{5} Sing praises to the LORD with the lyre,
> > with the lyre and the sound of melody.
> ^{6} With trumpets and the sound of the horn
> > make a joyful noise before the King, the LORD.
> ^{7} Let the sea roar, and all that fills it;
> > the world and those who live in it.
> ^{8} Let the floods clap their hands;
> > let the hills sing together for joy
> ^{9} at the presence of the LORD, for he is coming
> > to judge the earth.
> He will judge the world with righteousness,
> > and the peoples with equity.

Like Psalm 96, this psalm concentrates on the positive side of the hoped-for transition to a new age of global peace and justice under God's kingship. There is reference to God's victory in front of all the nations and the entire earth, which implies that a hostile confrontation has occurred (vv. 1–3), but the focus is on praise. Verses 7–9 speak of the joyous involvement of the elements of the natural world, which will sing at God's enthronement ceremony as King and Judge. This is the positive counterpart of the cataclysms that we've seen above (see Pss. 96:11–13; 46:2–3, 6–7; 97:5). The psalmist calls in v. 4 for "all the earth" to sing and be joyful at God's coming. In this we see the psalmist's hope that people from all parts of the earth will truly and willingly welcome God, who is going to bring justice for all peoples (v. 9).

Let's take stock of what we've discovered in the Psalms before going on to look at expectations of a new age in the books of the prophets. We looked at eight psalms that have in common the vision of God making a decisive claim to kingship over all nations and over the entire world. Some of them concentrate on the cataclysmic and violent process of transformation to God's Kingdom; others concentrate on the joy of welcoming God, the just Judge and King; others have an equal concentration of both. There is a surprising inclusiveness to be seen in many of the songs, which dare to hope that many from the Gentile nations will join the people of Israel in welcoming God when "he comes to judge the world with righteousness, and the peoples with equity" (e.g. Pss. 96:13; 98:9). We've seen some potential hints of an expectation of resurrection for the faithful wrapped up with this hope of God's coming to Earth as King (Pss. 22:27–29; 97:10–11), but we haven't seen the slightest indication of something like a general resurrection and judgment. These eight psalms are not the only ones in which the psalmist prays that God will intervene to judge the whole earth and vindicate the downtrodden (see e.g., Pss. 82:8; 94:1–11, 20–23). They are, however, the ones that create the clearest

The End of the Unrepentant

impression of a total transformation of the world at the establishment of God's universal reign on earth.

Let's now turn to the words of the prophets, in which we will see remarkably similar hopes expressed.

Isaiah 2

> ¹ The word that Isaiah son of Amoz saw concerning Judah and Jerusalem.
> ² In days to come
>   the mountain of the LORD's house
> shall be established as the highest of the mountains,
>   and shall be raised above the hills;
>   all the nations shall stream to it.
> ³ Many peoples shall come and say,
> "Come, let us go up to the mountain of the LORD,
>   to the house of the God of Jacob;
> that he may teach us his ways
>   and that we may walk in his paths."
> For out of Zion shall go forth instruction,
>   and the word of the LORD from Jerusalem.
> ⁴ He shall judge between the nations,
>   and shall arbitrate for many peoples;
> they shall beat their swords into ploughshares,
>   and their spears into pruning-hooks;
> nation shall not lift up sword against nation,
>   neither shall they learn war any more.[6]

As the rest of the chapter testifies, the transition to the beautiful age of worldwide peace and reconciliation under the tutelage of God will not be a smooth one:

> ¹⁰ Enter into the rock,
>   and hide in the dust
> from the terror of the LORD,
>   and from the glory of his majesty.
> ¹¹ The haughty eyes of people shall be brought low,
>   and the pride of everyone shall be humbled;
> and the LORD alone will be exalted
>   on that day.
> ¹² For the LORD of hosts has a day
>   against all that is proud and lofty,
>   against all that is lifted up and high . . .[7]

As we observed in a number of our Psalms, it appears that there are two sides to the transition to an age in which all nations are reconciled to God and to one another. There

---

6. Cf. Ps. 46:9.
7. See Isa. 2:5–22 for the full oracle of the crisis phase of the "Day of the Lord" (vv. 12, 20).

is the positive side for those who want to know the LORD (vv. 2–4), and there is the negative, confrontational side for the privileged, the powerful, and the idolaters (vv. 5–22).

Isaiah 11

> ¹ A shoot shall come out from the stock of Jesse,
> and a branch shall grow out of his roots.
> ² The spirit of the LORD shall rest on him,
> the spirit of wisdom and understanding,
> the spirit of counsel and might,
> the spirit of knowledge and the fear of the LORD.
> ³ His delight shall be in the fear of the LORD.
> He shall not judge by what his eyes see,
> or decide by what his ears hear;
> ⁴ but with righteousness he shall judge the poor,
> and decide with equity for the meek of the earth;
> he shall strike the earth with the rod of his mouth,
> and with the breath of his lips he shall kill the wicked.
> ⁵ Righteousness shall be the belt around his waist,
> and faithfulness the belt around his loins.
> ⁶ The wolf shall live with the lamb,
> the leopard shall lie down with the kid,
> the calf and the lion and the fatling together,
> and a little child shall lead them.
> ⁷ The cow and the bear shall graze,
> their young shall lie down together;
> and the lion shall eat straw like the ox.
> ⁸ The nursing child shall play over the hole of the asp,
> and the weaned child shall put its hand on the adder's den.
> ⁹ They will not hurt or destroy
> on all my holy mountain;
> for the earth will be full of the knowledge of the LORD
> as the waters cover the sea.
>
> ¹⁰ On that day the root of Jesse shall stand as a signal to the peoples; the nations shall inquire of him, and his dwelling shall be glorious.

We see here, as can also be seen in Psalms 2 and 110, the promise that God will accomplish the transition to a future age of peace and glory through the agency of a Messiah who is a descendent of David. Isaiah's vision pictures a just king who is full of wisdom, the Holy Spirit, and the power of God. The radical nature of the envisioned transformation is indicated by the complete removal of the wicked (v. 4), by the promise that there will no longer be violence of any kind, either in the human or in the natural realm (vv. 6–9a), and by the statement that the knowledge of God will absolutely drench the world (vv. 9b-10).

The End of the Unrepentant

Isaiah 24–27

This long passage is commonly known as "the Isaiah Apocalypse."[8] It almost reads like an epic poem, and it arguably gives us the single most detailed vision of the coming of the Kingdom of God in the OT. Among the literary prophets of the OT,[9] Isaiah stands as the clear favorite of Jesus, the four evangelists, the apostles Paul and Peter, and the author of the Book of Revelation.[10] Isaiah 26 also contains one of the clearest references to the hope of resurrection in the OT (Isa. 26:19; cf. Isa. 25:7–8). We are therefore going to proceed on the assumption that this passage has something important to contribute to our understanding of the relationship between the hope of the coming of the Kingdom of God, the hope of resurrection, and the hope that the unrepentant will someday pose no further danger to the faithful. Because the passage is lengthy, I will quote a portion of it at a time and offer comments.

Isaiah 24:1–3

> ^{24:1} Now the LORD is about to lay waste the earth and make it desolate,
>   and he will twist its surface and scatter its inhabitants.
> ² And it shall be, as with the people, so with the priest;
>   as with the slave, so with his master;
>   as with the maid, so with her mistress;
>   as with the buyer, so with the seller;
>   as with the lender, so with the borrower;
>   as with the creditor, so with the debtor.
> ³ The earth shall be utterly laid waste and utterly despoiled;
>   for the LORD has spoken this word.

---

8. An apocalypse is an account of someone's vision or visions of divine secrets, especially concerning the end of the world. The word is formed from the Greek word *apokalypsis*, which means an unveiling or an uncovering.

9. That is, the writers of the books of Isaiah through Malachi, as distinct from Moses, Elijah, Huldah, and so on.

10. The counting of quotations and allusions to the OT in the NT is not an exact science, but the dominance of Isaiah is obvious. The table below is compiled from the database at http://www.blueletterbible.org/study/misc/quotes.cfm.

Quotation Level and Scope	Total	Isa.	Jer.	Ezek.	Dan.	Pss.
Whole NT Direct Quotations	311	62	12	3	0	83
Whole NT Allusions	507	79	28	17	28	56
Whole NT Possible Allusions	138	22	4	22	29	11
Gospels, Quote or Allusion	260	47	11	1	13	48
Paul, Quote or Allusion	175	36	0	0	0	32
General Epistles, Quote or Allusion	144	9	2	0	0	25
Revelation, Quote or Allusion	136	42	21	17	14	17

The Changing of the Ages in the Old Testament

As we mentioned above, Isaiah 24–27 is a self-contained sequence of visions and prophetic oracles that essentially tells a story of the end of the world. It begins here with the announcement that a total global catastrophe is coming. The catastrophe is universal in geographic terms (vv. 1, 3), and it is universal in human terms (v. 2). That is, it affects the entire earth, and it affects every single human being.

Isaiah sees God's agency behind the crisis (vv. 1, 3), but that is not the same thing as saying that Isaiah understood what he was seeing as a supernatural occurrence. We will observe later in ch. 24 that the total destruction and despoiling of the earth are the work of humanity itself. It is typical in Isaiah and in the other prophetic books of the OT for God to take responsibility for humanly caused disasters (such as invasions by foreign empires like Assyria and Babylon). As creator, God knows what will become of the freedom that he has granted to his creatures. He foreknows what they will do, and he knowingly works with their choices—all the while warning human beings of the consequences of their actions.

Isaiah 24:4–6

> ^{4} The earth dries up and withers,
>   the world languishes and withers;
>   the heavens languish together with the earth.
> ^{5} The earth lies polluted
>   under its inhabitants;
> for they have transgressed laws,
>   violated the statutes,
>   broken the everlasting covenant.
> ^{6} Therefore a curse devours the earth,
>   and its inhabitants suffer for their guilt;
> therefore the inhabitants of the earth dwindled,
>   and few people are left.

The picture in vv. 4–6 is of a whole world dying of deadly heat and drought, and suffering from universal pollution caused by its human population (v. 5). The result is that humanity nearly causes itself to go extinct (v. 6c). The "everlasting[11] covenant" is the covenant that God made with all of humanity after flood of Noah's time (Gen. 8:21—9:17). In Genesis we read that within only nine generations from Adam, humanity had become so destructive and murderous on the earth that God was forced to intervene and trim humanity back to one single family (Gen. 6:5–13). After the flood, God covenanted never again to destroy all life on the earth with a flood. However, every covenant binds *two parties* together under mutual obligation. Implicit in God's promise never to destroy the earth is an obligation on the part of humanity never again to destroy the earth, as it had been actively doing when God was forced to intervene with the flood (Gen. 5:11–13).

Isaiah is prophesying that the end of the world will come when humanity as a whole breaks its age-old covenant obligation under the Noahic covenant. The picture is not that

---

11. More literally, "age-enduring," Heb. *ōlam*, Strong's #H5769.

The End of the Unrepentant

of God supernaturally harming the earth out of aggravation over being disobeyed by human beings; it is a picture of humanity destroying its own environment, and reaping the very curse (Isa. 24:6) that God promised never to send on the earth (Gen. 8:21–22). What God promised never to do to the earth, humanity has done.

Isaiah 24:7–12

> ⁷ The wine dries up,
>   the vine languishes,
>   all the merry-hearted sigh.
> ⁸ The mirth of the timbrels is stilled,
>   the noise of the jubilant has ceased,
>   the mirth of the lyre is stilled.
> ⁹ No longer do they drink wine with singing;
>   strong drink is bitter to those who drink it.
> ¹⁰ The city of chaos is broken down,
>   every house is shut up so that no one can enter.
> ¹¹ There is an outcry in the streets for lack of wine;
>   all joy has reached its eventide;
>   the gladness of the earth is banished.
> ¹² Desolation is left in the city,
>   the gates are battered into ruins.

When total drought occurs, everything stops. Those who are well off take it for granted that they will always be able to enjoy themselves with music, drinking, and socializing. But without food, everything stops. Isaiah sees one great city in the center of this dynamic, which he calls "the city of chaos" (v. 11).

We will get hints from elsewhere in this extended passage that he is not referring to Jerusalem, but to an empire that has enslaved God's people. The great empire that rules on the earth at the end of history will fall too, along with all of humanity.

Isaiah 24:13

> ¹³ For thus it shall be on the earth
>   and among the nations,
> as when an olive tree is beaten,
>   as at the gleaning when the grape harvest is ended.

Isaiah pictures here a process of destruction as sweeping and thorough as the harvest, which leaves everything picked, and only a scattered few bunches of grapes missed here, a few olives missed there.

Isaiah 24:14–16a

> ¹⁴ They lift up their voices, they sing for joy;
>   they shout from the west over the majesty of the Lord.
> ¹⁵ Therefore in the east give glory to the Lord;
>   in the coastlands of the sea glorify the name of the Lord, the God of Israel.
> ¹⁶ᵃ From the ends of the earth we hear songs of praise,
>   of glory to the Righteous One.

In the midst of all this destruction come hymns of triumph and celebration: God is here! God is arriving! People at opposite ends of the earth celebrate together, and even those who live in the faraway islands of the sea. The demise of humanity is not the end of the story, but the beginning of God's reign on earth—for those who welcome him (see 24:23).

Isaiah 24:16b–18a

> ¹⁶ᵇ But I say, I pine away,
>   I pine away. Woe is me!
> For the treacherous deal treacherously,
>   the treacherous deal very treacherously.
> ¹⁷ Terror, and the pit, and the snare
>   are upon you, O inhabitant of the earth!
> ¹⁸ᵃ Whoever flees at the sound of the terror
>   shall fall into the pit,
> and whoever climbs out of the pit
>   shall be caught in the snare.

Like Jeremiah and Ezekiel (see Jer. 15:16; Ezek. 3:3), Isaiah finds that there is a terrible pain of grief packed in close with the revelation of the joy of God's coming reign. A traumatic transition process on earth accompanies God's arrival, and despite the rejoicing of the saints in vv. 14–16, Isaiah experiences waves of dread and horror as he contemplates it. Human beings are plotting against one another and stabbing one another in the back on a scale that threatens to destroy the entire world.

Isaiah 24:18b–20

> ¹⁸ᵇ For the windows of heaven are opened,
>   and the foundations of the earth tremble.
> ¹⁹ The earth is utterly broken,
>   the earth is torn asunder,
>   the earth is violently shaken.
> ²⁰ The earth staggers like a drunkard,
>   it sways like a hut;

The End of the Unrepentant

> its transgression lies heavy upon it,
> > and it falls, and will not rise again.

Finally, the entire environment collapses, and mortal humanity's tenure on the earth comes to a decisive end. Humanity has caused the radical destruction of the entire living world that humankind was created to manage and nurture (see Gen. 1:26–28; 2:15; 3:25).

Isaiah 24:21–23

> ²¹ On that day the Lord will punish
> > the host of heaven in heaven,
> > and on earth the kings of the earth.
>
> ²² They will be gathered together
> > like prisoners in a pit;
>
> they will be shut up in a prison,
> > and after many days they will be punished.
>
> ²³ Then the moon will be abashed,
> > and the sun ashamed;
>
> for the Lord of hosts will reign
> > on Mount Zion and in Jerusalem,
> > and before his elders he will manifest his glory.

When God intervenes at the end of history, all but a remnant of humanity will have died (vv. 6, 13). God will take up his rule by calling to account all those destructive beings—both angelic and human—who have been leading the process of humanity's suicide. They will find themselves dethroned, and will face a sentence of imprisonment in the "pit" of the underworld (Sheol) along with all those whom they have just led over the cliff.[12]

At the moment when God comes to reign, his glory will be so great that it will make the sun and the moon embarrassed at the feebleness of their own light.

Isaiah 25:1–5

> ¹ O Lord, you are my God;
> I will exalt you, I will praise your name;
> for you have done wonderful things,
> > plans formed of old, faithful and sure.
>
> ² For you have made the city a heap,
> > the fortified city a ruin;
>
> the palace of aliens is a city no more,
> > it will never be rebuilt.
>
> ³ Therefore strong peoples will glorify you;
> > cities of ruthless nations will fear you.

---

12. Those who understand Isaiah 14 and Ezekiel 28 as referring to the defeat of the devil ought to see a strong parallel here (Isa. 24:21–22 || Isa. 14:5–20 || Ezek. 28:1–19 || Rev. 20:1–3).

⁴ For you have been a refuge to the poor,
    a refuge to the needy in their distress,
    a shelter from the rainstorm and a shade from the heat.
When the blast of the ruthless was like a winter rainstorm,
   ⁵ the noise of aliens like heat in a dry place,
you subdued the heat with the shade of clouds;
    the song of the ruthless was stilled.

Isaiah now sings a joyous psalm of praise. The empire that once oppressed the entire world has been judged and flattened. The great competition between empires through the course of history has now ceased, and God, the constant advocate of the poor and the oppressed, will reign in justice. The sudden relief granted by God's intervention will be like the instant relief one feels on an oppressively hot day when a thick cloud crosses in front of the sun.

Isaiah 25:6–10a

⁶ On this mountain the LORD of hosts will make for all peoples
    a feast of rich food, a feast of well-matured wines,
    of rich food filled with marrow,
    of well-matured wines strained clear.
⁷ And he will destroy on this mountain
    the shroud that is cast over all peoples,
    the sheet that is spread over all nations;
   ⁸ he will swallow up death for ever.
Then the Lord GOD will wipe away the tears from all faces,
    and the disgrace of his people he will take away from all the earth,
    for the LORD has spoken.
⁹ It will be said on that day,
    Lo, this is our God; we have waited for him, so that he might save us.
    This is the LORD for whom we have waited;
    let us be glad and rejoice in his salvation.
¹⁰ᵃ For the hand of the LORD will rest on this mountain.

God will inaugurate his reign by giving a great royal banquet on Mount Zion (vv. 6, 10), whose invitees will be from every nation and people. The faithful remnant of humanity will celebrate the end of mortality, death, sorrow, and disgrace (cf. Rev. 7:15–17; 21:3–4). Israel in particular will be freed from disgrace ("his people," v. 8, in comparison to "all peoples," v. 6). The prayers and hopes of all the oppressed will find their final fulfillment (v. 9).

The End of the Unrepentant

Isaiah 25:10b–12

> ^{10b} The Moabites shall be trodden down in their place
>   as straw is trodden down in a dung-pit.
> ¹¹ Though they spread out their hands in the midst of it,
>   as swimmers spread out their hands to swim,
>   their pride will be laid low despite the struggle of their hands.
> ¹² The high fortifications of his walls will be brought down,
>   laid low, cast to the ground, even to the dust.

Hostile nations such as Moab will not be invited inside, but will find themselves outside in the compost heap.

Isaiah 26:1–3

> ¹ On that day this song will be sung in the land of Judah:
> We have a strong city;
>   he sets up victory
>   like walls and bulwarks.
> ² Open the gates,
>   so that the righteous nation that keeps faith
>   may enter in.
> ³ Those of steadfast mind you keep in peace—
>   in peace because they trust in you.

There will be a new Zion, a New Jerusalem. It won't be a sinful human city that runs on the politics and power and intrigue, but a city built by God. Only the righteous and faithful will be able to come inside, and it will need no army because God will be its defender (cf. Rev. 21:24–25).

Isaiah 26:4–6

> ⁴ Trust in the Lord forever,
>   for in the Lord God
>   you have an everlasting rock.
> ⁵ For he has brought low
>   the inhabitants of the height;
>   the lofty city he lays low.
> He lays it low to the ground,
>   casts it to the dust.
> ⁶ The foot tramples it,
>   the feet of the poor,
>   the steps of the needy.

Isaiah calls out to the faithful to trust in God. They are to know that God is going to bring down the oppressor empire, and that the poor and needy will triumph over it through their faith.

Isaiah 26:7–9

> [7] The way of the righteous is level;
>   O Just One, you make smooth the path of the righteous.
> [8] In the path of your judgments,
>   O Lord, we wait for you;
> your name and your renown
>   are the soul's desire.
> [9] My soul yearns for you in the night,
>   my spirit within me earnestly seeks you.
> For when your judgments are in the earth,
>   the inhabitants of the world learn righteousness.

Now Isaiah praises God and expresses his determination to continue putting his hope and faith in God. He is determined that hope of God's coming as judge will be his focus, day and night. He believes that when God comes to intervene and reign, rebellious humanity will finally learn what God's justice and righteousness look like.

Isaiah 26:10–11

> [10] If favor is shown to the wicked,
>   they do not learn righteousness;
> in the land of uprightness they deal perversely
>   and do not see the majesty of the Lord.
> [11] O Lord, your hand is lifted up,
>   but they do not see it.
> Let them see your zeal for your people, and be ashamed.
>   Let the fire for your adversaries consume them.

But what will happen if the unrepentant are convicted by God and are later shown clemency? They totally misinterpret the clemency of God. They enter back into self-deception, and, in madness, mistake God's mercy for weakness. In utter recklessness, they presume to attack the peaceful New Jerusalem, whose only defense is God. Their fate is going to be instant and total destruction by fire from God (v. 11).

The End of the Unrepentant

Isaiah 26:12–13

> ¹² O Lord, you will ordain peace for us,
>   for indeed, all that we have done, you have done for us.
> ¹³ O Lord our God,
>   other lords besides you have ruled over us,
>   but we acknowledge your name alone.

Isaiah's imagination now comes back to the present, and he prays about the fact that, in this age, most of what the faithful experience is oppression under invading nations and empires. He looks ahead in hope to the moment of world-transition that has just been revealed to him, when God will establish peace once and for all for the faithful.

Isaiah 26:14

> ¹⁴ The dead do not live;
>   shades do not rise—
> because you have punished and destroyed them,
>   and wiped out all memory of them.

There will be no resurrection for the unrepentant, when God comes to vindicate and establish the righteous on the earth. Just the opposite: the destructive mortal nations will be wiped off the face of the earth along with their kings (see Isa. 24:21–22; Rev. 19:19–21), and there will no longer be any memory of them.

Isaiah 26:15

> ¹⁵ But you have increased the nation, O Lord,
>   you have increased the nation; you are glorified;
>   you have enlarged all the borders of the land.

The faithful, on the other hand (here represented in Isaiah's imagination as "the nation" of Israel), will grow and flourish. Rather than being pressed in and taken over, they will spread out.

Isaiah 26:16–17a

> ¹⁶ O Lord, in distress they sought you,
>   they poured out a prayer
>   when your chastening was on them,
> ¹⁷ᵃ like a woman with child,
>   who writhes and cries out in her pangs
>   when she is near her time.

The focus now goes back to the unrepentant (see v. 14), who are dead and cannot birth themselves back to life. They feel an anguish of remorse over the fact that they have had

Isaiah 26:17b–19

> ^{17b} So were we because of you, O Lord;
> ^{18} we were with child, we writhed,
>   but we gave birth only to wind.
> We have won no victories on earth,
>   and no one is born to inhabit the world.
> ^{19} Your dead shall live, their corpses shall rise.
>   O dwellers in the dust, awake and sing for joy!
> For your dew is a radiant dew,
>   and the earth will give birth to those long dead.

We too, says Isaiah, found ourselves helpless and in anguish when God handed us over be defeated by enemies who held us under oppression, and we had no ability to escape our captivity. We couldn't achieve the transition to a just world, or even defend ourselves against those who exploited us.

But God promises resurrection for the faithful—indeed, for all the faithful, including those of the distant past. The faithful are assured that when God's reign comes, death will not simply cease to be from that moment on (see Isa. 25:8 above), but God will resurrect all the faithful of history to participate in the New Jerusalem and the age of life that is invulnerable to death.

Isaiah 26:20–21

> ^{20} Come, my people, enter your chambers,
>   and shut your doors behind you;
> hide yourselves for a little while
>   until the wrath is past.
> ^{21} For the Lord comes out from his place
>   to punish the inhabitants of the earth for their iniquity;
> the earth will disclose the blood shed on it,
>   and will no longer cover its slain.

God now gently shepherds the faithful people of the New Jerusalem indoors. There is some unpleasant business to take care of: the unrepentant have been shown mercy, but they have cast that mercy back in God's face. They are attempting to attack the Peaceful City (see vv. 10, 11). This time their self-deception, and their usual tactic of simply hiding the bodies of their victims beneath the ground, are not going to succeed. Exactly who they are and what they've done are going to come out into the open.

The End of the Unrepentant

Isaiah 27:1

> ¹ On that day the Lord with his cruel and great and strong sword will punish Leviathan the fleeing serpent, Leviathan the twisting serpent, and he will kill the dragon that is in the sea.

Leviathan was the old, old sea monster of Jewish mythology (see Job 3:8; 41:1-9), who lived in the deep sea, the realm of chaos. There will come a time, says Isaiah, when the most fearsome and seemingly untamable forces of evil will be put to death once and for all.

It is evident that John the writer of Revelation understood this statement as referring to Satan (see Rev. 12:1-17; 20:1-3, 7-10). On the same day that God deals with the human forces of evil for the final time, God will deal with the cosmic forces of evil for the final time. All of history has seen these two forces operating in powerful collusion with one another, but in the context of God's reign, it will only take a brief moment for God to deal with the situation all by himself (26:11, 20).

Isaiah 27:2-5

> ² On that day:
> A pleasant vineyard, sing about it!
> ³ I, the Lord, am its keeper;
> every moment I water it.
> I guard it night and day
> so that no one can harm it.
> ⁴ I have no wrath.[13]
> If someone gives me thorns and briers,
> I will march to battle against him.
> I will burn him up.
> ⁵ Instead, let him join close to me for protection.
> Let him make peace with me.
> Let him make peace with me.[14]

The pleasant vineyard here represents God's people, in parallel with the prophetic parable at the beginning of Isaiah (Isa. 5:1-7; cf. 27:6). But now the setting is the age of renewal, in which God is the exclusive nurturer and protector of his people (v. 3).

---

13. NRSV punctuates with a semicolon after the word "wrath," effectively attaching the phrase "I have no wrath" to the end of v. 3. I agree with most translations that it belongs logically with what follows (vv. 4b-5).

14. NRSV translators understood the entity being warned by God here as being the vineyard itself, but that makes poor sense in the overall context of Isa. 24–27. Here is their rendering:

> If it gives me thorns and briers,
> I will march to battle against it.
> I will burn it up.
> Or else let it cling to me for protection,
> let it make peace with me,
> let it make peace with me.

The Changing of the Ages in the Old Testament

God addresses those who might wish to attack or sabotage the vineyard with which God is pleased (27:4). God says to the would-be saboteurs, "I have nothing against you. I am not angry with you, and I'm not your enemy. But if you attempt to harm my people, I will burn you up just as surely as you would burn up thorns and briars that someone tried to plant in your vineyard. Come! Be at peace with me! You're welcome to come under my protection." The repeated words, "Let him make peace with me" suggest that this is both a final invitation and a final warning (see again 26:11, 20).

Before we move on to discuss other passages, let's summarize what we've discovered from reading this extended visionary poem about the coming of God's Kingdom to the Earth.

- The final coming of the Kingdom of God (24:23) is to be attended by the death throes of rebellious and destructive humanity, which will have succeeded in making the Earth uninhabitable for itself, thus pulling the plug on its own existence (24:4–6, 17–20)
- The angelic beings and the human beings that have exercised the authority of leadership over humanity and the creation are going to be stripped of life and power, and imprisoned together in the underworld of death when God comes to reign (24:21–23; cf. Isa. 14:4b–20; Ps. 82; Rev. 19:17—20:6).
- When God comes to reign on Mount Zion, he will welcome people from all the peoples of the world to his rich banqueting table, and take away the pall of mortality from "all peoples" and "all nations" (25:6–8). But the invitees will only be the righteous, whether from the Jews or from the Gentiles (26:2–6; cf. Mt. 8:10–11; Lk. 13:28–30).
- In the context of God's glorious renewal of the world, which follows the paroxysms of the end of this age, God is going to show grace to the unrepentant. But they will have learned neither from the experience of self-destruction nor from the experience of grace. When God invites them to join "the righteous nation" (26:2, 7–9), they will perpetrate treachery and attempt to attack God's people, and will be destroyed by inundating fire (26:10–11, 20–21; cf. Rev. 20:7–9).
- The righteous will find that they simply do not have the power to cause God's new life and God's righteousness to reign on the earth. Their grief and sorrow over the demise of humanity and the Earth will be as painful to them as the delivery of a stillborn child. But God will accomplish their yearning: he will cause the earth to bring back human life: he will raise to life those who have died in his service (26:16–19).
- On the same day that God sends annihilating fire on those human beings who have utterly spurned his grace and rejected the hospitality of his kingdom, he will also put to death the ancient serpent that is humanity's age-old nemesis (27:1; cf. Rev. 20:7–10).
- God truly has nothing against those rebellious human beings to whom he grants amnesty after the establishment of his kingdom. He is not angry (27:4). He pleads with them to come to him in peace and enjoy his protection,[15] along with those who were once needy and downtrodden. But if they reject his invitation, and they have

---

15. Heb. *ma'ōz* (Strong's #H4581), a refuge, a place of safety and protection.

The End of the Unrepentant

it in mind to attack his people (symbolized as a beloved vineyard: 27:2–6), they risk being burnt up like a pile of thorny weeds (cf. 26:10–11).

Isaiah 64–66 (Excerpts from an Extended Poem on the Coming of God's Reign)

This passage, like Isaiah 24–27, can be read as an extended prophetic meditation on the transition to a new age of peace and blessing, which God himself brings about by means of a radical intervention as Creator.

Isaiah 64:1–2

> ¹ O that you would tear open the heavens and come down,
> so that the mountains would quake at your presence—
> ² as when fire kindles brushwood
> and the fire causes water to boil—
> to make your name known to your adversaries,
> so that the nations might tremble at your presence!

As we've seen in a number of psalms and in Isaiah 24–27, there is an expectation that God's coming will be attended by huge upheavals in the natural world and by a decisive confrontation with human enemies.

Isaiah 65:17–18

> ¹⁷ For I am about to create new heavens
> and a new earth;
> the former things shall not be remembered
> or come to mind.
> ¹⁸ But be glad and rejoice forever
> in what I am creating;
> for I am about to create Jerusalem as a joy,
> and its people as a delight.

A new heavens and a new earth imply the passing away of the current heavens and earth. This, combined with the statement that the former things will not be remembered, suggests the coming of an entirely new age and a radically new regime. Verse 18 seems to imply the permanence of the new regime.

Isaiah 65:25

> ²⁵ The wolf and the lamb shall feed together,
> the lion shall eat straw like the ox;
> but the serpent—its food shall be dust!

> They shall not hurt or destroy
> > on all my holy mountain,
> > says the LORD.

The peace and reconciliation of all creatures, as we saw when we looked at Isaiah 11, is an important element in God's promise to renew the world.

Isaiah 66:1–2

> ¹ Thus says the LORD:
> Heaven is my throne
> > and the earth is my footstool;
> what is the house that you would build for me,
> > and what is my resting-place?
> ² All these things my hand has made,
> > and so all these things are mine,[16]
> > says the LORD.
> But this is the one to whom I will look,
> > to the humble and contrite in spirit,
> > who trembles at my word.

Interestingly, this reference to God sitting on a throne stands as the only time in this extended passage (Isa. 64–66) that the text explicitly refers to the theme of God's kingship. Even so, the emphasis is immediately drawn to the personal relationship between God and those loyal to him: "this is the one to whom I will look, the humble and contrite . . ."

Isaiah 66:14–16

> ¹⁴ You shall see, and your heart shall rejoice;
> > your bodies[17] shall flourish like the grass;
> and it shall be known that the hand of the LORD is with his servants,
> > and his indignation is against his enemies.
> ¹⁵ For the LORD will come in fire,
> > and his chariots like the whirlwind,
> to pay back his anger in fury,
> > and his rebuke in flames of fire.
> ¹⁶ For by fire will the LORD execute judgment,
> > and by his sword, on all flesh;
> > and those slain by the LORD shall be many.

Verse 14 may be a hint of resurrection, but if so, is only a hint. Verses 14b-16 recall Isa. 26:11–12.

---

16. Following the LXX and Syriac; Hebrew has "these things came to be."
17. Heb. *bones*.

The End of the Unrepentant

Isaiah 66:19-21

> [19] ... From them I will send survivors to the nations ... to the coastlands far away that have not heard of my fame or seen my glory; and they shall declare my glory among the nations. [20] They shall bring all your kindred from all the nations as an offering to the LORD, on horses, and in chariots, and in litters, and on mules, and on dromedaries, to my holy mountain Jerusalem, says the LORD, just as the Israelites bring a grain-offering in a clean vessel to the house of the LORD. [21] And I will also take some of them as priests and as Levites, says the LORD.

As we've seen, the invitation and reconciliation of the Gentiles is a recurring theme in passages that look ahead to the final coming of God's Kingdom on earth. Nonetheless, these verses are nothing short of astounding. Isaiah goes far beyond prophesying that God will spare some of the Gentiles (and execute some of the Jews: see 66:3-4, 17). He dares here to prophesy that those Gentiles who are receptive to the reign of God will journey throughout the world and collect the Jews who have been scattered in exile, bringing them back to the Temple as an offering to God (vv. 19-20). God views this loving ministry on behalf of the returning exiles as tantamount to priestly or levitical service (v. 20b), and he plans to reward those who humbly serve his people in that way with nothing less than official status among the priests and Levites of Israel (v. 21)! There is perhaps no single statement more revolutionary in the entire OT.

Isaiah 66:22-24

> [22] For as the new heavens and the new earth,
>   which I will make,
> shall remain before me, says the LORD,
>   so shall your descendants and your name remain.
> [23] From new moon to new moon,
>   and from Sabbath to Sabbath,
> all flesh shall come to worship before me,
>   says the LORD.
>
> [24] And they shall go out and look at the dead bodies of the people who have rebelled against me; for their worm shall not die, their fire shall not be quenched, and they shall be an abhorrence to all flesh.

Those who are spared in the divine judgment that attends the transition from the current creation to the new creation will all worship God in the New Jerusalem. In other words, all of humanity will stand in right and worshipful relationship to God in the new creation. But the rebels will never come inside the walls of the new Jerusalem: they will be struck down by a fire that will not be quenched until its work is finished (cf. Isa. 26:11, 20-21; Rev. 20:7-10).

Ezekiel 37:1–10

> [1] The hand of the LORD came upon me, and he brought me out by the spirit of the LORD and set me down in the middle of a valley; it was full of bones. [2] He led me all round them; there were very many lying in the valley, and they were very dry. [3] He said to me, "Mortal, can these bones live?" I answered, "O Lord GOD, you know." [4] Then he said to me, "Prophesy to these bones, and say to them: O dry bones, hear the word of the LORD. [5] Thus says the Lord GOD to these bones: I will cause breath to enter you, and you shall live. [6] I will lay sinews on you, and will cause flesh to come upon you, and cover you with skin, and put breath in you, and you shall live; and you shall know that I am the LORD."
>
> [7] So I prophesied as I had been commanded; and as I prophesied, suddenly there was a noise, a rattling, and the bones came together, bone to its bone. [8] I looked, and there were sinews on them, and flesh had come upon them, and skin had covered them; but there was no breath in them. [9] Then he said to me, "Prophesy to the breath, prophesy, mortal, and say to the breath: Thus says the Lord GOD: Come from the four winds, O breath, and breathe upon these slain, that they may live." [10] I prophesied as he commanded me, and the breath came into them, and they lived, and stood on their feet, a vast multitude.

This passage is known as the "Valley of Dry Bones" vision. This vision and its interpretation (37:11–14) come immediately before a passage that pictures the full and final salvation of Israel (37:15–28, see below). It's therefore tempting to see this passage as a prophecy that concerns not simply the fifth-century BCE return of the exiles to Judah from Babylon (see vv. 12, 14 below), but also—and even primarily—the future moment of transition to the age to come.[18]

Is it fair to characterize Ezekiel's vision as a hint of the hope of resurrection? At first blush, that would seem to be an understatement. On its face, the dry bones vision *explicitly* pictures a resurrection of the dead. Ezekiel sees the bones of a great company of dead people lying on the valley floor one minute (37:1–2), and the next minute he sees them all standing up alive and breathing (37:7–10), brought back to life by the Spirit and power of God. Nonetheless, when God explains the vision to Ezekiel, it becomes clear that God has given him this vision of a great resurrection as a metaphor for the revival of hope on the part of the discouraged exiles of Judah:

Ezekiel 37:11–14

> [11] Then he said to me, "Mortal, these bones are the whole house of Israel. They say, 'Our bones are dried up, and our hope is lost; we are cut off completely.' [12] Therefore prophesy, and say to them, 'Thus says the Lord GOD: I am going to open your graves, and bring you up from your graves, O my people; and I will bring you back to the land of Israel. [13] And you shall know that I am the LORD,

---

18. Most of the rabbis quoted in the discussion of Ezekiel 37:1–10 in the Talmud take it as a tale of something that actually happened in Ezekiel's day, rather than as something that happened in a vision (*b. Sanh.* 92B).

The End of the Unrepentant

> when I open your graves, and bring you up from your graves, O my people. [14] I will put my spirit within you, and you shall live, and I will place you on your own soil; then you shall know that I, the Lord, have spoken and will act, says the Lord.' "

Paradoxically, the Vision of the Valley of Dry Bones does not actually propound the idea of a literal resurrection for the community of the faithful. What it does do is illustrate that the idea of resurrection, the idea of dead people being brought back to life, was reasonably familiar to the imagination of Ezekiel and his contemporaries. Otherwise, it could not have been pressed into service as a metaphor for a promised reinvigoration for the community of the exiles after a period of deep discouragement. This makes sense because as a Jew, Ezekiel very probably knew some traditional stories of individuals being raised back to (mortal) life by God's power (e.g. 1 Kgs 17:17-24; 2 Kgs 4:8-37; 13:20-21). He may also have been familiar with expressions of hope for resurrection or life beyond death in the Psalms and the earlier prophets (e.g. Pss. 16:8-11; 17:15; 49:14-15; 73:21-26; Hos. 6:2; cf. Job 14:10-15).

Ezekiel 37:24-28

> [24] My servant David shall be king over them; and they shall all have one shepherd. They shall follow my ordinances and be careful to observe my statutes. [25] They shall live in the land that I gave to my servant Jacob, in which your ancestors lived; they and their children and their children's children shall live there forever; and my servant David shall be their prince forever. [26] I will make a covenant of peace with them; it shall be an everlasting covenant with them; and I will bless[19] them and multiply them, and will set my sanctuary among them for evermore. [27] My dwelling-place shall be with them; and I will be their God, and they shall be my people. [28] Then the nations shall know that I the Lord sanctify Israel, when my sanctuary is among them for evermore.

The promises of a Davidic Messiah who will unite Israel and Judah and bring in an everlasting age of peace seem to position this as an age of renewal/Kingdom of God prophecy. Certain key elements that we have seen elsewhere are missing, however. For example, the kingship of God is not explicit. Neither is there any mention of a reconciling invitation to the Gentiles or of a renewal of the creation. Nor is there a picture of an earth-shaking cataclysm in the natural world or of a violent conflict with enemy nations. Ezekiel 38 and 39, which follow immediately after this passage, can be seen as belatedly supplying the latter two elements, but they do not do so in a way that readily resolves into a single coherent story. Let's look at them and see why this is the case.

After Ezekiel prophesies that there will be an everlasting peace for the Israelites under the Davidic Messiah, God commands Ezekiel to prophesy against Gog and a host of other far-flung nations (Ezek. 38-39). God's voice speaks to them and says:

---

19. Heb. *give*.

Ezekiel 38:8–16

> [8] After many days you [Gog] shall be mustered;[20] in the latter years you shall go against a land restored from war, a land where people were gathered from many nations on the mountains of Israel, which had long lain waste; its people were brought out from the nations and now are living in safety, all of them. [9] You shall advance, coming on like a storm; you shall be like a cloud covering the land, you and all your troops, and many peoples with you.
>
> [10] Thus says the Lord God: On that day thoughts will come into your mind, and you will devise an evil scheme. [11] You will say, "I will go up against the land of unwalled villages; I will fall upon the quiet people who live in safety, all of them living without walls, and having no bars or gates"; [12] to seize spoil and carry off plunder; to assail the waste places that are now inhabited, and the people who were gathered from the nations, who are acquiring cattle and goods, who live at the centre of the earth . . . .
>
> [14] Therefore, mortal, prophesy, and say to Gog: Thus says the Lord God: On that day when my people Israel are living securely, you will rouse yourself [15] and come from your place out of the remotest parts of the north, you and many peoples with you, all of them riding on horses, a great horde, a mighty army; [16] you will come up against my people Israel, like a cloud covering the earth. In the latter days I will bring you against my land, so that the nations may know me, when through you, O Gog, I display my holiness before their eyes.

This prophecy indicates that God will summon Gog and his hosts long after the inauguration of the peaceful period promised in Ezek. 37:24–28. As v. 8 says:

> [8] After many days you shall be mustered; in the latter years you shall go against a land restored from war, a land where people were gathered from many nations on the mountains of Israel, which had long lain waste; its people were brought out from the nations and now are living in safety, all of them.

God seems to be putting a test in front of Gog and his hosts: how will you respond when God draws you into the land of everlasting peace and prosperity?

> [10] Thus says the Lord God: On that day thoughts will come into your mind, and you will devise an evil scheme. [11] You will say, "I will go up against the land of unwalled villages; I will fall upon the quiet people who live in safety, all of them living without walls, and having no bars or gates" . . .

Will they recognize, when they see the quietness and peacefulness of the eternally blessed land, that there is no longer any need for violence as a way of being in the world? Or will they bring with them the "might makes right and winner takes all" philosophy that used to dominate in an age long gone, and see nothing but an easy target for conquest and plunder? Their destiny, says this prophecy, is to manifest, by falling into temptation

---

20. Heb. *paqad*, Strong's #H6485, lit. "to visit," which frequently means "to punish" or "to visit for judgment" in the OT (e.g. Lev. 26:16; Job 35:15; Ps. 59:5; 89:32; Isa. 10:12; 24:21; 26:14; 27:1; 29:6; Jer. 5:9, 29 [and very many more refs. in Jeremiah, Hosea, Amos, and Zephaniah]).

The End of the Unrepentant

(v. 10), their obstinately violent and predatory mentality. They may be stubborn in remaining blind to the peace of God, but they will not remain blind to the power of God:

Ezekiel 38:17–23

[17] Thus says the Lord GOD: Are you he of whom I spoke in former days by my servants the prophets of Israel, who in those days prophesied for years that I would bring you against them? [18] On that day, when Gog comes against the land of Israel, says the Lord GOD, my wrath shall be aroused. [19] For in my jealousy and in my blazing wrath I declare: On that day there shall be a great shaking in the land of Israel; [20] the fish of the sea, and the birds of the air, and the animals of the field, and all creeping things that creep on the ground, and all human beings that are on the face of the earth, shall quake at my presence, and the mountains shall be thrown down, and the cliffs shall fall, and every wall shall tumble to the ground. [21] I will summon the sword against Gog in all my mountains, says the Lord GOD; the swords of all will be against their comrades. [22] With pestilence and bloodshed I will enter into judgment with him; and I will pour down torrential rains and hailstones, fire and sulfur, upon him and his troops and the many peoples that are with him. [23] So I will display my greatness and my holiness and make myself known in the eyes of many nations. Then they shall know that I am the LORD.

Whereas Israel learned "that I am the LORD" when God forgave them and brought them back into the land of promise with grace and blessing (Ezek. 36:33–38; 37:13–14), Gog and his hosts will now learn "that I am the LORD" the hard way (38:23). It appears that the only language strong enough to teach these hardened violent marauders is the language of raw destructive power, a power that must destroy those whom it teaches.

Ezekiel 38, following on in an unbroken context from chs. 36 and 37, makes for a coherent and meaningful climax to the story of Israel's ultimate destiny. God rescues the people of Israel from the nations and brings them back from their exile to the land of Israel, where they enjoy unending peace and blessing under the divinely established kingship of the Messiah. Long after the Messiah's kingdom has been established, and when peace and prosperity of that age have long prevailed, God creates the circumstances for a final test for the violent, predatory nations of the world. They fail this test to their peril. Ezekiel's vision of a final attempted attack and a final miraculous rescue of the defenseless people of God creates an appropriate conclusion for the story of Israel's salvation. The age-old problems of Israel's sins and the violence of their enemies have both been solved permanently.

When we proceed to read Ezekiel 39, however, the story begins to look like a kind of narrative double exposure. In Ezekiel 39, we read yet again about a decisive confrontation with Gog and his hosts (vv. 1–20), but this time the confrontation is clearly not characterized as occurring long after the regathering of the exiles and well into the time of peace inaugurated with the coming of Messiah. It is instead unambiguously placed in the context of the regathering of the exiles:

Ezekiel 39:21–29

> [21] I will display my glory among the nations; and all the nations shall see my judgment that I have executed, and my hand that I have laid on them. [22] The house of Israel shall know that I am the LORD their God, from that day forward. [23] And the nations shall know that the house of Israel went into captivity for their iniquity, because they dealt treacherously with me. So I hid my face from them and gave them into the hand of their adversaries, and they all fell by the sword. [24] I dealt with them according to their uncleanness and their transgressions, and hid my face from them.
>
> [25] Therefore, thus says the Lord GOD: Now I will restore the fortunes of Jacob, and have mercy on the whole house of Israel; and I will be jealous for my holy name. [26] They shall forget their shame, and all the treachery they have practiced against me, when they live securely in their land with no one to make them afraid, [27] when I have brought them back from the peoples and gathered them from their enemies' lands, and through them have displayed my holiness in the sight of many nations. [28] Then they shall know that I am the LORD their God because I sent them into exile among the nations, and then gathered them into their own land. I will leave none of them behind; [29] and I will never again hide my face from them, when I pour out my spirit upon the house of Israel, says the Lord GOD.

In these paragraphs, we have clearly moved backwards on Ezekiel's storyline to the previous context of Ezekiel 36 and 37, in which the focus had been on the people of Israel—rather than the nations—coming to "know that I am the LORD." They learn this when they experience God's forgiveness and God's kindness in restoring them to their land (see Ezek. 36:33–38; 39:7a, 22, 26–29). To illustrate just how close (and exclusive of Ezek. 38) the affinity is between Ezekiel 36–37 and Ezekiel 39, here is a list of 11 distinctive themes and terms that are common to Ezekiel 36–37 and Ezekiel 39, but *are not* found in Ezekiel 38:

- Israel "will know that I am the LORD" (36:11 || 39:22, 28)
- God will act to protect his name from being profaned (36:20–23 || 39:7)
- The people of Israel went into exile because of their sins (36:17–19 || 39:23–24)
- God will restore the fortunes of Israel (36:36–38 || 39:25)
- God will give the Spirit to Israel (36:26–27; 37:14 || 39:29)
- "I have spoken!"[21] (36:36 || 39:5, cf. 39:7)
- "I will do it"/"I have done it"[22] (36:22, 27, 32, 36; 37:14, 22 || 39:21, 24)
- "The House of Israel" (36:10, 17, 21, 22, 32, 37; 37:11, 16 || 39:12, 22, 23, 25, 29)
- Israel's "iniquity"[23] (36:31, 33 || 39:23)
- Israel's "shame"[24] (36:31–32 || 39:26)

---

21. Heb. *dibbarti'*, from *dabar*, Strong's #H1696.
22. Heb. *'asiti, 'oseh*, Strong's #H6213.
23. Heb. *'avon*, Strong's #H5771.
24. Heb. *kalam, k'limah*, Strong's #H3637, #H3639.

The End of the Unrepentant

- "Cleanse"[25] (36:25, 33; 37:23 || 39:12, 14, 16)

What are we to make of this doubling of the contextual setting for the attack of Gog and his hosts in Ezekiel 38–39? The fact is that we are left with a puzzle no matter how we interpret these chapters.[26] If we interpret them as describing a single attack that happens at the transition between this age and age of peace under the Messiah, then we are left wondering why Ezekiel clearly evoked the situation long after the establishment of that age of peace when setting the context for the attack in Ezek. 38:8–14. If, on the other hand, we interpret the two chapters as describing two separate attacks, we are then left wondering why the earlier of the two is narrated second (in Ezek. 39), and why there is no direct clue that we are stepping back in time. When we illustrate the second of these options, it doesn't look unreasonably complicated:

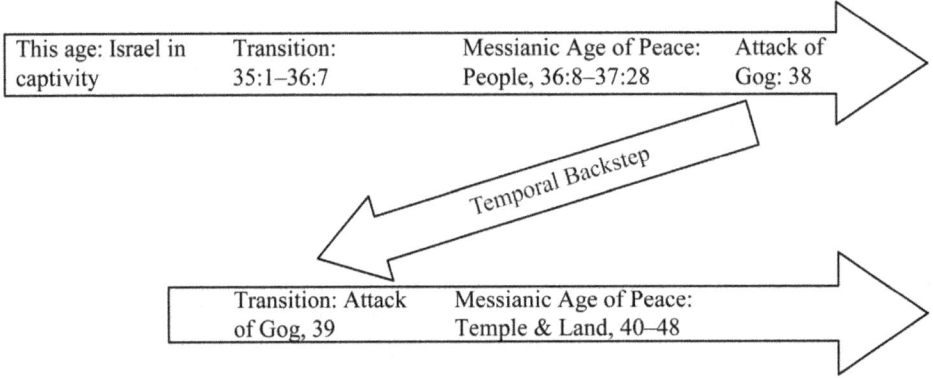

Nonetheless, Ezekiel has not given us any obvious temporal road map in his text to indicate that we are to make a U-turn, go back a ways, and go forward again. There is one thing that we do get which could possibly be considered as a hint that we are seeing the same horde of enemies appearing on two differing occasions. I refer to Ezekiel's cryptic question,

> Are you [Gog] he of whom I spoke in former days by my servants the prophets of Israel, who in those days prophesied for years that I would bring you against them? (38:17)

Notice that God is not indicating here through Ezekiel that the *attempted attack* of 38:1–16 has previously been prophesied by other biblical prophets. He is instead suggesting that the invading *enemy horde*, which he addresses here in the person of its leader, "Gog," is the same invading horde that has been referred to in prophecies that God has inspired in former times. In previous prophecies, God's miraculous defeat of invading multi-national hordes was typically characterized as *paving the way* for the inauguration of

---

25. Heb. *taher*, Strong's #H2891.

26. Testimony to this can be found in the fact that commentators on Ezekiel who are not committed to the presupposition of the text's unity and coherence see a patchwork of disparate materials by different authors from different periods in Ezekiel 38–39.

God's peaceful reign over the land of Israel and the whole earth (see e.g., Ps. 110; Isa. 34–35; Jer. 25:8–38; Joel 2:1–11, 18–20, 30–32; 3:9–21; Mic. 4:8–13; Zeph. 3:8–20). But here in Ezekiel 38, the attack comes when the land of Israel has already been "restored from war" (38:8), and the people have already been "living securely" (38:8, 14), presumably under the peaceful reign of Messiah (see Ezek. 37 as context). You can almost hear Ezekiel exclaim, "What? *You* again?" There is, indeed, a single clear instance within the corpus of the OT literary prophets (i.e. Isaiah–Malachi) in which the prediction of an enemy attack is clearly set within the context of the age of peace that comes with God's reign. That instance is Isaiah 26:10–11, which we read above:

Isaiah 26:10–11

> [10] If favor is shown to the wicked,
>   they do not learn righteousness;
> in the land of uprightness they deal perversely
>   and do not see the majesty of the LORD.
> [11] O LORD, your hand is lifted up,
>   but they do not see it.
> Let them see your zeal for your people, and be ashamed.
>   Let the fire for your adversaries consume them.

The same attack is alluded to again (sharing the same context) in Isa. 27:2–5:

> [2] On that day:
> A pleasant vineyard, sing about it!
>   [3] I, the LORD, am its keeper;
>   every moment I water it.
> I guard it night and day
>   so that no one can harm it;
>   [4] I have no wrath.
> If someone gives me thorns and briers,
>   I will march to battle against him.
>   I will burn him up.
> [5] Instead, let him join close to me for protection.
>   Let him make peace with me.
>   Let him make peace with me.

We will examine the relationship between Ezekiel 38 and Isaiah 24–27 in more detail below, when we turn to look at Revelation 20. For the moment, however, we can just remark that these two passages stand together as the only OT predictions of an attack on the people of God that explicitly happens *after* the inauguration of God's/Messiah's peaceful reign.

The End of the Unrepentant

Daniel 2:34–35, 44

> [34] As you looked on, a stone was cut out, not by human hands, and it struck the statue on its feet of iron and clay and broke them in pieces. [35] Then the iron, the clay, the bronze, the silver, and the gold, were all broken in pieces and became like the chaff of the summer threshing-floors; and the wind carried them away, so that not a trace of them could be found. But the stone that struck the statue became a great mountain and filled the whole earth.
>
> . . .
>
> [44] And in the days of those kings the God of heaven will set up a kingdom that shall never be destroyed, nor shall this kingdom be left to another people. It shall crush all these kingdoms and bring them to an end, and it shall stand for ever . . .

These verses belong to the story of Nebuchadnezzar's dream of the great statue of gold, silver, bronze, iron, and clay. The dream's contents and interpretation are revealed to Daniel by God's power (see Dan. 2:1–45). The dream and its interpretation affirm that a moment will come in the future history of the world in which God will remove all of the world's empires once for all and establish an everlasting kingdom that will "fill the whole earth" (v. 35). There is a possible hint of the theme of a violent confrontation in vv. 34–35, but this is not developed in the interpretation presented in v. 44.

Daniel 7:9–17

> [9] As I watched,
> thrones were set in place,
>   and an Ancient One took his throne;
> his clothing was white as snow,
>   and the hair of his head like pure wool;
> his throne was fiery flames,
>   and its wheels were burning fire.
> [10] A stream of fire issued
>   and flowed out from his presence.
> A thousand thousand served him,
>   and ten thousand times ten thousand stood attending him.
> The court sat in judgment,
>   and the books were opened.
>
> [11] I watched then because of the noise of the arrogant words that the horn was speaking. And as I watched, the beast was put to death, and its body destroyed and given over to be burned with fire. As for the rest of the beasts, their dominion was taken away, but their lives were prolonged for a season and a time. As I watched in the night visions,

The Changing of the Ages in the Old Testament

> I saw one like a human being
>> coming with the clouds of heaven.
> And he came to the Ancient One
>> and was presented before him.
> To him was given dominion
>> and glory and kingship,
> that all peoples, nations, and languages
>> should serve him.
> His dominion is an everlasting dominion
>> that shall not pass away,
> and his kingship is one
>> that shall never be destroyed.

> [15] As for me, Daniel, my spirit was troubled within me, and the visions of my head terrified me. [16] I approached one of the attendants to ask him the truth concerning all this. So he said that he would disclose to me the interpretation of the matter: [17] "As for these four great beasts, four kings shall arise out of the earth. [18] But the holy ones of the Most High shall receive the kingdom and possess the kingdom for ever—forever and ever."

Verses 9–10 unmistakably convey the idea that God's coming will constitute a radical and history-stopping intervention. The great court of God sits, and the four great beasts of Dan. 7:1–8, representing the last four great predatory empires of history, are all summarily removed from power. In their place, God grants the kingdom of the world to "the people of the holy ones of the Most High," which they will retain "forever—forever and ever," or, more literally, "for the age, and for an age of ages" (v. 18; cf. vv. 26–27). Some of our other themes, such as cataclysm in the natural world, the inauguration of unending world peace and blessing, and the invitation of the Gentiles,[27] are not explicitly articulated, nor is there any overt reference to resurrection.[28]

Daniel 12:1–3, 13

> [1] At that time Michael, the great prince, the protector of your people, shall arise. There shall be a time of anguish, such as has never occurred since nations first came into existence. But at that time your people shall be delivered, everyone who is found written in the book. [2] Many of those who sleep in the dust of the earth shall awake, some to everlasting life, and some to shame and everlasting contempt.[29] [3] Those who are wise shall shine like the

---

27. The angel interpreter tells Daniel that "all peoples, nations, and languages" will serve the Son of Man, and that "all dominions shall serve and obey them," i.e., the holy ones. But these statements do not necessarily imply that all nations and peoples will be included as full and willing members of the kingdom (as in Ps. 47 and Isa. 66).

28. Of course, if this passage is read concordantly with Rev. 20:4–6, it becomes very natural to understand that "the people of the holy ones of the Most High," who are invited to rule in Dan. 7:18, 22, 27, constitute or at least include those who have been killed by the beast (vv. 21, 25). Resurrection can then be understood to be implicit in the passage.

29. Interestingly, this word "contempt" (or "disgrace," Heb. *der'aōn*, Strong's #H1860) occurs in only

The End of the Unrepentant

> brightness of the sky, and those who lead many to righteousness, like the stars forever and ever.
>
> . . .
>
> ^{13} But you, go your way, and rest; you shall rise for your reward at the end of the days.

This passage is perhaps the one single passage in the OT that speaks more or less explicitly in terms of an end of the age ("the end of the days," v. 13). The implication is that beyond the great crisis that must occur at the end of the days of this age lie the days of a new age. The transition to this new age will be a moment of rescue for the people of Israel ("your people," v. 1), a moment of awakening to life and "reward" for the faithful (vv. 2a, 13), and a moment of awakening to "shame and everlasting contempt" (v. 2b) for others. It's hard to know how to interpret the words, "many of those who sleep in the dust of the earth shall awake." If "awakening" implies resurrection, then the angel's statement seems to be affirming that there will be a *selective* resurrection at the end of the days; after all, it would have been very easy to say, "*all* those who sleep in the dust of the earth shall awake," but the angel does not say that.[30] The angel's wording has in fact led many Jewish commentators to understand his words as meaning, "Many from among those who sleep in the dust of the earth will awake, and these (i.e. the ones who have awoken) will have resurrection life, whereas those (i.e. the ones who do not awake) will have shame and everlasting contempt."[31]

A better reading might result from giving due weight to the angel's way of characterizing death as a kind of sleep or rest (see vv. 2b, 13). He speaks of "the book," which is presumably the Book of Life that contains the rolls of those who are to be granted resurrection to life and citizenship in the age to come (v. 1b). He also refers to Daniel's "reward" (v. 13). Together, these references serve to recall the judgment scene of Dan. 7:9-10, in which "the books were opened" (7:10), and it was determined who would receive the kingdom of the world in the age to come. In other words, those who currently sleep in death must awake to face God the Judge, from whom they will receive either a positive verdict on their lives, resulting in an invitation to the unending life of the world come (12:3), or a negative verdict on their lives, resulting in shame and disgrace for the age to come (12:2b). If the awakening to which the angel refers is indeed this sort of summons from the sleep of death to the judgment seat of God, then this passage says nothing specific about whether or when the disgraced ones will be "resurrected." We can imagine them being called from the slumber of the grave to a judgment at which they are told that they have not been found worthy of resurrection to life, at which point they are

---

two places in the OT: here, and in Isa. 66:24, the last verse of the book of Isaiah.

30. Although there is nothing self-contradictory about a the idea of a selective resurrection that has positive (life) results for some participants and negative (shame, contempt) results for others, this concept coheres neither with the expectation of many Jews and Christians that there will be one final resurrection and judgment for all, nor with the expectation of many Christians that there will be a resurrection of the faithful at Christ's second coming, followed by a delayed resurrection of the rest of humanity (i.e. at the end of the thousand years narrated in of Rev. 20:1-10).

31. The most famous of these are R. Saadia Gaon (c. 892-982 CE) and R. Abraham Ibn Ezra (1089-1164 CE).

will be sent back to the realm of the dead in shame and disgrace.[32] Alternatively, we can imagine them being drawn from the slumber of the grave to participate in the judgment as resurrected people, following which they will be sent away as resurrected people to a place of shame and disgrace. Nothing in the angel's words forecloses either of these readings. If we do not overlay expectations generated elsewhere on this passage, we are left with a promise of life and glory "like the stars forever and ever" (Dan. 12:3) for the faithful, but no precise picture of the fate of the unrepentant.

Despite the puzzles that surround this passage, it is clearly the one and only passage in the OT that contemplates a universal judgment at the end of this age which includes both the living and the dead, and which determines who will be rewarded with life for the age to come, and who will face shame and disgrace.

Joel 3:1–3, 11–21

> [1] For then, in those days and at that time, when I restore the fortunes of Judah and Jerusalem, [2] I will gather all the nations and bring them down to the valley of Jehoshaphat, and I will enter into judgment with them there, on account of my people and my heritage Israel, because they have scattered them among the nations. They have divided my land, [3] and cast lots for my people, and traded boys for prostitutes, and sold girls for wine, and drunk it down.
>
> . . .
>
> [11] Come quickly,
>   all you nations all around,
>   gather yourselves there.
> Bring down your warriors, O LORD.
> [12] Let the nations rouse themselves,
>   and come up to the valley of Jehoshaphat;
> for there I will sit to judge
>   all the neighboring nations.
> [13] Put in the sickle,
>   for the harvest is ripe.
> Go in, tread,
>   for the wine press is full.
> The vats overflow,
>   for their wickedness is great.
> [14] Multitudes, multitudes,
>   in the valley of decision!
> For the day of the LORD is near
>   in the valley of decision.
> [15] The sun and the moon are darkened,
>   and the stars withdraw their shining.

---

32. For a possible NT example of this idea, see Mt. 11:21–24 || Lk. 10:13–15. Hades, throughout the NT, is not the realm of the resurrected, but the realm of those who are dead and awaiting resurrection.

The End of the Unrepentant

> ¹⁶ The Lord roars from Zion,
>> and utters his voice from Jerusalem,
>> and the heavens and the earth shake.
> But the Lord is a refuge for his people,
>> a stronghold for the people of Israel.
> ¹⁷ So you shall know that I, the Lord your God,
>> dwell in Zion, my holy mountain.
> And Jerusalem shall be holy,
>> and strangers shall never again pass through it.
> ¹⁸ On that day
> the mountains shall drip sweet wine,
>> the hills shall flow with milk,
> and all the stream beds of Judah
>> shall flow with water;
> a fountain shall come forth from the house of the Lord
>> and water the Wadi Shittim.
> ¹⁹ Egypt shall become a desolation
>> and Edom a desolate wilderness,
> because of the violence done to the people of Judah,
>> in whose land they have shed innocent blood.
> ²⁰ But Judah shall be inhabited forever,
>> and Jerusalem to all generations.
> ²¹ I will avenge their blood, and I will not clear the guilty,
>> for the Lord dwells in Zion.

We see here many, but not all, of the themes we've been encountering in the psalms and the prophets Isaiah and Ezekiel. We see the theme of a violent confrontation between God and a universal host of enemies ("all nations," vv. 2, 11). We see cataclysm in the natural world, or at least massive upheaval of the regular and reliable features of the heavens and the earth (vv. 15–16). We see the promise of unending peace for God's people (v. 17, 20) and of a renewed world of blessing and prosperity (v. 18). We see all of this put into the context of a restoration of God's people (i.e. Judah, Jerusalem, and Israel, vv. 1–2) to their land from exile (see Ezek. 39). What we do not see, which we have occasionally seen elsewhere, is the theme of the genuine reconciliation of the Gentiles, and the theme of resurrection.

Micah 4:1–8 (note the context, Micah 5:1–15)

> ¹ In days to come
>> the mountain of the Lord's house
> shall be established as the highest of the mountains,
>> and shall be raised up above the hills.
> Peoples shall stream to it,
>> ² and many nations shall come and say:
> "Come, let us go up to the mountain of the Lord,
>> to the house of the God of Jacob;

>   that he may teach us his ways
>   and that we may walk in his paths."
>   For out of Zion shall go forth instruction,
>   and the word of the Lord from Jerusalem.
>   ³ He shall judge between many peoples,
>   and shall arbitrate between strong nations far away;
>   they shall beat their swords into ploughshares,
>   and their spears into pruning-hooks;
>   nation shall not lift up sword against nation,
>   neither shall they learn war anymore;
>   ⁴ but they shall all sit under their own vines and under their own fig trees,
>   and no one shall make them afraid;
>   for the mouth of the Lord of hosts has spoken.
>   ⁵ For all the peoples walk,
>   each in the name of its god,
>   but we will walk in the name of the Lord our God
>   forever and ever.
>   ⁶ On that day, says the Lord,
>   I will assemble the lame
>   and gather those who have been driven away,
>   and those whom I have afflicted.
>   ⁷ The lame I will make the remnant,
>   and those who were cast off, a strong nation;
>   and the Lord will reign over them in Mount Zion
>   now and for evermore.
>   ⁸ And you, O tower of the flock,
>   hill of daughter Zion,
>   to you it shall come,
>   the former dominion shall come,
>   the sovereignty of daughter Jerusalem.

Verses 1–3 here repeat, with slight variations, the prophecy that we read in Isa. 2:2–4 (see above). In Micah's version, which is a little bit more explicit, God will reign over the whole world from his Temple in Zion (vv. 7–8), and all nations will eagerly come and learn his ways (vv. 1b–2). He will bring in an age of universal reconciliation and peace (vv. 3–4). The inauguration of this age of peace will coincide with the gathering of the scattered people of Israel ("On that day," vv. 6–7). It's amazing how inclusive Micah's vision is. His prophecy not only affirms the traditional hope of a prosperity in which everyone in Israel will be able to have their own grapevine and fig tree, but it also generously extends it to all the nations (v. 4, cf. 1 Kgs 4:25; Zech. 3:10). If we dig more deeply into the context, we can also observe the themes of violent conflict and divine victory (Mic. 5:7–15), and God's election of a saving Messiah (5:1–5). We do not see any hint of the theme of cataclysm in the natural world at the transition to God's peaceful reign.

The End of the Unrepentant

Zephaniah 1:14–18; 3:9–20

> ¹⁴ The great day of the LORD is near,
>   near and hastening fast;
> the sound of the day of the LORD is bitter,
>   the warrior cries aloud there.
> ¹⁵ That day will be a day of wrath,
>   a day of distress and anguish,
> a day of ruin and devastation,
>   a day of darkness and gloom,
> a day of clouds and thick darkness,
>   ¹⁶ a day of trumpet blast and battle cry
> against the fortified cities
>   and against the lofty battlements.
> ¹⁷ I will bring such distress upon people
>   that they shall walk like the blind;
>   because they have sinned against the LORD,
> their blood shall be poured out like dust,
>   and their flesh like dung.
> ¹⁸ Neither their silver nor their gold
>   will be able to save them
>   on the day of the LORD's wrath;
> in the fire of his passion
>   the whole earth shall be consumed;
> for a full, a terrible end
>   he will make of all the inhabitants of the earth.
>
> [2:1–3 issues a call to repentance]
>
> [2:4—3:8 presents oracles against enemy nations]

We see here the theme of a universal crisis involving a violent confrontation between God and his enemies. Verse 18 joins Isa. 24:17–20 in making the radical prediction that all of humanity will perish in the day of the LORD (see Zeph. 3:8).

Zephaniah 3:9–10

> ³:⁹ At that time I will change the speech of the peoples
>   to a pure speech,
> that all of them may call on the name of the LORD
>   and serve him with one accord.
> ¹⁰ From beyond the rivers of Ethiopia
>   my suppliants, my scattered ones,
>   shall bring my offering.

Here we see the theme of the genuine reconciliation of the Gentile nations. The promise that far-flung nations will bring an offering to God recalls Isa. 66:18–21.

The Changing of the Ages in the Old Testament

Zephaniah 3:11–13

> [11] On that day you shall not be put to shame
> because of all the deeds by which you have rebelled against me;
> for then I will remove from your midst
> your proudly exultant ones,
> and you shall no longer be haughty
> in my holy mountain.
> [12] For I will leave in the midst of you
> a people humble and lowly.
> They shall seek refuge in the name of the Lord—
> [13] the remnant of Israel;
> they shall do no wrong
> and utter no lies,
> nor shall a deceitful tongue
> be found in their mouths.
> Then they will pasture and lie down,
> and no one shall make them afraid.

Here we can see the themes of final judgment on the rebellious within Israel itself (once again recalling Isa. 66: cf. 66:3–5, 17), rescue of the faithful, and an end for the problem of Israel's sin and rebellion against God.

Zephaniah 3:14–19a

> [14] Sing aloud, O daughter Zion;
> shout, O Israel!
> Rejoice and exult with all your heart,
> O daughter Jerusalem!
> [15] The Lord has taken away the judgments against you,
> he has turned away your enemies.
> The king of Israel, the Lord, is in your midst;
> you shall fear disaster no more.
> [16] On that day it shall be said to Jerusalem:
> Do not fear, O Zion;
> do not let your hands grow weak.
> [17] The Lord, your God, is in your midst,
> a warrior who gives victory;
> he will rejoice over you with gladness,
> he will renew you in his love;
> he will exult over you with loud singing
> [18] as on a day of festival.
> I will remove disaster from you,
> so that you will not bear reproach for it.
> [19] I will deal with all your oppressors
> at that time.

The End of the Unrepentant

Here we have the theme of God's kingship and the theme of peace and security for the faithful under the God's new regime.

Zephaniah 3:19b–20

> [19b] And I will save the lame
>   and gather the outcast,
> and I will change their shame into praise
>   and renown in all the earth.
> [20] At that time I will bring you home,
>   at the time when I gather you;
> for I will make you renowned and praised
>   among all the peoples of the earth,
> when I restore your fortunes
>   before your eyes, says the LORD.

Zephaniah's book closes with a promise that the exiles of Israel will be gathered back to the land when God comes to reign.

We have now looked at every significant passage in the OT that envisions a future world transition that results in something like a new age, in which God's will and God's righteousness hold sway on the earth.[33] Many of our passages foresee a painful crisis at the end of the present age that leads into the coming world transition. Sometimes this crisis is pictured as involving shattering upheavals in the natural world[34] or severe persecution of the faithful,[35] and most often it is pictured as involving a violent and decisive confrontation in which God defeats all human enemies.[36] The psalmists and the prophets do not always picture the transition to a new age of peace and blessing as being mediated by the coming of a Davidic Messiah, but those that do put forward the hope of the coming of a Messiah envision his appearing in the context of a transition to a new age.

Isaiah 26 and Daniel 12 (and just possibly Ezekiel 37) express the prophetic hope of resurrection for those who are faithful to God, and among these three passages, Daniel 12 alone unambiguously locates the resurrection of the faithful in time at the transition point between this age and the age to come. In contrast to this, not even one single passage in the OT unambiguously pictures *a resurrection of those who have not been faithful to God in their lives.* Daniel's description of the great heavenly judgment scene in Daniel 7 does not contain so much as a hint that a judgment of the dead (as opposed to the living) might be being pictured. Indeed, it is only by reading Dan. 7:18, 22, 27 with

---

33. Admittedly, one can detect hints or fragmentary glimpses of these themes in other passages (e.g. Zech. 14:1–21). The passages that we've surveyed are those that have the most explicit and well-developed presentation of the whole complex of themes that amounts to the announcement of a new age.

34. Pss. 46:2–3; 97:3–5; Isa. 24:1, 3–6, 18b–20, 23; 64:1–2; Ezek. 38:19–20, 22; Joel 3:15–16.

35. Isa. 24:16; 25:4–5; 26:16–18; Dan. 7:21, 25; 12:1(?), 7; Zeph. 3:15, 18.

36. Pss. 2:9–11; 46:6, 8–9; 97:3; Isa. 2:10; 11:4; 24:21–22; 65:12–15; 66:6, 16; Ezek. 38:21—39:21; Dan. 2:44–45; 7:11, 26; Joel 3:9–14; Mic. 4:11–13; 5:7–15; Zeph. 1:2–3, 14–18; 3:6, 8.

The Changing of the Ages in the Old Testament

Dan. 12:1–2, 13 in mind that one begins to suspect that the deliverance of the holy ones might include the deliverance (from death itself) for those who have died for their faith.

Here is a table that lays out the passages we've surveyed and the themes we've noted. It indicates which of the themes come forward explicitly in each passage.

	God Comes as Judge	God Comes to Reign	Violent Confrontation	Upheaval in Natural World	Creation is Transformed	Salvation of the Oppressed	Return of Exiles	Gentiles Reconciled to God	Zion is Exalted	Worldwide Justice	Universal Peace	Protection for God's People	Messiah Reigns	Resurrection	God's Intimate Presence	No More Sin
Ps. 2		✓	✓						✓				✓			
Ps. 22		✓						✓		✓			✓			
Ps. 46		?	✓	✓		✓		✓	✓		✓	✓		✓		
Ps. 47	✓	✓														
Ps. 96	✓	✓						✓								
Ps. 97	✓	✓	✓	✓				✓						?		
Ps. 98	✓	✓						✓		✓						
Isa. 2	✓		✓					✓	✓	✓	✓					
Isa. 11		✓			✓	✓		✓		✓			✓			
Isa. 24–27	✓	✓	✓	✓	✓	✓		✓	✓	?		✓		✓	✓	
Isa. 64–66		✓	✓	✓	✓	✓	✓	✓	✓	✓		✓	?	✓	✓	✓
Ezek. 37–39		✓	✓	✓		✓	✓					✓	✓	?	✓	✓
Dan. 2		✓	✓	?												
Dan. 7	✓	✓	✓				✓			✓				?		
Dan. 12	✓					✓								✓		
Joel 3	✓		✓	✓	✓				✓			✓		✓		
Mic. 4:1–8		✓	✓				✓	✓	✓	✓	✓	?	✓			
Zeph. 1:14—2:3; 3:9–20		✓	✓			✓	✓					✓				✓

The combination of themes and expectations surrounding the coming of a new age that we see laid out in this table illustrates what Jesus and the apostles and writers of the NT found in the pages of their Bibles. It is also what their hearers and readers read in *their* Bibles.[37] As we turn to examine the ways in which Jesus and the writers of the New Testament talk about resurrection, judgment, and the coming of a new age in which God's

---

37. It's worth reminding ourselves that Jesus and the apostles, and the vast majority of the hearers of Jesus and the apostles, did not have anything close to our New Testament. Even though books of the NT were written starting about the middle of the first century, they did not come to be gathered into a uniform collection and made available to Christians as a single book until many generations later. The Bible of the first Christians was essentially the OT.

The End of the Unrepentant

Kingdom would reign throughout the earth through Christ, our knowledge of this OT background will consistently help us understand what they're saying.

Let's make the move to discussing the NT by first satisfying ourselves that the NT takes up all of the major themes associated with the idea of the coming of a new age in the OT.

- God Comes as Judge: Lk. 18:1–8; Acts 17:31; Rom. 2:5; 14:10; Jude 1:14–15; Rev. 11:15–19; 14:7
- God Comes to Reign: Mt. 6:10; Lk. 13:29 || Mt. 8:11 (|| Isa. 24:3; 25:6); Lk. 22:18; 1 Cor. 15:24; Rev. 11:15–19
- Violent Confrontation: Lk. 19:27; 2 Thess. 1:6–10; Rev. 19:11–21
- Upheaval in the Natural World: Mt. 24:7–8, 29 (|| Isa. 13:10; Ezek. 32:7), 35; Lk. 21:11, 25–26, 33; 2 Pet. 3:5–12; Rev. 6:12–17 etc.
- Creation is Transformed: Mt. 19:28; Rom. 8:18–23; 2 Pet. 3:13; Rev. 21:1—22:5
- Salvation for the Oppressed: Mt. 5:3–7 || Lk. 6:20–25; Lk. 18:1–8; 2 Thess. 1:5–10; Rev. 20:4–6
- Return of Exiles: Mt. 24:31 || Mk 13:27; Lk. 21:24; Jn 11:52
- Gentiles Reconciled to God: Mt. 12:18, 21; 28:19–20; Lk. 2:32; Jn 10:16; multiple instances in Pauline Epistles; Acts 11:18; 28:28; 1 Pet. 2:9–10; Rev. 7:9–17[38]
- Zion is Exalted: Mt. 5:35 (contrast, however, Jn 4:21); Rom. 11:26; Gal. 4:25–26; Heb. 12:22; Rev. 3:12; 14:1; 21:1—22:5.
- Worldwide Justice: 2 Pet. 3:13; Rev. 21:24–27
- Universal Peace (not in this age: Mt. 10:34; Lk. 12:51): Rom. 2:10; Eph. 2:11–22; Col. 1:20; Rev. 7:9–17; 21:1–4
- Protection for God's People: 1 Pet. 1:5; Rev. 20:7–10
- Messiah Reigns: e.g., Mt. 19:28; 25:31; Lk. 1:32; 2:11; Acts 2:30, 36; 2 Tim. 4:1; Heb. 1:8; 8:1; 12:2; Rev. 3:21; 7:17; 11:15
- Resurrection: Mt. 22:30–31; 27:52, 53; Mk. 12:25–26; Lk. 11:31; 14:14; 16:31; 20:35–36; Jn 5:21, 29; 6:39–40, 44, 54; 11:24; Acts 24:15; 1 Cor. 15; Phil. 3:11; 1 Thess. 1:10; 4:16; Heb. 6:2; 11:19; Rev. 20:4–6
- God's Intimate Presence: Rev. 7:9–17; 21:1–8, 22–23; 22:3–5
- No More Sin: Rom. 8:1–6; 1 Cor. 15:54–57; Heb. 8:8–13; 10:11–22

---

38. Note that most of these passages express the belief that the reconciliation of the Gentiles is already underway in the current age through the preaching of the Good News of Jesus Christ.

5

The Changing of the Ages in the New Testament

BOTH JOHN THE BAPTIZER and Jesus picture the coming of the Kingdom of God as imminent (Mt. 3:2; 4:17; 10:7; Mk 1:15; Lk. 10:11; 11:20; however, see Lk. 19:11–12). John the Baptizer expects Messiah to be the key instrument of God's winnowing of the human race (Mt. 3:12 || Lk. 3:17).[1] John also believes that Messiah will be instrumental in pouring out the Holy Spirit on those who are found faithful (see Mt. 3:11; Jn 1:33, cf. Acts 1:5). In the OT prophets, this outpouring of the Spirit signals a kind of spiritual rebirth of humanity that is associated with the transition to the Kingdom of God (see Isa. 44:3; 59:21; Ezek. 37:14; 39:29; Joel 2:28–29; Zech. 12:10). It's noteworthy that John never speaks in terms of resurrection and judgment, but only in terms of the (living) righteous and repentant being welcomed to participate in the coming Messianic age of righteousness, and the (living) unrepentant being utterly destroyed and so excluded from that age (see Mt. 3:7–12 || Lk. 3:7–9, 16–17).

Now there is a slightly tricky aspect to all of this, but it shouldn't have a major impact on the particular questions that we are trying to answer. The tricky aspect concerns what is known as "realized eschatology." Realized eschatology refers to prophetic promises that were traditionally understood to belong to the future and to the age to come, but which Jesus and the writers of the New Testament see as being, so to speak, brought forward into the present through the ministry of Jesus and the Christian community. Let's break the terms down. "Eschatology" (from Greek, meaning study or doctrine of the last things) concerns theories and beliefs about the "end of the world," such as things that belong to the coming age and the transition to it. "Realized" indicates that Jesus and the first Christians *experienced* and taught the *present reality* of a number of things traditionally relegated to "the end" in Jewish popular belief. Among these were the coming

---

1. Winnowing is the process of separating the edible parts of grain from the inedible parts. It is used as a metaphor for God's judgment, which makes a division between the righteous and faithful on the one hand, and the unrepentant and unfaithful, on the other hand.

The End of the Unrepentant

of Messiah,[2] the outpouring of the Holy Spirit,[3] the establishment of a new covenant,[4] and the conversion of the Gentiles, resulting in their welcoming and integration into the community of faith.[5] Even resurrection from the dead, that most remote-seeming of eschatological beliefs, is seen intruding into the present age through the ministry and resurrection of Jesus himself.[6] A swimming pool of ink has been spilled on this subject, but we need only to be aware of it and to understand the basic concept of it. Here is an illustration that may be of some benefit in forming a basic grasp of realized eschatology:

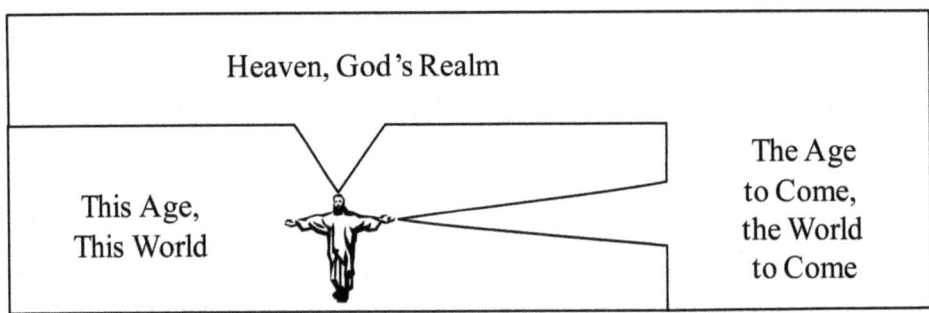

In popular Jewish belief and understanding, God's realm, the realm of divine power and justice, is currently in a state of separation from the realm of ordinary human experience. God's realm is heaven, conceived of as hidden beyond the blue dome of the sky. In Jesus (both in his person and in his words and actions), God's heavenly presence intrudes, pierces, into the human, earthly realm.[7] Similarly, in Jesus, the good things traditionally understood to belong to the future and the age to come pierce into the present age and the present time. These two intrusions are closely related because, as the illustration indicates, the great promise of the world to come is that heaven, God's realm, will no longer be separate from Earth, the realm of human beings.[8] Heaven does not yet take over Earth, nor does the age to come take over this age, but the blessings of God's

---

2. John the Baptizer was convinced that God had shown him that Jesus was the Messiah (Mt. 3:11–17 || Mk 1:7-11 || Lk. 3:15-16. 21-22 || Jn 1:26-34). Sharing the beliefs of most of his contemporaries, John probably expected Jesus to bring in a glorious new age by miraculously expelling the Romans from Judea and setting up a worldwide messianic Kingdom of God. That's why he was confused when he became imprisoned and heard that Jesus was simply traveling around preaching the good news of the Kingdom and healing people. Jesus sent a message to reassure him that the scriptural promises were being fulfilled, and Jesus acknowledged that there would be a temptation to be disillusioned by the fact that the transition to the new world was not going to happen all at once (see, e.g., Mt. 11:1-6 || Lk. 7:18-23).

3. Mt. 3:11 || Mk 1:8 || Lk. 3:16; Lk. 24:29; Acts 1:1-8; 2:1-21; Eph. 1:13.

4. Mt. 26:28 || Mk 14:24 || Lk. 22:20 || 1 Cor. 11:25; 2 Cor. 3:6; Heb. 6:8-13; 10:1-22; 12:24.

5. Mt. 8:11; Lk. 13:29; Jn 10:16 (all eschatological); but see Mt. 28:18-20; Acts 10:1-11:18; Eph. 2; 1 Pet. 1:3—2:12, etc.

6. In addition to the resurrection of Jesus himself, the Gospels show Jesus raising at least three dead people to life: Mt. 9:18-26 || Mk 5:22-43 || Lk. 8:40-56; Lk. 7:11-17; Jn 11. Matthew reports that many OT saints were also raised in connection with Jesus' death and his own resurrection: Mt. 27:50-53.

7. This is most dramatically illustrated at his baptism, when the heavens split open and God speaks (Mt. 3:17 || Mk 1:11 || Lk. 3:22).

8. Cf. Isa. 24:23-25:10; 64:1-2; 65:17; Ezek. 37:26-27; Rev. 21:1-7.

realm and the blessings of the new creation dramatically manifest themselves as present wherever Jesus is present. In Jesus and the ministry of the community of his followers, the people of this present age and this present world are invited to experience a foretaste of the good things of the world come.[9]

We have seen that many of the psalmists and the prophets of the OT looked ahead to a new age in which God's Kingdom and God's ways would be the ruling realities on earth. We have confirmed that NT authors take up and embrace all of the major themes associated with the coming of a new age in the OT. We have also noted that Daniel 12:13 contains the only *explicit* language in the OT regarding an "end" to the current age or period of history. By the era of Jesus and the apostles, however, it had become commonplace among the Jews to talk in terms of "this age" and "the age (or ages) to come." Let's now turn to look over the key NT passages that use this language. Once we've done this, we will combine what we learned in our survey of OT passages that look ahead to a new age with what we learn from reading those NT passages that specifically refer to the relationship between this age and the age or ages to come. We will thus be able to engage a survey of NT passages that refer to *resurrection* in the confidence that we have appropriate background knowledge.

Matthew 12:32

> $_{32}$But if someone says something against the Holy Spirit, they will not be forgiven—not in this age, nor in the next one.

This statement simply illustrates the fact that Jesus is comfortable talking about a current age and an age to come.

Matthew 13:38–49 (Jesus explains the parable of the darnel[10] weeds)

> $_{36}$Then Jesus left the crowds and went back to the house. His followers came up to him and said, "Explain the parable of the darnel weeds in the field to us." $_{37}$He answered:
>
> The one who plants the good-quality seed is the Human One, $_{38}$and the field is the world. The good-quality seed is those who belong to God's Reign.[11] The darnel weeds are those who belong to the Evil One.[12] $_{39}$The enemy that scattered them is the devil. The harvest is the wrapping up of the age, and the harvesters are angels. $_{40}$So, just as darnel weeds are gathered up and burned, the same will happen at the wrapping up of the age. $_{41}$The Human One will send out his angels, and they'll separate out of his Realm all the people who trip people up, and those who go around acting lawless. $_{42}$They'll throw them

---

9. Heb. 6:4–6.

10. Darnel is a green grass that looks somewhat similar to wheat until it becomes mature. Its seeds are poisonous.

11. Lit. "the children of the kingdom." It's a figure of speech.

12. Lit. "the children of the Evil One."

> in a burning furnace. In there there's going to be people crying and grinding their teeth. ₄₃Then the people of integrity[13] are going to shine like the sun in the kingdom of their Father.

This parable offers us a lot of insight about how Jesus sees the present age in relation to the coming transition to the age to come. He compares the present world and age to a field of growing wheat. We can imagine that Jesus owns this metaphorical field. By preaching and living out the good news of the Kingdom of God, Jesus plants in this world seeds whose destiny is to prove themselves to be "the children of the Kingdom," i.e., those who will ultimately grow up spiritually to love and serve God, and show a "family likeness" to him. Collectively, the mix of similar-looking but genetically unrelated (wheat and darnel) plants represents the visible church growing in the soil of the world. Just as wheat and darnel plants don't display their full nature and character until they're fully grown, so it is in the life of the church in this age: God's genuine children are not always immediately distinguishable from those ultimately destined to manifest a family likeness to the devil, God's enemy. In the parable, the good plants, the ones that bear the true wheat kernels, are gathered into the owner's barn, whereas the counterfeit plants, the toxic weeds, are burned (13:30; cf. 13:41–43). The natural expectation behind this parable is that those who genuinely adhere to God's and Christ's kingdom will be invited to take part in the age to come. In the harvest, which represents the end of this age (v. 40), many who have assumed that they will be welcome to participate in the new age will instead find to their horror that they are slated for destruction. The point: it's not good enough to hang around with children of God and to look a little bit like a child of God. You actually have to become one.

Note the allusion in v. 43 to Dan. 12:3, in which an angel says to Daniel,

> Those who are wise shall shine like the brightness of the sky, and those who lead many to righteousness, like the stars forever and ever.

The difference between Jesus and Daniel here is that Jesus appears to be talking about the judgment of the living at the end of this age, and not about the judgment of the dead. I say that because he says, "The Human One will send out his angels, and they'll separate out of his kingdom all the people who trip people up, and those who go around acting lawless" (v. 41). But he has already explained that "the field is the world" (v. 38). So if we allow the interpretation to be self-consistent, then the mixed plants, representing the visible church in this world, grow together until the end of this age. At that point the weeds are removed from this world and destroyed—whereas the wheat is harvested and safely stored in the barn, the latter result being symbolic of people being safely conducted through the transition to participate in the glorious age to come (compare vv. 30, 43).[14]

---

13. Traditionally: "the righteous."

14. Paul talks explicitly about what Jesus often seems content to leave implicit in his parables and teachings: the assumption that some Christians will be alive on earth at the moment of transition to the new age. The promise is that these living mortals will be gathered up and vested with eternal life without dying and having to be resurrected (see 1 Cor. 15:50–53; 1 Thess. 4:15–17). When Paul introduces his teaching in 1 Thess. 4:15 by saying he's teaching "by the word of the Lord," he is referring to the words of the Lord Jesus in Mt. 24:29–31.

As we'll see, Jesus will definitely talk about the judgment of the dead at the end of this age. But he also offers a number of parables and teachings that look forward to a process of separating true from false disciples *among the living* at the transition point between this age in the age to come.[15] This appears to be one such parable.

Matthew 24:3

> ₃ . . . when Jesus sat down at the Mount of Olives, his followers came up to him privately. They said, "Tell us, when will these things happen? Also, what's the sign[16] of your coming,[17] and of the wrapping up of the age?"

By this point in the ministry of Jesus, his closest followers seem to realize that he has no plans to revolutionize the world right away and all at once. Teachings such as his parables of the mustard seed and the yeast[18] have impressed them that he is not going to manifest himself in glory as Messiah until the end of the age. But the wording of their question is instructive. They talk about "the wrapping up of the age." They expect that this world and this age will have to be wrapped up, to be brought to an end; they do not expect there to be a gradual or step-by-step transition to the new conditions of the Kingdom of God. The things that Jesus says in response to their question (Mt. 24–25) make it clear that he shares the same way of thinking. This age will come to a dramatic and traumatic end.

Matthew 24:14

> ₁₄And this good news of the kingdom is going to be preached throughout the world as a testimony to all the nations. Then the end will come.

This age, says Jesus, has a purpose: the purpose of spreading the good news of God's Kingdom to all the nations of the world. When that task is complete, then it can be brought to a close. Beyond the "end," by implication, lies the full manifestation of the Kingdom of God on earth, as foreseen in the psalms and the prophets.

---

15. See Mt. 7:13–23; 22:1–14; 24:36—25:30; Lk. 13:23–30. Note the surprise expressed by of the rejected ones in most of these scenes. If we take seriously the picture of the intermediate state given us in the parable of Lazarus and the Rich Man (Lk. 16:19–31), we'll have good reason to assume that the unfaithful dead will not be expecting a positive result when they are raised for judgment.

16. Jews believed there would be certain striking events ("signs") that would give the clue that God was about to intervene to put an end to human history and renew the world through the Messiah.

17. In the present context, the Greek word *parousia* (Strong's #G3952) here means more than just "coming," "appearance," or "arrival." It can often mean the official arrival of a king or emperor. Since Matthew represents Jesus' followers as associating his arrival with the end of the age, it is clear that we are to understand that they see him as the hoped-for Messiah, who just hasn't gone public yet. It means here, "your coming to rule the earth as Messiah."

18. Mt. 13:31–33 || Mk 4:30–32 || Lk. 13:18–21.

The End of the Unrepentant

Mark 10:29–30 || Luke 18:30

> ₂₉Jesus was saying, "I'm telling you seriously: there's no one who has left a home, or brothers or sisters, or mother or father, or a child, or properties for me and the good news, ₃₀who won't receive a hundred times as much now in this age: homes, brothers, sisters, mothers, children, and properties—with persecutions. And in the age that's coming, eternal life."

This statement simply illustrates the fact that Jesus expected the gift of resurrection to eternal life to be given to the faithful in the age to come. This idea is not as self-evident as most Christians may assume it to be. Some Jewish literature contemporary with the NT expects a messianic age to follow the current age, and for the resurrection to occur after the end of that age.[19]

Luke 20:34–36

> ₃₄And Jesus said to them, "The people[20] of this age marry and get married. ₃₅But those who've been considered worthy to take part in[21] that age, and in the resurrection from among the dead—they don't marry, and they don't get married. And they can't die anymore. ₃₆Because they're like angels, and they're God's children. They belong to the resurrection.[22]

Here Jesus explains that there is a fundamental difference in the principle of life between this age and age to come. In this age, which functions on the principle of mortal life, human life on the earth can only be sustained over time through procreation. A new mortal generation is continuously being born to succeed its parent generation, thereby keeping the human species alive. In contrast, those raised from among the dead to participate in the coming age will be immortal. In that age, humanity's numbers will be complete,[23] and since there will be no further need to procreate, there will be no need to marry.[24]

---

19. See, e.g., *4 Ezra* 7:26–43; 8:52–54; *Apocalypse of Baruch* (= *2 Baruch*) 29–30; *Life of Adam and Eve* 29:7–10; 48:1–3; 51:1–2. All of these works appear to expect a general resurrection to occur *after* the hoped-for golden age or messianic age. Rabbinic opinion about the timing of the resurrection (and, indeed, about whether the unrepentant would be raised at all) was not at all unanimous. Some hoped for a resurrection for the faithful when Messiah appeared, and some expected a general resurrection of all human beings for judgment at the end of the messianic age. See M. Greenberg, D. Boyarin, and S. Siegel, "Resurrection," in *Encyclopaedia Judaica*, vol. 17 (ed. M. Berenbaum and F. Skolnik; 2nd edn; Detroit: Macmillan Reference USA, 2007), pp 240–44.

20. Lit. "children."

21. "To take part in": lit. "to reach," or "to attain."

22. Lit. "... God's children, being children of the resurrection."

23. The Book of Revelation (13:8) speaks of the Lamb's Book of Life that has had the names of the saved in it from the creation of the world. This implies that there is a specific number of people destined to live and a specific number of people destined to inherit eternal life. See also Exod. 32:32–33; Ps. 69:28; Dan. 12:1; Phil. 4:3; Rev. 3:5; 17:8; 20:12, 15; 21:27.

24. Gen. 2:24 says, "Therefore a man leaves his father and his mother and clings to his wife, and they become one flesh." The import of this statement is that the purpose of the social convention of marriage

Romans 16:27

> ₂₇To the One Wise God, through Jesus Christ, be the glory to the ages!²⁵ Amen.

Paul's blessing at the end of Romans illustrates the fact that he shares with the author of Daniel (see Dan. 7:18; 12:13) the conception that the world to come contains an indefinite number of future ages, not just one.

1 Corinthians 2:7–8

> ₇We're talking about God's secret, hidden wisdom. It's the wisdom that God had already decided on before all the ages,²⁶ for our glory. ₈It's the wisdom that none of this world's rulers knew about. After all, if they had known it, they wouldn't have hung the Lord of Glory²⁷ on a cross.

This passage illustrates the fact that Paul conceives of the past as divided up into various ages, and not just the future. He expresses the same understanding about the existence of past ages in 1 Cor. 10:11, in which he says that Christians are those "upon whom the ends of the ages have come."

Galatians 1:4

> ₃Grace and peace to you from God our Father and from the Lord Jesus Christ. ₄He gave himself for our sins, so that he could rescue us out of this current evil age.²⁸

Implicit in Paul's statement is the expectation that there is an age to come that is good and full of God's presence. Although it's conceivable that Paul thinks we have already been rescued in the present, even though we are still living in the current evil age, it's much more likely that he is looking forward to the transition to the age to come at Christ's second coming as the moment of rescue (see Phil. 3:20).

Ephesians 1:21 (quoted without comment)

> ₂₁Christ . . . is above every title you can name,²⁹ not just in this age, but in the coming age too . . .

---

is to create an appropriate social and personal relationship structure for the physical joining of sexual intercourse, whose core biological function is to accomplish reproduction.

25. Some early mss have, "to the ages of the ages."
26. More literally, "that God foreordained before the worlds/ages."
27. For background to this title, see, e.g., Ps. 24:8.
28. Or "world" (Gr. *aiōn*, Strong's #G165). The same word means both in Greek.
29. Lit. "above every name that is named."

The End of the Unrepentant

Titus 3:11–13 (quoted without comment)

> ₁₁Because God's grace has appeared, bringing salvation to all people.³⁰ ₁₂It's taught us to renounce godlessness, and the obsessions³¹ of this world. It's taught us to live soberly, justly, and reverently in this age . . .

Hebrews 1:1–2

> ₁Long ago, God spoke to our ancestors many times, and in many ways, through the prophets. ₂In these "last days," God has spoken to us through a Son. God has appointed the Son to inherit everything;³² and through him, God created the universe.³³

In the OT prophets, the expression "the last days" most often refers to the time of the transition to God's hoped-for intervention to renew the creation and put an end to injustice.³⁴ Here it refers to the last phase of the current age, which was inaugurated with the appearance of Jesus Christ.

Hebrews 2:5

> ₅After all, it's [to Christ, and] not to angels that God subjected the world to come.

The author of Hebrews knows that God's special king, the Messiah, figures in many of the prophetic characterizations of the age to come.³⁵ He agrees in this hope, and he understands such passages to be looking ahead to the reign of Jesus Christ.

Hebrews 6:4

> ₄Now, suppose people have already been enlightened: they've tasted the heavenly gift; they've shared in the Holy Spirit; ₅and they've tasted God's good word, and the powers of the coming age.

The author of Hebrews is thinking here of the outpouring of the Holy Spirit, which the OT prophets foresaw.³⁶ As we observed above, the apostles and the first Christians realized that a number of key blessings prophesied in connection with the coming of the

---

30. Later mss have, "Because God's saving grace has appeared to all people." See 1 Tim. 4:10 for a similarly broad statement about God as savior of all people.
31. Or "cravings," or "lusts." He's not just talking about sexual desire.
32. Lit. "has made him heir of all things."
33. Lit. "the ages," or "the worlds."
34. Isa. 2:2 || Mic. 4:1; Jer. 49:39; Hos. 3:5.
35. See, e.g., Ps. 2; Isa. 11; 42:1–3; Jer. 23:5–6; Ezek. 37; Dan. 7 (?); Mic. 4:1–8.
36. Cf. Isa. 44:3; 59:21; Ezek. 37:14; 39:29; Joel 2:28–29; Zech. 12:10.

The Changing of the Ages in the New Testament

new age were already being experienced in the here and now. The age to come, through Christ, was truly encroaching on the current godless age.

Hebrews 9:26

$_{26}$But now he [Christ] has appeared once, at the wrapping up of the ages.

Like Paul (see 1 Cor. 2:6 and 10:11 above), the author of Hebrews is capable of seeing the previous history of the world divided into ages.

1 Peter 1:20

$_{20}$He [Christ] was foreknown before the foundation of the world, but he's been revealed at the end of history[37] because of you!

Peter joins Paul and the author of Hebrews in feeling a sense that we are in the last phase of human history, more or less at the climax of the story of humanity. The "you" to which he refers is the Gentiles: Peter understands personally that Christ's coming has inaugurated the phase of God's plan for humanity in which he draws the Gentiles into the blessings of the covenant community of Israel (see Acts 10–11).

Jude 25

$_{25}$To the One God our savior, through Jesus Christ our Lord, be glory, greatness, power, and authority—before every age, and now, and to all the ages. Amen.

Jude manages in one statement to refer to a plurality of past ages, the present age, and a plurality of future ages.

Revelation 11:15

$_{15}$The seventh angel blew his trumpet. And there were loud voices in heaven, saying, "The kingdom of this world now belongs to our Lord and to his Christ! He's going to reign forever and ever!"[38]

$_{16}$And the twenty-four ancient ones, who are sitting on their thrones in front of God, fell on their faces and worshiped God. They were $_{17}$saying,

We thank you, Lord, All Powerful God,
Who is and who was,[39]
Because you've taken your great power and have begun to rule.

---

37. Lit. "upon the end of the times/ages."
38. Lit. "to the ages of the ages."
39. Lit. "the Is and the Was." See Rev. 1:8; 4:8.

The End of the Unrepentant

> ₁₈The nations were angry,
> And your anger came,
> And the time came to judge the dead,
> And to give rewards to your servants the prophets,
> And to the holy ones,
> And to those who revere your name, the weak and the powerful,[40]
> And to destroy those who are destroying the earth.

The voices in heaven announce a radical changeover of the visible and tangible sovereignty of the world. In other words, they announce the fulfillment, which is to say, *the coming in fullness*, of the Kingdom of God. This is the great moment that the OT psalmists and prophets foresaw, just as we read in our survey above. In v. 18, we see the familiar theme of a violent confrontation between God and his enemies, the result of which is "the destruction of those who are destroying the earth."[41] To English speakers, it may appear that the terms specifically related to a "changing of the ages" are absent here (as in all the OT passages we looked at except for Daniel 12). However, the terminology of "ages" is actually present in the Greek behind the English. It remains hidden in English because the English Bible translation tradition makes much of the language of "age/ages" invisible. The words "forever and ever" actually translate the Greek phrase *eis tous aiōnas tōn aiōnōn*, which means, word for word, "for (or into or throughout) the ages of the ages." The heavenly voices, responding to the seventh (and last) trumpet, announce that God and his Christ have taken up their reign on the earth, and will reign for all future ages.

An intriguing aspect of this passage is the announcement that the time has come for God to "judge the dead, and to give rewards to your servants . . . those who revere your name." There are a few ways to read this phrase. We can, for example, read it as saying (1) that it is time for God to judge all of the dead, and to hand down a verdict as to who deserves to be rewarded with resurrection (see Rev. 2:10; 3:5; 20:4–6). Or we can read it as saying (2) that it is time for God to judge the unrepentant dead, and, in the same process, to give a reward to those faithful ones of both the old and new covenants whose lives—even though they have died—are hidden in God, and so are not to be regarded as dead (see Rev. 6:9–11; 20:4–6). Perhaps slightly more awkward, but still possible, would be a reading according to which (3) the dead refers to all the dead, the unrepentant and the faithful, and the "servants" refers to those faithful who are alive on the earth at the moment that God's and Christ's kingdom comes. It may be that the language here is intentionally capable of conveying all and each of these ideas. The second advent of Christ, according to the oldest creeds of the church, is the moment at which "he will come again to judge the living and the dead." Rev. 11:18 appears to be affirming this general concept, without spelling it out in detail. Readers will have to wait for Revelation 19–20 to have this idea elaborated.

---

40. Lit. "the small and the great."

41. It's a principle worth meditating on that those who behave destructively towards God's creation set themselves as enemies of God, the Creator, who loves everything he has made (Ps. 145:7–9). Rev. 11:18 announces the eviction of all those who insist on living in a harmful way on planet earth.

Summary of the Things We've Learned So Far in Chapters 1–5

Let's step back for a moment and review what we've achieved so far. In Chapters 1–3, we examined every single passage from Genesis 1 to Revelation 22 that pictures the fate of the unrepentant as an experience of fiery destruction or as some form of being consumed. We've found that the overwhelming majority of these passages simply and unambiguously picture an instant and/or total destruction. A small handful of passages picture a lengthy and painful period of punishment—commencing either at an individual's death (Lk. 16:19–31; Jude 7 [?]), at the second coming of Christ (Mt. 25:31–46; Rev. 14:9–12), or at some point not specified (Mt. 5:23–26; 18:21–35; Lk. 12:57–59). Within this small handful of passages, exactly one passage, Rev. 14:9–12, explicitly threatens the unfaithful with unending torment.[42] Upon examination, that one passage turns out to possess unique and unmistakable links with Isa. 34:9–10, a prophetic passage that is clearly non-literal in its reference to a smoking fire that never goes out. Rev. 14:9–12 also has unmistakable links with Rev. 19:3, a passage in the book within Revelation itself that is also clearly non-literal in its reference to a smoking fire that never goes out. In addition to this, Rev. 14:9–12 also remarkably directs its threat not to outsiders or unbelievers, but to professing Christians who are facing the temptation to renounce their faithfulness to Jesus Christ because of the deadly threats being made by the beast and his minions.

In Chapter 4 we turned our attention to an examination of every passage in the OT that looks ahead to an end of the current regime of history and to the establishment of the unending reign of God on the earth. Noting a number of important shared themes and expectations, we confirmed at the end of that chapter that Jesus and the authors of the NT reaffirm each of these major themes and expectations. In the current chapter (Chapter 5) we have looked at every significant passage in the NT that refers to past ages, the current age, and the age or ages to come. With this information at our fingertips, we now stand in a good position to take a close look at all the NT passages that refer to, or teach about, the similarities and differences between the resurrection of the faithful and of the unrepentant. This will be our task in Chapter 6.

---

42. Rev. 20:10 is closely related, but its explicit import concerns the fate of Satan, the beast, and the false prophet, not the fate of the unrepentant as a group. In view of the fact that these three have been characterized in Revelation as the most intensely evil beings in the history of the world, it is not automatically to be assumed that their fate equals that of all of the unrepentant. Rev. 14:9–12 thus stands on its own, and does not receive numerical support from Rev. 20:10.

6

Future Judgment and Resurrection in the New Testament

THERE'S A CERTAIN AMOUNT of disagreement about when, how, and in what forms the Jews came to believe in a great future judgment and in the resurrection of the dead. In particular, around the time that the New Testament was being written, there were different schools of thought about whether "the resurrection of the righteous" would accompany the appearance of Messiah's kingdom. Probably a majority of Jews at that time hoped that the faithful who had died would be raised to participate in the Messianic age. Some, however, looked for a general resurrection and judgment of all the dead at the end of time, i.e., at the end of the Messiah's reign. I'm not going to tax your patience with that question; instead I'm just going to jump in and start looking at NT passages. We'll do our best to interpret them on the basis of their internal logic and inner-biblical connections.

Matthew 12:41–42 || Luke 11:31–32

> 12:41 The men of Nineveh[1] are going to stand up in the judgment and testify[2] against this generation, and they will condemn it. Because they changed their hearts[3] on the basis of Jonah's preaching. And look, there's something bigger than Jonah here. 42 The Queen of Sheba[4] will rise to testify[5] against this generation in the judgment, and she'll condemn it. Because she came from the far corners of the earth to hear the wisdom of Solomon. And look, there's something bigger than Solomon here.

---

1. Prn. ***ninn**-a-va*.
2. Lit. "will stand up in the judgment" (Gr.: *anastēsontai en tē krisei*). The verb here is *anistēmi* (Strong's #G450).
3. Traditionally: "they repented."
4. Lit. "the South."
5. Lit. "will be raised up in judgment" (Gr. *egerthēsetai en tē krisei*). The verb here is *egeirō* (Strong's #G1453). Interestingly, the words used here for "to stand up" and "be raised up" can also mean "rise" (from the grave or from Hades) or "be resurrected."

Future Judgment and Resurrection in the New Testament

> ₁₁:₃₁The Queen of Sheba[6] will rise to testify[7] against the men of this generation, and she's going to condemn them. Because she came from the far corners of the earth to hear the wisdom of Solomon. And look, there's something bigger than Solomon here. ₃₂The men of Nineveh are going to stand up in the judgment and testify[8] against this generation, and they will condemn it. Because they changed their hearts[9] on the basis of Jonah's preaching—and look, there's something bigger than Jonah here."

The first thing to be noted here is that Jesus is talking about "the judgment" (Mt. 12:41 || Lk. 11:32). This is most naturally understood as the great trial that is pictured as standing at the moment of transition between this age of mortal life and human history on the one hand, and the coming age of immortal life and resurrection on the other hand.

Are we to picture people taking part in that great judgment in a state of resurrection? After all, the words translated as "stand up" and "rise up" are each capable of referring to resurrection.[10] Or are we simply being given the picture of individuals bringing suit against one another and testifying against one another in front of God on the day of judgment, without any information as to whether resurrection is to be assumed? The language here, after all, closely parallels that in Ps. 94:16, which clearly has a legal meaning:

> Who rises up for me[11] against the wicked?
> Who stands up for me[12] against evildoers?

To "stand up" or "rise up" in ancient Jewish parlance means to appear in court to present testimony or argument. The same language is also used in the context of the trial of Jesus, at which (false) witnesses bear false witness against him before the Sanhedrin (Mk 14:57):

> Some people stood up[13] and falsely accused him: ₅₈"We heard him say, 'I am going to destroy this Temple that was made by human hands, and within three days I'm going to build another one, that's not built by human hands.'" ₅₉But even their testimony about that[14] wasn't the same.

Using similar language, the psalmist in Ps. 1:5 claims that the wicked will have "no standing" in the court of God's justice:

---

6. Lit. "the South." 1 Kgs 10:1–10; 2 Chron. 9:1–12.
7. See the nt. on Mt. 12:42 above.
8. See the nt. on Mt. 12:41 above.
9. Traditionally: "they repented."
10. See Dan. 12:2 (LXX), which has both these words: *anistēmi* (Strong's #G450) and *egeirō* ("stand up," and "rise," Strong's #G1453), and Dan. 12:13, which has *anistēmi* ("stand up"). Dan. 12:1 also has *anistēmi* with the meaning of "to take a stand." These words are common and everyday words, and it has to be established by reference to context whether they connote resurrection.
11. Gr. (LXX): *tis anastēsetai moi*, from *anistēmi*, Strong's #G450.
12. Gr. (LXX): *tis sumparastēsetai moi*, from the verb *sumparistēmi*, from the stem *anistēmi*.
13. Gr. *anistēmi*, the same verb as in Mt. 12:41 and Ps. 94:16.
14. "Even their testimony about that": lit. "even that way."

The End of the Unrepentant

> Therefore the wicked will not stand in the judgment,[15]
> nor sinners in the congregation of the righteous.

Some commentators resist seeing in Mt. 12:41–42 a picture of people accusing one another at the judgment. They suggest that Jesus means that *the example* of the Queen of Sheba and the Ninevites will condemn the unbelieving religious leaders. This is a possible way of reading the passage. On the other hand, Mt. 12:41–42 is not the first place that Jesus has pictured the coming judgment as a place where people will present legal arguments against one another. For example, see Mt. 5:23–26 || Lk. 12:57–59:

> $_{23}$So suppose you are just bringing your offering[16] to the altar, and right there you remember that your fellow human being has something against you. $_{24}$Leave your gift there in front of the altar! Go, get reconciled with the person! Then, come back and offer your gift. $_{25}$Be quick, make amends with the person who has a complaint against you,[17] while you are both on the way to court. Otherwise the person will turn you over to the judge. The judge will then turn you over to the guard,[18] and you'll be thrown in prison. $_{26}$I'm telling you seriously: you *will not*[19] get out of there until you've paid back the last cent!

The apostle Paul also seems willing to imagine the judgment as a trial in which people will dispute with one another:

Romans 2:11–16

> $_{11}$Because there's no such thing as special status with God. $_{12}$Those who sin[20] without the Law will perish without reference to the Law, and those who sin knowing the Law[21] will be judged on the basis of the Law. $_{13}$After all, it's not those who hear the Law read to them that are just: it's those who carry out the Law who are going to be declared just. $_{14}$For example, sometimes non-Jews, who don't have the Law, instinctively do the things the Law requires. These people, despite not having the Law, embody the Law in themselves. $_{15}$They demonstrate the result of the Law being engraved on their hearts, bearing witness to their consciences. As I understand the good news, it will be their own arguments and reasonings with one another—whether condemning or approving—that will judge them $_{16}$on the day when God judges the secrets of humanity through the agency of Jesus Christ.

How is it that we have people arguing back and forth at the judgment? Most Christians have been taught to believe that God (through Christ) will be the only judge on the Day

---

15. Gr. (LXX): *ouk anastēsontai* [from *anistēmi*] *asebeis en krisei*.
16. Or "gift."
17. Lit. "your opponent at law."
18. Or "bailiff"; lit. "attendant."
19. Lit. "you will not—will not—." In reading, the word "not" should be emphasized.
20. The Greek word here connotes a missing of the target, a going astray from the good.
21. Lit. "within the Law."

Future Judgment and Resurrection in the New Testament

of Judgment. But that in no way precludes the idea of witnesses being called, which is exactly what is being characterized in Mt. 12:41–42 and Lk. 11:31–32. The crucial question here is this: *what is it that is decided in the judgment?* Once again, most Christians tend to assume that they will not have to appear at the judgment—that they will have "a resurrection of life" (Jn 5:28–29), and that only the non-Christians and bad folks in general will have to appear in the judgment. That is not, however, what Paul teaches (2 Cor. 5:7–10):

> . . . we live our lives[22] by faith, not by sight. ₈And we also take courage as we sense that[23] it's better to be away from the home of our body and to be home with the Lord. ₉That's why we aspire, whether at home or away from home, to please him.[24] ₁₀After all, we all have to appear in front of Christ's judgment bench.[25] And each person is going to get paid back[26] for the things they've done while they were in their body,[27] whether good or bad.

This characterization coheres with the scene that we encountered in the teaching of Jesus himself in Mt. 25:31–46, which is often called The Judgment of the Nations. Despite the fact that some theologians argue against it, and most Christians feel uneasy about it, the principle is repeated numerous times in the NT that everyone—including those who consider themselves to be followers of Jesus—will face judgment at the second coming of Christ on the basis of their "works." That is, people will be evaluated as to their worthiness to take part in the world to come on the basis of their *behavior*, and not their *beliefs*.[28]

According to both Paul and Peter, Jesus is coming again to judge the living and the dead. Paul says to Timothy:

2 Timothy 4:1

> ₁I challenge you in front of God, and in front of Christ Jesus, who's going to judge the living and the dead—and I challenge you by his arrival and his kingdom: ₂Preach the message!

And Peter says:

---

22. Or "we conduct ourselves"; lit. "we walk."

23. Lit. ". . . courage, and we consider that."

24. Lit. "to be pleasing to him." The "him" here is the Lord Jesus (see 4:14). When Paul says "the Lord," he almost always means Jesus.

25. This is the language of the courtroom. We "have to appear," and Christ as judge sits at "the bench."

26. Lit. "so that each person can get paid back."

27. Lit. "the things done through the body."

28. To confirm this, carefully read Mt. 5:17–30; 7:1–2; 7:21–27; 12:32–37; 13:40–43; 16:27; 24:13; 24:45–51; 25:14–30; 25:31–46; Lk. 6:37; 14:13–14; Jn 5:22–29; 12:25–26; Rom. 2:1–13; 14:7–12; 1 Cor. 4:4–5; 10:1–12; 2 Cor. 5:9–10; Gal. 5:19–21; 6:7–8; Jas. 3:1; Rev. 22:12.

The End of the Unrepentant

1 Peter 4:5

> ₅They're going to have to give an account of themselves to the One who's just about[29] to judge the living and the dead.

I repeat the question: what is going to be decided when Jesus judges the living and the dead? Jesus (Mt. 25:31–46) agrees with Daniel (Dan. 7:14, 26–27) that what is to be decided is the question of *who is worthy to participate in the glorious Kingdom of God in the age to come, and in the eternal life that is characteristic of that age*. Paul himself agrees. As he says in Romans:

Romans 2:4–10

> ₄Don't you know that God's acts of kindness are supposed to lead you to a change of heart?[30] ₅But suppose your heart is stubborn and unrepentant. Aren't you piling up God's wrath towards you for the day when God's anger and just judgment are revealed?[31] ₆God is going to repay each person in line with their behavior. ₇For those who consistently do good, and so strive for glory and honor and incorruptible life,[32] there will be eternal life. ₈But for those who live selfishly,[33] and disobey the truth, while obeying what is unjust, ₉there will be anger and wrath. Trouble and distress will land on every human soul that does evil—the Jew first, and also the non-Jew. ₁₀But glory and honor and peace will come to everyone who does good—the Jew first, and also the non-Jew.

Paul's statements here imply that the gift of "eternal life" (v. 7) is the outcome of a positive verdict at the judgment. In other words, Paul believes that all the living and all the dead are going to appear before the judgment seat of God, and resurrection to "incorruptible life" (v. 7) is going to be the outcome for some, whereas "anger, wrath, trouble, and distress" (v. 9) will be the outcome for others.

In reading Mt. 12:41–42, it's not at all impossible to picture those who are arguing with one another as persons resurrected for judgment; however, Jesus speaks in such a way as to leave the door open for the interpretation that the "standing up" and the "rising up" have to do with being called as witnesses (or appearing as plaintiffs and respondents), rather than with resurrection. In that case, our passage would cohere with a number of other passages in the NT, including the following, which posit *not* that human beings are called to the judgment in a resurrected state, but that they are called to the judgment *to determine whether they are worthy of resurrection*.

---

29. Lit. "who holds ready."
30. Traditionally: "to repentance."
31. Lit. "aren't you storing up anger in a day of anger and revelation of just judgment of God."
32. Lit. "incorruptableness."
33. Or "promote themselves." The word connotes working situations for your own ends, intentionally setting others against each other.

Matthew 22:30 || Mark 12:25 || Luke 20:34-36

> 22:30 Because in the resurrection, people aren't married, and they don't get married. No, they're like angels in heaven.

> 12:25 Because when they rise from among the dead, people aren't married, and they don't get married. No, they're like angels in the heavens.

> 20:34 And Jesus said to them, "The people[34] of this age marry and get married. 35 But those who've been considered worthy to take part in[35] that age, and in the resurrection from among the dead—they don't marry, and they don't get married. And they can't die anymore. 36 Because they're like angels, and they're God's children. They belong to the resurrection.[36]

If we look carefully at the relationship between these three versions of Jesus' saying in response to the trick question about resurrection posed to him by the Sadducees,[37] it becomes apparent that the expression "the resurrection" refers to *the resurrection of the faithful* when it is used without further qualification in Jewish parlance. No Jew, Jesus included, would have been willing to say that *the resurrected unrepentant* would be invulnerable to death, that they would be "like angels in heaven," and that they would be "God's children." Luke, self-consciously writing for Gentiles, may have used this version of the saying in order to make sure that his readers don't assume Jesus is talking about the resurrection of everyone, but only about the resurrection of those who are found worthy of eternal life. He knows that this teaching is about the obsoleteness of marriage in "the resurrection of the just" (see Lk. 14:14), and that Jesus is not making an affirmation of universal resurrection to eternal life.

Luke's version of this saying is very instructive for our purposes, because it makes an equivalency between being found worthy (in the judgment) to participate in the age to come, on the one hand, and "resurrection from among the dead" on the other hand:

Luke 20:35

> 35 But those who've been considered worthy to take part in[38] that age, and in the resurrection from among the dead—they don't marry...

"That age" obviously means the age to come, the age of God's Kingdom on earth that is destined to follow this current age of history. The unjust, or, if you like, the unrepentant, must at some point be judged, and a verdict of "unworthy of participation in the age to come and eternal life" must be determined in their case. What happens to such people? Jesus doesn't elaborate on their fate in this saying, for the simple reason that the fate of the unrepentant is not what the conversation is about. But he does indicate what *does not*

---

34. Lit. "children."
35. "To take part in": lit. "to reach," or "to attain."
36. Lit. "...God's children, being children of the resurrection."
37. For the whole exchange, see Mt. 22:22-30; Mk 12:18-27; Lk. 20:27-40.
38. "To take part in": lit. "to reach," or "to attain."

happen to them when the faithful are raised. To speak of a "resurrection from among the dead" (Gr. *anastasis ek nekrōn*)[39] is automatically to affirm about the rest of the dead *that they remain dead. They are not raised.*

It's important to understand that the familiar phrase "resurrection from the dead" from our English Bibles simply does not mean "resurrection from a state of death," as most people automatically tend to assume.[40] The Greek substantive adjective *nekros* (dead) in the expression *ek (tōn)*[41] *nekrōn*, "from the dead," is plural, and refers to dead people. This fact is underlined in v. 38, when Jesus says, "God is not the God of dead people (*theos de ouk estin nekrōn*), but of the living (*alla zōntōn*). Because everyone lives to him." To speak of a resurrection "from the dead" (Gr. *ek nekrōn* or *ek tōn nekrōn*), in other words, is transparently to speak of a resurrection from among those who are dead—a resurrection that leaves the rest of the dead people . . . dead. You simply can't have a resurrection from among the dead if everyone is being raised at the same time. The burden of proof in this matter rests squarely upon the shoulders of the person who wishes to assert that *ek nekrōn* means something like "from death" or "from the realm of the dead." I have carefully researched the early Christian letters, sermons, treatises, and apocalypses written in Greek, and I'm prepared to put forward the claim that this expression is never employed when (1) a general resurrection or (2) a resurrection to judgment (rather than life) is in view.

Jesus' characterization of a selective resurrection that only happens to the faithful coheres closely with the words of Isaiah in Isa. 26:13–19, which we considered in detail above. Isaiah prophesies that the moment of redemption for the persecuted faithful (26:13, 18) will be a moment of resurrection for them (26:19), but *not* for the dead in general (26:14). The latter will remain dead, serving out a sentence of punishment and destruction. It's remarkable that so many Christian interpreters seem to give little or no weight to this passage from Isaiah, despite the fact (as I pointed out above) that Jesus and all of the writers of the NT held Isaiah in the highest possible regard as a conduit of authoritative divine revelation. They were unanimous in regarding the prophecies of Isaiah as the word of God, as solid biblical truth, and as crucial revelations from God about the future that *must* come to fulfillment. I can affirm this not simply about Isaiah in general, but about chs. 24–27 in particular.[42] Consequently, anyone who wishes to deny the idea of a selective resurrection for the faithful based on a harmonistic approach to the Scriptures automatically assumes a dual burden of proof here. They must plausibly demonstrate (1) that Isa. 26:13–19 did not originally refer to a refusal of resurrection to

---

39. The Greek words here are *anastasis* ("resurrection," Strong's #G386; see also the verb *anistēmi*, "rise," #G450), *ek* ("from," Strong's #G1537), and *nekros* ("corpse," "dead," Strong's #G3498).

40. The idea of "from the state of death" is easy to express in Greek, and it is indeed expressed in the NT. See Jn 5:24 and Heb. 5:7, which use the expression *ek thanatou* (Strong's #G2288), "from death."

41. The word *tōn* is the genitive form of the Greek article, Strong's #G3588. The expression sometimes has it (*ek tōn nekrōn*) and sometimes does not have it (*ek nekrōn*), There is evidently no particular difference in meaning between the two forms of the expression.

42. The scripture index in the *UBS Greek New Testament* shows twelve direct NT quotations from this four-chapter section of Isaiah. This does not include the many allusions to the section in Rev. 19–21 and elsewhere in the NT.

Future Judgment and Resurrection in the New Testament

the oppressors and the granting of resurrection to the persecuted faithful, and (2) that Jesus and the writers of the NT also did not read it in that way.

Since we've begun considering the subject of selective resurrection at the transition to the age to come, let's turn now to see what evidence we can find from elsewhere in the NT for this concept.

To begin with, we can note that the apostle Paul uses the terminology we've been discussing—that is, the terminology of "resurrection from among the dead"—when he expresses the hope that he personally will experience resurrection to eternal life:

Philippians 3:10–11

> $_{10}$It's about knowing Christ, and the power of his resurrection, and knowing what it is to share in his sufferings. It's about being molded into the pattern of his death, $_{11}$so I can somehow make it[43] to the resurrection from among the dead.[44]

I think we can agree for the purposes of this study that Paul believed in the principle that all of the dead would be resurrected at some point, and not just those who are being saved.[45] Paul does not simply aspire to be raised from death, which he regards as the destiny of everyone, good and bad, saved and lost. He wants to be raised *to eternal life* along with those who belong to Christ at his coming. Paul talks at some length about resurrection in First Corinthians:

1 Corinthians 15:12, 20–24

> $_{12}$But if Christ is being preached as raised from among the dead, how is it that some of you say that there's no resurrection of the dead? . . . $_{20}$But the fact is, Christ *has* risen from among the dead. He's the first harvest of those who've passed away.[46] $_{21}$After all, since death came through a human being, resurrection of the dead also came through a human being. $_{22}$Because just as in Adam everyone dies, so in Christ everyone will be brought to life—$_{23}$but each in their own proper order:[47] Christ the first harvest, then those who belong to him, at

---

43. Or ". . . death, if I can somehow make it."

44. For instances of the phrase "from among the dead" referring to the resurrection of Jesus, see Rom. 1:4; 4:24; 6:4, 9, 13; 7:4; 8:11; 10:7, 9; 11:16 ; 15:12, 20; Gal. 1:1; Eph. 1:20; 5:14; Col. 1:18; 2:12; 1 Thess. 1:10; 2 Tim. 2:8; Heb. 13:20; 1 Pet. 1:3, 21; Rev. 1:5.

45. See Acts 24:15, in which he affirms the belief in a "resurrection of both the just and the unjust." It is not uncommon among biblical scholars to doubt that Luke, or any other person who actually knew Paul, wrote Acts. Such scholars would often maintain that characterizations of Paul's views in Acts should not be given any value independent of what can be learned from Paul's own (undisputed) letters. I personally am comfortable with the idea that Luke, friend and companion of Paul, wrote Acts. I trust his characterization of Paul's views.

46. Paul's using a metaphor from Jewish worship. A gift was to be given to God from the best of the early summer harvest. That gift would "redeem" the rest of the crop and guarantee God's blessing on it.

47. Paul is using the analogy of a parade. The word "order" implies that each person has their proper place in the formation.

The End of the Unrepentant

> his coming, ₂₄then the end. That's when he hands the kingdom over to God the Father.[48] It's when he does away with all rule and authority and power.

It isn't Paul's purpose here to go into detail about all the things that happen at the end of the world. But it's a simple enough point to note that he does not affirm the resurrection of all of humanity at the second coming of Christ. He only affirms the resurrection of those who belong to Christ (v. 23).

Let's turn now to the book of Revelation, which presents by far the most detailed picture of what happens to the living and the dead when Christ comes again to reign.

SELECTIVE RESURRECTION IN REVELATION 20: ESTABLISHING THE CONTEXT

It's worth beginning our examination with Rev. 19:19–21 and 20:1–3, so that we can establish the immediate context for the very explicit scene of selective resurrection in Rev. 20:4–6.

Revelation 19:19–21

> ₁₉And I saw the beast, together with the kings of the earth and their armies. They'd gotten together to make war against the One who sat on the horse, and against his armies. ₂₀The beast was captured, along with the false prophet. He was the one who'd done those miracles[49] with the beast's approval. He'd used them to deceive[50] those who accepted the beast's stamp, and those who worshiped his image. Those two were thrown alive into the lake that's on fire with burning sulfur.[51] ₂₁All the rest were killed by the sword of the One who sat on the horse—the sword that came out of his mouth.

We heard earlier in the book of Revelation that "the beast" was going to be given authority over the entire earth, and that everyone whose name was not "written in the Lamb's book of life since the foundation of the world" was going to worship him (Rev. 13:7–8). If we read the above passage concordantly with what we read in the seventh and twelfth chapters of Daniel, it becomes abundantly clear that what is being pictured here is the end of the current age and the expulsion of this age's last world emperor. John certainly believes in the continuity of prophetic revelation, and he gives us too many clues to enumerate here that he believes that he is being shown the same thing that Daniel saw in Daniel 7.

What we essentially have here (in Rev. 19:11–21) is a picture of the judgment *of the living* at Christ's return. This is not a literal battle, since it is no more or less than the truthful testimony of Christ the Judge that results in the slaying of those who assemble

---

48. Lit. "to God, even the Father."
49. Traditionally: "signs."
50. Lit. "... who'd done the signs in front of him, by which he deceived."
51. Lit. "the lake of fire burning with sulfur." Sulfur was proverbial for burning extremely hot.

to resist his coming to establish the kingdom of God on earth (v. 21). The beast and the false prophet have been introduced earlier (ch. 13) as Satan's human agents, who work together to stir up humanity into a total rebellion against God. Here they are captured in the midst of leading that rebellion, and are "thrown alive into the lake of fire," which will later be interpreted as "the second death."[52] We might expect to see Satan dealt with similarly, but we do not. Instead, we are going to see him imprisoned in the abyss (20:1–3), recalling Isa. 24:21–23. He will later be released from the abyss, and will go to his final judgment and demise (Rev. 20:7–10). We already know from various places in the book of Revelation that human beings who die (or at least those who are unrepentant and who die) also go to the underworld, the keys to which belong to Christ, the Lord of life and death (Rev. 1:18). The "kings of the earth" (19:19 || Isa. 24:21), joined by all of their subjects, are thus presumably consigned to the underworld of the dead when we see them slain in 19:21. All of this, of course, closely parallels Isa. 24:21–23. Here is John's description of Satan's imprisonment:

Revelation 20:1–3

> ₁And I saw another angel coming down from heaven. He had the key to the bottomless pit in his hand, and a huge chain. ₂He grabbed the dragon, the ancient serpent,[53] who is the devil and Satan, and he chained him up for a thousand years. ₃He threw him in the bottomless pit, and closed[54] it and sealed it over him. That way, he couldn't deceive the nations anymore, until the thousand years were over. After that, he has to be set free for a little while.

It is extremely curious that many interpreters of the book of Revelation attempt to understand these words without reference to the obvious and intimate relationship between Rev. 20:1–10 as a whole and Isa. 24:21—27:5. As we've mentioned before, the book of Revelation is absolutely soaked in allusions to the OT prophets, and to Isaiah in particular. John obviously looks at the prophet Isaiah as a tremendously esteemed senior colleague in the fellowship of the prophets, one to whom God had revealed many of the same realities as he, John, was shown in his own visions. When we understand that, it makes no sense at all to attempt to interpret John's words without chasing down his allusions and attempting to understand from those allusions what he thinks his revelation might be adding to what God has already revealed to other prophets. What, then, does John have to add to the picture in Isa. 24:21–23? In a word, the fact that Satan's imprisonment makes him powerless to convince the nations any longer that he deserves to be worshiped. John probably has the scene from Isa. 14:9–15 in mind:

> ⁹Sheol beneath is stirred up
>   to meet you when you come;
> it rouses the shades to greet you,
>   all who were leaders of the earth;

---

52. Cf. Rev. 20:14.
53. See Gen. 3.
54. Or "locked."

The End of the Unrepentant

> it raises from their thrones
> > all who were kings of the nations.
>
> ¹⁰ All of them will speak and say to you:
> > "You too have become as weak as we are!
> > You have become like us!"
>
> . . .
>
> ¹² How you are fallen from heaven,
> > O Day Star, son of Dawn!
>
> How you are cut down to the ground,
> > you who laid the nations low!
>
> ¹³ You said in your heart,
> > "I will ascend to heaven;
>
> I will raise my throne
> > above the stars of God;
>
> I will sit on the mount of assembly
> > on the heights of Zaphon;
> > > ¹⁴ I will ascend to the tops of the clouds,
> > > I will make myself like the Most High."
> > > ¹⁵ But you are brought down to Sheol,
> > > > to the depths of the Pit.

Satan's schemes to foment a universal rebellion against God, first in heaven (Rev. 12:7–8), and then on earth (Rev. 12:12–17), employing the human agency of the beast and the false prophet (Rev. 13–19), have utterly failed. His previously successful[55] campaign to get all humanity to worship him (Rev. 13:4) is now revealed as nothing more than an insanely grandiose and globally murderous fraud. The curtain has been pulled back, revealing the ultimate weakness of the fearsome Wizard. He has no power to deceive anyone anymore.

Selective Resurrection in Revelation 20: Key Text

Revelation 20:4–6

> ₄And I saw thrones, and people sat on them.[56] They were given the task of passing judgment.[57] And I saw the souls of the people who'd been executed[58] because of the testimony of Jesus, and because of the word of God—whoever[59] hadn't worshiped the beast and his image, and hadn't taken his stamp on their forehead and their hand. They came alive[60] and ruled with Christ for a

---

55. His success does not extend to those who love and serve Christ.
56. See Dan. 7.
57. Lit. "and judgment was given to them." The Greek words here can also mean, "and judgment was passed in their favor," or "and judgment was passed by them." This double—or triple—meaning may well be intentional.
58. Or "beheaded": lit. "given the ax."
59. Or "and whoever."
60. Or "And they lived."

thousand years. ₅The rest of the dead didn't come to life⁶¹ until the thousand years were over. This is the first resurrection. ₆The person who gets to take part⁶² in the first resurrection is blessed and holy. The second death doesn't have any power at all over them. They're going to be priests of God and of Christ, and they're going to rule with him for the thousand years.⁶³

In this section, we are still very close to Isaiah 24–27. The defeat and imprisonment of the hosts of heaven and the kings of the earth in Isa. 24:21–22 results in a new age inaugurated by the establishment of the glorious reign of God (Isa. 24:23; 25:6 || Rev. 11:15–18 || 20:4). The age of God's reign sees the vindication and resurrection of those who had suffered and even died for their faithfulness under conditions of oppression by enemies (Isa. 25:6–9; 26:16–19 || Rev. 20:4), and *no resurrection* for those who had held the power on earth in the previous age (Isa. 26:13–14 || Rev. 20:5).

In addition to Isaiah 24–27, John also clearly understands that what he is seeing relates closely to the vision of Daniel 7. Many parallels are discernible. For example:

- The deadly career of the beast in both Daniel and Revelation spans 3 1/2 years (Dan. 7:25; 12:11–12 || Rev. 12:6, 14; 13:5–6)
- Utter defeat of the beast, who receives a unique fiery destruction (Dan. 7:11–12 || Rev. 19:20)
- Thrones are set up for God's panel of delegate judges (Dan. 7:9–10 || Rev. 20:4)
- The holy ones who have been being defeated by the beast are vindicated, receive the kingdom, and reign (Dan. 7:21, 26–27 || Rev. 13:7; 20:4–6)

A story is being told here that makes perfectly clear sense. The only difficulty is that it seems to be saying that virtually every follower of Jesus Christ who lives in the handful of years leading up to the end of this age will be put to death by the beast. John's vision gives new and disturbing meaning to some of the warnings Jesus gave his followers:

> If any of you wishes to be my follower, you have to take up your cross and follow me (Mt. 16:24 || Mk 8:34 || Lk. 9:23).

> If that time weren't cut short, not one living soul⁶⁴ would be saved. But for the sake of the chosen ones, that time will be cut short (Mt. 24:21–22 || Mk 13:19–20).

John's affirmation in Rev. 20:4 that the holy ones will reign for a thousand years is not a denial that they will also reign for all eternity (see Rev. 22:5; Dan. 7:18).⁶⁵ It is simply an indication that the age immediately following the current age will be characterized by (1) the resurrection of those who have been persecuted for their testimony to the truth

---

61. Lit. "didn't live."
62. Lit. "has a portion."
63. Some mss have, "for a thousand years."
64. Lit. "no flesh" (by implication, this includes the elect).
65. As the angel tells Daniel in Dan. 7:18, "The holy ones of the Most High shall receive the kingdom and possess the kingdom for the age, and for the age of the ages."

The End of the Unrepentant

of God and have remained loyal to Jesus Christ, and (2) the refusal of resurrection to everyone else, who will spend that age imprisoned in the underworld along with Satan.

Strikingly, John describes the timing of the release of Satan from his underworld prison and the timing of the resurrection of those imprisoned in the underworld with him in precisely the same words: "when the thousand years are finished" (20:3, 5, 7). This makes a perfect setup for the next section (20:7–10) to describe what happens when "the hosts of heaven on high and the kings of the earth on the earth" are released from their co-imprisonment in the underworld (see Isa. 24:21–22). Let's read it.

Revelation 20:7–10

> 7And when the thousand years are over, Satan's going to be let out of his prison. 8He's going to go out to deceive the nations that are at the four corners of the earth: Gog and Magog.[66] He's going to gather them together for battle.[67] They're as numerous as the sands of the ocean.[68] 9And they came up, covering the breadth of the earth.[69] They surrounded the camp of the holy ones, the Beloved City.[70] And fire came down out of heaven[71] and burned them up.[72]
> 10And the devil, who was deceiving them, was thrown into the lake of fire and sulfur—where both the beast and the false prophet are. They're going to be tormented day and night, forever and ever.

After a very lengthy imprisonment, Satan and all the unrepentant are released from the prison of the underworld—together, just as Isa. 24:21–22 implies. As Isa. 24:21–22 additionally implies, they come out *for judgment*. They have been found unworthy of taking part in the first thousand-year "day" (Ps. 90:4; 2 Pet. 3:8) of God's endless reign of blessing, and they have been paying a painful price for misusing the gifts and powers of created being. Complete exclusion from participation in the life of creation, and helpless imprisonment, have been their lot for an entire age. What happens now is, so to speak, a picture of their release on probation. Ahead of them lies the promise of an endless succession of peaceful and blessed ages in the reign of God and his holy ones (see Dan. 7:18 || Rev. 22:5). Will they humble themselves, bury the past, and take up the joy of the present and future?

Sadly, they will not. The unrepentant prove themselves unwilling to enter into God's peace. Readily deceived all over again by Satan, who is himself incorrigibly self-deceived, they immediately re-offend. Instead of embracing the grace of God, who has granted them a new start and who invites them to take part in the good things of his

---

66. Prn. gog and may-*gog*. See Ezek. 38.
67. Or "for the war."
68. Lit. "the sea."
69. Lit. "And they came up upon the breadth [or the plain] of the earth." See Hab. 1:6 for this imagery.
70. Lit. "and the Beloved City." "And" here means "that is." Jerusalem is referred to metaphorically as a "camp" in 2 Chron. 22:1; Heb. 13:11–14.
71. Some mss add, "from God."
72. See 2 Kgs 1:10; Ezek. 38; Isa. 26.

kingdom, they display a determined attitude of murderous self-deception. John wants us to understand that what he is seeing has been revealed before to Isaiah:

Isaiah 26:10–11

> [10] If favor is shown to the wicked,
>   they do not learn righteousness;
> in the land of uprightness they deal perversely
>   and do not see the majesty of the Lord.
> [11] O Lord, your hand is lifted up,
>   but they do not see it.
> Let them see your zeal for your people, and be ashamed.
>   Let the fire for your adversaries consume them.

Isaiah 27:1–5

> [1] On that day the Lord with his cruel and great and strong sword will punish Leviathan the fleeing serpent, Leviathan the twisting serpent, and he will kill the dragon that is in the sea.
>
> [2] On that day:
> A pleasant vineyard, sing about it!
>   [3] I, the Lord, am its keeper;
>   every moment I water it.
> I guard it night and day
>   so that no one can harm it.
> [4] I have no wrath.
> If someone gives me thorns and briers,
>   I will march to battle against him.
>   I will burn him up.
> [5] Instead, let him join close to me for protection.
>   Let him make peace with me.
>   Let him make peace with me.

Isaiah 57:15–19

> [15] For thus says the high and lofty one
>   who inhabits eternity, whose name is Holy:
> I dwell in the high and holy place,
>   and also with those who are contrite and humble in spirit,
> to revive the spirit of the humble,
>   and to revive the heart of the contrite.
> [16] For I will not continually accuse,
>   nor will I always be angry;

The End of the Unrepentant

> for then the spirits would grow faint before me,
>> even the souls that I have made.
> ¹⁷ Because of their wicked covetousness I was angry;
>> I struck them, I hid and was angry;
>> but they kept turning back to their own ways.
> ¹⁸ I have seen their ways, but I will heal them;
>> I will lead them and repay them with comfort,
>> creating for their mourners the fruit of the lips.
> ¹⁹ Peace, peace, to the far and the near, says the LORD;
>> and I will heal them.
> ²⁰ But the wicked are like the tossing sea
>> that cannot keep still;
>> its waters toss up mire and mud.
> ²¹ There is no peace, says my God, for the wicked.

That which gives rise to the ultimate destruction of the unrepentant is not, after all, any lack of love for them on God's part, nor does it stem from any lack of divine patience and mercy. *The perdition of the unrepentant stems from their adamant refusal to take part constructively in God's creation—even when they are granted the ultimate gift of resurrection.*

John's vision in Rev. 20:7–10 graphically reveals what Jesus meant when he said that he would eventually accomplish the resurrection of everyone who had ever died—even the unrepentant:

John 5:21, 25, 28–29

> ₂₁Because just as the Father raises the dead, and brings them to life, so the Son also brings to life whoever he wants. . . . ₂₅I'm telling you very seriously: There's a time[73] coming—and it's here now—when the dead are going to hear the voice of the Son of God. And the ones who've heard are going to live. . . . ₂₈Don't be shocked by that. Because a time[74] is coming when all those who are in their graves are going to hear his voice, ₂₉and they're going to come out. Those who've done good things are going to come out for a resurrection of life; those who've done bad things are going to come out for a resurrection of judgment.

Jesus does not say that all of the dead are going to come out of their tombs at exactly the same moment. What he says is: (1) that they will *all* come out, (2) that the time[75] for them to start coming out is *right now*,[76] (3) that they will all come out *because they are going to are going to hear his voice*, and (4) *that the outcome* of the dead being called

---

73. Lit. "an hour."
74. Lit. "an hour."
75. The normal Greek expression for this idea is "the hour" (Gr. *ōra*, Strong's #G5610).
76. The Gospels record three instances of Jesus raising people from the dead: Jairus's daughter (Mt. 9:18–26 || Mk 5:21–43 || Lk. 8:40–56), the son of the widow of Nain (Lk. 7:11–17), and his friend Lazarus (Jn 11:1–45). He also presumably gets credit for many other people rising at his resurrection (Mt. 27:50–53).

forth from the tombs *is going to differ*, depending on what individuals have done in their mortal lives. Jesus affirms that those who have done good things—which is to say, those who have lived their mortal lives in such a way as to make it just and loving for God to give them an eternal portion of life—will come out to experience eternal life. Those, on the other hand, who have done bad things—which is to say, those who have lived their mortal lives in such a way as to make it unjust and unloving for God to entrust them with eternal life—will come out to face the judgment of God.

John's vision in Rev. 20:1–10 is consonant with this principle of dual outcomes to resurrection. By indicating that the "rest of the dead" do not come to life at Christ's coming as God's Son, earth's King and Judge, and by alluding to Isaiah 24–27, John gives us a way of understanding the distinction. Those who are not called forth to "live and reign with Christ" (20:4–6) must, in accordance with the conceptual world of Revelation, be understood to be consigned to the underworld for a thousand-year period of imprisonment. Jesus holds the keys of Hades, and it is he who possesses the divine authority to confine people there and to release people from there (see Rev. 1:18; 20:13). Ultimately, the unrepentant will be given one last chance "when the thousand years are over." They will be summoned to one final evaluation, "a resurrection of judgment." They will be granted release subject to probation, and will be offered the opportunity of participating in the unlimited blessing of God's Kingdom. By their actions as resurrected people, they will have the chance to demonstrate a newfound readiness to live in love and mutual faithfulness with their brothers and sisters in eternal life. John's vision—and Isaiah's—warn us that those who face this test are destined to fail it and to experience final and irrevocable destruction.

There is something wrenching about the idea that God would bring human beings to the threshold of eternal life, foreknowing (and even revealing ahead of time) that they would stumble and fall on that very threshold. Nonetheless, I believe that this is exactly the paradox that Jesus points to when he warns us that "many are called, but few are chosen" (Mt. 22:14). Unlike most human beings, God extends his love and grace without pulling back in anticipation of the reception that it will receive. Judgment of all—the repentant and the unrepentant—thus finally resolves to the question, "What will you do when God shows you kindness and mercy?"

We will have more to say later about the surprising and deeply perplexing conclusion to the story of unrepentant humanity that we encounter in Rev. 20:7–10. For the moment, however, let's focus on more ways in which John gives us the clue that he is not revealing something for the first time, but instead understands himself to be receiving further revelation about matters that have already been revealed to one or more prophets of the past.

Consider Ezekiel 38, for example. John makes an unmistakable allusion to Ezekiel's vision when he describes the uncountable horde of his vision as "Gog and Magog" (Rev. 20:8; cf. Ezek. 38:1–2). Does Ezekiel give us any clues that he understands that what he is seeing is a scene of *temptation*, and not simply the classical prophetic picture of enemies trampling the land of Israel because they are bigger and stronger? Yes, he does:

The End of the Unrepentant
Ezekiel 38:8-12

> ³⁸ After many days you [Gog] shall be mustered;⁷⁷ in the latter years you shall go against a land restored from war, a land where people were gathered from many nations on the mountains of Israel, which had long lain waste; its people were brought out from the nations and now are living in safety, all of them. ⁹ You shall advance, coming on like a storm; you shall be like a cloud covering the land, you and all your troops, and many peoples with you.
> ¹⁰ Thus says the Lord GOD: On that day thoughts will come into your mind, and you will devise an evil scheme. ¹¹ You will say, "I will go up against the land of unwalled villages; I will fall upon the quiet people who live in safety, all of them living without walls, and having no bars or gates"; ¹² to seize spoil and carry off plunder; to assail the waste places that are now inhabited, and the people who were gathered from the nations, who are acquiring cattle and goods, who live at the center⁷⁸ of the earth.

Gog and his hosts stumble and fall because they fall into *temptation*. Just like the self-deluded intruders of Isa. 26:10-11, who respond perversely to God's grace, Gog's hordes encounter a test of their hearts, motives, and attitudes that it is their destiny to fail. I believe that John recognizes, and invites his readers to recognize with him, that these passages from Isaiah and Ezekiel ultimately point to the same thing: the resurrection and final judgment of the unrepentant. Clues that this is what is going on can be detected on a number of levels. For example:

- God speaks to Gog, saying that "after many days you will be visited." This wording lies remarkably close to the very phrase Isaiah used in Isa. 24:21-22: "after many days they will be visited."⁷⁹
- "Meshech and Tubal," Gog's first-named cohorts in Ezek. 38:2-3, have already appeared earlier in Ezekiel, *lying dead in the underworld pit of Sheol* (32:25-26). This is the same "pit" (Heb. *bōr*) in which the hosts of heaven and the kings of the earth were to be imprisoned in Isa 24:21-22.
- John says in Rev. 20:9a that "*they came up* on the broad plain of the earth." It simply doesn't make sense to talk about "coming up" onto a broad plain. You come up onto a hill or a mountain, or you go down onto a plain. The only way that you can come up onto a plain is if you are underneath it—in an underground parking garage, or *in the underworld*. And sure enough, John has a number of similar uses of the expression "to come up" in Revelation: for example, he uses it for the beast "coming up" out of the sea, for the second beast, the false prophet, "coming up" out of the earth (both of

---

77. Lit. "visited" (Heb. *paqad*, Strong's #H6485).
78. Heb. "navel" (Heb. *tabbūr*, Strong's #H2872).
79. These two sentences are as close in Hebrew as they are in English, and are not paralleled elsewhere in the OT. The three words, "many" (*rob*, Strong's #H7230), "days" (*yōm*, Strong's #H3117), and "visit" (*paqad*, Strong's #H6485) appear in both statements. Similarly, Isa. 26:11 and Ezek. 38:18-19 share another key set of three Hebrew words: "zeal" (*qin'ah*, Strong's #H7068), "wrath" (*'af*, Strong's #H639), and "fire" (*'esh*, Strong's #H784).

which are symbolic of return from the realm of the dead), and for the beast "coming up" out of the abyss.[80]

- John says "They came up on *the broad plain of the earth*"[81] (Rev. 20:9a). The phrase "broad plain of the earth" is rare in the Greek OT, occurring only in Hab. 1:6, Sir. 1:3, and Dan. 12:2 (Old Greek). Of the three occurrences, the closest in the overall context to Revelation 20 is Dan. 12:2, which predicts that "many of those who sleep in *the broad plain of the earth* will arise: some to eternal life, some to disgrace, and some to dispersion and eternal humiliation."

The Story of the End of the Unrepentant

In studying Rev. 19:11—20:10 alongside Isaiah 24–27, we have uncovered profound parallels and resonances between John's and Isaiah's stories of the end. In view of these parallels, and in view of the fact that Isaiah is John's clear favorite among the OT prophets, we've recognized the power of both texts to interpret and clarify one another. Admittedly, it's possible to proceed on the assumption that the close relationship between John and Isaiah results from John using Isaiah as a template or as a model in the literary composition of his material. But that is not what I see going on here. I don't believe that John is creatively composing his visions as imaginative literary fictions. I believe that he is reporting, with a great deal of literary skill, visions that he has actually seen. And he recognizes, as he experiences his visions, that what he is seeing is something that the Spirit has already revealed at some level or another—whether in his own previous visions, or through the visions and oracles of other prophets in the past. John's use of verbal allusions is thus best understood as his way of letting his readers know that what he is now describing is something that he has already described before, or something that he understands Isaiah, Ezekiel, or Daniel to have seen and described before him. It is precisely because he is often trying to give us a lot of this kind of information that his prophecy is so rich. His vision narrative typically manifests itself in a dense network of allusions to related prophetic passages, both inside and outside of his own work.

Just as Isaiah's great vision of the end in Isaiah 24–27 draws the story of the unrepentant to a meaningful conclusion in Isa. 26:20—27:5, so John brings the story of the unrepentant to a meaningful conclusion in Rev. 20:7–10. In fact, nearly every episode, theme, or event of any kind that has been predicted or foreshadowed earlier in the text of Revelation up to this point has now been explicated.[82] No major episodes lie ahead; as far

---

80. See Rev. 11:7; 13:1, 11; 17:8. The Greek word for "going up" or "coming up" in all these instances (including Rev. 20:9) is *anabainō*, Strong's #G305. See also Rev. 9:3, where it is used of demonic locusts coming up out of the abyss. The sea is one of the named realms of the dead in Rev. 20:13, and the beast's "coming up out of the sea" parallels his "coming up out of the abyss." The second beast's "coming up" out of the earth correspondingly suggests the idea of rising from being buried in the grave.

81. Gr. *platos tēs gēs* (from Strong's #G4114, *platos*, and #G1093, *gē*).

82. I count at least 37 times in Revelation where an event or theme is foreshadowed or announced ahead of time, and only three of these still remain undeveloped as of 20:10: 1. Jesus promises that he will give the faithful permission to eat from the tree of life in the paradise of God (2:7); this is not developed until 22:1–5. 2. Jesus refers to the City of God coming down from heaven (3:12); there is a brief reference to the presence of the Beloved City on earth in 20:9 (cf. "the broad plain of the earth," 20:8), but

The End of the Unrepentant

as John's readers are concerned, nothing further needs to happen in the story of the end. For example, the resurrected holy ones are alive and well, having been protected from one last onslaught of evil by the intervening power of God (20:7–10; cf. 2 Kgs 1:10; Isa. 26:20–21). The unrepentant have been resurrected, judged, and destroyed. Presumably, the holy ones will continue to reign with Christ without end (see Rev. 5:10; 22:5 || Dan. 7:18, 27), given that all those violent ones who wished them harm have either been inundated with annihilating fire from heaven or drowned in an annihilating lake of fire and sulfur (20:9–10). These enemies—including Satan, the strongest and oldest of them all, *are never coming back.*

Of course, the fact that we have reached the end of the story chronologically does not mean that there is no potential for more depth of detail to be brought out. In the same way that Ezekiel chapters 40–48 elaborate the promise summarized earlier in Ezek. 37:24–28, so everything that follows on from Rev. 20:10 has the potential to fill out one or another story element that has not yet been fully revealed. For example, in Rev. 3:12 Jesus promises the overcomers citizenship in the New Jerusalem, and this theme will be given thorough elaboration in Revelation 21 and 22.

Let's now look at John's vision of resurrection and judgment in Rev. 20:11–15, and see whether this section appears to add something entirely new to the story of the end, or whether it appears to be an elaboration of something that has been announced or a new viewpoint on something that has already been narrated.

Revelation 20:11–15

> 11 And I saw a great white throne, and the One who sat on it. From the presence of that One, earth and heaven had fled away, and there'd been no room found for them.

The first thing we can say is that this opening verse of the section sits squarely within the changing-of-the-ages tradition that we've traced above through the Psalms, the Prophets, and the writers of the NT. The tradition expects the transition to the fulfillment of God's Kingdom on earth to be attended by a total cataclysm of the created world. As here, the cataclysm expected is so radical that it is sometimes pictured as literally unmaking the world in preparation for the coming of a new creation (e.g. Pss. 46:2–3, 6–7; 97:1–5; Isa. 24:3–6, 18b-20; 64:1–2; 65:17–18; Zeph. 3:18; 2 Pet. 3:13). Revelation itself has a number of profoundly cataclysmic scenes, all of which are linked to the appearance of God's throne, which signals the coming of God and Christ as judge. Let's look at the descriptions that follow the opening of the sixth seal in Rev. 6:12–17, the blowing of the seventh trumpet in 11:15–19, and the emptying out of the seventh bowl in 16:17–21:

---

this theme is only fully developed in 21:1—22:5. 3. Rev. 11:15 promises that God and Christ will reign forever and ever; this is not specifically affirmed again by 20:10. It is later developed in 22:3–5.

Future Judgment and Resurrection in the New Testament

Revelation 6:12–17

₁₂And I looked when the Lamb opened the sixth seal, and there was a huge earthquake. The sun went dark, as if it had been covered by sackcloth made of goat hair.[83] The whole moon went blood-red.[84] ₁₃And the stars fell out of heaven onto the earth, just like when a fig tree drops its unripe figs when it's shaken by a powerful wind. ₁₄And the sky was split apart like a scroll curling up. And every mountain and island was thrown out of place.[85] ₁₅And the rulers of the earth, and the influential, and the commanders, and the rich, and the powerful,[86] and every slave and free person,[87] hid themselves. They hid in caves, and among the rocks in the mountains. ₁₆They said to the mountains and the rocks, "Fall on us! Hide us[88] from the One[89] who sits on the throne, and from the anger of the Lamb! ₁₇Because the great day of their[90] anger has come. Who can stand in front of them?"

Revelation 11:15–19

₁₅The seventh angel blew his trumpet. And there were loud voices in heaven, saying, "The rulership of this world now belongs to our Lord God,[91] and to his Christ! He's going to reign forever and ever!" ₁₆And the twenty-four ancient ones, who are sitting on their thrones in front of God, fell on their faces and worshiped God. They were ₁₇saying,

We thank you, Lord, All Powerful God,
Who is and who was,[92]
Because you've taken your great power and have begun to rule.
₁₈The nations were angry,
And your anger came,
And the time came to judge the dead,
And to give rewards to your servants the prophets,
And to the holy ones,
And to those who revere your name, the weak and the powerful,[93]
And to destroy those who are destroying the earth.

---

83. Lit. "became black as a hair sack." Goat hair is thick and black, and was used for rough sacking.
84. Lit. "became as blood."
85. Lit. "were moved out of their places."
86. Lit. "the strong."
87. In other words everybody, from the very top to the very bottom of the social ladder.
88. See Isa. 2:10, 19, 21; Jer. 4:29; Hos. 10:8.
89. Lit. "from the face/presence of the One."
90. Some mss have "his."
91. Lit. "The realm/rulership of the world has become of our Lord, and of his Christ."
92. Lit. "the Is and the Was." See Rev. 1:8; 4:8.
93. Lit. "the small and the great."

The End of the Unrepentant

> ₁₉And the temple of God in heaven opened up, and the ark of the covenant[94] appeared in God's sanctuary. There were lightning flashes, sounds, rumblings of thunder, an earthquake, and a huge hailstorm.

Revelation 16:17–21

> ₁₇The seventh angel poured out his bowl on the air. And a loud voice came out of the temple, from the throne. It was saying, "It's done." ₁₈And there were lightning flashes, sounds, and rumbles of thunder. And there was a huge earthquake—so big that there's never been one like it, ever since humanity appeared on earth. That's how huge an earthquake it was. ₁₉The great city split into three parts, and all the nations' cities collapsed. And Babylon the Great got remembered in God's presence, and it was given the wine cup of God's furious anger. ₂₀And every island ran away, and the mountains were nowhere to be found. ₂₁And huge hailstones, weighing about a hundred pounds, came down out of the sky on people.

What's going on in these passages is that John is being shown the cataclysmic moment of Christ's second coming from various different and complementary angles. This moment, as we've seen, is the great changing of the ages prophesied in the psalms and the prophets: the great crisis-point for the creation that signals the transition to a new creation "in which justice lives" (2 Pet. 3:13). The seals, trumpets, and bowls thus all climax with some kind of revelation of the second coming. Some interpreters try to see these passages as merely hinting at or prefiguring the second coming, as though it will only *really* be narrated in Rev. 19:11–21. But there is nothing in the nature of a "hint" in any of these passages. John sees the whole world being dissolved, being reduced to an uninhabitable chaos. The sky splits apart like a scroll and rushes away (6:14; cf. 19:11), and there is an earthquake so radical that all the familiar features of the earth are removed—every mountain and island (6:14; 16:20). It's possible to look at these passages as examples of a complex compositional technique John is using: a kind of narrative spiraling in on the second coming. Alternatively, you can interpret them at face value, and conclude that God gave John multiple visions of the moment of transition to the new age of God's Kingdom because there is so much depth to be revealed in this subject that it can't be presented to the human imagination in one vision episode. It requires unfolding into a multidimensional picture. In any case, when John describes the appearance of the Enthroned One in Rev. 20:11, he does so in such a way as to encourage us to remember all the previous times that he saw the coming of God and Christ and the dissolution of the physical world.

Where, then, are we to understand ourselves to be located now, along Revelation's timeline of the end of things? As we have already seen in Rev. 11:15–18 and 19:11—20:6, the time appointed for living *and the dead* to be judged is at this climactic moment of transition from the current age to the age of the Kingdom of God and of Christ. This coheres with what is taught in numerous other places in the NT (e.g. Lk. 20:34–35; Acts

---

94. See Exod. 25:10–22; 1 Kgs 8:1, 6; 2 Chron. 5:7

Future Judgment and Resurrection in the New Testament

10:42; 17:31; Rom. 2:1-16; 14:9-12; 2 Cor. 5:10; 2 Tim. 4:1; 1 Pet. 4:5; 2 Pet. 3:2-13). In Rev. 6:12-18 we've been shown the judgment of the living as a kind of instant cosmic court session, in which the defendants suddenly find themselves at the bar of God's judgment, and they cower and scramble to hide from the wrath of their Creator who has appeared as Judge.[95] In 19:11-21, we've seen the judgment of the living pictured as a battle, providing a very clear NT example of the familiar OT age-transition theme of a violent confrontation between God and his human enemies.[96] In Rev. 20:4-6, we've seen the vindication of the holy ones as a court proceeding, recalling Daniel 7. Implicitly in the scene, the dead in Christ are judged and found *worthy* of life, and the unrepentant dead (including those who have just been slain in 19:21) are judged and found *unworthy* of life. But the *emphasis* in 20:4-6 is on the positive side. The scene's main focus is on celebrating the "first resurrection" and its participants. Next, we've seen the belated resurrection and final judgment of the unrepentant dead in terms of a violent confrontation (Rev. 20:7-10 || Isa. 26:10-11; 27:1-5 || Heb. 10:27). *What John has not yet seen* in relation to these judgment themes by the end of Rev. 20:10 is (1) a scene elaborating the theme of the judgment of the unrepentant dead at Christ's coming in terms of a courtroom scene,[97] and (2) a scene elaborating the delayed resurrection and final judgment of the unrepentant as a courtroom scene. This, I propose, is exactly what we are now going to get:

Revelation 20:11-15

> ₁₁And I saw a great white throne, and the One who sat on it. From the presence of that One, earth and heaven had fled away, and there'd been no room found for them. ₁₂And I saw the dead, the powerful and the weak,[98] standing in front of the throne. And books were opened. And another book was opened: the Book of Life. The dead were judged on the basis of the things written in the books—on the basis of their actions.[99]

---

95. The seven-sealed scroll of 5:1—8:5 (minus the interlude of ch. 7) is best understood as a certificate of debt, which contains full documentation of the debts that humanity owes its Creator. Humanity's sins, in other words, can be conceived of as deficits in the rightful behavior that we owe to God as created beings (cf. "forgive us our debts," Mt. 6:12 || Lk. 11:4). Christ, as the sinless, fully human Son of God, has personally experienced the murderousness of human beings, and has paid the price to redeem them from their crushing debt to God. Because he is fully divine, fully human, and fully sinless, Christ stands as the only party in heaven or on earth with the incontestable right to expose the truth about human behavior (Rev. 5:1-10; cf. Rom. 8:1-4). The opening of the sixth seal reveals a humanity liquid with fear at being caught red handed in its murderous behavior. Sinful humans would rather die than face up to the depth of their indebtedness.

96. For another clear NT example of this theme, see 2 Thess. 1:6-10.

97. We are not, incidentally, going to expect to see the judgment of the unrepentant dead at Christ's second coming as a battle scene or as a scene of violent confrontation, because these dead ones simply remain helplessly imprisoned in Hades. They can't present a threat to anyone until and unless they are released.

98. Lit. "the great and the small."

99. Traditionally: "their works."

The End of the Unrepentant

> 13 And the ocean[100] gave up the dead that were in *it*, and Death and Hades gave up the dead that were in *them*, and they were judged on the basis of their actions. 14 And Death and Hades[101] were thrown in the lake of fire. That's the second death, the lake of fire. 15 If somebody wasn't found recorded[102] in the Book of Life, they were thrown in the lake of fire.

In ancient Hebrew cosmology, the world was imagined to consist of three great regions arranged vertically, one beneath the other: heaven (God's realm), the earth and the air (the realm of humans and other living beings), and the underworld (the realm of the dead). Forming the border between heaven on the one hand and the earth and the air on the other hand, there was imagined to be a great dome, a great blue lid above the sky. Similarly, the bedrock beneath the soil of the earth was imagined to form the border between earth and the underworld.[103] What John sees in v. 11 is thus the stripping away of the two dividing layers (heaven and earth) that separate God's throne from the realm of the unrepentant dead. Accordingly, in v. 12 John sees everyone in Hades standing exposed before God the Judge—in the same way that John saw the unrepentant living on earth standing exposed before God the Judge in Rev. 6:12-17. As in Daniel 7, the books are now opened (Dan. 7:10). Reading v. 12 concordantly with nearby 20:4-6, as well as with Dan. 7:13-14, 22, 26-27 and very many NT teachings, we can assume that the matter to be decided here is whether these dead people will be found worthy to rise from Hades and participate as resurrected people in the "renewal of all things" that is about to dawn. After all, God has dissolved the heavens and the earth precisely in order to prepare for creating them anew (see Rev. 21:1-8; Mt. 19:28; 2 Pet. 3:10-13).

In earlier passages such as Rev. 6:9-11 and 15:1-4, the faithful who "die in the Lord" (14:13) or who are martyred are pictured as being in heaven, rather than in Hades.[104] For this reason, we're probably justified in understanding the group standing in Hades as the unrepentant dead, as opposed to all of the dead including the faithful. This also coheres with the fact that we've already had a description of the judgment/vindication of the faithful in Rev. 20:4-6. Verse 12 thus functions as that section's negative counterpart.

---

100. Lit. "the sea."
101. Prn. ***hay-deez***.
102. Lit. "written."

103. See Gen. 1:6-10; 7:11; Job 38:16; Ps. 104:6; 135:6; Prov. 3:20; 8:24, 27-28; Ezek. 26:19; 31:15. The Gen. 7 and 8 passages (and various others) show that rain was conceived of as coming down through holes in the solid heavenly dome, whereas springs were conceived of as coming up from the underworld through holes in the solid rock of the earth. By the time of the NT, the underworld was often pictured as a fiery underground cavern rather than as a watery place like the deep ocean (see the parable of Lazarus and the rich man, Lk. 16:19-31). The fact that the world was pictured this way does not necessarily imply that individuals such as Jesus and the writers of the NT believed naively in a literal three-storey universe. To give a contemporary analogy, most moderns probably conceive of an atom as a tight cluster of little hard balls (protons and neutrons) orbited by little fuzzy packets of light (electrons). Many of us know that this kind of thing is a rudimentary construction of the imagination that helps us get our heads around a reality that is in some ways impenetrably mysterious. Not everyone naively absolutizes the models that are given them for understanding the physical universe.

104. This coheres with Paul's concept in 2 Cor. 5:8 that death will unite him with Christ in heaven.

It may come as somewhat of a surprise that what happens next is not the announcement of a verdict, but rather a description of the resurrection of these dead ones, followed by a judgment of each according to their actions:

Revelation 20:13

> ₁₃And the ocean[105] gave up the dead that were in *it*, and Death and Hades gave up the dead that were in *them*, and they were each judged on the basis of their actions.

Our concordant reading of Rev. 20:7–10 and Isaiah 24–27 has already led us to understand that God's sentence upon the unrepentant, upon taking up his reign, had been that they should not be allowed to take part in the inaugural era of his unending reign on earth. The living unrepentant were to be consigned to the underworld (Isa. 24; Rev. 11:18; 19:21); the unrepentant dead were refused resurrection (Isa. 26:14, 16; Rev. 20:5), and so were sentenced to remain in the underworld. Convicted under a common verdict, both groups share a common sentence: *they must serve a long period of incarceration in the underworld, and be summoned later, at God's discretion, to a (final) judgment.* This is what John now describes in straightforward terms in Rev. 20:13. Where is the 1000-year-long prison sentence of the unrepentant in this visionary scene? It is left out, like a sub-point of an outline that disappears from view when the outline is collapsed to its main points. In Rev. 20:12-13, John simply sees the two phases of the judgment of the unrepentant juxtaposed: judgment in a state of death, based on the evidence in books that record their actions in mortal life, followed by resurrection and judgment, based on each person's actions in a resurrected state.

Later in Revelation, John is going to give us unmistakable clues that the "great white throne" that we've just seen in 20:11 is nothing less than the New Jerusalem, God's eternal dwelling place, and the "seat" of his rule. When we recognize this identity between the Throne and the City, both the setting and the outcome of the second and final phase of the judgment of the unrepentant will turn out to be equivalent. How do we come to this identification? First, we have OT prophetic precedent.

Jeremiah 3:17

> ¹⁷ At that time Jerusalem shall be called the throne of the LORD . . .

Jeremiah 17:12–13

> ¹² O glorious throne, exalted from the beginning,
>   shrine of our sanctuary!
> ¹³ O hope of Israel! O LORD!
>   All who forsake you shall be put to shame;

---

105. Lit. "the sea."

The End of the Unrepentant

> those who turn away from you shall be recorded in the underworld,
> for they have forsaken the fountain of living water, the LORD.[106]

Secondly, we have John's own descriptions, which tie the two together.

Revelation 4:2–3

> ₂A throne stood in heaven, and One sitting on the throne. ₃And the One sitting looked like a diamond[107] and a carnelian . . .

Revelation 7:15b–17

> ₁₅ᵦAnd the One who sits on the throne is going to put his Tent over them. ₁₆They won't be hungry or thirsty ever again, and the sun won't beat down on them, or any heat.[108] ₁₇Because the Lamb who's right there at the throne will be their shepherd, and he'll guide them to springs of flowing water.[109] And God will wipe away every tear from their eyes.[110]

Revelation 21:2–6

> ₂And I saw the New Jerusalem coming down out of heaven from God . . . ₃And I heard a loud voice from the throne saying, "Look! God's Tent is with humanity, and he's going to live with them . . . and he's going to wipe away every tear from their eyes . . . ₅And the One sitting on the throne said, "Look! I'm making everything new! ₆[. . .] To the person who's thirsty, I'm going to give free permission to drink from the spring of the water of life."

---

106. Cf. Rev. 22:1.

107. Lit. "a jasper stone." Culturally speaking, the most highly prized gemstone in John's world—comparable in prestige and beauty to today's diamond—would probably have been a stone of perfectly clear jasper. Diamond as a substance was slightly known in the ancient Mediterranean world—not as a beautiful gemstone, however, but only as the hardest known material.

108. Isa. 49:10.

109. Lit. "springs of living waters." He means artesian springs. See Ps. 23:1–2; Ezek. 34:23; Isa. 49:10; Jer. 2:13; Mic. 2:12–13 (compare the contexts).

110. Isa. 25:8.

Revelation 21:10–11

₁₀He showed me the Holy City, Jerusalem. It was coming down out of heaven from God, ₁₁shining with[111] God's glory.[112] The source of her light[113] was like a priceless gem, like a crystal-clear diamond.[114]

Revelation 21:23

₂₃The City doesn't need the sun or the moon to shine on it, because God's glory illuminates it, and its lamp is the Lamb.

Revelation 22:1

₁And the angel showed me the river of the water of life,[115] sparkling like crystal. It was coming from the throne of God and the Lamb.

When we listen to the verbal clues that John has laced into these and other passages in Revelation, we get the message that God's and Christ's Throne (3:21; 6:16; 7:9–17; 14:3; 16:17; 20:11; 21:3; 22:1, 3) ultimately refers to the same reality as all of these resonant symbols from Israel's heritage:

- God's Tent (7:15; 21:3)
- The Tent of Witness, symbol of God's personal presence among the Israelites in the desert of Sinai (15:5)
- The Holy City (11:2; 21:2, 10; 22:19)
- The Beloved City (20:9)
- The Camp of the Holy Ones (20:9)
- The New Jerusalem (3:12; 21:2, 10)

All these symbols together point to God's sovereign choice to be intimately and powerfully present among faithful human beings.

Let's look at Rev. 20:9, 11, 13–15 again:

---

111. "Shining with": lit. "having."

112. See Isa. 60:1, 2, 19.

113. In other words, God, whose glory illuminates her. God has already been compared to a shining gemstone in Rev. 4:4.

114. Lit. "jasper." See above on Rev. 4:2–3.

115. Or "And the angel showed me a river of spring water." The expression "river of living water" naturally refers to an artesian spring, but "the water of life" also evokes the second meaning of water that nurtures (resurrection) life. See Ezek. 47:1–12, which describes Ezekiel's vision of a miraculous river that comes up under the foundation of the Temple: "Everything will live wherever the river goes" (47:9).

The End of the Unrepentant

> ₉They surrounded the camp of the holy ones, the Beloved City.[116] And fire came down out of heaven[117] and burned them up.
>
> ₁₁And I saw a great white throne, and the One who sat on it. . . . ₁₂And I saw the dead, the powerful and the weak,[118] standing in front of the throne. . . . ₁₅If somebody wasn't found recorded[119] in the Book of Life, they were thrown in the lake of fire.

When we view these two descriptions of resurrection and judgment with the awareness that the same reality is frequently presented from multiple angles in Revelation, we see that their seeming differences do not distinguish them as separate episodes. Rather than pointing us to any essential difference in content, their differences serve to create a kind of narrative three-dimensionality. In other words, if these two descriptions seem different to the casual reader, it's not because their essential content is different, but only because the angle from which they are viewed is different. Differences of terminology aside, the Beloved City of 20:9 is identical with the Great White Throne of 20:11. The "nations that are in the four corners of the earth" of v. 8 are the resurrected unrepentant dead of v. 13, whose names are not written in the Book of Life, because they are not citizens of the Beloved City.[120] The actions of surrounding the Holy City and attacking it, after being incited by Satan (v. 9), are the actions for which the unrepentant dead are judged and cast into the lake of fire (vv. 13–15). What I'm saying here is that Revelation offers us a stereoscopic view of the final judgment and disposition of the unrepentant, whose military and judicial aspects ultimately complement one another. We have clear and directly relevant precedent for this understanding in the fact that John has already seen multiple visions and revelations of the second coming both as a courtroom proceeding and as a military confrontation (Rev. 1:16; 2:16; 2:26–27; 6:15–17; 11:18; 12:5; 19:1–2, 11–21; 20:4–6). For greater detail and a thoroughly systematic treatment of the whole subject of the relationship between Rev. 20:7–10 and Rev. 20:11–15, see my book, *After the Thousand Years: Resurrection and Judgment in Revelation 20*.[121]

RESURRECTION, JUDGMENT, AND NEW CREATION (REVELATION 21:1–8; ISAIAH 66:22–24)

Shortly we are going to go back and complete our survey of NT passages that mention resurrection, then we're going to go back and look for a second time at the handful of

---

116. Lit. "and the Beloved City." "And" here means "that is." As noted previously, Jerusalem is referred to metaphorically as a "camp" in 2 Chron. 22:1; Heb. 13:11–14. Jerusalem is described as beloved in the Psalms (78:68; 87:2; 122:6), and the New Jerusalem of the age of renewal is described in the prophets as beloved—both by God and by its citizens (Isa. 66:10; Zeph. 3:17).

117. Some mss add, "from God."

118. Lit. "the great and the small."

119. Lit. "written."

120. The Book of Life is the citizen rolls of the Holy City, whose inhabitants are the total community of the holy ones. See Rev. 21:27.

121. J. W. Mealy, *After the Thousand Years: Resurrection and Judgment in Revelation 20* (JSNTSup, 70; Sheffield: Sheffield Academic Press, 1992).

passages from the Gospels that we did not finish discussing in the first section. These were the passages about which we didn't have enough information to decide with confidence whether the punishment(s) they pictured were to be understood as lengthy, but temporally limited, or everlasting. But before we leave the Book of Revelation, I want to spend a moment looking at John's vision of a new creation and the appearance of the New Jerusalem. This is the scene that follows immediately after the double courtroom-style judgment scene of Rev. 20:11–12, 13–15.

Revelation 21:1–8

₁And I saw a renewed heaven, and a renewed earth: the first heaven and the first earth had gone away, and the sea[122] wasn't there anymore. ₂And I saw the Holy City, the New Jerusalem, coming down out of heaven from God. She was all dressed up, like a bride all ready for her husband. ₃And I heard a loud voice from the throne, saying,

Look! God's home[123] is with humanity![124]
God is going to live with them,
And they're going to be God's people,[125]
And God, their God, will be with them in person.[126]
₄God is going to wipe every tear from their eyes,[127]
And death will no longer exist.[128]
Nor will grief, nor crying, nor pain, exist any longer,[129]
Because the previous[130] things are gone.
₅And the One who sat on the throne said,
Look! I'm making everything new!
He said to me,[131]
Write! Because these words are faithful and true.
₆He said to me,
It's done!
I'm the Alpha and the Omega,[132]

---

122. Or, possibly, "the ocean."

123. Lit. "tent"; this is the presence of God on earth that was hinted at and hoped for in the divinely revealed symbols of the Tent of Meeting/Witness (e.g. Exod. 25–27 and 40:34–38) and the Temple (e.g. 1 Kgs 5–8; 2 Chron. 6:18; 7:1–3). For the promise of God's final dwelling with humanity, see Ezek. 37:27.

124. Lit. "with human beings."

125. Zech. 2:10–11.

126. Lev. 26:11. Some mss lack the words, "their God."

127. Isa. 25:8.

128. Isa. 25:6–10.

129. Isa. 35:10; 65:17–19.

130. Or "the former things," or "the first things." See Isa. 35:10; 43:18; 65:19.

131. Some mss lack the words, "to me."

132. These are the first and last letters of the Greek alphabet.

The End of the Unrepentant

> The Beginning and the End.[133]
> To the person who's thirsty,
> I'm going to give free permission to drink from the spring of the water of life.[134]
>
> 7 The person that wins the battle is going to inherit all of this.[135]
> I'm going to be their God,
> And they're going to be my child.[136]
>
> 8 But as for the cowards, and the untrustworthy,[137] and the filthy,[138] and the murderers, and the sexually immoral, and the sorcerers, and the idolaters, and all the liars, their inheritance is going to be in the lake that burns with fire and sulfur—which is the second death.

Here is the main question I want to ask in relation these opening verses of Revelation 21: What clues does John give us to help us understand whether the renewal of the creation and the appearance of the New Jerusalem occur (1) at the second coming of Jesus Christ, or (2) after the age-long reign of the holy ones that follows the second coming (20:4–10)? I ask this because although John may well be narrating his visions in the order in which he saw them, the sequential order of his visions does not tell us the relative sequence of the things that he sees. If that were true, we would end up expecting there to be multiple cataclysmic and history-stopping interventions of God and Jesus Christ. What the sensitive reader comes to realize is that the angel (Rev. 1:1; 22:8–9) has shown John the second coming of Jesus and its aftermath a number of times, and from a number of different angles. So we can't simply say that by Rev. 20:15 the story of the end of things has proceeded to a point after the end of the thousand-year reign of the holy ones, and so whatever John sees next will happen after that. Instead, we have to ask whether this new passage connects to things revealed earlier in Revelation, and if so, *how* it connects to them. Answering that question will give us the information we need in order to decide where the new creation fits chronologically in the final scheme of things. Let's begin.

First, John gives us a picture in Rev. 21:1 of a dissolution–recreation *complex*: the first heaven and earth have "gone away," and a new creation now appears. We've already seen the total dissolution of the creation in Rev. 6:12–17 at the second coming of Christ. This involved the sudden tearing away of the heavens, as though a well-worn scroll lying open for reading on a table unexpectedly snapped apart in the middle and curled away on both sides. The dissolution of the present creation also involved the displacement of every mountain and island, or, in other words, all the features of the surface of the earth as we know it. As we discussed above, we saw the dissolution of the heavens and the

---

133. Isa. 44:6; 48:12.
134. Isa. 55:1; Jer. 2:13; Ps. 36:9; see Jn 7:37.
135. Lit. "these things."
136. See 2 Sam. 7:14, now extended to all the faithful.
137. Or "the faithless," or "the unbelievers." In John's world, all these amount to the same thing. Those who don't trust God and Christ will eventually prove themselves unwilling to risk their lives for the hope of resurrection, and so they will prove themselves untrustworthy by abandoning their faith under persecution and worshiping the beast.
138. Lit. "vile." By implication, they're filthy and disgusting because of practices to do with idolatry.

Future Judgment and Resurrection in the New Testament

earth pictured a second time in connection with the second coming of Christ in Rev. 16:20, and yet again in 20:11. We also encounter another probable reference to it in the second coming scene of Rev. 11:19, where, as in 6:12, we hear of an earthquake, and as in 6:16, we see the dramatic appearance of God on his throne through an opening that suddenly appears in the veil of the sky. Some people miss the connection here because in Rev. 11:19 the glorious self-revelation of God is expressed in Tent of Witness/Temple imagery. But this should not throw us off, because the ark of the covenant, with its winged cherubim, turns out to be another major representation of the throne of God (cf. Rev. 4:6-8).[139] Given that Revelation gives us no indication of a gap or disconnect between the dissolution of the present creation and the new creation, we can infer, at least to start with, that the recreation of the world happens, like its dissolution, at the second coming.

Next John sees the holy city, the New Jerusalem, coming down out of heaven from God. In his letter to the church at Philadelphia, Jesus has promised the reader,

Revelation 3:12

> [12]I'm going to make the winner in this battle a pillar in the temple of my God. They'll never go outside it ever again. And I'm going to write on them the name of my God, and the name of the City of my God, the New Jerusalem, that is coming down out of heaven from my God, and my new name.[140]

The general pattern in the letters to the seven churches is that in each Jesus promises Christians some reward that they will receive when he comes, if they hold out to the end. That pattern creates a certain amount of expectation that the coming of the New Jerusalem will coincide with the coming of Jesus. Underlining this is the fact that he says in ch. 22:

Revelation 22:12-13

> [12]"Look! I'm coming soon, and I have my rewards with me![141] I'm going to give each person what their behavior deserves.[142] [13]I'm the Alpha and the Omega,[143] the First and the Last, the Beginning and the End. [14]Those who

---

139. For the ark as a representation of God's throne, see Exod. 25:22; 1 Sam. 4:4; Pss. 80:1; 99:1; Isa. 37:16; 40:22; Ezek. 1:5-25; 10:1-22. It's worth restating the principle that heaven is not a physical place, with physical furniture such as thrones, lamps, altars, and covenant boxes. These things, like their earthly models in the Tent of Witness and the Temple, are given to us as symbolic representations God's character and relationship with the creation. In reality, they are not "things" at all, but revelations, through the medium of the visual imagination, of God's being and God's ways.

140. This alludes to Jer. 23:6; 33:15-16. At the time of the renewal, Messiah is going to be given the name, "YHWH is our Righteousness," which is identical to the new name to be given to Jerusalem at that time. This name thus contains all three of the names that Jesus promises in Rev. 3:12 to write on those who overcome: His father's name (YHWH), the name of the New Jerusalem, and his own "new name."

141. See Isa. 40:10; 62:11.

142. Lit. "I'm going to reward each person as is their work." This "reward" can be positive or negative.

143. These are the first and last letters of the Greek alphabet.

The End of the Unrepentant

wash their robes[144] are blessed, because[145] they're going to have a right to the tree of life. And they're going to go through the gates into the City.

Since entrance to the City is one of the rewards of remaining faithful to Jesus, and since Jesus is coming "with his rewards with him," the presumption is that the faithful will fully enjoy the City immediately when he comes. The allusion to Jer. 23:6 and 33:15–16 in Rev. 3:12 goes hand in hand with this, since the Jeremiah passages are prophecies of the coming of Messiah as the glorious king of a new Jerusalem.[146]

Next John likens the New Jerusalem to a radiant bride on her wedding day. This, of course, immediately recalls the words of Revelation 19:

Revelation 19:6–9

$_6$Hallelujah!
Our Lord God, the All Powerful, now reigns![147]
$_7$Let's celebrate and be happy,
Let's give[148] God the glory,
Because it's the Lamb's wedding day,
And his bride has gotten herself all ready.
$_8$She's been given the authority to wear fine, sparkling clean linen.

(The fine linen represents all the proofs of the integrity of the holy ones.)

$_9$And the angel said to me, "Write, 'Those who've been invited to the Lamb's wedding are blessed!'"

Given the way the visual symbols work together in Revelation, I'm very confident that we're to understand the beautiful wedding clothes of the New Jerusalem, the community of the holy ones, as being made up of the clean, bright garments of each of the holy ones as individuals. The coming of the New Jerusalem as the bride thus connects not only (1) with the representation of Christ's reunion with his holy ones "in white" at his second coming in Rev. 19:6–14, but also (2) with the promise in Rev. 3:4–5 that those who are worthy will "walk with me in white garments." Once again, the occasion for the fulfillment of this latter promise is the moment of Christ's coming (cf. 3:3).

Finally, the promises in Rev. 21:3–4 connect with OT prophecies that concern the moment of transition to an age of global justice and peace. The promise of God dwelling with the holy ones quotes Ezek. 37:27 (cf. Zech. 2:10), which has in view the inauguration of the new age of Messiah (see Ezek. 37:15–28). The promise that God will wipe away every tear quotes Isa. 25:8 for the second time, alluding in the process to its first quotation in Rev. 7:17. John clearly sees the global cataclysm that marks the end of this current

---

144. Some mss have, "Those who keep his commands are blessed," which sounds similar in Greek. It looks like a copyist's mistake.
145. Lit. "so that."
146. See the nt. on Rev. 3:12 above.
147. Lit. "has taken up the rulership."
148. Some mss have, "And we will give."

age in Isaiah 24, and the transition to the glorious age to come in Isaiah 24:21—25:9. He also clearly understands that this transition is identical to the second coming of Christ.

The puzzle pieces are fitting together cleanly here. The New Jerusalem, settled on earth in the new creation, and beloved as the bride of Christ, is to be recognized as the "beloved city" of Rev. 20:9. The thousand-year reign of the holy ones, in other words, begins at the second coming of Jesus Christ, at the inauguration of the new creation. The resurrection and last rebellion of the unrepentant in Rev. 20:7–10 has the new creation as its setting.

But wait just a minute, someone will say. How can the unrepentant hordes be given access to the renewed and cleansed earth in a resurrected state? How can they, after all that has happened, be given the power to force the holy ones to flee into the New Jerusalem, polluting the pure ground of the new creation with their unholy footsteps?[149] The answer to this question may become apparent if we simply paraphrase it. How can God grant access to a perfect and sinless creation to beings whom he foreknows will end up turning against it and becoming a danger to it? If you think about it, that choice is exactly what the story of humanity's beginnings in Genesis 1–3 implies, if we bring to it the biblical concept of divine foreknowledge. God's mercy is not limited ahead of time by his foreknowledge of the human response to it. It is God's prerogative to decide to whom and for how long to grant further chances. Moreover, if God is as radically loving and merciful as he proclaims himself to be (e.g. Exod. 34:6–7; Ps. 145:9), then it would not be out of character for God to offer the unrepentant one last chance to taste life, even foreknowing that they will ultimately spit it out. "Many are called, but few are chosen," says Jesus (Mt. 22:14). Given that it is not *unjust* for God to extend this radical level of grace and amnesty—since it appears to be extended equally to all the undeserving, and in this case it does not result in harm to the innocent—only one question remains: *Is this too generous to be in character for God?*

Exodus 33:19

> [19] And he said, "I will make all my goodness pass before you, and will proclaim before you the name, 'The Lord'; and I will be gracious to whom I will be gracious, and will show mercy on whom I will show mercy."

What will we lose if we read these words as saying that God will not be deterred from showing as much mercy to as many people as he wishes, rather than, as most of us ungenerously interpret it, that God reserves the right to refuse mercy to whomever he chooses to turn his back on? What will we have lost if our God should actually turn out to be *more persistent than we are* in extending mercy and grace to the unrepentant? Perhaps God is not going to be finished with his attempts to offer relationship with lost human beings as quickly as we might suppose. Hear Isaiah's prophecies again:

---

149. I here paraphrase the argument of Uriah Smith, the famous nineteenth-century SDA interpreter of Revelation. He goes on to say, "Besides outraging all ideas of propriety, there is no scripture from which even an inference can be drawn to support this proposition" (*Daniel and the Revelation* [Nashville: Southern Publishing Assn, 1944 (1881)], p. 749). But there most certainly is, as I will demonstrate.

The End of the Unrepentant

Isaiah 27:4–5

> ⁴ I have no wrath.
> If someone gives me thorns and briers,
>   I will march to battle against him.
>   I will burn him up.
> ⁵ Instead, let him join close to me for protection.
>   Let him make peace with me.
>   Let him make peace with me.

Isaiah 57:16–21

> ¹⁶ For I will not continually accuse,
>   nor will I always be angry;
> for then the spirits would grow faint before me,
>   even the souls that I have made.
> ¹⁷ Because of their wicked covetousness I was angry;
>   I struck them, I hid and was angry;
>   but they kept turning back to their own ways.
> ¹⁸ I have seen their ways, but I will heal them;
>   I will lead them and repay them with comfort,
>   creating for their mourners the fruit of the lips.
> ¹⁹ Peace, peace, to the far and the near, says the LORD;
>   and I will heal them.
> ²⁰ But the wicked are like the tossing sea
>   that cannot keep still;
>   its waters toss up mire and mud.
> ²¹ There is no peace, says my God, for the wicked.

The prophecies of Isaiah do not predict that everything is going to come out fine for everyone. They affirm that God will be finished reaching out to the unrepentant when he decides to be finished, and not before. So what is going to be the context of the final, decisive encounter between God and the unrepentant? Once again, nothing is clearer than the prophecy of Isaiah himself:

Isaiah 66:22–24

> ²² For as the new heavens and the new earth,
>   which I will make,
> shall remain before me, says the LORD,
>   so shall your descendants and your name remain.
> ²³ From new moon to new moon,
>   and from Sabbath to Sabbath,
>   all flesh shall come to worship before me,
>   says the LORD.

> ²⁴ And they shall go out and look at the dead bodies of the people who have rebelled against me; for their worm shall not die, their fire shall not be quenched, and they shall be an abhorrence to all flesh.

Judgment and Resurrection in the New Testament: Summary of Results

Let's take stock of what we've accomplished. We've discovered that Jesus, Paul, and the Book of Revelation agree with the prophet Isaiah in the view that the great moment of transition to the new age of God's Kingdom is going to be characterized by resurrection to incorruptible life for the faithful, but by a refusal of resurrection to the unrepentant. That which Jesus refers to very briefly as "a resurrection of judgment" (Jn 5:29), and which Paul refers to cryptically as "the end" (1 Cor. 15:24), the visions of Isaiah and John reveal in striking clarity. These two prophets foresee that the unrepentant dead will be given a delayed resurrection, and with it an invitation to participate peacefully in the world to come—a chance that they will violently refuse. Paul's words in 1 Cor. 15:24–26 actually make very good (if less than totally explicit) sense when viewed according to this paradigm:

1 Corinthians 15:24–26

> ₂₄Then comes the end. That's when Jesus hands the kingdom over to God the Father.¹⁵⁰ It's when he does away with all rule and authority and power. ₂₅Because he has to rule as king until he puts all his enemies under his feet.¹⁵¹ ₂₆The last enemy he'll overthrow is death.

It is precisely the *deathliness* of the unrepentant—which is to say, the destructiveness with which they treat their own lives and the lives of their fellow created beings—that will earn them the sentence of a delayed resurrection. When the Spirit has granted everlasting and incorruptible life to those who love God, and when, after a just prison sentence, all the forces of deathliness are released from the bonds of death and attempt to destroy the forces of life all over again, that will be the moment when death itself, and all of its murderous emissaries, will be overthrown and removed for good.

Finishing the NT Survey: Examining the Remaining References to Resurrection

I promised that after we studied the concept of a transition to a new age, we would look at every significant NT reference to resurrection. When we found evidence of a distinction between the resurrection of the faithful and the resurrection of the unrepentant, we spent some time concentrating on passages that clearly brought out that distinction,

---

150. Lit. "to God, even the Father."
151. See Ps. 8:6.

The End of the Unrepentant

including and especially the Book of Revelation. We now turn to examine passages that mention resurrection but may not necessarily make any clear distinction or division between two types of resurrection. Of course, not everyone who mentions resurrection can be assumed to have an intention to explain the intricacies of the topic. But now that we've demonstrated a clear, consistent, and coherent pattern of expectation between Isaiah, Jesus, Paul, and the Book of Revelation, the question before us in relation to the following passages is not, "Is it possible to interpret the passage in such a way as to contradict the pattern," but rather, "Is it possible to interpret this passage, with minimal tension, to cohere with the pattern?"

Matthew 27:51–53

> $_{51}$Suddenly the great veil in the Temple was torn in two from top to bottom. The ground shook, and rocks were being split apart. $_{52}$Tombs were being opened up, and the bodies of many dead holy ones were raised.[152] $_{53}$They went out of the tombs after Jesus was raised, and went into the holy city and appeared to a lot of people.

This passage is evocative of the surprising words of Jesus in Jn 5:25 (which we looked at above). Whereas most of the Jewish people expected there to be a great resurrection at some time in the vague future at the end of time, Jesus affirmed that the era of resurrection *had already begun* with the coming of his ministry. He told his hearers that he was going to call people out of their tombs *starting now*, and he set about doing so.[153]

Luke 14:14

> $_{14}$... when you have a party,[154] invite poor people, people with disabilities, people that can't walk, blind people. $_{14}$Then[155] you'll be blessed, because they don't have a way to pay you back, and[156] you'll be paid back in the resurrection of the just.

The expression "the resurrection of the just" doesn't, in and of itself, necessarily convey the idea that there will be a chronological separation between that resurrection and the resurrection of the unrepentant. But it certainly goes well with the idea of two separate resurrections that we've found in Isaiah and a number of places in the NT.

---

152. Lit. "and many bodies of the sleeping holy ones were raised."
153. See Mt. 9:18–26 (|| Mk 5:21–43 || Lk. 8:40–56); Lk. 7:11–17; Jn 11:1–45 for examples of resurrections recorded in the Gospels. Peter himself also revived a dead person by means of prayer: Acts 9:36–43.
154. Lit. "make a reception."
155. Lit. "And."
156. Lit. "for."

Luke 16:31 (Abraham argues with the Rich Man who is Dead in Hades)

₂₉Abraham said, "[Your brothers] have Moses and the prophets. They should listen to them." ₃₀But he said, "Please, no, father Abraham! But if somebody goes to them from among the dead, then they'll change their hearts."[157] ₃₁But he said to him, "If they don't listen to Moses and the prophets, they won't pay attention even if somebody rises from among the dead."

The parable of Lazarus and the Rich Man (Lk. 16:19–31) does not give us any information about whether the unrepentant will rise *en masse* from their graves at the same time as the faithful, or later than the faithful. What this parable does, however, is to characterize the fate of an unrepentant person at the moment when he is separated from his body at death, *and not* the fate of an unrepentant person who has been reunited with his body in resurrection. A number of factors make this conclusion irresistible. First, there is no mention in this story of a final judgment that befalls the rich man, leading to his punishment. Secondly, he is explicitly described as being in Hades (v. 23), which, like Sheol, represents the holding place of those who have died and who await future resurrection and judgment. Thirdly, the rich man refers to his father's house, which still stands, and to his brothers, who are living their ordinary (unrepentant) mortal lives on the earth (v. 27). These factors combine to place the time-frame of the rich man's conversation with Father Abraham firmly in the current age. Lastly, Abraham's denial of the rich man's request refers to the idea that sending Lazarus to the rich man's brothers would amount to "someone rising from among the dead" (*tis ek nekrōn anastē*, Lk. 16:31). In other words, no large-scale resurrection and judgment have yet happened, and Hades is still populated by the dead. Nonetheless, the rich man is already in torment. At the very least, it looks as though his current state of misery is going to last throughout the rest of the current age, up to the transition to the age to come. At that point, we can imagine that he will join the living and the dead in facing the judgment seat of Christ. As of this moment, however, he only exists in a kind of pre-trial custody. There is a very important principle to be gleaned from this parable. *We cannot conclude, from the fact that we are seeing a characterization of post-mortem misery or torment, that we are seeing a characterization of resurrection or of a final or endless state.* Jesus appears to be warning his hearers that the fruitless remorse or frustration of the unrepentant dead will make them intensely miserable even in their pre-resurrected state.[158]

John 5:21, 24–25, 28–29; 6:39–40, 44, 54

₂₁Because just as the Father raises the dead, and brings them to life, so the Son also brings to life whoever he wants. [. . .] ₂₄I'm telling you very seriously:

---

157. Traditionally: "repent."

158. Another approach to the story of Lazarus and the Rich Man would be to treat it as pure fiction, as a kind of moral warning story that offers us no information about the actual future of human beings. In that case, it would simply be off the table when it comes to forming a scriptural view of the condition of the dead.

The End of the Unrepentant

> the person that hears my message[159] and believes in the One who sent me has eternal life. They don't come to judgment—no, they've crossed over from death to life. ₂₅I'm telling you very seriously: There's a time coming—and it's here now—when the dead are going to hear the voice of the Son of God. And the ones who've heard are going to live. [. . .] ₂₈Don't be shocked by that. Because a time is coming when those who are in their graves are going to hear his voice, ₂₉and they're going to come out. Those who've done good things are going to come out for a resurrection of life; those who've done bad things are going to come out for a resurrection of judgment.
>
> ₃₉And this is what the One who sent me wants: that I won't lose anything from what he gave me, but raise it all up on the last day. ₄₀Because this is what my Father wants: for everyone who sees the Son and believes in him to have eternal life. I'm going to raise that person up on the last day."
>
> ₄₄Nobody can come to me unless the Father who sent me draws them, and I'm going to raise them up on the last day.
>
> ₅₄The person that eats my flesh and drinks my blood has eternal life, and I'm going to raise them up on the last day.

Just as Jesus spoke in Lk. 14:14 of the resurrection of the just, suggesting the possibility that there would be a different resurrection for the unjust, Jesus looks ahead here to two qualitatively different kinds of resurrection: a resurrection of life for those who have done good things, and a resurrection of judgment for those who have done bad things. To be frank, nothing here tells us that these two kinds of resurrection happen at different times. On the other hand, nothing here teaches us that these two kinds of resurrection necessarily happen on the same occasion. As I noted above, the only clear chronological information that Jesus gives is that the era of resurrection *has already begun* (Jn 5:25). It is interesting, moreover, that Jesus does *not* say that he will raise up *every* human being on "the last day." Instead, he repeats four times that he will raise *those whom the Father has given him* on "the last day" (6:39, 40, 44, 54). What is "the last day"? The last day of what? Presumably, it is the last day of this current age, the final day of the present creation, the moment that signals the cataclysmic transition to the age to come and the renewal of the creation. Perhaps not coincidentally, Paul also sees the moment of resurrection for "those who belong to Christ" as happening at the moment of crisis when Jesus comes to rescue the faithful on earth at the very endpoint of this age (1 Cor. 15:23, 50–52; 1 Thess. 5:13–18).

John 11:24 (quoted without comment)

> ₂₄Martha said to him, "I know that he's going to rise again in the resurrection on the last day."

---

159. Lit. "word."

John 12:47–50

> ₄₇I don't[160] judge the person that hears my words but doesn't obey them. Because I didn't come to judge the world, but to save[161] the world. ₄₈If a person thinks nothing of me, and doesn't accept my words, they have their judge. It's the word that I've spoken. That will judge them on the last day. ₄₉Because I haven't spoken from myself. No, the One who sent me, the Father himself, has told me what to talk about and what to say. ₅₀And I know that his command is eternal life. So what I say is what the Father has said to me. That's exactly what I say.

At this point in John's Gospel, we already know that Jesus will raise those who belong to him at "the last day." Now we find that those who reject Jesus, who do not receive his words, will be *judged* on "the last day," rather than hearing Jesus speak "the command of eternal life" to them, raising them from death. It's an error to assume that where future judgment is in view, the resurrection of those judged is in view. *Judgment* does not in fact imply or require *resurrection*. As we saw in Lk. 20:35 and Rev. 20:4–6, the great judgment that stands at the threshold of the coming age of incorruptible life is a judgment that decides who is worthy to receive the gift of being raised from among the dead. The sentence for those who fail that judgment consists in the very fact that *they are not raised* at that time.

Acts 24:15

> ₁₅I'm putting my hope in God—just as my accusers themselves are[162]—that there's going to be resurrection of both the just and the unjust.[163]

As in the case of Jn 5:28–29, nothing in this statement by Paul tells us that there will be two separate moments of resurrection—one for the just, and a later one for the unjust. But then again, as in Jn 5:28–29, Paul's words also don't affirm that there will be a single moment of resurrection for all. The main thing that Paul's words affirm is that *he and his accusers* (who belong to the party of the Pharisees) *share the same belief*: the belief that there is going to be resurrection of both the just and the unjust. Paul is on trial before Felix, the Roman governor of Judea and Samaria. In this setting, Paul has no intention to put forward any distinctively Christian opinions about the doctrine of resurrection—but only to hammer home one point: he is being accused for the very beliefs that his Jewish accusers share.

There is a very specific reason why Paul says what he says here, and that is that it's the keystone of his defense. Even more important in his eyes, it's the keystone of his defense of the legality of Christianity itself. In the law of the Roman Empire, under which Paul and all Christians lived, it was a capital offense to start or to belong to a new

---

160. Or "I'm not going to."
161. Or "heal."
162. Lit. "which hope also these themselves look forward to."
163. Traditionally: "of the righteous and the unrighteous."

The End of the Unrepentant

religion.[164] Nonetheless, when the Romans invaded a region and took over, they had a policy of respecting existing religions. Judaism, in particular, was covered under this policy. It was a certified legal religion, a *religio licita*. The Jewish authorities exhibited a strong drive to stamp out "the Way," as belief in Jesus as Messiah was originally known.[165] If they, or, for that matter, Paul's Gentile opponents,[166] could persuade the Roman authorities that adherence to Jesus Christ[167] was a new religion, they would look upon it as illegal and potentially seditious. The deadly power of the Roman state would therefore move into action against Christians. Christians could be (and later were) required either to give up their faith or face execution. For that specific reason, Paul, when putting his case before a Roman official, takes care to frame what he says in such a way as to leave no room for anyone to pry his beliefs apart from those of mainstream (Pharisaic) Judaism.

Paul, in fact, repeats the same line of defense every time he has an opportunity to state his case. For example:

Acts 23:6

> [6]Now, Paul knew that some of them [members of the Jewish high council] were Sadducees,[168] and others were Pharisees.[169] He started shouting in the council, "Gentlemen, brothers![170] I am a Pharisee, and a son of Pharisees. I'm on trial about my hope in the resurrection of the dead!"

These are Paul's words when he was on trial in front of the Jewish High Council (the Sanhedrin).

Acts 24:20-21

> [20] ... these people here[171] should say what crime they discovered[172] when I was tried by[173] the high council. [21]Or is it about that one single thing I said, when I stood on trial in front of them and shouted, "I'm being judged by you today over the resurrection of the dead"?

These words were spoken at the same hearing as the statement in Acts 24:15 (see above).

---

164. Cf. R. Martin Novak, *Christianity and the Roman Empire: Background Texts* (Harrisburg, PA: TPI, 2001), pp. 51–53; F.F. Bruce, *New Testament History* (Garden City, NY: Doubleday, 1972), 355–61.

165. See Acts 9:1–3.

166. E.g., Acts 19:23–41.

167. The word "Christ" means "anointed" in Greek. Belief in Jesus Christ thus means belief in Jesus as Messiah.

168. Prn. **sadd**-*yoo-seez*.

169. Prn. *ferr-a-seez*. Lit. " ... that one part is Sadducees and the other Pharisees."

170. Lit. "Brother men."

171. Lit. "themselves."

172. Some mss have "discovered in me."

173. Lit. "when I stood before."

Future Judgment and Resurrection in the New Testament

Acts 25:18–19

> ₁₈[Paul's accusers] didn't bring any of the criminal charges I had been expecting. ₁₉Instead, they had some disputes against him about their own religion—and about a certain dead man named Jesus, that Paul insisted was alive.

This is from a letter from Festus, Felix's successor, to King Agrippa about Paul. In it is the very kind of language that Paul would have desired: "they had some disputes against him about their own religion," i.e., the religion that Paul shared with his Jewish accusers, despite being a follower of Jesus.

Acts 26:4–8

> ₄All Jews are well aware of my life from childhood onwards—with my fellow Jews[174] and among the people of Jerusalem. ₅They've known me all along—if they were just willing to testify. They know that I lived by the rules of the strictest sect of our religion: I was a Pharisee.[175] ₆And now I stand here on trial for my hope in the promise made by God to our ancestors. ₇It's that promise that our twelve tribes hope to attain by diligently serving[176] God night and day. It's for that hope, King Agrippa, that I'm being accused by the Jews. ₈Why do you all find it unbelievable[177] that God should raise the dead?

These are Paul's words when he was on trial in front of King Agrippa. You can see how careful he is to stay on message: I am a Jew, and my (Christian) beliefs are native to Judaism.

Acts 28:20

> ₂₀It's because of the hope of Israel that I'm wearing these chains.

This statement is the opening words to of Paul's speech to the Jews of Rome, when he has arrived in Rome to present his case in front of Caesar. Yet again he stays with the approach that he has chosen.

Understanding the context obviously doesn't make our original text, Acts 24:15, say that there are two temporally separate resurrections, one for the faithful and one for the unrepentant. *What it does do is remove all force whatever from the argument that Paul would have spoken differently here if he had understood there to be a chronological gap between the two resurrections.* The Roman legal context of Acts 24:15 makes it crystal clear that Paul is not trying to teach his accusers what Christians think about how or when the resurrection of the just and the unjust come about. Instead, he is appealing as

---

174. Lit. "in my nation/country." This probably means Israel, not Cilicia, the country of Paul's birth (see Acts 21:39), because Jews thought of their nation as being Israel, no matter where they lived (see Acts 24:17).

175. Prn. *ferr-a-see*.

176. Or "... attain, as they diligently serve." "Serve" here can also mean "worship."

177. Lit. "Why is it reckoned unbelievable by you [pl.]."

The End of the Unrepentant

strongly as he can to the commonality of belief between himself and the ruling Pharisaic party of the Jews. People who overwrite the ordinary force of Paul's *teaching* language in 1 Cor. 15:21–23 on the basis of his careful legal rhetoric in Acts 24:15 simply fail to think the matter through from Paul's perspective. When you treat his summary self-defense statement crafted for Jewish and Roman authorities as though it were a piece of teaching crafted for Christian disciples, you end up mis-assigning the interpretive priorities between it and 1 Cor. 15:21–23.

Concluding Remarks on Resurrection in the Teachings of Jesus and the New Testament

We have now finished our survey and discussion of NT passages that talk explicitly about the future resurrection of the faithful in a way that potentially sheds light on the question of the disposition of the unrepentant.[178] This book is devoted to bringing forth what the scriptures say, so I am not going to spend time proving what post-NT writers thought about this subject. Nevertheless, those who are interested can confirm that, among the earliest Christian writings and among the orthodox Christian writers honored as "Fathers of the Church," those that address the subject at all express belief in a future millennium or the idea of a selective resurrection (for the faithful alone) at the second coming of Christ.[179] It is only with Augustine of Hippo, in the late fourth century, that the idea of a single general resurrection (at the second coming of Christ) begins to become the dominant view. I will allow myself one quotation from what is very probably the earliest extant post-NT document on the subject. The *Didache*[180] is a well-respected teaching document for the training of new Christians. I include it in this survey because it spells out explicitly, in its very last verses, what Paul says less explicitly in 1 Cor. 15:22–24: that only the faithful will experience resurrection when Jesus comes again.

---

178. For completeness, I list here the remaining NT references to resurrection of the faithful: 2 Cor. 4:14; 1 Thess. 1:10 [Jesus]; 4:16; 2 Tim. 2:18; Heb. 6:2; 11:19; 1 Pet. 1:3. None of these statements has any impact on our discussion.

179. For those interested, here is the list of orthodox writers who are known for their premillennial views, and who may therefore be presumed to have subscribed to a two-stage view of the future resurrection. Papias of Hierapolis, quoted in Eusebius, *Ecclesiastical History* 3.39.11–12; Polycarp of Smyrna, *Ep. Phil.* 2.1; 5:2; 7:1 (both these men were known to have sat at the feet of John); *Ep. Barn.* 15; Justin Martyr, *Dial. Tryph.* 80–81; Irenaeus of Lyons, *Against Heresies* 5.29.2; 5.32.1; 5.35.1; 5.36.3; Tertullian, *Against Marcion* 3; Hippolytus of Rome, *Scholion on Daniel* 7:17, 22; 10:16; 12:2; *Comm. on Daniel* 4; Commodianus, *In Favor of Christian Discipline against the Gods of the Heathens* 43–46; Victorinus of Pettau, *Comm. on Rev., in loc.* (make sure to get the earliest version of his commentary, not the one edited by Jerome so as to remove references to a belief in a future millennium); Lactantius, *Divine Institutes* 7:24–26. To this list we can add the respected name of Melito of Sardis, a theologian whose works have not survived (see Jerome, *Commentary on Exodus* 36).

180. Also known as "The Teaching of the Twelve Apostles." It was written sometime late in the first century CE or early in the second century CE.

Didache 16:4–8

⁴ As lawlessness increases, people will hate one another, persecute one another, and betray one another. And then the one who leads the entire world astray will appear, claiming to be the son of God. He'll do signs and wonders, and the earth will be given over into his hand. He'll commit blasphemies that have never happened before since the beginning of the world. ⁵ Then created humanity will go into the refining fire of testing, and many will fall away and be lost. But those who hold out in their faith will be saved by the very thing that is being cursed. ⁶ And then the true signs will appear: first the sign spread out in heaven, then the sign of the trumpet blast, and thirdly the resurrection of the dead—⁷ but not of all of them. No, as it was said: "The Lord is coming, and all of his holy ones with him."[181] ⁸ Then the world will see the Lord coming on the clouds of heaven.

---

181. See Zech. 14:5; Jude 1:14; *1 Enoch* 1:9.

7

Answering Unresolved Questions from Chapter 2

THE FINAL EXEGETICAL TASK now before us is to go back and re-examine the small handful of NT passages that picture an extended period of miserable or tormented imprisonment for the unrepentant. Given what we've learned about resurrection and judgment, we will now have appropriate interpretive tools to assess in each case whether we are being invited to understand this state of imprisonment as endless.

MATTHEW 25:31–46, SECOND LOOK AT THE JUDGMENT OF THE NATIONS

In Chapters 1–3, we carried out a Genesis-to-Revelation survey of passages that picture the future fate of the unrepentant in images of fire or being consumed. In Chapter 2, we looked carefully at Mt. 25:31–46, the Judgment of the Nations. We found that there were two questions that we could not answer without first undertaking the two research tasks that we've accomplished in Chapters 4–6. The first task (undertaken in Chapters 4–5) was to survey all significant OT and NT passages that look ahead to a transition from this age to a new age of God's Kingdom, and the second task (undertaken in Chapter 6) was to examine all significant biblical passages that discuss the resurrection of the faithful and the unrepentant in relation to this transition. Having finished these tasks, we're now in a position to answer the two questions.

Question 1

Does Jesus show signs that he views the age of renewal that follows the current age of history as a single, endless age that contains, so to speak, no further eschatological calendar items such as resurrections and judgments and fundamental changes of disposition for groups of human beings? Or is there evidence that Jesus, in agreement with Isaiah, sees the transition to the coming age of renewal as one that signals the lengthy co-imprisonment of unrepentant angelic and human beings—an imprisonment that presumably leads after a long delay ("after many days," Isa. 24:23) to a trial, followed by a final punishment (Isa. 24:21–23)?

Answer to Question 1

We have indeed discovered solid evidence that Jesus agreed with Isaiah in expecting that the great judgment between this age and the age to come *would not* consign human beings (and angels) to their final fate. For example, Jesus, in agreement with Isa. 24:21–23 and 26:14, pictures the future age-transition judgment as a moment for the unrepentant living people to go down to Hades (Mt. 11:23 || Lk. 10:15). This is significant because first-century Jews, including Jesus, held as common knowledge the idea that imprisonment in Hades represents *an interim state*—the state between death and resurrection. For example, we have seen that the parable of Lazarus and the Rich Man (Lk. 16:19–31) clearly illustrates this. Jesus also indicates that certain ones of the dead (presumably the unrepentant) are going to be found unworthy of resurrection at the age-transition judgment, and will thus be left imprisoned in the realm of the dead for "that age," i.e., the coming age of incorruptible life in God's Kingdom (Lk. 20:34–35). In addition, Jesus more than once suggests that unrepentant people risk being sentenced to a very lengthy—*but not infinite*—prison sentence (presumably in the underworld) at the age-transition judgment (Mt. 5:21–26; 18:21–35; Lk. 12:57–59). Finally, the parable of Lazarus and the Rich Man suggests that Hades, the underworld realm of the dead—at least as far as the unrepentant are concerned—is already a place of fiery torment *in this present age* (Lk. 16:19–31). In consequence, *it is not valid to infer*, from the fact that Jesus pictures fiery punishment and/or imprisonment for the unrepentant at the coming world-transition judgment, that he must therefore be referring to resurrection or to the final or permanent fate of the unrepentant.

Let's now look again at the key verses in the Judgment of the Nations teaching (Mt. 25:31–46). First there is Mt. 25:41, in which Jesus, agreeing with Isa. 24:21–23, refers to human beings being consigned at the age-transition judgment to "the age-long fire that has been prepared for the devil and his angels" (Gr. *to pur to aiōnion to etoimasmenon* . . .). Secondly, there is Mt. 25:46, in which he refers to the unrepentant "goats" being sent off into "age-long punishment" at this age-transition judgment. Each of these verses now makes good and consistent sense when viewed in the context of the worldview that we have been discussing. If you overlook the clues to a strong relationship between Isaiah 24–27 and the teachings of Jesus and the NT, then this passage will appear to be talking about endless punishment. But if you read the Scriptures attentively, it then appears to be referring to the imprisonment that unrepentant human beings and angels face at the transition to the age to come—which leaves the question open as to what happens *after that age*.

The interpretive paradigm gleaned from Isaiah 24–27 does more than clarify what's going on in Matthew 25 and Revelation 20. It also serves to illuminate a number of things in the NT that once stood on their own as individual oddities, which now make coherent sense together, alongside Mt. 25:41, 46. For example:

The End of the Unrepentant

- Demons in the story of the Gadarene demoniac(s) scream at Jesus, "Have you come to torture us before the time?" (Mt. 8:29). Luke's version of the story adds the detail that "they were begging him not to order them to go off into the abyss" (Lk. 8:31).[1] In other words, in Luke the demons appear to understand that they are destined, when God's Kingdom ultimately comes, to be sent off into the underworld abyss for punishment (once again recalling Isa. 24:21–22). They plead with Jesus not to send them there "before the time."
- Jude 6 says that angels who disobeyed God in the days of Noah are being "kept in permanent[2] chains for a great day of judgment."
- Similarly, 2 Pet. 2:4 says that God threw disobedient angels from the time of Noah "into dark caves[3] in the deepest part of the underworld, and handed them over to be kept there until the judgment."
- Jude 7 says that the people of Sodom and Gomorrah stand as an example of "a judgment of age-long[4] fire."
- 2 Pet. 2:9 uses the fate of disobedient angels from the time of Noah and that of the people of Sodom and Gomorrah to illustrate God's ability to "keep unjust people under punishment for the day of judgment."
- Jesus' parable of Lazarus and the Rich Man pictures an unrepentant person as suffering tormenting flames in the underworld as soon as he dies (Lk. 16:24).

When you add all these elements up, the result is a picture in which rebellious or unrepentant human beings and angelic beings are *both* seen as imprisoned in the underworld, and this imprisonment is imagined as being painful for both. Furthermore, humanity's last generation, according to Isaiah 24:21–23, is going to be added to those already in the "pit" of the underworld along with hosts of rebellious angelic beings. These will all be released and judged together on an occasion vaguely characterized by Peter as "a day of judgment" (2 Pet. 2:9), and by Jude as "the great day of judgment" (Jude 6). Thus, the judgment that Jesus pictures in Matthew 25 in his teaching on the Judgment of the Nations is identifiable as the moment of Isa. 24:21–23, when the Kingdom of God and of Christ comes to fulfillment on Earth. At that time, all rebellious and unrepentant human beings and angels who have not already been consigned to the abyss will be sent there *en masse*, for an age-long period of imprisonment. The day on which they are all (including those who had been imprisoned there previously) released for one final trial looms far in the future at that moment—as the great, and final, judgment (Isa. 26:10—27:5 || Rev. 20:7–10 || Heb. 10:27).

Although this very last statement makes good and plausible sense as part of a Bible-wide, coherent paradigm of the end of things, the truth is that it can't be proven from the words of Jesus himself. Jesus never actually speaks about what will happen when all those unrepentant humans and angels are released from the pit. He only insists that

---

1. We might call this "realized eschatology from a demonic perspective."
2. Gr. *aïdios*, Strong's #G126, which is a stronger word than *aiōnios*, #G166.
3. Many mss have, "in bonds of darkness," the Greek words for "bonds" and "caves" being very close in spelling.
4. Gr. *aiōnios*, #G166.

many of the living, many of the dead, and many of the angelic beings (such as the devil and his angelic adherents) will not be considered worthy of taking part in the glorious age to come. And he repeats many times and in many ways that those found unworthy are going to be punished and kept "outside," and that they're going to be feeling a great deal of fruitless remorse, pain, and frustration.

As for what happens after that, Jesus remains silent. Nevertheless, it is a serious mistake to form your view of these matters on the basis of what Jesus *does not say*. The reason you can't safely make this kind of move is that in the Gospels, Jesus shows that he's not concerned with offering a programmed and systematic set of teachings on what happens to the unrepentant at the coming world-transition judgment and beyond. He frequently uses or alludes to concepts recognizable in the OT prophets, but he speaks aphoristically, in parables and short sayings. He never sets out to walk us step by step through all the stages of the coming judgment and disposition of the unrepentant. He also never drops more than a brief mention of major subjects like the coming of the man of lawlessness (also known as the antichrist), the new creation, and Babylon the Great, the great and final empire of the world. Each of these is treated at significant length and in significant detail by one or more OT prophets, by Paul, or by the Book of Revelation. Given this lack of a systematic set of teachings by Jesus, we may well conclude that he did not have the intention of giving us complete and detailed information as to the happenings that surround the coming transition to a new age and its aftermath.

But that conclusion can only be valid in relation to *his incarnate ministry on earth*. *The resurrected Jesus*, on the other hand, arguably has a great deal more to reveal. John claims that Jesus himself is the ultimate source of the visions and revelations in the Book of Revelation (Rev. 1:1; 21:16). If we consider the New Testament Scriptures in their canonical form, it only seems fair to say that Jesus *does* have the intention to give us extensive information about this topic. In particular, John, the Holy-Spirit-inspired author of the Book of Revelation, clearly wishes us to appreciate the intricate relationships that exist between the things the risen Jesus revealed to him, and the things the Spirit has revealed in the past to Isaiah and the other prophets. Therefore it is simply not a defect of the concordant view proposed here that Jesus doesn't lay that view out systematically anywhere in the four Gospels. John, author of the Book of Revelation, would certainly have insisted that Jesus had not finished revealing things to his followers about the future of the world when he completed his earthly ministry.

If it be granted that Jesus wasn't trying to cover all the bases in his teachings about the future judgment of the world, his teachings and sayings nonetheless turn out to be coherent with one another, with what we have noted in our survey of the prophets, and with what we have noted elsewhere in the NT. When we assemble the various puzzle pieces, they combine to create a coherent and meaningful pattern that agrees with Isaiah 24-27 and Revelation 20 in particular, not to mention 2 Pet. 2:4, 9 and Jude 6-7. Here's an outline of the total picture that emerges when you put it all together.

- Human beings who die unrepentant in the current age are sent to the abyss of Hades,[5] where they may be imagined to lead a miserable imprisoned existence as bodiless beings (Lk. 16:22-23 || 2 Pet. 2:9 || Jude 7).

---

5. In general, the NT term Hades (*hadēs*, Strong's #G86) corresponds to the OT Hebrew term Sheol

The End of the Unrepentant

- Certain angelic beings that disobeyed God back in the time of Noah have also been consigned to imprisonment in the abyss (2 Pet. 2:4 || Jude 6).
- At the coming age-transition judgment known as the second coming of Jesus Christ, all the living unrepentant will perish, and will thus be added to the number of those incarcerated in Hades (Isa. 24:1–6, 13, 17–22[6] || Mt. 13:40–42 || Mt. 25:41, 46 || Rev. 19:17–18, 21).
- At the same age-transition judgment, all of the unrepentant dead that are already in Hades will be judged and found unworthy of being raised to participate in "that age and the resurrection from among the dead" (Isa. 26:14 || Lk. 20:34–35 || Rev. 11:18 || Rev. 20:4–6 || Rev. 20:12[7]).
- Satan, presumably joined by all those angelic beings who stood with him in rebelling against God in the period leading up to the end of this age (Rev. 12:7–9, 12–17), will also be consigned to the abyss at that time (Isa. 24:21–22 || Mt. 25:41 || Rev. 20:1–3).
- The "age-long fire," into which both angelic and human beings are to be sent at the age-transition judgment (Mt. 25:41 || Lk. 16:24), signifies (1) the miserable frustration of having one's power of agency utterly removed,[8] together with (2) the agony of being faced with one's culpability and the consequences of it, without being able to indulge in blame-shifting or denial.[9] When all the forces of unrepentance—angelic and human—find themselves incarcerated *together*, they will have no more ability to deceive themselves and one another.
- At the same world-transition judgment, God, through Jesus Christ, will vindicate and bring to life the faithful who have died, and he will transform the bodies of those faithful ones who remain alive (e.g. Lk. 20:34–36 || 1 Cor. 15:50–55 || Rev. 11:18 ||

(Strong's #H7585). Both terms signify the underworld as a prison for the spirits of dead human beings. "The abyss" (*abussos*, Strong's #G12), sometimes styled "the bottomless pit," is yet another term for the underworld. It is sometimes used in the NT to signify the underworld prison for the spirits of the dead (Rom. 10:7; Rev. 11:7; 17:8) and for demonic beings (Lk. 8:31; Rev. 9:1–2; 20:1–3). Greeks and certain Jewish apocalyptic writers speculated about various compartments or levels in the underworld, but no such distinctions are discussed in the Bible. I suspect that the only biblical distinction between Hades and the abyss is terminological. Hades is not distinct from the abyss in a cosmological sense, but is simply the *term* for the underworld that is used when talking exclusively about the human dead.

6. The "few" who are pictured as surviving this scene are to be understood as the faithful (see Mt. 24:23). With the exception of those faithful who survive and are rescued by being lifted up to meet Jesus in the air (Mt. 24:29–31 || 1 Thess. 4:13—5:4), no one on earth survives the fiery transition from the current creation to the new creation (Isa. 24:17–20; 2 Pet. 3:5–13).

7. As I explained above, my view is that Rev. 20:12 recapitulates the judgment of 20:4–6, focusing on the unrepentant. I also think that it pictures a separate phase of judgment from 20:13–15. This view is not widely held, but no major consequences result for the overall thesis of this book if Rev. 20:11–15 is interpreted as one final judgment that follows the millennium. I simply believe that the latter is a less sensitive reading of the passage.

8. The central (but not exclusive) meaning of the biblical metaphor of fire concerns *destruction*. In the case of human beings sent to a fiery underworld, the image of a constant fire points to the fact that their physical bodies have been (and remain) destroyed. As long as they are denied bodily existence, they experience the chronic pain of frustration at lost agency.

9. See Prov. 25:22; Rom. 12:20 for the burning pain of a convicted conscience. And compare Zech. 12:10 and Rev. 1:7 for the idea that the second coming in particular will bring intense conscience pain for many.

Rev. 20:4–6). All will be gifted with incorruptible life. They will live and reign in peace on the cleansed and re-created earth (Isa. 65:17–19; 66:14–16, 22–23 || Mt. 19:28 || 1 Pet. 3:11–13 || Rev. 20:4–6 || Rev. 21:1–7 || Rev. 22:1–5).

- After an age-long delay, those human and angelic beings who have been imprisoned in the underworld will be granted release from the underworld together, and will be granted the gift and responsibility of agency once again. Intoxicated with their newfound power, and oblivious to the fact that their life still completely depends on the creative love and mercy of God, they conceive the idea of conquering the people of God and taking over the new earth. Unbeknownst to them, the freedom they are currently experiencing constitutes their final chance to prove themselves willing to live harmoniously with their fellow created beings. This is a final test, a final divine judgment. They fail this test, and so show themselves unworthy of participation in the community of creation. God irrevocably annihilates them (Isa. 26:10–12, 20–21 || Isa. 27:1–5 || Isa. 66:24 || Ezek. 38:1–23 || Rev. 20:7–10 || Rev. 20:13–15).

Question 2

If we find evidence that Jesus *did not* regard the coming transition to an age of renewal as the moment at which the unrepentant would be resurrected and consigned to their final disposition, can we detect his understanding of the difference between their condition in the extended state of imprisonment, on the one hand, and their condition following the subsequent trial that would determine their ultimate fate, on the other hand?

Answer to Question 2

As I admitted above, we cannot directly infer his answer to this question from his teachings in the Gospels. Jesus never (in his earthly ministry) develops the idea of a great last judgment that (1) follows the age to come, (2) involves an attack on the faithful by the resurrected unrepentant, and (3) results in the defeat and destruction of the unrepentant. Instead, Jesus gives us two kinds of pictures, which he does not connect together explicitly: (1) He gives us pictures of people being slain, imprisoned, banished to Hades,[10] or otherwise excluded and severely punished at the age-transition of the second coming. Such people are often shown being forcibly removed from, or prevented from entering, the kingdom or the messianic banquet.[11] Teachings such as this often include indications that those so cast out or imprisoned will be intensely miserable. (2) Jesus gives us pictures of people being utterly destroyed, body and soul, in Gehenna.[12] Consonant with the pattern we've detected in Isaiah and the Book of Revelation, *Jesus never once characterizes Gehenna as a place of misery, where people will be crying and grinding*

---

10. See Mt. 11:23 || Lk. 10:15. Luke's version of the saying about the faithless cities (Lk. 10:11-15) seems to put in parallel "that day," the coming of God's Kingdom, and "the day of judgment."

11. See Mt. 5:21-26; 8:11-12; 13:24-30, 36-43 (cf. Isa. 65:11-15); 13:47-50; 18:21-35; 22:1-14; 24:45-51 (= Lk. 12:41-46); 25:14-30 (= Lk. 19:11-27); 25:31-46; Lk. 12:57-59; 13:24-28.

12. See Mt. 5:21-22; 7:19; 10:28 (= Lk. 12:4-5); Mt. 18:6-9 (= Mk 9:42-50 = Mt. 5:29-30); cf. Jn 15:6.

The End of the Unrepentant

their teeth. His references to Gehenna, after all, refer back to Isa. 66:24, where the fuel for the fire and the food for the worms are the *inert corpses* of God's enemies. It's also true that, by appealing to Isa. 66:24 ("their worm doesn't die, and the fire doesn't get put out," Mk 9:48), Jesus implicitly invites us to consider *the context* in Isaiah. The picture of burning corpses in Isa. 66:24 is explicitly set in the new creation, and also seems to involve the results of a siege and assault on Jerusalem—especially if you connect it with Isa. 26:10–11, 20–21; 27:1–5; 66:6, 14–16. The teachings of Jesus are consistent with the paradigm that we've been discussing, and they may *hint* at it, but nothing more definitive than this can be said.

Let's now look at the rest of the passages that we bookmarked in Chapter 2 for a second look, and see if each of them fits within the Isaiah 24–27 paradigm that we've been discussing.

Matthew 18:8–9 || Matthew 5:29–30 || Mark 9:43–48, Second Look

> $_8$And if your hand or your foot trips you up, cut it off and throw it away from you. It's better for you to come into life maimed or with a disability, rather than having two hands or two feet to be thrown into the age-long fire. $_9$And if your eye trips you up, take it out, and throw it away from you. It's better for you to come into life one-eyed, rather than to get thrown with two eyes into the fire of Gehenna.

When we looked at this passage and its parallel in Mark's Gospel, I mentioned the possibility that Jesus had spoken this saying on various occasions with slight variations. That possibility stands to reason, given the high probability that Jesus went from place to place all over Judea and Galilee, preaching the same core set of teachings wherever he went. Also, given the fact that Jesus crafts a number of sayings so that they exhibit an escalating parallelism structure,[13] it seems feasible that the Mt. 18:8–9 variant of this saying could be crafted with an escalating parallelism structure. In that case, the saying would fit well within the Isaiah–Revelation paradigm. Being "thrown into the age-long fire" would characterize the fate of the person who is consigned to the underworld at the transition to the new age of God's Kingdom. Such persons, like the rich man in the parable of Lazarus and the Rich Man, would find themselves intensely miserable in the underworld of Hades for the whole long age to come. They would be tormented by the flames of fruitless remorse (at having thrown away the opportunity for life) and of the total frustration of having lost all bodily agency. Being "thrown into Gehenna" would count as an escalation in relation to being "thrown into the age-long fire," because this would imply not simply a long and miserable imprisonment in the underworld, but resurrection from the underworld followed judgment and total, final, and irrevocable destruction. How then do we decide whether this is an escalating parallelism or an ordinary parallelism? Here is the honest answer. Although the escalating parallelism analysis

---

13. Those trained in the scholarly discipline of redaction criticism may well prefer to see this as a preference on the part of Matthew. In terms of its function in my argument, nothing hinges on whether it is Jesus or Matthew who enjoys crafting sayings in an escalating parallelism form.

fits perfectly with the Isaiah–Revelation paradigm, and it conforms to the escalating parallelism style that Jesus is known to use, there is nothing in this saying itself to give us the clue that Jesus is not simply crafting an ordinary parallelism with no major shift of meaning between the two outcomes: age-long fire, and Gehenna. If we're to going to decide in favor of the escalating parallelism interpretation, we're going to have to do so on the basis of broader biblical and theological considerations, as distinct from considerations internal to this saying on its own.

A. The Broader Biblical Pattern

We've seen that the Isaiah–Revelation paradigm ties together, in a way that is both coherent and satisfying as a story, a whole range of NT sayings and teachings about the future of the unrepentant. In particular, it makes sense of the *common fate* of unrepentant angelic and human beings in Mt. 25:31–46, the Judgment of the Nations. In contrast, if we take the expression "the age-long fire" of Mt. 18:8 as referring to the fire of Gehenna, which destroys the resurrected person, then consistency dictates that we take it as meaning the same thing in the scene of Mt. 25:31–46 (see v. 41). In that case, however, the interim period of underworld imprisonment that we see characterized in Isa. 24:21–23, Lk. 20:35, and Rev. 20:1–10 would be missing in Mt. 25:31–46, and it would appear that Christ is sending people straight from this mortal life to Gehenna, the place of final, resurrected, destruction. Two strange consequences arise from this.

First, the prophetic narrative of Isaiah 24–27, which is very powerful as an interpretive overlay that can draw together and integrate the many and diverse NT teachings about the future, would become irrelevant and meaningless. It would be demoted from a key eschatological prophecy to a kind of white elephant that no one knew what to do with.[14]

Secondly, in addition to this negative consequence, we would have to supply, completely on inference, the otherwise unsupported idea that the bodies of the unrepentant among the living will be transformed to a resurrected state so they can appear at the Judgment of the Nations at Christ's second coming, along the lines of Paul's statement that there is going to be a transformation for the faithful from ordinary mortal life to incorruptible life at the second coming (1 Cor. 15:50–53). Alternatively, we would have to supply, again completely on inference, the otherwise unsupported idea that Jesus Christ will kill all the living and then instantly resurrect them along with all those who have previously died, in order to set the scene for the Judgment of the Nations. Over against these two odd ideas stands the Book of Revelation's insistence that all of unrepentant humanity perishes at the second coming and *is not raised* until the coming age is over (Rev. 19:11–18, 21; 20:5, 7–10). It is only the beast and the false prophet who are pictured as going immediately to their final destruction at the age-transition at Christ's second coming (Rev. 19:19–20; 20:10). Indeed, there is apparently a specific and exclusive reason for

---

14. This can be illustrated by looking up Isa. 24–27 in the scripture index of a few well-respected amillennial Revelation commentators, and see if they are able to say anything that makes sense of this passage as a whole in relation to its unmistakable parallels the Book of Revelation.

the exception in their case: each appears already to have come back from the realm of the dead.[15]

In summary, when we understand Mt. 18:8 || Mt. 25:41 as referring to the consignment of unrepentant (angels and) humans to imprisonment in the underworld at the age-transition of Christ's second coming, the two passages fit neatly into the cohesive Isaiah 24–Revelation 20 narrative scheme that ties together virtually all statements in the NT about the future of the unrepentant. If we interpret these two verses as referring to the final state of the unrepentant, this cohesiveness is disrupted, formerly powerful elements become extraneous, and contradictions and oddities are generated. We therefore *infer* the escalating parallelism literary form of Jesus' teaching in Mt. 18:8–9 from the fact that this makes far better sense within the matrix of all his teachings, as well as those of the other canonical scriptures.

B. Theological Consequences

If we assume that Mt. 18:8 and Mt. 25:41 refer to the final condition of the unrepentant, then no future event lies on the narrative horizon that might signal an end or a change to their condition. In that case, the word *aiōnios* in these two cases presumably takes up its possible connotation of "everlasting," and we find ourselves confronted with a major doctrinal consequence. We find Jesus teaching everlasting torture. This doctrine, which we've mentioned in our introduction, and which we will discuss briefly in the next chapter, is radically objectionable in theological terms. Whenever we are faced with two possible readings of a statement in scripture—one that leads to a view of God that is consistent with the core teachings of Jesus and the writers of the NT about God, and another reading that leads to a view of God that is starkly inconsistent with these teachings—then the reading to be preferred is the reading that is consistent with the core teachings of Jesus and the NT. This principle applies even when, taking the statement in isolation, the somewhat more plausible reading is the one that leads to the problematical view. I'll offer three brief examples of this principle as practiced by orthodox Christian biblical interpreters. (It would be easy to produce a dozen or more similar examples.)

1. In Col. 1:15, Paul calls Jesus "the firstborn of all creation." If orthodox interpreters did not come to understand from many other passages in the NT that Jesus is *not* a created being, this statement on its own would naturally lead them to understand that Paul saw Jesus as the first created being.

2. Jesus asks a questioner in Mk 10:18, "Why do you call me good? None is good but God alone." Orthodox Christian interpreters never argue that Jesus is denying his own goodness in this statement. Instead, they will often suggest that Jesus is turning aside an attempt at flattery that is offered to him on the basis an *incorrect* assumption that he is a mere human being. Jesus' question to the man, while rejecting the offer of human flattery, nonetheless presents an opportunity to recognize Jesus' divine identity. A person

---

15. See Rev. 11:7; 13:1; 17:8 for the beast, and Rev. 13:11 for the second beast, later characterized as the false prophet.

not otherwise committed to the divinity of Jesus would certainly not derive this meaning from his remark. Nonetheless, within the rational agreements of a Christian biblical criticism that self-consciously reads scripture *as scripture*, this is a possible, and even a standard, reading.

3. John says in 1 Jn 5:18, "We know that no one who is born of God sins." John says this plainly, in so many words.[16] Nonetheless, few canonical interpreters are ready to say John teaches that Christians never sin. After all, earlier in his own letter he says, "If we say we don't have sin, we are deceiving ourselves, and the truth isn't in us" (1 Jn 1:8). Even if John hadn't said that in the very same letter, theologians and biblical interpreters would still have enough information about the human fallibility of Christians from elsewhere in the NT (backed up by common experience) that they would not be willing to interpret his statement in 1 Jn 5:18 at face value.

The interpretive approaches that we see in the three examples above are both normal and reasonable. There's nothing particularly unusual or intellectually problematic about selecting an interpretive option for a passage that is somewhat weaker when viewed from a strictly internal point of reference. What's essential is that we honestly discuss the tensions in the text without explaining difficult items away or pretending they don't exist. After all, notwithstanding what we might *like* it to be, the Bible we actually have is a diverse library of materials stemming from and speaking to very different ages and cultures. Moreover, all of those ages and cultures lie at a significant distance from our own age and culture. As a result, it stands to reason—even on the widely-agreed Christian assumption that the Spirit's inspiration lies behind all of the Bible's writings—that *any* overarching interpretive scheme we develop is going to encounter passages that appear to fit perfectly, passages that fit well, passages that fit adequately, and passages that seem to show a level of tension with the scheme. Anyone who believes that their scheme does not include this sort of range of levels of "fit" is certainly failing to read the scriptures with the same attentiveness in all instances.

Here's the bottom line. Like *any* such system, the Isaiah 24–27 and Revelation 20 paradigm makes great sense of a lot of the NT information about the future, it makes good sense of a lot of it, it makes adequate sense of a few passages, and it stands in a modest amount of tension with one or two passages. Any honest theological and canonical interpreter of scripture will admit that this is par for the course. I'm admitting it to you: the expression *to pur to aiōnion*, "the age-long fire," in Mt. 18:8–9 is probably the weakest link in my entire interpretive system. Nonetheless, in Christian biblical criticism, an overarching interpretive system is *not* as weak as its weakest link. (Imagine the consequences of that assumption in relation to the three examples put forward above.) The interpretive system as a whole must simply be robust enough to merit granting the benefit of the doubt to the weak portion, since there will *always* be a weak portion.

---

16. Many Bible translation committees are so certain that John cannot be saying what he appears to be saying that they supply a corrective mistranslation: "We know that no one born of God continues to sin," or "habitually sins," etc. There is no lexical or grammatical justification for these paraphrases, only a theological and pastoral justification.

The End of the Unrepentant

Let's now return for a second look at one final passage that envisages something like an extended future period of punishment or imprisonment for the unrepentant, and we'll be ready to wrap up the chapter.

Matthew 5:23–26 ‖ Luke 12:57–59, ‖ Matthew 18:34–35, Second Look

$_{23}$Suppose you are just bringing your offering[17] to the altar, and right there you remember that your fellow human being has something against you. $_{24}$Leave your gift there in front of the altar! Go, get reconciled with the person! Then, come back and offer your gift. $_{25}$Be quick, make amends with the person who has a complaint against you,[18] while you are both on the way to court. Otherwise the person will turn you over to the judge. The judge will then turn you over to the guard,[19] and you'll be thrown in prison. $_{26}$I'm telling you seriously: you are *not*[20] going to get out of there until you've paid back the last cent!

There is something interesting about this passage and its parallels, in light of all that we've discovered in this chapter. It's the fact that Jesus manages to convey the idea that the punishment of the unrepentant will be temporally limited, while offering not the slightest amount of consolation on this basis. No one, on hearing these teachings, will manage to think, "Ah, well, maybe the ultimate consequences of living an unrepentant life won't be all that bad." Moreover, given the outcome foreseen by Isaiah and John for those who are imprisoned and later released from the underworld through resurrection, it is well that no one is led to console themselves with the idea that the punishment of those condemned at the judgment will not be everlasting. Without explaining the whole Isaiah 24–27 story, which is not his intent, Jesus leaves his hearers with the indelible impression that condemnation in the coming judgment leads to an unimaginably bad fate, a fate worse than death.

Within the teaching materials available to us in the Gospels, Jesus never goes beyond these pictures of lengthy imprisonment, and the occasional brief allusion to the incinerating fire and consuming worms of Isaiah 66:24, to synthesize his pictures of future judgment and punishment into one connected and sequential narrative of "how it all goes." He never once, in fact, speaks in so many words about what is going to happen when the unrepentant are resurrected.[21] In the single place where he actually affirms that the unrepentant will be resurrected, he merely says that theirs will be a "resurrection of judgment" (Jn 5:28–29) rather than life, and he leaves it at that. In a way, the impression you get when you read all of his sayings on the topic of future negative judgment is this: *you really don't want to find out what it is to be rejected and punished in the coming judgment. It's a worse fate than you can imagine.* As I'll be arguing in the next chapter,

---

17. Or "gift."
18. Lit. "your opponent at law."
19. Or "bailiff"; lit. "attendant."
20. Lit. "you will not—will not—." In reading, this word should be emphasized.
21. Although Jesus speaks of Gehenna as the place where God can destroy "body and soul" (Mt. 10:28), he never explicitly uses the language of resurrection in connection with it.

this is a far cry from the idea that God infinitely hates the unrepentant and intends to torment them literally without end. For now, I'll just pose it as a question: is it possible that the many horrifying pictures of the fate of the unrepentant in the Gospels are there *to convey to our limited imaginations the infinite tragedy of throwing away the priceless gift of everlasting life*, rather than to convey God's infinite desire to torment those with whom he is displeased?

Summary: What We Have Accomplished

In Chapter 1, we looked carefully at every one of the fifty-seven OT passages that use the language of fire and being consumed to convey the results of divine judgment. We found that all of them, without exception, convey the central theme of *destruction*. Within this broad theme, we found that a number of more specific sub-themes come out repeatedly, and often multiple sub-themes appear in a single passage. Some passages emphasize the idea that the fire of judgment will bring a destruction that is *instant*; many bring out the idea that it will be *complete, irrevocable, permanent,* or *final*. A number use the image of raging and unquenchable fire to warn that the destruction will be *unpreventable*, and many use the figure of fire to illustrate the *impermanence of human life*. Not one of these OT passages contains the idea of a post-death state of torment at all, let alone the idea of unending torment. Only two of them (Isa. 50:11; Ezek. 30:14–16) mention pain, and in each case the pain described is plainly that of being burned to death in a fire.

In Chapters 2 and 3, we took our inquiry to the NT, where we found these results: Nearly all of the thirty passages referring to fire in the NT—including Jesus' famous references to Gehenna—bring forward the OT theme of *destruction*, together with various ones of its sub-themes. A handful of passages in the Gospels (Mt. 25:31–46; Lk. 16:19–31)[22] and two passages in the Book of Revelation (Rev. 14:6–12; 20:10) presented exceptions to this pattern. Each of these passages pictures an extended period of fiery torment or miserable imprisonment for the unrepentant in the hereafter. In relation to the two passages in the Book of Revelation, we discovered that they are intentionally invoking a prophetic image from Isa. 34:9–10. In that passage, the picture of a fire that never stops smoldering is clearly not literal, but serves to convey the idea that the destruction being described is *complete, permanent,* and *irreversible*. In relation to the passages in the Gospels, we found that we could not, without further information, determine with confidence whether the fiery torment being pictured was to be imagined as going on for a very long time, or whether it was to be pictured as going on without end. Neither the information internal to the teachings, nor the built-up context from the OT passages that we had surveyed, gave us the answer to this question.

We therefore turned in Chapters 4 and 5 to examine all passages in the OT and the NT that look forward to the coming of a new age of renewal characterized by the establishment of God's global reign of peace and justice on the earth. And in Chapter 6, we looked at New Testament passages that express belief in resurrection. In the process

---

22. A few more gospel passages picture a long (but theoretically limited) imprisonment (Mt. 5:23–26; 18:21–35; Lk. 12:57–59). These technically lie outside the scope of our study, which concentrates on passages that contain the figure of fire. They present a similar puzzle.

of synthesizing the results from our survey of passages expressing hope in the coming of a new age and passages expressing belief in the future coming of judgment and resurrection, we found that a striking and coherent pattern of expectation emerges, which we characterized as the Isaiah 24–27 and Revelation 20 paradigm. This paradigm pictures the fate of the unrepentant as lengthy imprisonment in the underworld, followed by resurrection, judgment, and fiery annihilation. We found that this paradigm forms a meaningful and illuminating backdrop for all of Jesus' teachings about resurrection and judgment. In fact, it turns out to make uniquely coherent sense of the fact that neither Jesus nor Paul expects the unrepentant to be resurrected along with the faithful when Jesus comes again. This paradigm also explains why Jesus sometimes pictures the future fate of the unrepentant as a long and miserable imprisonment, and sometimes pictures it as total, fiery destruction.

Between the covers of the Bible, we came upon exactly two passages (Rev. 14:6–12; 20:10) that unambiguously picture not lengthy and miserable imprisonment, not instant annihilation, but everlasting torment for some parties. Both of these passages undoubtedly allude to Isa. 34:9–10, where the picture of a fire that never stops smoldering is clearly not literal, but rather serves to convey the idea that the destruction being described is *complete*, *permanent*, and *irreversible*. Furthermore, the second of the two Revelation passages stands in immediate juxtaposition with an alternative picture of instant annihilation for the same parties (Rev. 20:9). Since only one of these images can be taken literally, the following question presents itself: will we (1) choose to take the annihilation image literally, understanding that it is linked to approximately eighty-five prophetic and apostolic texts that picture fiery destruction for the unrepentant, and well over a hundred other biblical texts that warn of total and irrevocable destruction for the unrepentant without using this particular imagery, or (2) decide to take the everlasting torment picture literally, not only ignoring the powerful and consistent pattern of expectation throughout the scriptures, but also ignoring the fact that this picture itself is founded on an earlier (non-literal) prophetic image representing irreversible destruction?

The simple truth is that if you want to believe that God intends to torment people without end, you have in your possession a Bible that can justify your desire to believe that. You simply have to tune out the 99 percent of the Bible that contradicts your belief and concentrate on the 1 percent that appears to support your belief—until you take into account its prophetic context. The most perplexing question, however, is why anyone would *wish* to believe in a God who would torment forever any being that he created.

8

The End of the Unrepentant: Hermeneutical and Theological Conclusion

Summary of What We've Discovered in Our Surveys

WE'VE DISCOVERED THAT THE overwhelming majority of the more than eighty Bible passages that refer to the unrepentant being burned in fire, or being consumed, are using those images to convey the idea of total destruction. Four passages (Mt. 15:41–42; 18:8; 25:41, 46; Lk. 16:24) use the image of fire in a way that suggests a long and intensely miserable period of bodiless existence in the underworld of Hades. Only two passages (Rev. 14:10–11; 20:10) explicitly picture unending torment for unrepentant human or angelic beings. These two passages, however, trace their own biblical roots to the prophecy of Isaiah 34, where the non-literal picture of a burned-out land (Edom) that never stops smoldering is used to assure the readers that the threat from that age-old enemy nation will never return. The text offers the reader a way of imagining a future completely and everlastingly free from the current dangers. In other words, the picture of a fire that never stops smoldering is not put forward with the intent that it be understood literally, but rather for the purpose of reassuring the readers/hearers that the danger posed by perennial enemies will someday be permanently removed. This interpretation makes excellent sense not only in Isaiah, but also in the Book of Revelation itself (see Rev. 19:3; 20:7–10), in which Babylon the Great is characterized as the greatest persecutor of Christians in the history of the world.

Prophecy, Parable, and Taking Things Literally

Many complications and unanswerable questions arise if we do attempt to take passages like Isaiah 34:8–10 and Revelation 19:3 literally. What is going to happen, for example, when the entire present creation is burned up and replaced with a pristine new creation (2 Pet. 3:3–12)? Are we to imagine that God is going to miraculously lift Edom off the earth, together with the entire empire of Babylon the Great (Rev. 19:3), when

The End of the Unrepentant

this fallen creation is cleansed, and set their toxic, smoldering ruins down in the new creation—just so that those of us who want everything in the Bible to be literal can be proven right? Hardly. Our wishing that all revelation should be straightforward and immediately understandable is natural enough, but it does not constrain God to do one thing or the other. *We* are the learners here. Moreover, God never once taught us that everything he reveals in visions will be literal—quite the opposite. For example, the first thing God does in order to begin Jeremiah's training as a prophet is to teach him that visionary revelation comes in symbolic, non-literal forms (Jer. 1:4–15).

Does this observation cut both ways? Yes, it does. Perhaps we can't simply take the Bible's images of instant, fiery destruction literally either. For example, when Jesus says that angels will come and throw the unrepentant into a "burning furnace" at the end of this age, it's clear that he's not talking about a literal giant furnace—otherwise people would not be in there "crying and grinding their teeth" (Mt. 13:42, 50). People thrown into a literal giant furnace would more or less immediately lose consciousness, and would burn to a crisp within seconds. Attempting to interpret these words of Jesus realistically plainly will not work. But the solution is not to take away the image of the fiery furnace and replace it in our imaginations with something like an overly hot sauna or some other image that seems easier to imagine when taken literally. Nor is the solution to conclude that Jesus must be talking about a *magical* furnace that torments people with *magical, indestructible bodies*. He's simply not giving us that kind of information. So what is he saying? I personally believe Jesus is saying that the unrepentant are going to have the gift of bodily life abruptly taken away from them, and that they are going to be intensely miserable as a result. Well, someone will ask, what makes you so sure that you can take even *that* idea literally? The fact is that I'm *not* sure. But it's my best estimate of what Jesus is saying. That's all I can offer.

I'm convinced that the images of the future in the Bible are there to open up our thinking to realities that transcend our current experience. They are not entrusted to us so that we can file them away as though they were simple facts analogous to things we already know: they are rather given to us to be pondered, to be embraced in the imagination. They are there to ruminate on. They are not given to us in such a way that we can easily (without dishonestly oversimplifying them) pin them down and force them to conform to our existing ways of thinking. Indeed, the whole point of them is to *shake up* our existing ways of thinking. My sense is that sometimes God wants to give us a glimpse of realities that are literally beyond our current ability to grasp on an ordinary level as limited human beings. Sometimes these things are too vast or too complex; sometimes they are entirely beyond the limits of our experience. In any of these situations, there are no ordinary ways for God to communicate to us about them. The Spirit of God therefore reveals things about them to us by means of symbols, parables, metaphors, and images (see Isa. 64:4; 1 Cor. 2:9). It is a sign of intellectual laziness—and ultimately of weak faith—to insist on a system of interpretation that flattens such deeper realities, making them comfortable and congenial to us.

The End of the Unrepentant: Hermeneutical and Theological Conclusion

THE THEOLOGY OF TOTAL DOMINATION AND INFINITE VINDICTIVENESS

It's certainly true that, if you concentrate your attention exclusively on a small number of passages in the Scriptures, you can form the impression that God intends to torment many of his creatures without end. The truth is, however, that this idea cannot be embraced literally without destroying the most foundational principles of the Christian faith: God's justice, his love for all his creatures, and his lack of arbitrary vindictiveness.

If you start from the idea—founded on a superficial reading of a tiny sliver of the witness of Scripture—that God is the sort of deity who is glorified by tormenting his creatures forever, then you can certainly build a theology on that foundation. Your theology will be one whose first principle is that of *control*. It will be a theology of God as the imperious master, whose greatest concern is to retain complete domination. Any coherent definition of love and justice will be impossible in such a system, since the deification of control per se will ultimately require the denial of genuine agency to any created being. Agape love—by and for human beings—will become meaningless in such a system, for two reasons. First, on a theological level, agape love is the free choice to value the well-being of the other, and in this system only one being (God) will truly be capable of choosing freely. Secondly, on a practical level, subscribers to this deity will very often be confused as to whether they should love this or that person or group. After all, they will not know whether the potential recipients of their love belong to the reprobates, whom God hates, or to the blessed, whom God loves—and it is inconceivable that the creature should love more than the Creator. In this system, God is characterized as though he is the Great Narcissist, who makes creatures in his own image so that they can adulate him. He loves them not for their own sake, but for the sake of what they can give him. The love of a deity whose greatest concerns are adulation from and control over his creatures offers no example for loving your neighbor as yourself.

I say this as a person who has had far too many conversations with professing Christians who could not understand what point there would be in bringing the Gospel to the world, if the only consequence that faced the unrepentant were extinction and the loss of eternal life. These people had embraced a system of religion that gave them no basis for concerning themselves with the very real suffering experienced by human beings living without the love of God in the here and now. In their world, if God is on your side, then everything is predestined in your favor, so presumably God will provide for your needs. For that matter, maybe the suffering you are experiencing has been decreed by God for your own good. On the other hand, if God is against you, then nothing would be gained by trying to help you. After all, God's plan for you is that you should suffer exquisitely forever anyway. In this system of religion, human agape love is hamstrung. It suffers mutilation.

Thankfully, not everyone who has been taught to think like this demonstrates a heartless attitude. Many people somehow manage to stay focused on Christ's command that we love one another and love our neighbor as ourselves. My observation is that such people often carry a sense of confusion and contradiction around with them, but their Christian instincts keep them oriented in the right direction. This book is for people like them. No one who has truly learned to desire the wellbeing of their fellow human beings in the name of Jesus Christ can be comfortable with the doctrine of everlasting torment.

Are Human Beings Created with an Everlasting Nature?

Rather than spending more energy critiquing the theology of a God who chooses to torment his creatures without end, I'm going to turn now and spend some time outlining my own understanding of the Gospel—which underlies the model I have presented for the final destiny of the unrepentant. But first I want to lay to rest one idea that is sometimes tried by those who sense the deep injustice of the doctrine of everlasting torment, but who do not know how to avoid believing in it. Their tactic is to suggest that human beings have been created with an indestructible mode of being. According to this thinking, the reason why the unrepentant exist forever is that they are by nature impossible to uncreate. As much as I respect the motivation behind this suggestion, there is not one statement in Scripture that supports it, and there are very many that flatly contradict it.[1] Furthermore, speaking theologically, unless there were some strong reason to begin thinking otherwise, the general principle of God's rights and powers as Creator must stand: that which is brought into being out of nothing by the will of God can be returned to nothing by the will of God.[2] The idea of human indestructibility is crafted ad hoc to ameliorate the problem of everlasting torment; it cannot stand on its own, and it can be laid aside when the problem of everlasting torment is removed.

Are Humans Dimensionally Deeper Than They Realize?

There will be some who believe in the divinely inspired authority of the Bible, and who can't escape the sense that the Bible simply wouldn't contain language about everlasting torment unless something greater than plain annihilation were in the offing. For such people, I believe that there is a biblical approach that is far more sound than trying to posit the indestructibility of human beings.

This alternative approach to the issue of everlasting torment starts from the insight that we human beings are dimensionally deeper than we realize. It then asks, how can the Spirit convey to our imagination the infinite tragedy of losing a potential life that is, so to speak, this life *squared*? Paul gives us a hint of the deeper dimensionality of ourselves (at least in the life to come) in 1 Corinthians 15:

1. E.g., Isa. 2:22; 50:9; 51:6–8, 12; 66:22–24; Mal. 4:1–3; Mt. 3:8–12 || Lk. 3:7–9; Mk 9:43–48; Heb. 12:25–29; Jas 5:1–5.

2. In his fantasy novel *The Great Divorce* (San Francisco: HarperOne, 2001 [1945]), C.S. Lewis imagines the inmates of hell as retaining a bare whiff of conscious existence that eternally dwindles towards nothingness according to a kind of "half-life" principle. For whatever it's worth, this scenario has some substantial plausibility within the contemporary scientific theory of morphic fields (see Rupert Sheldrake, *The Presence of the Past* (rev. edn; London: Faber & Faber, 2011 [1988]). Under that theory, a consciousness (such as that of an angel or human being) that was denied embodiment might progressively fade away like an echo, rather than abruptly ceasing to exist altogether. This study is founded in the Bible, which concerns itself with the *what* rather than with the *how* of annihilation. Nothing in my study rests on speculation.

The End of the Unrepentant: Hermeneutical and Theological Conclusion

1 Corinthians 15:36–38, 42–43

> $_{36}$The seed you plant isn't brought to life unless it dies. $_{37}$And what you plant isn't the body that is going to be, but just a bare seed—such as wheat, maybe, or some other grain. $_{38}$And God gives it a body just as he wishes. In other words, God gives each seed its own body . . . $_{42}$That's how it is with the resurrection of the dead. The body is planted in a process of breaking down; it's raised invulnerable to breaking down.³ $_{43}$It's planted in dishonor; it's raised in glory. It's planted in weakness; it's raised in power. $_{44}$It's planted a soul-based body; it's raised a Spirit-based body.⁴ If there's a soul-based body, there's also a Spirit-based body.

Paul here compares the difference between the power of the coming resurrection body and that of our current body to the difference between a fully grown plant and the bare seed from which it grows. He's pointing to a magnitude of difference in glory and power that is so great as to be literally impossible to imagine. As he says earlier in the same letter:

1 Corinthians 2:9 (quoting Isa. 64:4; 52:15)

> $_9$Things that no eye has ever seen,
> And no ear has ever heard,
> And that never came up in any human heart,
> God has prepared for those that love him.

It's conceivable that there is only one way even to get a hint of the depth of the tragedy that is the loss of eternal life, and that is to contemplate images of exceptionally long or even never-ending torment. In that case, everlasting torment language, though not literal, would still be pointing to a reality vastly worse than what we imagine when we contemplate the prospect of simple extinction. Everlasting fiery torment, after all, is itself already a figurative concept. Perhaps few Christians would go so far as to say they believe God is going to supply literal flaming ovens and magic re-growing flesh to those who are resurrected and condemned. *We have little choice but to interpret the language of fiery torment symbolically, one way or another.* So let us search for ways of interpreting it that are compatible with the love and justice of God. Those who readily overturn everything Jesus and the apostles have revealed to us about God's loving, merciful, and generous character on the basis of a tiny handful of passages reveal a great deal about themselves, and very little about God.

---

3. Lit. "It's planted in perishability, raised in imperishability," referring to the body.

4. Or: "It's planted a natural/soulish body; it's raised a spiritual body." Paul is not saying—as our use of such words might imply—that the resurrection body is a non-physical body. To him, "spiritual" means based on or powered by the Holy Spirit, not "immaterial."

The Point of Departure for My Theology: The Bible on the Fundamental Nature of God

So what is my theology, what is my understanding of the Good News, if I don't believe in a tyrannical deity whose central concerns are those of exercising total control over, and receiving total adulation from, the beings he creates? I have always been an avid student of John the Beloved Disciple, who is arguably the most profound theological thinker in the Christian Bible. I have founded my theology on the radical principle that John enunciated in his first letter: God is love.[5] I can imagine the control-centered thinkers screwing up their faces in disgust upon reading this. "Pah! You don't like the sovereignty of God, so you fly like a bee to land on the flower with the sweetest nectar. How weak, how insipid, how convenient to your flesh!" We shall see.

Before I talk about what it means to me to say that God is love, I need to take a single step backwards, and begin by affirming the mystery that God is the Creator of all that is. This is the consistent testimony of Jesus and the apostles and prophets of the Bible, and I embrace it wholeheartedly. I honor and thank God for choosing to bring into being this wondrous and awesome universe, and I humbly honor God for causing this fragile bodily life of mine to be formed in my mother's womb. I thank and honor God for granting me the gift of life on the earth at this time and in this place. To be alive and to be sentient, to have the capacity to see, to know, to love, and to enjoy my fellow created beings—these are gifts precious beyond understanding, beyond expression. I pray that I may learn to accept them and employ them with the gratitude and respect that they deserve.

Once again, "God is love." What does that mean? I have known many people who understood it to mean that the total potential of human love is what people are searching for, what people are affirming in a symbolic way, when they speak of God. This is not at all what John meant, nor is it what I mean. When I assert that "God is love," I am not reducing God to the ideal of perfect love nor to the dynamic totality of love among living beings in the universe. To explain what I do mean, let me first define (agape) love. Love, as Jesus uses the term (and as John uses the term in his Gospel and epistles), refers to *the free desire for and commitment to the well-being of the other*. Agape love is thus not a feeling, but an active posture of the will, a living commitment. To say that "God is love" is to affirm that God is the Being whose one, pure motivation is desire for the well-being of the other. This is a great deal of what James is saying when he says:

James 1:13–17

> ₁₃Nobody who's being tempted should say, "I'm being tempted by God." Because God is not tempted by anything bad, and God doesn't tempt anybody. No, each person is tempted by their own obsessions, and they get seduced and trapped by them. Then their obsession, which has conceived, gives birth to sin. And sin, when it's full grown, gives birth to death. Don't be led astray, my dear brothers and sisters. Every good act of giving, and every perfect gift, comes

---

5. 1 Jn 4:8, 16.

The End of the Unrepentant: Hermeneutical and Theological Conclusion

down from the Father of Lights. With him, there's no shifting or shadow of a change.

God, says James, *always* gives good things. You can be sure that God will never try to trip up someone who is trying to do good, because nothing God does has the slightest tinge of ill will.[6] That being the case, how has humanity as a whole and how have individual human beings come to the place of alienation from God and addiction to unloving and destructive behaviors? In other words, *what went wrong*?

To answer this question is to frame the fundamental problem of human sin. But before we get there, I need to lay a foundation of the nature and identity of humanity.

THE POTENTIAL: THE BIBLE ON GOD'S WILL FOR HUMANITY IN CONTEXT OF CREATION

The scriptures affirm something astounding about us human beings: we were brought into being as God's own offspring. The Book of Genesis says:

Genesis 1:26–28

> [26] Then God said, "Let us make humankind in our image, according to our likeness; and let them have dominion over the fish of the sea, and over the birds of the air, and over the cattle, and over all the wild animals of the earth, and over every creeping thing that creeps upon the earth."
>
> [27] So God created humankind in his image,
>   in the image of God he created them;
>   male and female he created them.
>
> [28] God blessed them, and God said to them, "Be fruitful and multiply, and fill the earth and subdue it; and have dominion over the fish of the sea and over the birds of the air and over every living thing that moves upon the earth."

Our role on this earth is stated simply and clearly: we are given the responsibility of managing all the living beings and living systems on this planet! A *huge* responsibility—yet we have demonstrated that we as a species have the potential ability to shoulder it. We have learned many of the deepest secrets of life on this planet, down to the cellular, molecular, atomic, and even subatomic level. We have learned to exert significant control over nearly every species that we have desired to control, and it only requires looking

---

6. This does not imply that God will never trip *anyone* up. If the only way God, who loves you, can keep you from harming someone else he loves is to trip you up, then God may well trip you up. The story of the Exodus illustrates this, as do various sayings in Psalms and Proverbs. For example:

> They [the unrepentant] make a pit, digging it out,
>   and fall into the hole that they have made.
> Their mischief returns upon their own heads,
>   and on their own heads their violence descends.
>   (Ps. 7:15; see also Pss. 9:15; 37:14–15; 57:6; 141:10; Prov. 26:27)

out the window of an airplane to realize that we have put our stamp on this planet like no other species.

The most remarkable thing about us, however, is not the responsibility we were given as a species when we were created, but the *identity* that we were given. Countless gallons of ink have been spilled over the words "created in the image of God," but their significance is very easy to determine. The author of Genesis lays it in our lap a very few chapters later:

Genesis 5:1–3

> ¹ When God created humankind, he made them in the likeness of God. ² Male and female he created them, and he blessed them and named them "Humankind" when they were created.
> ³ When Adam had lived for one hundred and thirty years, he became the father of a son in his likeness, according to his image, and named him Seth.

God brought human beings into being as offspring! We are God's children! It's true that there is some language in the NT about people *becoming* children of God, but we are also given clear teaching—from both Jesus and Paul—that affirms our fundamental identity as God's children, whether we abide in the benefits of our divine parentage or not (e.g. Lk. 15:11-32; Acts 17:28). Thus, if people with no relationship with God are sometimes talked about as though they weren't God's children, it is not because they were not created to be God's children, but because they have become estranged from their divine Father. They have divorced him and emancipated themselves. When you think of it, Jesus' central teaching that we are to look in trust to God as *our Father* is itself nothing more or less than an affirmation of our identity as God's children.

THE PROBLEM: THE BIBLE ON THE ORIGIN AND NATURE OF HUMAN SIN

We've started out on the good, solid biblical foundation of God as the One who has only love, which is to say good will, for his creatures, and ourselves as beings created to be his children. As the psalmist says, "The LORD is good to all, and his compassion is over all that he has made" (Ps. 145:9). So once again, *what went wrong*? On this foundation, there is one thing guaranteed to destroy the harmony and intimacy between human beings and God, their loving creator: *hate*, otherwise describable as *envy*, *spite*, or *ill will*. Agape love, the love that comes from God, is a free choice, an intentional posture of the will. God freely chooses to love human beings for their own sake, not for anything that they can achieve or give him. The most fundamental thing you can say about God is that he chooses, he always chooses, to love those whom he creates. We human beings have been created with the intention that we eventually grow up into adulthood as God's children, therefore we have the same capacity to choose love built into us. "We love," says John, "because he loved us first" (1 Jn 4:19). "Love is from God. Everyone who loves is born from God and knows God" (1 Jn 4:7). Every time created beings follow the Creator's example and love their fellow created beings, they fulfill their identity as children of the God who is Love, and God's love is multiplied in the creation. God deservedly receives the glory and credit for this, because it is God who has brought them into existence, and they have demonstrated a family likeness to God by loving just as their Father loves. The Creator's deepest character has come to manifestation in the world through the creature, to the praise and honor of his name.

To indulge in *hate*, then, is to renounce your birthright and to set yourself in direct opposition against your Father and Creator. By embracing a callous, loveless attitude, or even an active ill will, towards your fellow beings, you set yourself in a posture of enmity towards your Father, who loves them just as he loves you. If lack of love for your fellow created beings implies that you do not love the God who lovingly created them, it is equally true that lack of love or even hatred towards your Creator must sooner or later manifest itself in lack of love or hatred for your fellow created beings. In other words, hatred for the Creator naturally results in hatred for what the Creator creates. The story of humanity's fall from innocence in Genesis 3 illustrates this.

Adam (shortly to be joined by Eve) is given a beautiful garden to tend (Gen. 2:15).[7] God says that humanity is welcome to eat the fruit of every tree in the garden, *including the fruit of the Tree of Life*. Only one kind of fruit is forbidden: the fruit of the Tree of the Knowledge of Good and Evil. Why? Because the fruit of that tree is deadly (Gen. 2:16–17). The story makes good sense when interpreted on the basis of our theological foundation: God tells them not to eat this kind of fruit for the simple reason that he loves them. He warns them that not every tree in the garden bears edible fruit, because he wants to protect them from harm. God desires the best for them.[8]

The snake, on the other hand, has a different interpretation of God's command, one that has exactly the opposite polarity. His proposal is that God's reason for forbidding this fruit is *not* because eating it is lethal (Gen. 3:4), but because God doesn't want human beings to be like God (Gen. 3:5). The snake, a crafty being (v. 1), pitches his most important messages at a subliminal level: (1) knowledge of good and evil is a *good* thing to have, and that's the very reason that God wants to keep it away from you; therefore (2) God *does not* love you, God *does not* want the best for you; and (3) God *does not* want you to be like him, *does not* look on you as beloved children who bear his likeness, but as peons, and he wants to keep the powers and attributes befitting the highest dignity for himself alone. God is a stingy, status-conscious, power-hoarding tyrant. In a word, he's your enemy.

---

7. Note that this verse symbolically restates humanity's responsibility of managing the creation (see Gen. 1:28).

8. Someone will ask, "If God truly loves them, and this fruit is really poisonous, then why has God planted this tree in the garden in the first place (Gen. 2:8)?" I have two responses: (1) This question poses a problem no matter what interpretation we give to the fruit of the tree of the knowledge of good and evil and the command not to eat from it. For that matter, the fact that the snake has been permitted to enter the garden is equally problematic. (2) Admitting that this is not supported directly in the text, I enter imaginatively into the story and propose that God did intend for his human children to be able, when mature, to metabolize the grievous knowledge that both good and evil (both love and ill will) are represented in the creation. What was harmful to them was not that they came to share their Creator's knowledge that evil exists, but (1) that they learned it in infanthood when they were not ready to digest it, and (2) that they learned about evil by joining in it.

The End of the Unrepentant

Adam and Eve had a choice when they were confronted with the snake's proposed version of reality. They could laugh and say,

> Snake, you are not making sense! God loves us. He has given us this beautiful garden, together with an unlimited supply of fruit from the Tree of Life. He would never keep anything good away from us. Why should we be offended if God possesses this unknown thing called "knowledge of good and evil" that we have never experienced? It must be good for him but not for us, otherwise he would share it with us. We are his children, and he loves us. You are confused!

This is not, however, how they choose to respond. They choose to accept the snake's lying words and to believe that God has lied to them. In choosing to believe that God stands *against* their best interests, they become hostile to God, and they make an enemy of God in their own minds. This is the general human condition according to Paul: "Once you used to be estranged from God, enemies in your attitude" (Col. 1:21).

The snake calculates that his best shot at deceiving Adam and Eve is to approach Eve, who does not have firsthand knowledge of the command about the Tree of the Knowledge of Good and Evil (Gen. 2:17). She represents all of us, who learn the ways and commands of God through the testimony of others. As soon as Eve (read: *we*) began to accept the false idea that God was her enemy, she unknowingly cut off her lifeline to the three kinds of spiritual sustenance that human beings are created to live on: faith, hope, and love (1 Cor. 13:13). Bereft of her connection to God, Eve fell headlong into idolatry, the attempt to replace God with things in the creation. John summarizes the whole range of human idolatry in this way:

1 John 2:15–17

> 15 Don't love the world or the things in the world. If somebody loves the world, they don't have the Father's love in them. 16 Everything in the world—the lust[9] of the flesh, the lust[10] of the eyes, and the boastful pride of life—is not from the Father, but from the world. 17 And the world is disappearing, and so are its obsessions.[11] But the person that does God's will lasts forever.

Eve turned away from *faith* in God, and in her insecurity, she began to be attracted to the idea of having the forbidden fruit as a possession: "She saw that it was a delight to the eyes." This is "the lust of the eyes."

Eve turned away from *hope* in God to provide for her future needs, so she began to become obsessed with the immediate satisfaction of bodily hunger: "the woman saw that the tree was good for food." This is "the lust of the flesh."

---

9. Or "craving," or "obsession."
10. Or "craving," or "obsession."
11. Or "lusts," or "cravings."

The End of the Unrepentant: Hermeneutical and Theological Conclusion

Eve turned away from the *love* of God that had given her a free sense of self-esteem, so she began to desire wisdom in order to gain a sense of worth: "the woman . . . saw that the tree was to be desired to make one wise." This is "the boastful pride of life."

This story is about all of us. When we cut off our relationship with God, we try to replace God's spiritual sustenance with what we ourselves can provide with our own strength. Idolatry is a trap that can never satisfy our need for the three permanent gifts of God: faith, hope, and love. When we are rightly connected to God and to one another, these three together constitute a kind of living spiritual metabolism. We love God and our fellow created beings, and we ourselves receive love. We trust God and our fellow created beings, and we ourselves live in trustworthiness. We expend ourselves in hope, and our strength is replenished through God's Spirit and through the community. That which we receive, we freely return and freely give forward.

Idolatry, in contrast, is a parasitic process; it turns us into vampires within the creation.

When we shut out the love of God, we become incapable of receiving *love*. We deny ourselves God's free and unconditional affirmation of our esteem, and in that very motion we make ourselves incapable of metabolizing the love of our fellow created beings. We therefore find ourselves trying to generate a sense of our own esteem at the expense of others. We try to feel good about ourselves by comparing ourselves to others and finding ourselves better than they are.[12] Esteem becomes a zero-sum game. All forms of pride and competition, both individual and social, are examples of this dynamic. I might, for example, name racism, sexism, nationalism, anthropocentrism,[13] intellectual pride, pride in good looks or sex appeal, pride in physical strength or skill in fighting arts, pride in wealth or family heritage, pride in spiritual prowess or position in spiritual community. Pride is the idol that we serve when we lose our connection to God and thereby starve for agape love. Pride attempts to take away esteem from our fellow created beings in order to garner it for ourselves. It is a negative, destructive dynamic in the creation. There is only one cure for pride, and that is to drink in the free and unmerited love of God.

When we turn from trusting God and the community of creation, we lose *faith* and become insecure, and we attempt to garner security by grasping for control. We manipulate people, and we become obsessed with "getting" things and people. We form ideas in our head about how things should be, and we become obsessed with having them that way and no other. The idol of "the lust of the eyes" names our craving for unlimited mastery and our obsession with bringing about states of affairs that we picture in our mind's eye, whether they are good for us or not.

The story of Amnon's rape of Tamar (2 Sam. 13) is a textbook example of the lust of the eyes. King David's son Amnon gets it in his head that he "loves" Tamar, his half

---

12. Jesus' parable of the Pharisee and the Tax Collector draws a bold caricature of this attitude (Lk. 18:9-14). We contemporary Christians may harbor every bit as much pride as the Pharisee in the parable, but we are well trained to hide this fact from ourselves.

13. When we consciously or unconsciously treat the rest of creation as a kind of disposable playground, and when we look upon ourselves as the only beings in the universe who matter to God, we give evidence of the fact the we are attempting to take our esteem from the false notion that we are better, more important, than all other created beings.

sister. He becomes so fixated on the notion of having her that he makes himself sick. Ultimately, when various kinds of conniving and conspiring do not get him what he desires, he rapes Tamar and "possesses" her by force. But as soon as he has conquered her, he loses all interest in her, and sends her away in disgrace. By the end of the story, Tamar's life is ruined and Amnon is dead, murdered by her vengeful brother Absalom.

Just as in this story, we too create wreckage around ourselves in our intense yearning for that which we imagine. We want this house, that car, this gadget, that sexual or romantic relationship. Much of the time, the very achievement of our desire causes the anticipated satisfaction to vanish and reappear beyond our reach like a mirage. We have lost faith in God, so we exhaust ourselves trying to build fortresses of "things just so" around ourselves, as though this will make us complete and secure. Everyone perceives the world out of a different pair of eyes and a different imagination, and each of us is sure that our idea should prevail. In struggling for mastery of our world rather than living in cooperation and trust, we bring about injustice, strife, and chaos. We have destroyed the harmony of creation. There is but one solution for the chronic insecurity that plagues us: simple, vulnerable faith in God (Mt. 6:19–34).

When we disconnect ourselves from the flow of life from the Holy Spirit, we lose *hope*, and we despair of being replenished. We become enslaved to the idol of the "lust of the flesh," which names all the ways in which we try to gain pleasure, convenience, and comfort for their own sake, and avoid exerting ourselves. We short-circuit the nervous systems of the bodies that God gave us, which are designed to reward us with pleasure when we use our bodies rightly and take good care of them. We turn from the healthy behaviors that bring pleasure along with them as a free gift, and we attempt to distill bodily pleasure and use it as a drug. Food addiction, substance and alcohol addiction, sex addiction, media addiction, thrill seeking, and common, everyday laziness (sloth) are all manifestations of this idolatry. It is the idolatry of immediate gratification and ease.

These three idols, I believe, concisely sum up what drives human beings and human culture in alienation from God. The paradox of this analysis lies in the logic that human beings theoretically ought to lack love for their own lives if they turn away from God. If we no longer love our Creator, then our love for all things, including ourselves, ought to dry up. In some mysterious way, these three idols—the lust of the flesh, the lust of the eyes, and the pride of life—work in combination to motivate most human beings to carry on living and reproducing and learning about their environment. God has graciously designed creation so that his original command (to fill the earth and subdue it) would be carried out, even by a humanity that is largely self-alienated from his love. He knows that we are on a treadmill and that we are miserable and self-destructive without him. The good news is that he has visited us in the person of his Son Jesus Christ, whose mission is to reclaim us from our alienated state. I'll expound in due course on what Jesus has done, but for the moment I want to spend a little more time contrasting my own analysis of the Fall with the analysis that leads to a doctrine of everlasting torment.

Those who insist on a doctrine of everlasting torment most often read in Genesis 2–3 the story of humanity's rejection by a deity who is concerned above all else with domination. He first lays a temptation trap in Paradise, to see if his creatures will obey every command, even ones they cannot understand. He then allows a tempter (the snake) to confuse and mislead them. When his creatures fall into his trap, he becomes furious. He cuts them off from relationship, takes an implacable posture of enmity towards them, and subjects them to death and to suffering of all kinds. This supposed response would be called criminal child abuse if any human parent did it, but those for whom control is the highest principle call it the holiness of God.

As I've said, the sense I make of the scriptures comes from the Johannine insight that God's core motivation, God's greatest concern, is not control, but desire for the wellbeing of his creatures. He loves them unconditionally and without reserve. When read through this lens, the story of the Fall becomes not the story of God's loss of temper at being disobeyed and of his angry rejection of humanity, but the story of our rejection of God. Thus Genesis 3 does *not* say that God "curses" the human beings, as most people expect it to, nor does it say that God subjected them to punishments of suffering and death because of their disobedience. It is the snake who is punished by being cursed (Gen. 3:14–15).[14] For the human beings, the consequence of eating the fruit of the Tree of the Knowledge of Good and Evil is that they are granted precisely what they have chosen for themselves in defiance of God's wise warning: the experiential knowledge of good *and* evil. The paradox is that if Adam and Eve had rejected the snake's subliminal message that God was their enemy, the perplexing encounter with the snake would have presented them with a first opportunity to begin realizing that not all beings created by God are as honest as God is, not all are loving as he is, and not all are trustworthy as he is. Adam and Eve would have been on their way to learning the "facts of life" about good and evil in a wise and measured way—not by falling headlong into evil themselves, but by observing its presence, being confused by it, and taking their questions to their loving Father.

My thesis is that Genesis 3 narrates humanity's moment of turning away from belief in and relationship with the God who is Love. Already knowing by constant experience what good was like, they insisted on learning what evil was like. Their Father and Creator, grieved but respectful of their freedom to choose, granted them their wish. The nature of evil is bound up with the generation of *unnecessary suffering*: the suffering of heightened physical pain (Gen. 3:16a, 18), the suffering of fraught relationships (Gen. 3:16b), the suffering of frustration in work (Gen. 3:18), and the suffering of death and dying (Gen. 3:19). None of these kinds of suffering would have to have been brought upon human beings if they had abided in faith, hope, and love.

In addition to granting Adam and Eve the experience of suffering, God expels them from paradise (Gen. 3:22–24). Those who interpret the text within the paradigm of God as the Master-Controller assume that the expulsion of the human beings expresses God's

---

14. Gen. 3:17 also says that the ground is cursed because Adam has eaten the fruit of the tree of the knowledge of good and evil. We're not by any means forced to think that Adam's experience of painful frustration in working the ground is a form of retributive punishment for his disobedience. On one hand, Adam has chosen to experience evil, and the experience of frustration and painful labor is one of its forms (Eve's harsh pain in childbirth is another). On the other hand, now that he has chosen to exist outside of God's love, he is henceforth such a danger to the creation that God now has to put severe limits on both the life power and the cooperativeness of the creation over which Adam still retains managerial power and authority (Rom. 8:19–23).

rejection of them, God's assumption of an enduring posture of enmity towards them. Yet nothing in the text suggests this. The text neither says nor assumes that God lives (exclusively) in the garden, such that kicking them out of the garden is the same as kicking them out of his home. On the contrary, the text says that God planted the garden as a home for *them* (Gen. 2:8). Moreover, the text (Gen. 3:23) is explicit about the reason for their exclusion from the garden: God[15] did not consider it appropriate for them to have access to the Tree of Life and live forever, now that they knew good and evil. And why might that be? As I read the text with the understanding that God is love, and that God's actions are always motivated by love, the answer is not far to seek.

When human beings embraced the snake's cynical lie about God, they turned away from love and embraced the snake's attitude of enmity and competition—not only towards God, but towards everything God had created, including one another. God had designed life on earth as a living community in which all beings would exist in harmony, blessing, and mutual support.[16] It was thus manifestly unjust and unwise for God to allow these beings, who had now chosen to experiment with a way of being characterized by suspicion and "every being for itself," to possess unlimited powers of life. Attempting to live without God and without love, human beings now stood poised to enslave, and wreak destruction upon, the priceless ("very good," Gen. 1:31) living world that God had commissioned them to manage (Gen. 1:26–28). To give them access to the Tree of Life would be to empower them not only to threaten the existence of their fellow life forms, but also to torment one another and war with one another without end. It was God's love and compassion for human beings, and his love and compassion for their fellow living species on the earth, that led God to put severe limits on their life power until such time as human beings again learned to be a blessing in the creation (see Rom. 8:18–22).

The control-based theology reads Genesis 3 as the story of God becoming the enemy of humanity; a Johannine love-based theology sees in this chapter the story of human beings becoming enemies of God, of one another, and of the living creation itself. Let's see which theory makes better sense of the story of Genesis as it unfolds going forward from Genesis 3.

The Predicament: Humanity's Descent into Deadliness

My argument has been that humanity, by setting itself against the God of love, has now generated within itself the potential to become a deadly force on the earth. As we read on in Genesis, this idea is immediately confirmed. In Genesis 4, *practically the next thing that happens is a murder*. Cain, Adam and Eve's firstborn son, apparently infuriated by his failure to attain a competitive victory over his younger brother Abel in the realm of religious service, hates him and kills him (Gen. 4:1–10).[17] Later in Genesis 4 we hear

---

15. Or, possibly, God in consultation with the council of angelic beings: note the use of "we" and "us."

16. Note that in Gen. 1–2 living things contribute to one another's nutrition, but no being depends for its sustenance on harm or death coming to any other. Human beings eat fruits and seeds (1:29; 2:9, 16); other creatures eat grass, which continuously replenishes itself by growing from underneath (1:30).

17. There's cautionary wisdom in here somewhere about religious figures who form murderously hostile attitudes towards those who serve God differently from themselves.

Lamech, Cain's great-great-great-grandson, boasting that he takes great pride in killing and in being more murderous than his opponents (Gen. 4:23–24). After a genealogical interlude in Genesis 5, we read in Genesis 6 that in the generation of Noah, a scant nine generations down from Adam, humanity has become poised to wipe out all life on the earth.

Genesis 6:11–13

> [11] Now the earth was corrupt in God's sight, and the earth was filled with violence. [12] And God saw that the earth was corrupt; for all flesh had corrupted its ways upon the earth. [13] And God said to Noah, "I am being confronted by the end of every living thing,[18] for the earth is filled with violence because of them; now I am going to destroy them along with the earth."

According to this account, it took a mere ten generations for the human race to progress from alienated from God, to inherently murderous, to globally, corporately suicidal and even ecocidal. The text says that God couldn't bear to watch the human race destroy itself and all of life ("the end of all flesh has come before my face, for the earth is filled with violence because of them," Gen. 6:13). Just as a prudent gardener trims a rose bush all the way back in the winter, or the vine dresser in a vineyard prunes all the shoots from a grape arbor after the harvest, God determines that he must trim the human race all the way back to the root. In the same way, says Jesus, looking to the future, "If those days hadn't been shortened, no flesh would have been saved" (Mt. 24:22). The last thing the author of Genesis or Jesus means is that unless God pulls back from expressing his full aggravation towards humanity, he will destroy it. To the contrary, in each case it is being said that, without God's intervention, the human race would proceed to destroy not only itself, but also all living things on the earth. That is how desperate the human condition is according to the Bible.

Modern history bears witness to the extreme dangerousness of humanity on the earth. Biologists tell us that, thanks to human activities over the past handful of generations, the earth is now experiencing a die-off of species unparalleled in the previous 65 million years.[19] We are destroying the world's rain forests at a rate of more than an acre a second. Within the space of two generations we have designed and stockpiled enough weapons of mass destruction (both nuclear and biological) to destroy all animal life on the earth many times over. We are fishing out our oceans with breathtaking rapidity. We

---

18. I've edited the NRSV's rendering here, which is "I have determined to make an end of all flesh." This is an over-translation of the Hebrew, which is literally, "The end of all flesh has come before my face." This phrase appears to mean either "I am being confronted with the extinction of all flesh and blood beings," or "I am being confronted with the choice of whether to allow all flesh and blood beings to be brought to an end."

19. "Today, many scientists think the evidence indicates a sixth mass extinction is under way. The blame for this one, perhaps the fastest in Earth's history, falls firmly on the shoulders of humans. By the year 2100, human activities such as pollution, land clearing, and overfishing may have driven more than half of the world's marine and land species to extinction" (http://science.nationalgeographic.com/science/prehistoric-world/mass-extinction). See also A. D. Barnosky, *et al.*, "Has the Earth's Sixth Mass Extinction Already Arrived?" *Nature* 471 (March 3, 2011), 51–57.

are very rapidly depleting our water tables around the world with no sign of any will to restrain ourselves. We are furiously burning hydrocarbons formed over millions of years within a handful of human generations, utterly throwing our planet's ecosystem out of equilibrium and threatening catastrophic mass extinction of life in our oceans through acidification. Whatever may be going on elsewhere in the world, it's at least clear that the vast majority of us in the "developed nations" show no indication of willingness to change our lifestyles for the sake of our fellow human beings, let alone our fellow species on earth.

Sadly, it is probably true to say that, as a broad group, middle class North American Christians show no more awareness of the destruction they are wreaking on the earth than their non-Christian neighbors. They rush back and forth in their huge vehicles, worship in their huge, expensive buildings, and consume ten or more times as many resources as their poor neighbors around the planet. Like the Christians at Laodicea, they're blindly assuming that their material prosperity is a sign of God's blessing on them and their group. But they might well listen to the words of Jesus to the Laodiceans:

Revelation 3:15–19

> 15 I know what you're doing. You're not cool, and you're not hot. 16 So, since you're lukewarm, and you're neither cool nor hot, I'm about to spit you out of my mouth! 17 Because you're saying, "I'm rich," and "I'm already wealthy," and "I don't need anything"—and you don't know *you're* the one that's destitute, miserable, poor, blind, and naked! 18 I advise you to buy from me gold that's been refined by fire. Then you'll be rich. And buy white clothes from me, so that you can put them on. That way, your embarrassing nakedness won't be made public. And buy eye ointment from me, so that you can see. 19 I challenge and discipline everyone that I love. So get serious and change your heart.

The Gospels tell the familiar story of a rich man who "went away sad" because he couldn't give up his attachment to his "great wealth" when Jesus challenged him to sell it all (Mt. 19:22 || Mk 10:22). If that man could have been put in a time machine and transported to present day North America and shown the luxury, abundance and ease experienced as normalcy by most contemporary Christians in the USA, he might well have fainted from bedazzlement at the opulence of it all. At the same time, perhaps two billion people today live in levels of poverty and destitution no different from those faced by the poor of the first century. That is, they literally cannot adequately feed themselves and their children, they literally cannot give them safe water or adequate clothing and shelter. Just because massively unsustainable levels of consumption and luxury have become the norm where you live does not make your lifestyle any less wealthy, any less idolatrous, or any less destructive to God's creation. We live in a civilization of idolaters, and it is not going to exonerate anyone on judgment day to say, "Well you see, it wasn't the custom in my culture to think of ourselves as wealthy."[20] Jesus may well say to you,

---

20. In 2008, presidential candidate John McCain hesitated to call himself a wealthy person despite the fact that he owned so many houses (somewhere between six and nine) that he couldn't even keep track of them. He also expressed the opinion that a person only qualified as rich if he or she had an

Didn't my servant John warn you that the whole world lies in the power of the evil one [1 Jn 5:19]? Didn't he paint you an unmistakable picture of a whole civilization lost in addiction to luxury [Rev. 17–18]? Why did you not open your eyes to the suffering of your fellow human beings and to the destruction that your lifestyle was causing to the living planet that I entrusted to your care [Mt. 25:31–46; Rev. 11:18]?

As you can see, subscribers to the control-centered theological paradigm don't have a monopoly on the conviction that contemporary Christians dangerously underestimate the seriousness of sin.

The Position:
Humanity Subject to God's Love, Holiness, Righteousness, Justice, Wrath

At this point someone will say, "It's all well and good to talk about God's love, but it's a dangerous error to focus on God's love to such an extent that you undermine God's holiness, God's justice, and God's wrath." I agree completely with this sentiment, and the following paragraphs lay out my understanding of the relationship between these biblical attributes of God.

What is Holiness, and How Does God's Holiness Relate to God's Love?

For reasons that totally escape me, proponents of everlasting torment seem to feel that vague appeals to God's holiness can somehow justify a doctrine that would otherwise be grotesquely unjust on its face. (I don't, incidentally, mean unjust to a secular conscience; I mean unjust to a *Christian* and *biblically formed* conscience.) These writers seem to believe that agape love and holiness can be set over against one another as conflicting principles. Even an elementary study of holiness in the Bible reveals that this argument is a smokescreen and nothing more. When we survey the many hundreds of occurrences of words relating to holiness in the Bible,[21] it becomes clear that the core concept of holiness is that of *purity*. Purity is often seen as being achieved or maintained by that which is holy being separated from or kept separate from things that do not have the same special character. For example, once a vessel has been dedicated for service to God, it is no longer supposed to be exposed to substances or vessels that belong to the *common* (i.e. *every day*) sphere. Similarly, holy people (such as priests) might have to maintain a

---

annual income of $5 million dollars or more. It's worth asking ourselves *why* there is such strong social pressure in the modern West not to think of ourselves as wealthy. Could it have to do with the suppressed awareness of *privilege* and *injustice*?

21. In the OT, see especially the Hebrew words *qadash*, "to consecrate," "to sanctify" (Strong's #H6942, 172 occurrences); *qodesh*, "holiness," "sacredness" (Strong's #H6944, 468 occurrences); *qadōsh*, "holy" (Strong's #H6918, 116 occurrences). The Aramaic word *qaddīsh* (Strong's #H6922, 13 occurrences, all in Daniel) is synonymous with the Hebrew word *qadōsh*. In the NT, see especially the Greek words *hagiazō*, "make holy," "sanctify" (Strong's #G37, 29 occurrences); *hagiasmos*, "sanctification," "consecration" (Strong's #G38, 10 occurrences); *hagios*, "holy" (Strong's #G39, 11 occurrences); and *hagiōsunē*, "holiness," "purity" (Strong's #G42, 3 occurrences).

The End of the Unrepentant

separation from certain situations or classes of people in order to maintain their purity. The *separateness*, in other words, is established or maintained in service of *purity*.

As this relates to God and the future of the unrepentant, I'll mention two points. First, nothing would create greater separation between God and the unrepentant than their annihilation. Secondly, agape love concerns a desire for someone's well-being that is independent of the desire for personal relationship with them. Holiness might indeed come into tension with the expression of other kinds of love, such as familial or friendship love, but it doesn't come into tension with agape love or with the justice that is founded on it (see below). A look at how words relating to holiness are actually used in the Scriptures confirms this:[22]

---

22. In order to give some quantitative backing to my qualitative sense of the results after scanning nearly 1000 biblical passages touching on the concept of holiness, I performed a number of statistical spot checks using the two term Bible/Dictionary Search at www.blueletterbible.org. For this purpose I used the ESV, which presumably cannot be suspected of watering down biblical references to God's wrath and the like. I discovered that:

"Holy" occurs 665 times in 595 verses in the ESV.

"Holy" and "wrath," where God's holiness is being referred to, occurs only once in the ESV:

> I will not execute my burning anger; I will not again destroy Ephraim; for I am God and not a man, the Holy One in your midst, and I will not come in wrath. (Hos. 11:9 ESV)

"Holy" and "die" occur in the same verse 8 times in the ESV: Exod. 28:35; 28:43; Lev. 16:2; Num. 4:15; 4:19; 4:20; 18:32; Hab. 1:12. In most of these verses, people are being commanded not to touch the holy thing on pain of death. There is simply no conceivable basis for extrapolating from this sort of warning to the concept of unending torment.

"Holy" and "anger," where God's holiness is being referred to, occurs only twice in the ESV:

> By setting their threshold by my threshold and their doorposts beside my doorposts, with only a wall between me and them. They have defiled my holy name by their abominations that they have committed, so I have consumed them in my anger. (Ezek. 43:8 ESV)

> I will not execute my burning anger; I will not again destroy Ephraim; for I am God and not a man, the Holy One in your midst, and I will not come in wrath. (Hos. 11:9 ESV)

"Holy" and "destroy" occur in the same verse only 7 times in the ESV, the most relevant instances of which are:

> They shall not hurt or destroy in all my holy mountain; for the earth shall be full of the knowledge of the Lord as the waters cover the sea. (Isa 11:9 ESV)

> The wolf and the lamb shall graze together; the lion shall eat straw like the ox, and dust shall be the serpent's food. They shall not hurt or destroy in all my holy mountain," says the Lord. (Isa 65:25 ESV)

> I will not execute my burning anger; I will not again destroy Ephraim; for I am God and not a man, the Holy One in your midst, and I will not come in wrath. (Hos. 11:9 ESV)

> If anyone destroys God's temple, God will destroy him. For God's temple is holy, and you are that temple. (1 Cor. 3:17 ESV)

"Holiness" occurs 33 times in 32 verses in the ESV.

"Holiness" and "wrath" occur in the same verse 0 times in the ESV.

"Holiness" and "punish" (56), "punishment" (58), "anger" (269), "destroy" (214), "destroyed" (133), and "strike" (115) occur in the same verse 0 times in the ESV.

Isaiah 5:16

> ¹⁶ But the Lord of hosts is exalted by justice, and the Holy God shows himself holy by righteousness.

Ezekiel 36:22

> ²² Therefore say to the house of Israel, Thus says the Lord God: It is not for your sake, O house of Israel, that I am about to act, but for the sake of my holy name, which you have profaned among the nations to which you came.²³

Hosea 11:9

> ⁹ I will not execute my fierce anger, I will not again destroy Ephraim; for I am God and no mortal, the Holy One in your midst, and I will not come in wrath.

The reason why passages like this can appeal to God's holiness as the explanation for the fact that he's going to act in justice and in love is that God's holiness is nothing more or less than God's *purity*. God is love, and there is no trace of lovelessness in him. God is just, and there is no trace of injustice in him. It is a mark of profound biblical and theological confusion to appeal to God's holiness as though that could justify your belief that God is capable of something infinitely unloving and infinitely unjust.

What Is Righteousness, and How Does Righteousness Relate to Love?

I want to propose that righteousness is what agape love looks like in practice.²⁴ Listen to what God says through the prophet Ezekiel:

Ezekiel 18:5–9

> ⁵ If a man is righteous and does what is lawful and right— ⁶ if he does not eat upon the mountains or lift up his eyes to the idols of the house of Israel, does not defile his neighbor's wife or approach a woman during her menstrual

---

23. Note that the act referred to is a loving act of rescue and forgiveness: see vv. 23–32.

24. In the OT, see especially the Hebrew words *tsedakah*, "righteousness," "justice" (Strong's #H6666, 157 occurrences); *tsedek*, "righteousness," "justice" (Strong's #H6664, 116 occurrences); *tsadīk*, "just," "lawful," "righteous" (Strong's #H6662, 206 occurrences); *tsadak*, "to be just," "to justify," "to be righteous" (Strong's #H6663, 41 occurrences). The Aramaic word *tsidkah* (Strong's #H6665, 1 occurrence, in Daniel) is synonymous with the Hebrew word *tsedakah*, but has the added connotation of *beneficence*. In the NT, see especially the Greek words *dikaios*, "just," "righteous" (Strong's #G1342, 81 occurrences); *dikaiosunē*, "righteousness," "integrity," "that which is appropriate or right" (Strong's #G1343, 92 occurrences); *dikaiōs*, "righteously," "justly" (Strong's #G1346, 5 occurrences); and *dikaioō*, "to justify," "to declare or prove someone to be in the right," or "to declare or prove the justness of someone's actions" (Strong's #G1344, 40 occurrences).

The End of the Unrepentant

> period, ⁷ does not oppress anyone, but restores to the debtor his pledge, commits no robbery, gives his bread to the hungry and covers the naked with a garment, ⁸ does not take advance or accrued interest, withholds his hand from iniquity, executes true justice between contending parties, ⁹ follows my statutes, and is careful to observe my ordinances, acting faithfully—such a one is righteous; he shall surely live, says the Lord God.

If you truly love the Lord your God with all your heart, then you're not going to be worshiping other gods, and you are going to obey his commands. By the same token, if you truly love your fellow human beings, then you're not going to do anything that is unjust or unloving to anyone else, and you're going to be active in helping those who are in need. God's statement in Ezekiel 18 is well interpreted by his famous plea through the prophet Micah:

Micah 6:8

> ⁸ He has told you, O mortal, what is good;
>   and what does the Lord require of you
> but to do justice, and to love kindness,
>   and to walk humbly with your God?

This is what human righteousness looks like. By analogy, when we affirm that God is righteous, we are affirming that God always acts in a way that is loving and fair in all his dealings with human beings,[25] for the simple reason that God's justice and righteousness flow directly out of God's love. Thus God is the model and standard for our righteousness. Notice, by the way, that true justice, God's justice, is better evoked by the open-ended ideal of mutual service than by the legalistic notion of equal treatment. An illustration of this can be seen in the preaching of John the Baptizer. In warning people about the coming of divine judgment, John describes a perfect micro-example of human justice: "If you have two shirts, share with the person who doesn't have one. And if you have things to eat, do the same." (Lk. 3:21). The biblical command to "love your neighbor as yourself" lies behind this advice by the Baptizer, implying that each of us should act out of the same motivation to see the well-being of our fellow human beings as we have to live and prosper ourselves. As Paul says, "Love is the fulfillment of the Law" (Rom. 13:10; Gal. 5:14).

How Does God's Anger Relate to God's Love?

I maintain that just as God's righteousness expresses God's love, so God's anger flows directly out of God's love. Some people would flatly deny that a loving God could indulge in anger. Even people who firmly believe that God gets angry may have an uneasy feeling that these two attitudes (love and anger) are incompatible. The key to straightening out our confusion about anger is to recall that love is a motivation, a commitment to

---

25. On God as the one who never shows partiality, see Deut. 16:19; Job 34:19; Acts 10:34; Rom. 2:11; Eph. 6:9; Col. 3:25; Jas 2:1–13; 1 Pet. 1:17.

the well-being of the beloved, and to recognize that anger, as it applies to God, is also a motivation. It is a motivation to act that arises from this commitment, and not an attitude of ill will or a desire for anyone's harm. If we look at it this way, anger will become recognizable as a direct manifestation of God's love, provided that it is understood wisely. Consider this definition of anger: *Anger is a kind of pain or discomfort that drives the one who loves to protect the beloved from unjust suffering.* Bear with me as I unpack this statement.

Pain Protects from Harm—In an almost uncountable variety of ways, pain subtly guides us as bodily persons and keeps us out of harm's way. For example, if I reach for something hot enough to burn me, I am immediately and forcefully motivated to draw my hand away by pain. If I respond to pain's motivating power rather than ignoring it, I am in nearly all cases protected from injury. Thus, as I adjust my position or activity in such a way as to remove the threat of injury, the pain goes away, signaling me that I am safe again. The wonderful nature of pain is thus its wisdom. You don't have to think about what to do when you experience pain: in most cases your body knows exactly what needs to be done, and you do it.[26]

Anger is a Form of Social Pain—Not the Same Thing as Aggravation—Suppose someone unintentionally inconveniences me by spilling a cup of hot coffee down my front. I may get irritated or aggravated at them, and say that I am angry, but being irritated at some discomfort or inconvenience (and perhaps even finding a way of "blaming" the person who has inconvenienced me) is not anger in the sense that is useful for theological purposes. Again, suppose I am trying to repair some appliance, and I can't find the tool I need. I might well become upset and agitated, but that is aggravation or exasperation that grows out of frustrated effort or powerlessness, not anger.

Genuine, positive anger, which is attributable to God as well as to human beings, is the pain that arises when someone I love is hurt, or is under threat of being hurt, unjustly. For example, suppose I see my two children arguing, and I realize that one is insulting the other or tormenting her. If I love my children, then seeing that going on will make me angry. When I experience this kind of pain, I say I am "angry at" the one who is doing or threatening the injury to the other. This pain, rather than motivating me to remove *myself* from the threat of injury, instead motivates me to intervene towards a person in such a way as to stop them from continuing a process that leads to the injury of *another*. Just as our bodies often know exactly what action is necessary to avoid injury to ourselves (I called this the "wisdom" of pain), so anger based on love has its wisdom. Now, the sad reality is that a great deal of unloving and self-centered behavior gets mixed into everyone's experience of human anger, and so we don't typically associate anger with love. Nonetheless, there is clearly a kind of anger that directly expresses love. This kind of anger motivates the one who loves to intervene in such a way as to stop a hurtful process, without in turn harming the perpetrator. In other words, in the scene mentioned above, my love for both my children is the same, and my anger does not in

---

26. A deeply helpful book on this subject of pain as a positive thing is *Fearfully and Wonderfully Made* (Grand Rapids: Zondervan, 1980), by the famous Christian surgeon and Hanson's disease (leprosy) expert Paul Brand.

any way change my love towards the one who is doing some injustice against the other. I oppose the one I love, but I do so by instinct in such a way as to bring the child's harmful behavior to a stop without causing any injury. For example, I may say "Stop that!" in a sharp voice, or I may even shout or grab my child by the arm and pull her away from her sister, depending on the level of danger I sense in the situation. What I will *not* do is call my child a name that tears down her self-esteem, nor will I physically injure her—that would be to join in the process of harm rather than stopping it.

A Loving God is an Angry God—Given the understanding that I have just expressed, I must believe that God is angry, since I know very well that this world is full of human injustices. I assert the complementary principle no less: a God who was not angry in our unjust world would not be a loving God, and would not deserve my worship. If we don't believe that God is motivated in his deepest nature to act against injustice on behalf of the oppressed, then it is surely empty to say that God loves the poor.[27]

What is the Wrath of God?—I think "rage" would be a fair synonym for this obsolescent word in contemporary English. Wrath/rage is more than simply intensified anger. In human terms, wrath/rage is what happens when an angry or aggravated person "loses their temper" and becomes dangerous and potentially destructive. The concept of "temper" comes from the fact that steel has a certain resiliency, called temper, which allows it to bend and spring back without breaking. When a person loses their temper, what is bent beyond the breaking point is their patience, their ability or willingness to negotiate in a non-harmful way with whatever is angering or aggravating them. The wrathful or enraged person lashes out to strike what is angering or aggravating them.

I have argued above that aggravation is a sinful human response that God does not share. As God says of himself in Exodus 34:6, "The LORD, the LORD, a God merciful and gracious, slow to anger, and abounding in steadfast love and faithfulness." Nonetheless, there is very definitely a point at which God's anger, truly defined as a manifestation of his love, can become wrathful. By this, of course, I don't mean that God loses his self-control and turns away from reasonableness and forms an irrational desire to do harm to his children. On the contrary, I mean that *God's anger sometimes becomes dangerous to the perpetrator of harm precisely because of its basis in love*. After all, even though love always desires to protect all of the beloved, not just the beloved being harmed, in our world it is not always possible to protect the one being harmed without harming the one doing the injury. For example, when Adolf Hitler began in earnest to take over Europe in 1939, was it any longer possible to act for the protection of those experiencing invasion and genocide, and at the same time to protect from harm all German people—including the German soldiers? The answer is *no*, even assuming one's complete goodwill towards the German people. Or consider a hostage situation, in which a mentally deranged gunman has made it clear through action that he intends to kill each of his hostages one by

---

27. This of course immediately raises "the problem of evil," which is expressed in the question, "If God loves all people, and is angry about injustice, why is so much injustice allowed to go on?" I know of no completely satisfying answer to this question, but it's too far off topic to address here. For some thoughts, see my essay, "God, Love, Justice and Anger: Some Theological Reflections," available on my website, www.simplegospel.net.

one. The gunman might be the police chief's own son, yet the only possible course could still resolve to sending in a SWAT team. The concept of wrath exposes the grievous truth that love is not always able to avoid harming the beloved. Such is the cost to God of bringing truly personal and free beings into the world.

The Provision:
The Salvation (i.e. the Rescue) That God Has Accomplished for Us in Jesus Christ

At this point I have sketched out the foundation for my understanding of the Good News. I've discussed the nature of God and the identity into which and purpose for which God created humanity. I have talked about the Fall, carefully exposing the Bible's story of the primal breach of relationship between ourselves and God. I've opened up the Bible's revelation of the utterly deadly nature and consequences of human sin, and I've backed that revelation up with undeniable examples from contemporary civilization. I've explicated the relationship between God's love, justice, holiness, and anger. With this foundation laid, what remains is to give a presentation of the Good News as I understand it. What follows is the story of salvation through Jesus Christ, in my own words.

First of all, what do I mean by "salvation"? The truth is that "salvation" is simply a religious word that means *rescue*. As I have characterized condition of humanity, humanity stands in desperate need of rescue. We have turned our backs on our loving Father and Creator, and, in our hostility towards him, we have become lost from right relationship with one another and with the living world that we were created to take part in and serve. We are not simply poorly behaved beings; we have literally become deadly to ourselves and to our entire planet. I am not saying this simply by way of contemporary social commentary: I learned it first by reading the Scriptures, which opened my eyes to see what I and my fellow human beings were doing on the planet.[28] The premise of the story of salvation is that we are lost, and we neither have it within ourselves to find our way back to God nor to come back into right relationship with our fellow created beings. Knowing that we cannot help ourselves, God, who loves us, has taken action on our behalf to rescue us from our condition of destructiveness.

As a Christian, it is my faith that God's action on our behalf has its center in the coming of Jesus Christ into the world. But the story of God's saving action begins about 2000 years before that. It starts with God's choosing of Abraham[29] and the family of his grandson Jacob/Israel, which eventually grew into a nation. That family and that nation weren't noticeably better than those around them; just like everybody else they were capable of being heartless,[30] they were swindlers and thieves,[31] they were liars,[32] violent

---

28. E.g., Gen. 6:5–6, 11–13; Isa. 24; Rev. 11:18.
29. See Gen. 12:1–3; 15:5–6; 28:10–17; 35:9–13.
30. E.g., Gen. 21:8–19.
31. E.g., Gen. 25:29–34; 27:1–38; 31:19.
32. E.g., Gen. 31:35; 34:1–31.

The End of the Unrepentant

and murderous,[33] sexually immoral,[34] and idolaters.[35] Nevertheless God loved them, and intended, through them, to express his love to the whole world.[36] When they had grown into a people, God displayed his power and mercy by rescuing them from attempted genocide at the hands of a great and powerful empire, ancient Egypt.

Through the mediation of angels, God gave the Israelites a set of laws appropriate to that time and place, a means to relate to him in worship, and a land of their own.[37] In that land, Canaan (now known as Palestine), where they took their place as a nation of the Middle East, they once again acted pretty much like everybody else, but God worked with them and disciplined them for their own good.[38] They experienced wild swings of fortune through the centuries. They had short periods of relative unity, peace, and tranquility, and once (under Solomon) they even got a taste of significant power in their region. But they also experienced many moments of oppression and civil war; they quickly split (under Solomon's son Rehoboam) into two warring kingdoms, each of which eventually experienced exile: most of the Northern Kingdom of Israel was deported by the Assyrians, and much of the Southern Kingdom of Judah was deported by the Babylonians.[39] Subsequently, those who returned to the land experienced hundreds of years of occupation under the Persians, the Greeks, and the Romans. Finally, during the reign of Caesar Augustus, the first Roman emperor, a man named Jesus ben Joseph was born, and eventually came to live in Nazareth. It was in preparation for the coming of this long-expected man that God had called Abraham some two millennia previously. Isaiah had prophesied many centuries earlier about Jesus:

Isaiah 52:6–7, 10, 13

> [6] Therefore my people shall know my name; therefore on that day they shall
>   know that it is I who speak; here am I.
> [7] How beautiful upon the mountains
>   are the feet of the messenger who announces peace,
> who brings good news,
>   who announces salvation,
>   who says to Zion, "Your God reigns."
>
> . . .
>
> [10] The LORD has bared his holy arm
>   before the eyes of all the nations;
> and all the ends of the earth shall see
>   the salvation of our God.

---

33. E.g., Gen. 27:41–42; 34:1–31; 37:1–20.
34. E.g., Gen. 38:12–16.
35. E.g., Gen. 31:19–21.
36. E.g., Gen. 12:1–2.
37. See the books of Exodus through Joshua. For the mediating role of angels in God's revelation of the Law to Moses, see Exod. 3:2; Acts 30:30–38, 53; Gal. 3:19.
38. See the books of Judges through 2 Samuel.
39. See the books of 1 Kings through 2 Chronicles.

The End of the Unrepentant: Hermeneutical and Theological Conclusion

...
¹³ See, my servant shall prosper;
> he shall be exalted and lifted up,
> and shall be very high.

God is here announcing that he is going to come and save the people of Zion/Jerusalem *in person* (vv. 6, 10). He announces (i.e. preaches) *good news* (i.e. the Gospel) *of salvation and of the reign* (i.e. Kingdom) *of God* (v. 7).[40] But then, intriguingly, God goes on to draw attention to his *Servant* (v. 13), who is destined for very great honor and dignity. Who is this? I suspect that we have heard the servant's voice speaking somewhat earlier in Isaiah:

Isaiah 48:12–16

¹² Listen to me, O Jacob,
> and Israel, whom I called:
I am He; I am the first,
> and I am the last.
¹³ My hand laid the foundation of the earth,
> and my right hand spread out the heavens;
when I summon them,
> they stand at attention.
¹⁴ Assemble, all of you, and hear!
> Who among them has declared these things?
The LORD loves him;
> he shall perform his purpose on Babylon,
> and his arm shall be against the Chaldeans.
¹⁵ I, even I, have spoken and called him,
> I have brought him, and he will prosper in his way.
¹⁶ Draw near to me, hear this!
> From the beginning I have not spoken in secret,
> from the time it came to be I have been there.
And now the Lord GOD has sent me and his Spirit.

Who is this One, who can speak both as the Creator, who has been from before the creation of the world (vv. 12, 13), and also as the LORD's Servant, whom God is going to send, together with his Spirit (v. 16)? I agree with the testimony of the apostle John, who identified this One as the Word of God, the unique Son of God and God the Unique Son (Jn 1:1–17), whom God the Father sent into the world as a flesh and blood human being to rescue us.

Let's hear some more of Isaiah's prophecy of the good news of God's reign and God's salvation through the Servant.

---

40. Cf. Mt. 4:23–24; 9:35; 24:14; Mk 1:15; Lk. 4:43; 8:1; 9:2, 60; Acts 28:31.

The End of the Unrepentant

Isaiah 52:14–15

> ¹⁴ Just as there were many who were astonished at him
> —so marred was his appearance, beyond human semblance,
> and his form beyond that of mortals—
> ¹⁵ so he shall startle[41] many nations;
> kings shall shut their mouths because of him;
> for that which had not been told them they shall see,
> and that which they had not heard they shall contemplate.

What is this? How did the beloved Servant come to experience appalling disfigurement?

Isaiah 53:1–3

> ¹ Who has believed what we have heard?
> And to whom has the arm of the Lord been revealed?
> ² For he grew up before him like a young plant,
> and like a root out of dry ground;
> he had no form or majesty that we should look at him,
> nothing in his appearance that we should desire him.
> ³ He was despised and rejected by others;
> a man of suffering and acquainted with infirmity;
> and as one from whom others hide their faces
> he was despised, and we held him of no account.

Here we see that the "arm of the Lord," the dramatic personal manifestation of the Lord's saving power and presence, is to be seen in none other than the Servant himself (v. 1). Astonishingly, incomprehensibly, he is despised and rejected by those he came to save. How can it be that the Servant, who brings God's very own personal presence, is treated as a stranger, and finds himself despised by human beings?

Isaiah 53:4–6

> ⁴ Surely he has borne our infirmities
> and carried our diseases;
> yet we accounted him stricken,
> struck down by God, and afflicted.

---

41. Or "sprinkle," Heb. *nazah*, Strong's #H5137. The idea of sprinkling is a familiar Hebrew metaphor for cleansing.

The End of the Unrepentant: Hermeneutical and Theological Conclusion

> ⁵ But he was wounded because of our transgressions,⁴²
>   crushed because of⁴³ our iniquities;
> upon him was the punishment that made us whole,
>   and by his bruises we are healed.
> ⁶ All we like sheep have gone astray;
>   we have all turned to our own way,
> and the LORD has laid on him
>   the iniquity of us all.

Verse 4 tells us that the Servant is a healer. In some way, however, he accomplishes the healing of wounded human beings by bearing their woundedness in his own body. God the Sender calls God the Sent One, to encounter, in his own body, the injuries of those he comes to save. Verse 6 tells us that our transgressions, our iniquities, can all be summarized in the single idea that we have run away from God, and are now going our own way.

Isaiah 53:7–9

> ⁷ He was oppressed, and he was afflicted,
>   yet he did not open his mouth;
> like a lamb that is led to the slaughter,
>   and like a sheep that before its shearers is silent,
>   so he did not open his mouth.
> ⁸ By a perversion of justice he was taken away.
>   Who could have imagined his future?
> For he was cut off from the land of the living,
>   stricken because of the transgression of my people.⁴⁴
> ⁹ They made his grave with the wicked
>   and his tomb with the rich,
> although he had done no violence,
>   and there was no deceit in his mouth.

By whom is the Servant *oppressed* and *afflicted* (v. 7)? By whom is he falsely accused, condemned, and subjected to judicial murder (v. 8)? Could it be the very lost ones whom he came to save and heal?

---

42. NRSV: "for our transgressions." The Hebrew reads, literally, "from our transgressions," which appears to mean that he was wounded *because of our* transgressions, as in the sentence, "She was wounded from her husband hitting her," or "He was injured because of my negligence." NRSV renders the Hebrew inseparable preposition *m-* (a contracted version of the preposition *min*) as "for" here, but *min* (Strong's #H4480) simply does not mean "for." The LXX renders it with *dia* (Strong's #G1223) plus the accusative, meaning "because of."

43. NRSV: "for." See previous note.

44. NRSV: "for the transgression of my people." See the note above on v. 5.

The End of the Unrepentant

Isaiah 53:10–12

> ^{10} Yet it was the will of the LORD to crush him with pain.[45]
> When you[46] make his life an offering for sin,
>> he shall see his offspring, and shall prolong his days;
>
> through him the will of the LORD shall prosper.
> ^{11} Out of his anguish he shall see light;
>> he shall find satisfaction through his knowledge.
>
> The righteous one, my servant, shall make many righteous,
>> and he shall bear their iniquities.
>
> ^{12} Therefore I will allot him a portion with the great,
>> and he shall divide the spoil with the strong;
>
> because he poured out himself to death,
>> and was numbered with the transgressors;
>
> yet he bore the sin of many,
>> and made intercession for the transgressors.

The picture that ultimately emerges here is deeply shocking. The scene opened with the picture of people running over the mountains with wonderful news, news that God reigns and is acting powerfully to save. We heard that "The LORD has bared his holy arm in the sight of all nations," and we expected that we would now see the Creator of the World coming with sleeves rolled up, dealing crushing blows to the murderers and oppressors of this world. We expected to see a public display of God's direct and awesome power to destroy evil. But the focus immediately changed, and we heard of "my Servant," the cherished servant that the LORD loves, with whom the LORD is very pleased. Inexplicably, we now hear that the servant has suffered terrible disfigurement and rejection, grief and undeserved punishment. Has the LORD turned against the Servant, attacking him for "our" sins? Absolutely not! The terrible reversal is that the Servant of the LORD is rejected by the very ones he came to serve and to save. He experiences sorrow, rejection, pain, and false accusation at the hands of the human race, and it is he himself, the Servant, in his steadfast love and forgiveness and intercession for the attackers (v. 12), who embodies the powerful and holy Arm of the LORD reaching out to accomplish our salvation. God's Arm is not exposed here in the act of reaching out to strike the sinful, and even less to strike the Servant, since the Arm is a symbol of the Servant himself (v. 1, "To whom has the arm of the LORD been revealed?"). The "arm of God," the personal saving power of God, is revealed to those who can recognize God's awesome decision to face violence and murder at the hands of humanity, in the person of the Servant. If the LORD wounds the Servant and makes him to suffer (v. 10),[47] it is precisely by asking the

---

45. An equally possible reading is "Yet the Lord was pleased with his wounded one, whom he had made to suffer." This is similar to how the translators of the Septuagint, the earliest translation of the Hebrew Bible, understood the phrase: "And the Lord desires to cleanse him of his wound."

46. Note that this is *plural*, indicating that *the readers* are the ones who have, by murdering the Servant, turned his life into a sin offering.

47. It's not at all certain that this is the force of the difficult Hebrew of v. 10 (see the footnotes on that verse above).

Servant to represent the LORD to us, the lost, estranged, hostile human race, and not to turn back before the consequences.

If we now recognize Jesus Christ in the Servant prophesied here, it is clear that Jesus saves and heals us, the guilty and broken ones, not by standing in for us and absorbing the vengeance of a hostile, angry God, as the champions of the control-based theology would have it, *but by standing for God before an angry, hostile human race.*[48] Jesus draws our very worst hostility for the very reason that he fully represents the loving God whom we have rejected. In facing and making himself vulnerable to our hatred, he *bears our sins*—not only metaphorically, in the sense of going through what we deserve, but literally—because we sin against him and act out our murderous rejection of him upon his very body. He willingly chooses, in obedience to God the Father, to submit to our "manhandling," even to the point of dying at our hands, and in doing so he releases for us, the very perpetrators, an unstoppable power of forgiveness, healing, and restoration.

This is the paradox of the death of Jesus on the cross: it was God's plan and intention (see Isa. 53:6, 10) that the wounding and the murder that Jesus experienced at our hands should be the saving encounter between ourselves and him. At the cross, God, in Jesus Christ, presents the living proof of his power to extend full forgiveness, and the reconciliation that leads us back to the eternal life that we have lost. Think about it. How could humanity possibly have proved itself more guilty, than to have attacked and killed their own Maker?[49] And how could God possibly have gone further to prove his choice to proclaim us not guilty?

Someone who is used to hearing the control-centered version of events will now be asking, "Wait a minute . . . wasn't Jesus supposed to have died to remove the wrath of God from us? Didn't the Father turn his face away from him, and didn't he have to experience the torments of hell in our place?" Actually, the clear biblical answers are *No* and *No*. To confirm this, let's now look at the other great Old Testament prophecy of the sufferings of Jesus Christ, Psalm 22.

Psalm 22:1–2

> [1] My God, my God, why have you forsaken me?
>   Why are you so far from helping me, from the words of my groaning?
> [2] O my God, I cry by day, but you do not answer;
>   and by night, but find no rest.

The psalmist here prays in an agony of fear and dread to God, asking why God has left him in the hands of murderers. He asks for rescue from deadly enemies, who are in the process of attacking him:

---

48. Isa. 53:4 makes it clear that it was a *profound misperception on our part* to assume that the sufferings of the Servant were perpetrated upon him by God.

49. See Jn 1:1–4; Col. 1:15–17; Heb. 1:1–4; 3:3–4.

The End of the Unrepentant

Psalm 22:11–13, 19–21

> ¹¹ Do not be far from me,
>   for trouble is near
>   and there is no one to help.
> ¹² Many bulls encircle me,
>   strong bulls of Bashan surround me;
> ¹³ they open wide their mouths at me,
>   like a ravening and roaring lion.
>   . . .
> ¹⁹ But you, O Lord, do not be far away!
>   O my help, come quickly to my aid!
> ²⁰ Deliver my soul from the sword,
>   my life from the power of the dog!
> ²¹ Save me from the mouth of the lion!

What is the psalmist's attitude here? Does he say, "God, why are you doing this to me"? No, he says, "God, why are you allowing this to happen to me? Please help me!" Who are the attackers? It is abundantly clear that they are human beings: "I am . . . scorned by people, and despised by the nation . . . " (vv. 6–7). His fellow Israelites are not the literal killers, but they are cheering on the process, leering and gloating. He calls the Gentiles who are physically attacking him "bulls," "lions," "dogs," "a band of evil men," "wild oxen." They are the ones who "divide my clothing and throw dice for my clothes" (v. 18). Is God seen as acting against the one who prays, even indirectly, through the agency of the human attackers? Absolutely not. After having prayed desperately for help, the psalmist breaks into joy and thanksgiving for the fact that he has been heard and rescued by God:

Psalm 22:21b–24

> ²¹ᵇ From the horns of the wild oxen you have rescued me.
> ²² I will tell of your name to my brothers and sisters;
>   in the midst of the congregation I will praise you:
> ²³ You who fear the Lord, praise him!
>   All you offspring of Jacob, glorify him;
>   stand in awe of him, all you offspring of Israel!
> ²⁴ For he did not despise or abhor
>   the affliction of the afflicted;
> he did not hide his face from me,
>   but heard when I cried to him.

This is what the author of Hebrews is referring to when he says:

Hebrews 5:7–8

> ₇When he lived physically on earth, Jesus came to God praying and pleading for help, with loud cries and tears. He knew God was able to save him from death, and his prayers were answered because of his reverence. ₈Even though he was a son, he learned obedience from the things he suffered. ₉And he's been perfected, and has become the source of eternal salvation for all those who obey him.

The author of Hebrews clearly understood Psalm 22 as a prophecy of the suffering and death of Jesus on the cross. He would say unequivocally that the Father was not the tormenter or killer of Jesus when he died on the cross, but his *rescuer*. Paradoxically, the Father rescues Jesus by being with him through his dying, rather than by keeping him from dying. The prophecy of Isa. 57:1–2, which follows on in the context of Isaiah 53 (which we read above), reveals the mystery that God sometimes rescues the faithful through death itself:

Isaiah 57:1–2

> ¹ The righteous perish,
>   and no one takes it to heart;
> the devout are taken away,
>   while no one understands.
> For the righteous are taken away from calamity,
>   ² and they enter into peace;
> those who walk uprightly
>   will rest on their couches.

The same is said of Jesus' followers in the Book of Revelation:

Revelation 14:13

> ₁₃And I heard a voice from heaven, saying, "Write this down: Those who die in the Lord from now on are blessed. Yes, says the Spirit! They're going to be able to rest from their hard work."

As Jesus himself says from the cross in his dying moments, "Father, I am entrusting my spirit into your hands" (Lk. 23:46). This is a quotation from another psalm that is prophetic of Jesus' sufferings on the cross: Psalm 31. As in Psalm 22, the psalmist is facing deadly violence, and fears for his life. There are also moments in which he wrestles in faith with a dread of God's abandonment (vv. 12, 22). But he ends with a sense of triumph:

The End of the Unrepentant

Psalm 31:21–22

> ²¹ Blessed be the Lord,
>   for he has wondrously shown his steadfast love to me
>   when I was beset as a city under siege.
> ²² I had said in my alarm,
>   "I am driven far from your sight."
> But you heard my supplications
>   when I cried out to you for help.

Reading this Psalm as a prophecy of the sufferings of Jesus, it's clear that God the Father is the loving rescuer, not the wrathful organizer and ultimate perpetrator of the violence. Yes, the encounter is predestined, and it is God's will.[50] But that does not imply that God is the one who needed to do violence in order help humanity in its lost state. The control-oriented reading of the sufferings of Christ is precisely inside out. It poses the human problem inside out, and it equally poses the solution inside out. The fundamental problem with humanity is not that it has been rejected by God and stands under God's infinite vindictiveness. As I've shown, it is that humanity has turned to enmity against God, and has become violent and deadly to itself and its world. The control-oriented solution to the problem as it poses it (God's implacable enmity towards humanity) is for Jesus to suffer God's wrath in our place. The biblical solution (to the problem as the Bible poses it: our irrational and violent hatred towards God and the creation) is for Jesus to meet us, and to show us, in the very place of our greatest hatred and deadliness, the proof of his love for us. My claim is that God's intention, in relation to the sufferings of Jesus on the cross, was to break down *our* enmity, not his.

Let's take our study to the New Testament, and see if this is so. John says this of the coming of Jesus into the world:

John 1:10–11

> ₁₀He was in the world, and the world came into being through him, but the world didn't know him. ₁₁He came to his own, and his own didn't accept him.

This passage isn't just about Jesus being rejected by the Jewish people; it's about his rejection by the human race. This is what Peter and John are getting at when they pray the following prayer in the book of Acts:

Acts 4:25–28

> ₂₅You spoke through the mouth of your servant, our ancestor David. Through the Holy Spirit, you said,
> Why were the nations enraged?

---

50. The whole shape of Christ's public life—both his preaching of the Good News of the Kingdom of God and the fact that healing was the centerpiece of his ministry—testifies to the fact that he understood himself to be the predestined Healer Servant of Isa. 52–53. See also Acts 4:27–28, below.

The End of the Unrepentant: Hermeneutical and Theological Conclusion

> Why did the peoples plan foolish things?
> ²⁶Earth's rulers took their stand,
> And the leaders gathered all together,
> Against the Lord G<small>OD</small>, and against his Messiah.[51]
>
> ²⁷And it's true: in this city, Herod and Pontius Pilate got together with the other nations and with the peoples of Israel. They came against your holy Servant Jesus, the One you anointed—₂₈and they did what your hand and your will had foreordained would happen.

Peter and John perceive behind the events of Good Friday a confrontation not just between God and some Jewish leaders, but between God and the whole hostile human race. John the author of Revelation sees this too:

Revelation 1:7

> ⁷Look! He's coming with the clouds,[52]
> And every eye will see him—
> Even the people that pierced him;
> And all the tribes of the earth will cry bitterly[53] over him.[54]

John here sees a universal application of the Old Testament prophecy of Zechariah, who speaks about the day when God saves the city of Jerusalem:

Zechariah 12:9—13:1 (paraphrased)

> ⁹ On that day . . . ¹⁰ I am going to pour out on the house of David and the inhabitants of Jerusalem a spirit of grace, a spirit enabling them to ask for my help. They will look on me, the one they pierced, and they will mourn for me [literally, "him"] like one grieves for a first-born son who has died. ¹¹ That day there will be lots of weeping in Jerusalem . . . ¹² The land will grieve, each family grieving by itself, husbands and wives by themselves, . . . ¹⁴ all the families, all the men, all the women, each and every one, weeping.
> ¹³:¹ On that day a fountain will be made available to the house of David and the inhabitants of Jerusalem: a fountain of cleansing from sin and the stain of wrongdoing.

In Christ, we see God the pierced one, God whose mercy and love drove him to endure being torn by the very ones he loved. That is the good news. The cross itself is the "fountain of cleansing" that God has appointed. It is the place of facing ourselves and the enemies that we have become towards our own Creator. It is the place at which God has chosen to meet us sinners, and to release for us his great power for repentance

---

51. Ps. 2:1–2, 5.
52. Dan. 7:13 || Mt. 24:30; 26:64 || Mk 13:26; 14:62 || Lk. 21:27; 22:69.
53. Lit. "will beat their breasts." See Lk. 23:48.
54. Zech. 12:10, 12, 14.

The End of the Unrepentant

and reconciliation—not just reconciliation to him, but also to one another (see Eph. 2:11–22). John says this:

1 John 4:8–10

$_8$The person that doesn't love doesn't know God, because God *is* love. $_9$This is how God's love has been shown to[55] us: God has sent his only Son into the world, so that we can live through him. $_{10}$This is what love is about:[56] not that we've loved God, but that he loved us, and sent his Son as an offering that makes amends[57] for our sins.

The thing that is worth noticing about this passage, and all similar passages in the New Testament, is that God gives Jesus to us as an amends maker ("propitiation") for our sins, and Jesus does not offer himself to God as a whipping boy or scapegoat. Various NT writers (e.g. the author of Hebrews) say that Jesus offered himself to God, but they say it in such a way that it is clearly not as someone who offers to undergo vicarious punishment or rejection at the hands of God. Hebrews says Jesus underwent vicarious purification and refinement through suffering, in order to flesh out and complete his identification with our need, confirming his flawlessly loving and forgiving nature as High Priest (Heb. 5:8–10). There is not a word in Hebrews about Jesus vicariously experiencing anger or condemning punishment—except from us:

Hebrews 12:2–3

$_2$Let's keep our eyes on Jesus, who's the originator[58] and perfecter of our faith. For the joy that lay ahead of him, he endured the cross. He gave no notice to the shame of it, and has sat down on the right side of God's throne. $_3$Just think about him—how he has endured such hostility from sinners against himself.[59] That way, you won't get tired and give up in your spirits.[60]

The New Testament writers agree that in his dying Jesus offered up the very life of his body, all of himself as a person, in love to God (as we are also commanded to do, Rom. 12:1). And God was infinitely pleased with that offering (see Eph. 5:2: "Christ loved us, and gave himself up for us as a fragrant offering and sacrifice to God"). In obedience, Jesus offered his sufferings at our hands to God as an outpouring of the inmost desire of his heart: that we would be forgiven, healed, reconciled, and saved. In doing this, God called out to God, revealing in shocking public vulnerability his desire for our wholeness and reconciliation.

55. Lit. "among."
56. Lit. "In this is love."
57. Traditionally: "as a propitiation."
58. Or "pioneer," or "champion," or "author."
59. Some early mss have "from people sinning against themselves," which is surprising, but could be what the author actually wrote.
60. Lit. "souls."

The End of the Unrepentant: Hermeneutical and Theological Conclusion

The control-oriented model of Christ's work on the cross characterizes it as a passive absorption of hostility and wrath from God, rather than as his active response in love and forgiveness to hostility and wrath from us. According to that model, Jesus experiences God's wrath and rejection so that we will not experience God's wrath and rejection. Thus it doesn't know what to do with passages such as these, and it leads Christians into deep confusion about their role in the world, by posing an absolute disjunction between Christ's experience and ours. Jesus and the writers of the New Testament, on the other hand, consistently pose a strong *commonality* between his experience and ours. For example, let's listen to Peter encouraging the faithful:

1 Peter 2:19–25

19After all, it's a credit to a person if they endure unfair suffering[61] because of their awareness of God. 20Because how heroic is it, if you do wrong, and you endure it when you get a beating? But if you're doing something good, and you endure suffering for it, that gets credit with God. 21After all, that's what you're called to. Because Christ also suffered for you. He was leaving you an example, for you to follow in his footsteps.

22He did nothing wrong,
And no lie was found in his mouth.[62]

23When he was insulted, he didn't insult anybody back. When he was suffering, he didn't make threats. But he entrusted himself to the One who judges justly. 24He himself carried our sins with his own body[63] on the wood of the cross. He did it so that we could die to our sins and live in integrity.[64] It was by his wounds[65] that you were healed.[66] 25Because you used to be going astray like sheep;[67] but now you've turned back to the shepherd and guardian of your souls.

The wrath-centered understanding of the cross makes absurd Peter's statement that Christ, by suffering on the cross, "was leaving you an example, for you to follow in his footsteps" (v. 21). Are we now to step forward for wrath and punishment from God too? That makes absolutely no sense. Peter also adds later:

---

61. Lit. "the pains of unfair suffering."
62. Isa. 53:9.
63. Isa. 53:4.
64. Traditionally: "righteousness."
65. Or "welt/bruise." The word refers to the wounds from being beaten or whipped.
66. Lit. "by whose bruise/welt you were healed" (Isa. 53:4).
67. Isa. 53:9.

The End of the Unrepentant

1 Peter 4:12-13

> [12] Dear friends, don't be surprised by the trial by fire[68] that's happening to you. It's not as though something strange were happening to you—[13] far from it. As you join in Christ's sufferings, celebrate. That way, you'll also be able to celebrate and be overjoyed at his glorious appearance.

Similarly, Paul says that he wants to know the fellowship of Christ's sufferings, and to become like him in his death (Phil. 3:10), and he also says that in his sufferings at the hands of hostile unbelievers he helps fill up in his flesh the measure of Christ's sufferings (Col. 1:24). *The only way that Peter and Paul can talk this way—and presume a continuity between their sufferings and those of Christ—is if they understand Christ's sufferings in terms of his being rejected and persecuted by the hostile human race.* In this they are simply embracing the clear and insistent teaching of Jesus himself, who warned his followers that they must take up their own cross and follow him.[69] On the night before he died, Jesus explained both why he was going to the cross and why his followers were also going to face deadly persecution:

John 14:18, 25

> [18] If the world hates you, understand that it already hates me first.... But now they've seen me, and they've hated both me and my Father. [25] That way, the saying in their Law gets fulfilled: "They hated me for nothing."[70]

The fundamental problem facing humanity is that it hates God for no reason, and in hating God, it either consciously or unconsciously sets itself against everything associated with God. Jesus died on the cross because he was willing to meet humanity exactly where it was, and to proclaim God's love and forgiveness in that place—the place of humanity's deadly hostility. The good news of God in Jesus Christ is that those who become lost in their hostility to God can be reconciled and turned around to belong again and to love God and their fellow created beings again. As Paul says in Colossians:

Colossians 1:19-22

> [19] It was God's will for all the fullness of the divine to dwell in him, [20] and through him to reconcile all things back to himself. God had made peace with all beings through the blood of Jesus shed on the cross—whether earthly beings or heavenly beings. [21] And once you used to be estranged from God, enemies in your attitude, living in your evil ways. [22] But now you've been reconciled by Christ's physical body, through his death. Christ's goal is to present you in front of God as people who are holy, and free from all blame and accusation.

---

68. This is a metaphor. He's talking about the process of testing the purity of a precious metal by melting it at high heat in a furnace.
69. Mt. 10:38-39; 16:24 || Mk 8:34 || Lk. 9:23; 14:27.
70. Or "for no reason." See Pss. 35:19; 69:4.

The End of the Unrepentant: Hermeneutical and Theological Conclusion

In this understanding of Christ's work on the cross, *we* are the hostile ones, *we* are the ones who need to be reconciled, not God. All our "evil ways" (v. 21) towards our fellow human beings ultimately stem from the fact that we have turned our backs on the love of God. There is therefore no disjunction between Christ's work of reconciling us to God, on the one hand, and Christ's work of reconciling us to one another, on the other hand. There are not two separate problems—God's enmity towards us, and our enmity towards one another. That is why Paul has no problem talking as he does in Ephesians:

Ephesians 2:12–16

> $_{12}$... At that time, you were separated from Christ. You were shut out from the community of Israel, and you were foreigners to God's promised covenants.[71] You had no hope, and you were without God in the world. $_{13}$But now, in Christ Jesus, you're not far away anymore: you've been brought in close by the blood of Christ.[72] $_{14}$Because he himself is our peace! He's the one who has made the two into one. And he's broken down the dividing wall, the hostility, in his own flesh. $_{15}$He has abolished the law of commands and rules, in order to create, from the two, one new human being in himself. He made the peace! $_{16}$And he reconciled the two, in one body, to God through the cross. He had put their hostility to death on the cross![73]

Paul's explanation of his role in the ministry of the gospel in 2 Corinthians confirms this:

2 Corinthians 5:14–20

> $_{14}$Christ's love compels us, when we conclude that One died on behalf of everyone. That implies that everybody died.[74] $_{15}$And when he died for everyone, it was so that those who live would not live for themselves anymore, but for the One who died and rose on their behalf. . . . $_{17}$The conclusion is that if somebody's in Christ, they're a new creation. The old is gone; now the new has come. $_{18}$And it's all from God, who reconciled us to himself through Christ. And he has given us the ministry of reconciliation. $_{19}$Just as God was in Christ, reconciling the world himself—not counting their offenses against them—so he has also put the message of reconciliation in us. $_{20}$So we're ambassadors on Christ's behalf. It's as though God were pleading through us, when we ask on behalf of Christ: come back[75] to God!

---

71. Lit. "foreigners to the covenants of the promise."

72. Lit. "But now, in Christ Jesus, you who were once far away have been brought near by the blood of Christ."

73. Or "in himself."

74. In other words, Christ died everybody's death for them, so now they're counted as dead. Paul is going to develop this idea at some length in his letter to the community at Rome (see Rom. 5:12—6:14; 7:1–6), which he may have written only a few weeks after he wrote this.

75. Lit. "be reconciled."

The End of the Unrepentant

The party to be reconciled here is *us,* not God. God is the one who, through Christ, is reaching out to reconcile *us.* Ah, well, someone will ask, Haven't you just stopped short of the part that proves that Jesus had to experience God's rejection on the cross for us? Let's look and see.

2 Corinthians 5:21

> 21 God appointed the One who never sinned
> To be sin [or: a sin offering] on our behalf,
> So that in him
> We could come to embody God's righteousness.

It makes neither biblical nor theological sense to try to take this verse as saying something to the effect that God looked at Jesus and saw nothing but our sins. What God the Father saw, when he looked upon Jesus in his sufferings on the cross, was a pleasing "fragrant offering" (Eph. 5:2). He saw his precious Son offering up, in perfect purity and obedience, the priceless gift of his own lifeblood on our behalf (Heb. 5:7; 9:11–14). Jesus was received as acceptable on our behalf; he was not rejected as unacceptable in our place. If this is so, then what are we to make of the idea that God appointed him "to be sin"? The answer is that Paul is being poetic here, and is creating a wordplay based on the Suffering Servant poem of Isaiah 53, in which it is prophesied,

Isaiah 53:10–11

> ¹⁰ Yet the LORD was pleased with his wounded one,
>   whom he had made to suffer.[76]
> When you[77] make his life an offering for sin,
>   he shall see his offspring, and shall prolong his days;
> through him the will of the LORD shall prosper.
> ¹¹ Out of his anguish he shall see light;
>   he shall find satisfaction through his knowledge.
> The righteous one, my servant, shall make many righteous,
>   and he shall bear their iniquities.

In this verse the English words "offering for sin" translate the single Hebrew word *'asham,*[78] which, just like the Hebrew word *chatta'ah,*[79] can mean both "sin" and "an

---

76. NRSV renders this as "Yet it was the will of the Lord to crush him with pain." See the earlier nt. on Isa. 53:10.

77. Note that this is *plural,* indicating that *the readers* are the ones who have, by murdering the Servant, turned his life into a sin offering.

78. Strong's #H817.

79. Strong's #H2401; see also the synonym *chatta'at,* #H2403 (#H2402 is the equivalent word in Aramaic). Paul writes in Greek, and in the LXX, the Greek version of the OT, the phrase *peri hamartias* (lit. "in reference to sin") is most often used to translate the Hebrew words *chatta'ah* and *chatta'at.* There are, however, a number of instances where the single word *hamartia,* by itself, means "an/the offering for sin" (e.g. Lev. 4:8, 20, 21, 24, 25, 29, 33, 34; 6:17, 25 [2x], 30; 7:7 LXX).

The End of the Unrepentant: Hermeneutical and Theological Conclusion

offering for sin."[80] This meaning for Paul's words in 2 Cor. 5:21 not only makes perfect sense in and of itself, but it also coheres completely with Paul's perspective on the death of Christ elsewhere (e.g. Rom. 8:1–3; cf. Heb. 7:27; 9:28; 10:8–10, 14–16). God appointed Christ to be a sin offering on our behalf in order that we might be drawn back into right relationship with God and become righteous by the Holy Spirit's work of renewal and cleansing.

It might surprise the reader to learn that the instructions for the presentation of sin offerings in the book of Leviticus specify that it is *those who have sinned* who bring forward and slay the offering that will make amends for their sin (read Leviticus 4). Jesus knew, and God knew, that we *were unable* to turn from our own attitude of sin and hostility towards God. Therefore Jesus paradoxically conducted us through the process of offering amends by humbly putting himself, our own sin offering, in our hands to be slain (Isa. 53:7, 12). In saying this, I'm certainly not implying that God and Jesus maneuvered humanity into harming Jesus so that God could harm Jesus on our behalf. On the contrary, God appointed Jesus to represent God to us in complete transparency and honesty. Knowing our hostility, God foreordained and appointed Jesus to be the sin offering who, by dying at our hands, would singlehandedly open our way back to right relationship with God.

What, then, about the passage where God sees Jesus hanging on the cross and looks on him as a curse in our place? Let's read it.

Galatians 3:10, 13

> [10] After all, those who operate on the basis of doing what the Law requires are under a curse. Because scripture says:[81]
>
> > Everyone who doesn't hold to all the things written in the book of the Law, by doing them,[82] will be under a curse.[83]
>
> . . .
>
> [13] Christ has paid the price to set us free from the curse of the Law. He became a curse for us, for the scripture says,[84] "Everyone hung on a stake[85] is cursed."

When Paul says that Jesus "became a curse for us," is he saying that *God* cursed him? And is he thus implicitly saying that God *rejected* Christ instead of us? Looking at the scriptural background of Paul's statement will make clear that he's not saying either of those things. Let's have a look at the passage in Deuteronomy that Paul is quoting:

---

80. Out of some 61 occurrences of the word *'asham/'ashmah* in the Hebrew OT, the majority (approx. 36) refer to "an offering for sin," and only the minority refer to "sin."

81. Lit. "For it is written"—the standard way of citing Scripture.

82. Lit. "to do them."

83. Deut. 27:26.

84. Lit. "Because it is written."

85. Or "on a tree" (see Deut. 21:23). For the Hebrews, execution by hanging on a stake or from a tree was the most disgraceful manner of death.

The End of the Unrepentant

Deuteronomy 21:22–23 (NJPS Version)[86]

> [22] If a man is guilty of a capital offense and is put to death, and you impale him on a stake, [23] you must not let his corpse remain on the stake overnight, but must bury him the same day. For an impaled body is an affront to God:[87] you shall not defile the land that the LORD your God is giving you to possess.

First, what is a curse? In Deuteronomy, a curse is something horrible that can happen to a person or group, and by extension, a verbal threat that something horrible is going to happen. Thus, to *become* a curse means that you become a textbook example of a person who experiences horrible circumstances. To "be a curse," in other words, is to find yourself in more or less in the worst possible situation.[88] For example, note this prophecy of Jeremiah:

Jeremiah 24:9

> [9] I will make them a horror, an evil thing, to all the kingdoms of the earth—a disgrace, a byword, a taunt, and a curse in all the places where I shall drive them.

You *become* a curse when you embody a human experience so awful that your case immediately comes to mind when someone wants to wish a bad fate on somebody: "May you end up like so-and-so!"

According to the book of Deuteronomy, the entire Jewish community bound itself under a wide array of horrible consequences (i.e. curses) that they agreed would come down on them if they did not keep the whole Law (see Deut. 27:9—28:60). A great deal of what Paul is saying in Galatians 3 is that Jesus purchased the freedom of those who had been subject to all of these curses—because no one actually succeeds in keeping the whole Law. Jesus, in dying on the cross, put paid to the entire weight of the Deuteronomic curses for Jewish believers. Why, then, implies Paul, would you Galatians, who are Gentiles, be foolish enough to go backwards and put yourselves under the Law, and so subject yourselves to curses that even the Jews could not avoid by their own efforts?

This, I believe, is the application that Paul intends to make of Deut. 21:22–23, which he quotes in Gal. 3:13. According to this text, a criminal is not to be left hanging on a tree overnight, because such a person is "a curse to God." It is important to understand that this is not at all the same thing as being cursed *by* God. There is not some mysterious rule in the universe that says that you have to be cursed by God if ever God should see you hung on a tree. God is not the sort who enjoys adding insult to injury. Moreover, in what way would the alleged cursing by God here make it inappropriate for the person's

---

86. New Jewish Publication Society translation of the Tanach (the Hebrew Bible), available online at http://www.taggedtanach.org.

87. Lit. "a curse to God." NRSV overtranslates the Hebrew phrase *qilelat 'elohīm* as "accursed by God." For the word translated here as "an affront" (NJPS, above) and as "accursed" (NRSV), see Strong's #H7045, *qelalah*.

88. See Isa. 65:15; Jer. 24:9; 25:18; 26:6; 29:18–22; 42:18; 44:8, 12, 22; 49:13.

The End of the Unrepentant: Hermeneutical and Theological Conclusion

corpse to remain hanging overnight? That entire line of thinking has simply wandered down the wrong path.

The point of Deut. 21:22–23 is that God regards being killed and having your dead body hung up for public derision as being the worst possible state of degradation and humiliation. It is a dehumanizing fate, a fate beyond all bounds of human decency. It is a totally *accursed* thing to have happen to you. God commands, therefore, that no one's corpse is to be left hanging overnight, because to do so would be an insult to the inherent dignity of the person as a human being, a dignity which is not forfeited, and which is not to be denied, even if a person has committed a capital offense. Such an insult to the dignity of an executed individual becomes an insult to God, to the community as a whole, and, indeed, an injury to the dignity of the land itself: "You shall not defile the land that the LORD your God is giving you to possess" (v. 23).

In view of this background, let us return and have a look at Paul's statement again:

Galatians 3:13

₁₃Christ has paid the price to set us free from the curse of the Law. He became a curse for us, for the scripture says, "Everyone hung on a stake is cursed."

What did Jesus Christ experience on the cross? Was it God's displeasure? Was it God's rejection, God's punishment, God's hostility, God's "curse"? Neither Paul nor any other New Testament author ever says these things. In Gal. 3:13 Paul is saying that in his crucifixion, Jesus faced the worst, the most cursed, experience that human beings are capable of forcing on each other. For the crime of living out his total, passionate love towards us, he was executed in total disgrace. Beaten and spat upon for much of the night, then stripped naked and nailed to a cross with iron spikes, he was hung up publicly to die amidst insults and sneering (see Mt. 27:39; Mk 15:26). Jesus our Savior experienced the ultimate form of degradation that is possible to suffer at the hands of other human beings, *because he was determined to continue proving out his love to us no matter what we did to him.* The Gospels tell us that Jesus had sensed all along that he was destined to be rejected, mistreated and killed, yet he went forward and willingly gave up every last ounce of his dignity and power and submitted to the experience of being "a curse" for us. It was not the Father that cursed Jesus and subjected him to "being a curse"; it was we ourselves.

This is the mystery of the good news: not that God turned his alleged hatred for us against Jesus Christ, but that God, in Jesus Christ, turned his love towards us, even as we were acting out against him the worst possible form of the hatred that had split us off from him and all creation in the first place. This is the triumph of Jesus Christ, the Suffering Servant who wins by surrendering, who gains all by giving up all.

THE PROMISE: THE REDEMPTION OF THE WHOLE CREATION

How, then, did Jesus Christ solve our deadly problem? He did it by meeting us where we were and overcoming our hatred with his love. He reconciled us to himself at the cost

The End of the Unrepentant

of his own life. At the same time, he also sovereignly paid all our unpaid and unpayable bills—our debts to God, and our debts to our fellow created beings.

Colossians 2:13–15

₁₃When you were all dead in your offenses, and the uncircumcision of your flesh, God brought you[89] to life together with Christ. He has forgiven us all our offenses. ₁₄He has cancelled[90] the statement of unpaid debt that was against us and hostile to us, and has publicly taken it away and nailed it to the cross. ₁₅In that way, he has publicly disarmed the spiritual rulers and authorities, and has paraded them as defeated enemies[91] through Christ.[92]

According to the apostle Paul, God has done even more than this. He has reconciled *every being in the universe* to himself:

Colossians 1:19–22

₁₉Because it was God's will for all the fullness of the divine to dwell in Jesus Christ, ₂₀and through him to reconcile all things back to God. God had made peace with all beings through the blood of Jesus shed on the cross—whether earthly beings or heavenly beings.[93] ₂₁And once *you* used to be estranged from God, enemies in your attitude, living in your evil ways. ₂₂But now you've been reconciled[94] by Christ's physical body, through his death.

When this work of reconciliation is fully accomplished, God will be able, through Christ, to re-empower the whole creation, which had been trimmed back to a fraction of its potential aliveness:

Romans 8:18–24a

₁₈In my opinion, our current sufferings can't even be compared with the glory that's about to be revealed to us. ₁₉Because the creation is really yearning for[95] the children of God to be revealed. ₂₀After all, when the creation was subjected to human folly,[96] it certainly wasn't because it wanted to be. No, God subjected it[97] in hope—₂₁that the creation itself will be set free from slavery to decay, into

---

89. Some mss have "us."
90. Or "erased."
91. Or "publicly humiliated them," or "triumphed over them."
92. Or "by the cross."
93. Lit. "whether the things on the earth or the things in the heavens." Many mss have, "Through him [or "it," i.e., the cross], whether the things on the earth or the things in the heavens."
94. Many mss have "But now God has reconciled you."
95. Lit. "For the earnest expectation of the creation is looking forward to."
96. "Human foolishness": or "vanity," "emptiness," or "foolishness."
97. Lit. " . . . by its own will, but by the will of the One who subjected it."

The End of the Unrepentant: Hermeneutical and Theological Conclusion

the freedom of the glory of the children of God. ₂₂We know that the whole creation is groaning together, and going through labor pains together, right up to this moment. ₂₃And not only that: those of us who have the first harvest⁹⁸ of the Spirit groan within ourselves too. We're looking forward to our adoption, to the setting free⁹⁹ of our bodies. ₂₄We're saved in hope!

According to Paul, our redemption is part of a creation-wide process. God is not saving us and tossing out the rest of the created world; God is saving us within and together with our world. That's why it says,

Revelation 21:1–5

₁And I saw a renewed heaven, and a renewed earth: the first heaven and the first earth had gone away, and the sea wasn't there anymore. ₂And I saw the New Jerusalem coming down out of heaven from God. . . . And I heard a loud voice from the throne saying, "Look! God's home¹⁰⁰ is with humanity, and he's going to live with them . . . and he's going to wipe away every tear from their eyes . . . ₅And the One sitting on the throne said, "Look! I'm making everything new!"

John's vision pictures the fulfillment of the promise of God in Isaiah (65:17–25; 66:22). This world, this beautiful, "very good" world (Gen. 1:31), which God breathed into being in the beginning, will be free to revel in the unending and God-filled life that is its birthright. And the redeemed of humanity will be its loving, priestly custodians as God intended, no longer its wanton destroyers (Rev. 22:1–5; cf. Mt. 19:28; 2 Pet. 3:3–13; Isa. 24:4–6; Rev. 11:18).

This is the biblical picture of the positive "end" for the redeemed of humanity. It is not a coincidence that those who opt for the control-oriented paradigm typically cannot see these very words on the page of Scripture. Most of them take it for granted that the achievement of human salvation will render the physical world irrelevant. In defiance of what the scriptures teach, they assume that the redeemed will go off to heaven, there to gaze at God in rapt adoration for all eternity.¹⁰¹ They are like children in their belief that

---

98. Lit. "the firstfruits," i.e., the early harvest that was celebrated in the Jewish Festival of Booths.

99. Lit. "redemption." Paul's metaphor is that our bodies are in bondage to mortality, and that they are some day going to be purchased into freedom.

100. Lit. "tent," implying an intimate presence.

101. See, e.g., (1) The Heidelberg Catechism, 1563, answer to Question 52: "He will cast all His and my enemies into everlasting condemnation, but He will take me and all His chosen ones to Himself into heavenly joy and glory." (2) The Westminster Confession of Faith, 1646, article XXXII paras. I, II, and III, which appear to say that the souls of the redeemed will go to the highest heaven after they die, and the souls of the damned will immediately go to hell, after which, at the general resurrection, bodies of each class will go to be united with their souls in whatever location they are—the redeemed in heaven, the damned in hell. (3) The Westminster Larger Catechism, 1647, makes explicit what is implicit in the Confession (Answer to Question 90): "At the day of judgment, the righteous, being caught up to Christ in the clouds, shall be set on his right hand, and there openly acknowledged and acquitted, shall join with him in the judging of reprobate angels and men, and shall be received into heaven, where they shall be fully and forever freed from all sin and misery; filled with inconceivable joys, made perfectly holy and

The End of the Unrepentant

the whole universe revolves around them. To them, the rest of creation is redundant, disposable, like a paper cup. They have no interest in a new creation, because to them the physical world is simply an elaborate theatrical set—props and scenery for the great play between themselves and their Master God, upon whom they project their infantile craving to have their way without limitation and to be the center of all attention. If you have been confused and made uneasy by such a worldview, this book is for you, and the Scriptures are for you. Read them afresh, and be refreshed. The Gospel really is Good News.

Concluding Remarks

I could, of course, go on from here to spend many pages talking about the bodily resurrection and exaltation of Jesus, the infilling and renewal of the Holy Spirit, the fellowship of Christian believers, and the various ministries of the Good News in this age. But none of that is urgent to discuss in *this* book. What is important to me is to have shown that the most central New Testament interpretations of the saving work of Jesus on the cross make far better sense when viewed through the paradigm of God who is pure and perfect love than through the paradigm of God as the infinitely controlling and vindictive tyrant.[102] There is a reason why I have been unwilling to capitulate to the notion that God intends to torment people forever, and that reason is not that I prefer to cozy up to God's loving side, rather than stand in reverent fear of his just and holy side. It's because God has but one side, *love*, and his justice, his holiness, and even his wrath itself, are all expressions of his love.

Don't get me wrong. In my theology, there certainly is something to be afraid of. Jesus and the apostles of the New Testament tell me that I was created with the potential to live forever as a child of God in harmony and mutual service within a creation absolutely full of life. My first introduction to the life of God is through a frail and mortal bodily life. The greatest thing to fear is that, ignoring the infinitely valuable gift of everlasting life ahead of me, I would spend my short days gathering around me the petty objects, powers, and pleasures of this passing world, and that I would close my heart to

---

happy both in body and soul, in the company of innumerable saints and holy angels, but especially in the immediate vision and fruition of God the Father, of our Lord Jesus Christ, and of the Holy Spirit, to all eternity." (4) The New Hampshire Baptist Confession, 1833, Article 18. Of the World to Come: "We believe that the end of the world is approaching; that at the last day Christ will descend from heaven, and raise the dead from the grave to final retribution; that a solemn separation will then take place; that the wicked will be adjudged to endless punishment, and the righteous to endless joy; and that this judgment will fix forever the final state of men in heaven or hell, on principles of righteousness." (5) Faith and Message Statement of the (USA) Southern Baptist Convention, 2000, Article X. Last Things: "God, in His own time and in His own way, will bring the world to its appropriate end. According to His promise, Jesus Christ will return personally and visibly in glory to the earth; the dead will be raised; and Christ will judge all men in righteousness. The unrighteous will be consigned to Hell, the place of everlasting punishment. The righteous in their resurrected and glorified bodies will receive their reward and will dwell forever in Heaven with the Lord."

102. For more of my theology, see the essays at http://www.simplegospel.net. For a thoroughgoing biblical critique of the wrath-oriented model of the atonement, see http://www.simplegospel.net/Calvin-Critique.htm.

The End of the Unrepentant: Hermeneutical and Theological Conclusion

the crying need of my fellow human beings. The greatest thing to dread would be to miss the entire point of existence, and squander the gift of everlasting life in petty self-serving.

I'm persuaded that the horrific images in the Bible are trying to warn us that the tragedy of a lost eternal life is greater than we can ever imagine. But to turn these images into a theology of an infinitely vindictive God is to sell your birthright and trade the infinitely good news of the God of love, grace, and justice for the idea of a petty tyrant who never tires of tormenting those with whom he is displeased. We need to rethink our theology and the good news of Jesus Christ from the ground up if this is what we've been taught. After all, there can hardly be a more grotesque theological idea than that of a creator who brings beings into existence with the intention of letting them live for a fleeting moment[103] and then tormenting them utterly without end. In the name of all Christian decency, *that has to be wrong.*

The wrath of God is real. Beings that God creates are absolutely accountable to him for how they conduct themselves within the frame of existence that he grants them. This goes for human beings, angels, and any other kinds of beings that God creates. In no sense do I believe in a sleepy, laissez-faire deity whose philosophy is "whatever." The Bible affirms many times and in many places that God is profoundly patient, forgiving, and generous in offering chances for the sinner to start anew. What it does *not* say is that God's patience will never run out. God's infinite love, informed by God's infinite wisdom, determines a point, for each individual, and for the human race as a whole, when it is no longer loving and just to continue renewing the lease on the life of the unrepentant. Perhaps the single most foolhardy thing that a created being can do is gamble its invitation to eternal life in order to gain a few moments of pleasure, security, or ease in this mortal life. Those who lose such a gamble will not simply wink out like a person who trips under a bus. My reading of the Scriptures convinces me that God has an agreement with all of his creatures that such beings will first have to realize two things: the damage that they have done, and the literally infinite beauty and goodness that they have irrevocably thrown away. "Weeping and gnashing of teeth" doesn't even begin to evoke the horror of such a realization. In the face of this kind of threat, what kind of a Christian would feel they needed a worse fate with which to frighten themselves and others?

---

103. For the extreme brevity of mortal life, see Job 7:6–7; 14:1–2; Pss. 37:2; 39:5; 90:5–7; 103:15–16; 144:4; Isa. 40:6–8; 51:12; Jas 1:10–11; 4:14; 1 Pet. 1:24.

Appendix

Passages That Refer to Fire or Being Consumed, Organized by Recurring Themes

Theme 1. Instantness (20 passages). Gen. 19:12–29; Num. 16:23–35; Ps. 11:5-6; 2 Kgs 1:9–15; Isa. 26:10–11; 47:14–15; Ezek. 21:28, 31–32; Dan. 7:9–14; Amos 5:6; Mt. 13:47–50; Lk. 17:28–30; 2 Thess. 1:7–8; Heb. 10:27; Jas 5:1–5; 2 Pet. 2:3b–12; 3:3–12; Jude 5–7; Rev. 18:8–21; 19:19–21; 20:7–10

Theme 2. Completeness (55 passages). Gen. 19:12–29; Num. 16:23–35; Deut. 28:26; 29:19–28; 1 Kgs 14:10; 2 Kgs 1:9–15; 2 Kgs 22:16–17; 2 Chron. 34:25; Pss. 11:5-6; 21:8–11; Isa. 1:28; 26:10–11; 33:11–12; 33:14; 34:9–10; 47:14–15; 51:6–8; 66:14–16; 66:22–24; Jer. 4:4; 7:20; 17:27; 34:22; Lam. 4:11; Ezek. 15:1–8; 20:47; 21:28, 31–32; 28:18–19; 37:21–28; 38:8; Dan. 7:9–14; Amos 5:6; Obad. 18; Zeph. 1:18; 3:8; Mal. 4:1–3; Mt. 5:29–30; 7:19; 10:28; 13:47–50; 18:8–9; Mk 9:43–48; Lk. 12:4–5; Jn 15:6; 2 Thess. 1:7–8; Heb. 6:4–8; 10:27; 12:25–29; 2 Pet. 2:3b–12; 3:3–12; Jude 5–7; Rev. 17:16; 18:8–21; 19:19–21; 20:7–10; 20:11–15

Theme 3. Irrevocability (42 passages). Gen. 19:12–29; Deut. 28:26; 29:19–28; 2 Kgs 22:16–17; 2 Chron. 34:25; Ps. 21:8–11; Isa. 47:14–15; 51:6–8; 65:11–15; 66:22–24; Jer. 4:4; 17:27; 34:22; 37:8, 10; Ezek. 15:1–8; 20:47; 21:28, 31–32; 28:18–19; 37:21–28; 38:8; Amos 5:6; Mt. 3:8–12; 5:29–30; 7:19; 10:28; 13:24–30, 36–43; 13:47–50; 18:8–9; Mk 9:43–48; Lk. 3:7–9; 12:4–5; 17:28–30; Jn 15:6; 2 Thess. 1:7–8; Heb. 6:4–8; 2 Pet. 2:3b–12; 3:3–12; Rev. 17:16; 18:8–21; 19:3; 19:19–21; 20:7–10; 20:11–15

Theme 4. Permanence (27 passages). Gen. 19:12–29; Deut. 29:19–28; Ps. 21:8–11; Isa. 34:9–10; 66:22–24; Ezek. 21:28, 31–32; 28:18–19; 37:21–28; 38:8; Dan. 7:9–14; Mt. 3:8–12; 5:29–30; 7:19; 13:24–30, 36–43; 13:47–50; 18:8–9; Mk 9:43–48; Lk. 3:7–9; 17:28–30; Jn 15:6; 2 Thess. 1:7–8; Heb. 6:4–8; Jude 5–7; 18:8–21; 19:3; 19:19–21; 20:7–10; 20:11–15

Theme 5. Finality (29 passages). Gen. 19:12–29; 1 Kgs 14:10; Isa. 34:9–10; 66:22–24; Jer. 4:4; 17:4; Ezek. 28:18–19; 37:21–28; 38:8; Dan. 7:9–14; Zeph. 1:18; Mt. 3:8–12; Mt. 5:29–30; Mt. 13:24–30, 36–43; Mt. 13:47–50; Mt. 18:8–9; Mk 9:43–48; Lk. 3:7–9; 17:28–30; Jn

The End of the Unrepentant

15:6; 2 Thess. 1:7–8; Heb. 6:4–8; 12:25–29; 2 Pet. 2:3b–12; Jude 5–7; Rev. 18:8–21; 19:3; 19:19–21; 20:7–10; 20:11–15

Theme 6. The Disposal of Trash or Waste (23 passages). 1 Kgs 14:10; Isa. 33:11–12; 34:2–3; 47:14–15; 50:9; 51:6–8; 66:22–24; Ezek. 15:1–8; Dan. 7:9–14; Obad. 18; Mal. 4:1–3; Mt. 3:8–12; 5:29–30; 7:19; 13:24–30, 36–43; 13:47–50; 18:8–9; Mk 9:43–48; Lk. 3:7–9; 12:4–5; Jn 15:6; Heb. 6:4–8

Theme 7. The Unpreventable or Unstoppable Nature of the Destruction (36 passages). Num. 16:23–35; Deut. 28:26; 29:19–28; 2 Kgs 1:9–15; 22:16–17; 2 Chron. 34:25; Isa. 47:14–15; 50:11; 51:6–8; 66:22–24; Jer. 4:4; 7:20; 15:14; 17:27; 34:22; 37:8, 10; Ezek. 15:1–8; 20:47; 21:28, 31–32; 37:21–28; 38:8; Amos 5:6; Mt. 3:8–12; 10:28; 13:47–50; 18:8–9; 18:21–35; Mk 9:43–48; Lk. 3:7–9; 12:4–5; 17:28–30; 2 Thess. 1:7–8; Jas 3:5–6; 2 Pet. 3:3–12; Jude 5–7; Rev. 19:19–21; 20:7–10

Theme 8. The Impermanence of Human Life (16 passages). Isa. 50:9; 51:6–8; 51:12; 66:22–24; Mal. 4:1–3; Mt. 3:8–12; 5:29–30; 13:24–30, 36–43; 18:8–9; Mk 9:43–48; Lk. 3:7–9; 2 Thess. 1:7–8; Heb. 12:25–29; Jas 5:1–5; 2 Pet. 3:3–12; Rev. 20:11–15

Theme 9. Anguish (6 passages). Isa. 50:11; 65:11–15; Ezek. 30:14–16; Mt. 13:47–50; Lk. 16:19–31; Rev. 18:8–21

Scripture Index

OLD TESTAMENT

Genesis

Ref	Pages
1–3	181
1–2	218
1	5
1:2	93
1:6–10	172
1:26–28	110, 211, 218
1:29	218
1:30	218
1:31	218, 247
2–3	216
2:4–9	72
2:6	72
2:8	213, 218
2:9	72, 218
2:12	72
2:15	110, 213
2:16	218
2:17	214
2:24	144
3	159, 213, 217, 218
3:4	213
3:5	213
3:14–15	217
3:16	217
3:17–18	65
3:18	217
3:19	217
3:22–24	217
3:23	218
3:25	110
4:1–10	218
4:23–24	219
5	219
5:1–3	212
6–7	71
6:1—7:24	95
6:1–4	49
6:5–13	107
6:5–6	227
6:7	97
6:11–13	107, 219, 227
6:13	219
7	172
7:11	172
8	172
8:21—9:17	107
8:21–22	108
12:1–3	227
12:1–2	228
15:5–6	227
18:20–21	61
19	7, 12, 13
19:1–29	61, 72
19:2–28	79
19:4–25	73
19:12–29	9
19:24–28	9
21:8–19	227
25:29–34	81, 227
25:32	81
27:1–38	227
27:41–42	228
28:10–17	227
31:19–21	228
31:19	227
31:35	227
34:1–31	227, 228
35:9–13	227
37:1–20	228
38:12–16	228

Exodus

Ref	Pages
3:2	228
20:13	36
25–27	177
25:10–22	170
25:22	179
28:35	222
28:43	222
32:32–33	144
33:19	181
34:6–7	181
34:6	226
40:34–38	177

Leviticus

Ref	Pages
4:8	242
4:20	242
4:21	242
4:24	242
4:25	242
4:29	242
4:33	242
4:34	242
6:17	242
6:25	242
6:30	242
7:7	242
16:2	222
26:11	177
26:16	123

Numbers

Ref	Pages
4:15	222
4:19	222
4:20	222
16	12
16:1–35	95
16:1–3	9
16:1–22	9
16:16–17	9
16:23–35	9
18:32	222

253

Scripture Index

Deuteronomy

4:24	67
5:17	36
9:3	67
16:19	224
21:22–23	244, 245
21:23	243, 245
27–30	97
27:26	243
28:1–14	11
28:16–68	11
28:20	11
28:23	11
28:26	8, 10
28:27	11
29	12
29:19–28	10
32:35	66
32:36	66

Joshua

7:19	78

1 Samuel

4:4	179

2 Samuel

7:14	94, 178
13	215, 216

1 Kings

4:25	133
5–8	177
8:1	170
8:6	170
10:1–10	151
14:10	7, 8, 11
17:17–24	122

2 Kings

1:9–15	11, 12
1:10–14	7, 90
1:10	89, 162, 168
4:8–37	122
13:20–21	122
19:26	38
22:16–17	7, 8, 12
22:16	12
22:17	12
23:10	36

2 Chronicles

5:7	170
6:18	177
6:36–39	97
7:1–3	177
9:1–12	151
22:1	162, 176
34:25	8, 12

Job

1:6—2:8	49, 51
3:8	116
7:6–7	249
14:1–2	249
14:10–15	122
34:19	224
35:15	123
38:16	172
41:1–9	116
41:31–32	93

Psalms

1:5	151, 152, 237
2	98–101, 105, 137, 146
2:1–2	237
2:2–4	105
2:2	99
2:5–22	105
2:9–11	136
7:15	211
8:3–4	61
8:6	183
9:15	211
11	105
11:1–10	105
11:4	105
11:5–6	13
11:6–9	105
11:6	7, 13
11:9–10	105
16:8–11	122
17:15	122
21:10	13
21:8–11	13, 14
21:9	13
22	137, 233, 235
22:1–2	233
22:6–7	234
22:11–13	234
22:18	234
22:19–21	234
22:21–24	234
22:21	99
22:25–31	99
22:26–28	99
22:26	99
22:27–29	103
22:29	99
23:1–2	174
24:8	145
28:1	51
30:3	51
31	235
31:12	235
31:21–22	236
31:22	235
35:19	240
36:9	94, 178
37:2	38, 249
37:14–15	211
39:5	249
46	100, 101, 137
46:2–3	100, 103, 136, 168
46:5	100
46:6–7	103, 168
46:6–6	100
46:6	136
46:8–11	100
46:8	100
46:9	104
46:10	100, 101
47	129, 137
47:3	101
47:8	101
47:9	101
47:10	101
49:14–15	122
57:6	211
59:5	123
69:4	240
69:28	144
73:21–26	122
78:68	176
80:1	179

Scripture Index

Psalms (cont.)

82	48–50, 117
82:1–7	49
82:1	49
82:5	49
82:6	49
82:7	49
82:8	49, 103
87:2	176
88:4–6	51
89:32	123
90:4	70, 162
90:5–7	249
90:5–6	38
92:7	38
94:1–11	103
94:16	151
94:20–3	103
96	101, 103, 137
96:10–13	101
96:11–13	103
96:13	103
97	102, 137
97:1–5	102, 168
97:1	102
97:2	102
97:3–5	136
97:3	102, 136
97:4–5	102
97:5	103
97:10–12	102
97:10–11	102
97:10–1	103
98	102, 103, 137
98:1–3	103
98:4	103
98:7–9	103
98:9	103
99:1	179
102:26	17
103:15–16	249
103:15	38
104:6	93, 172
110	99, 105, 127
110:2	99
110:5–6	99
112:9–10	40
122:6	176
129:6	38
135:6	172
135:14	66
141:10	211
143:7	51
144:4	249
145:7–9	148
145:9	181, 212

Proverbs

1:12	51
3:20	172
8:24	172
8:27–28	172
25:22	196
26:27	211

Ecclesiastes

3:11	96

Isaiah

1:28	13
2	104, 137
2:1–4	104
2:1	146
2:2–4	133
2:2	69
2:5–22	104
2:10–22	64
2:10–12	104
2:10	62, 64, 136, 169
2:12	104
2:19	62, 64, 169
2:20	104
2:21	62, 64, 169
2:22	64, 208
5:1–7	116
5:16	223
6:24	198
10:12	123
11	137, 146
11:4	136
11:9	222
13:10	138
14	50, 110
14:3–21	49
14:4–20	117
14:5–20	110
14:9–15	159, 160
14:13–14	50
14:14–20	50
14:15	51, 53
14:16–19	50
14:18–20	10
14:19	51
24–27	3, 90, 106, 107, 116, 118, 127, 137, 156, 161, 165, 167, 173, 193, 195, 198, 199, 201, 202, 204
24	51, 107, 173, 181, 200, 227
24:1—27:5	51, 159
24:1–20	86
24:1–6	51, 196
24:1–2	106
24:1	107, 136
24:2	107
24:3–6	136, 168
24:3	107
24:4–6	107, 117, 247
24:5	107
24:6	51, 107, 108, 110
24:7–12	108
24:11	108
24:13	108, 110, 196
24:14–23	88
24:14–16	109
24:14–15	40
24:16–18	109
24:16	136
24:17–22	196
24:17–20	51, 117, 134, 196
24:18–20	109, 110, 136, 168
24:21—25:9	181
24:21–23	50, 51, 55, 77, 110, 117, 159, 193, 194, 199
24:21–22	51, 110, 114, 136, 161, 162, 166, 194, 196
24:21	51, 52, 123, 159
24:22	49, 58
24:23—25:10	140
24:23	52, 55, 109, 117, 136, 161
25	40
25:1–5	110, 111
25:4–5	136

Scripture Index

Isaiah (cont.)

Reference	Pages
25:6–10	52, 91, 93, 111, 177
25:6–9	161
25:6–8	117
25:6	111, 161
25:7–8	106
25:8	111, 115, 174, 177, 180
25:9	111
25:10–12	112
25:10	111
26	106, 136, 162
26:1–3	112
26:2–6	117
26:2	117
26:4–6	112, 113
26:7–9	113, 117
26:10—27:5	194
26:10–12	197
26:10–11	14, 91, 113, 118, 127, 163, 166, 171, 198
26:10	91, 115
26:11–12	119
26:11	66, 89, 113, 115–17, 120, 166
26:12–13	114
26:13–19	156
26:13–14	161
26:13	156
26:14	114, 123, 156, 173, 193, 196
26:15	114
26:16–19	117, 161
26:16–18	136
26:16–17	114
26:16	173
26:17–19	115
26:18	156
26:19	106, 156
26:20—27:5	167
26:20—27:1	91
26:20–21	115, 120, 168, 197, 198
26:20	116, 117
26:21	70
27:1–5	163, 171, 197, 198
27:1	116, 117, 123
27:2–6	118
27:2–5	116, 127
27:3	116
27:4–5	116, 182
27:4	117
27:6	116
29:6	123
30	87
30:33	36, 87, 88
33	15
33:11–12	14
33:14	14, 15, 67
34–35	127
34	8, 21, 79, 80, 85, 205
34:1–5	80
34:1	80
34:2–3	15
34:4	80
34:8–10	205
34:9–10	8, 15, 21, 80, 82, 149, 203, 204
34:10	85, 91, 92
34:11–12	95, 96
35:10	177
37:16	179
37:27	38
38:18	51
40:6–8	38, 249
40:10	179
40:22	179
42:1–3	146
43:18	177
44:3	139, 146
44:6	94, 178
47:14–15	16, 68
48:12–16	229
48:12	94, 178, 229
48:13	229
48:16	229
49:10	174
50:9	16, 208
50:11	8, 14, 17, 39, 68, 203
51:6–8	18, 208
51:8	8, 16
51:12	18, 38, 208, 249
52–53	236
52:6–7	228
52:6	229
52:7	229
52:10	228, 229
52:13	228, 229
52:14–15	230
52:15	209
53	235, 239, 242
53:1–3	230
53:1	230, 232
53:4–6	230, 231
53:4	231, 233, 239
53:6	231, 233
53:7–9	231
53:7	69, 231, 243
53:8	231
53:9	239
53:10–12	232
53:10–11	242
53:10	232, 233
53:12	232, 243
55:1	94, 178
57:1–2	235
57:15–19	163, 164
57:16–21	182
59:21	139, 146
60:1	175
60:2	175
60:19	175
62:11	179
64–66	118, 119, 137
64:1–2	64, 86, 118, 136, 140, 168
64:4	206, 209
65:9–10	39
65:11–15	17, 21, 39, 197
65:11	39
65:12–15	136
65:12	19
65:13–15	18
65:15	244
65:17—66:24	44, 45
65:17–25	20, 247
65:17–19	86, 177, 197
65:17–18	118, 168
65:17	64, 70, 140
65:19	177
65:25	118, 119, 222
66	2, 21, 36, 129, 135
66:1–6	21
66:1–2	119
66:3–5	135

Isaiah (cont.)

66:3–4	120
66:6	136, 198
66:10	176
66:14–18	21
66:14–16	18, 44, 63, 119, 197, 198
66:14	20, 64, 119
66:15–16	64
66:15	19, 62, 86
66:16	18, 64, 136
66:17	120, 135
66:18–21	134
66:19–21	120
66:19–20	120
66:20	120
66:21	120
66:22–24	8, 20, 45, 120, 176, 182, 183, 208
66:22–23	197
66:22	20, 64, 70, 86, 247
66:24	1, 2, 19–21, 44–46, 92, 130, 197, 202

Jeremiah

1:4–15	206
2:13	94, 174, 178
3:17	173
4:4	21, 68
4:29	169
5:9	123
5:29	123
7:20	22, 68
7:31–32	36
10:25	62
11:16	35
11:19	69
15:2	82, 83
15:14	22, 68
15:16	109
17:4	22
17:12–13	173, 174
17:27	7, 23, 68
19:6	36
19:11–14	36
21:10–14	7
21:10	23
21:12–14	23
23:5–6	146
23:6	179, 180
24:9	244
25:8–38	127
25:18	244
26:6	244
29:18–22	244
32:29	23, 24
33:15–16	179, 180
34:2	23, 24
34:22	24
37:8	24
37:10	24
38:17–18	24
38:23	24
39:8	24
42:18	244
43:11	82
43:12–13	25
44:8	244
44:12	244
44:22	244
48:45	25
49:2	25
49:13	244
49:27	25
49:39	146
50:32	26
51:40	69
51:58	26
52:12–13	26
52:13	24

Lamentations

4:11	26

Ezekiel

1:5–25	179
3:3	109
8	29
8:1–19	110
10:1–22	179
15:1–8	8, 26, 27
18:5–9	223, 224
18:23	70
20:47–68	68
20:47	27
21:1–5	27
21:28	27, 28
21:31–32	27, 28
21:31	28
21:32	28
26:19	93, 172
26:20	51
27	84
28	50, 110
28:1–19	50
28:8–10	50
28:16–18	50
28:18–19	28
28:18	28
28:19	28
30:14–16	29, 203
31:15	172
31:16	51
32:7	138
32:17–32	49
32:18	51
32:25–26	166
332:23–30	51
33:11	70
34:23	174
35:1—36:7	126
36–37	125
36	124, 125
36:8—37:28	126
36:10	125
36:11	125
36:17–19	125
36:17	125
36:20–23	125
36:21–22	125
36:21	125
36:22	125, 223
36:23–32	223
36:25	126
36:26–27	125
36:27	125
36:31	125
36:32	125
36:33–38	124, 125
36:33	125, 126
36:36–38	125
36:36	125
36:37	125
37–39	137
37	124, 125, 127, 136, 146
37:1–10	121
37:1–2	121
37:7–10	121

Scripture Index

Ezekiel (cont.)

Reference	Pages
37:11–14	121, 122
37:11	125
37:12	121
37:13–14	124
37:14	121, 125, 139, 146
37:15–28	121, 180
37:16	125
37:21–28	29, 30
37:22	125
37:23	126
37:24–28	122, 123, 168
37:24	91
37:26–27	140
37:27	177, 180
38–39	122, 126
38	89, 90, 122, 124–27, 162, 165
38:1–23	197
38:1–16	126
38:1–2	165
38:2–3	166
38:2	90
38:8–16	123
38:8–14	126
38:8–12	166
38:8	29, 30, 91, 123, 127
38:10	90, 123, 124
38:14	127
38:17–23	124
38:17	126
38:18–19	166
38:19–20	136
38:21—39:21	136
38:21–22	29
38:22	30, 136
38:23	124
39	122, 124–26, 132
39:1–20	124
39:3–6	29
39:4	30
39:5	125
39:7	125
39:12	125, 126
39:14	126
39:16	126
39:21–29	125
39:21	125
39:22	125
39:23–24	125
39:23	125
39:24	125
39:25	125
39:26–29	125
39:26	125
39:28	125
39:29	125, 139, 146
40–48	126, 168
43:8	222
47:1–12	175
47:9	175

Daniel

Reference	Pages
2	137
2:1–45	128
2:34–35	128
2:35	128
2:44–45	136
2:44	128
7	51, 55, 60, 88, 92, 136, 137, 146, 158, 160, 161, 171, 172
7:1–27	61
7:1–8	129
7:9–17	128, 129
7:9–14	30, 31, 62
7:9–10	61, 129, 130, 161
7:10	62, 88, 130, 172
7:11–12	161
7:11	31, 61, 62, 79, 88, 136
7:13–14	55, 62, 63, 92, 172
7:13	61, 63, 237
7:14	154
7:17	31
7:18	129, 136, 145, 161, 162, 168
7:21–22	63
7:21	62, 80, 129, 136, 161
7:22	129, 136, 172
7:23–26	61
7:23	31, 88
7:25–27	63
7:25	80, 129, 136, 161
7:26–28	55
7:26–27	63, 92, 129, 154, 161, 172
7:26	79, 136
7:27	129, 136, 168
10:1—11:1	49
12	136, 137, 148
12:1–3	129, 130
12:1	130, 136, 144, 151
12:2	130, 137, 151, 167
12:3	130, 131, 142
12:7	136
12:11–12	161
12:13	129, 130, 137, 141, 145, 151

Hosea

Reference	Pages
3:5	146
6:2	122
10:8	169
11:9	222, 223

Joel

Reference	Pages
2:1–11	127
2:18–20	127
2:28–29	139, 146
2:30–32	127
3	137
3:1–3	131, 132
3:1–2	132
3:2	132
3:9–21	127
3:9–14	136
3:11–21	131, 132
3:11	132
3:15–16	132, 136
3:17	132
3:18	132
3:20	132

Amos

Reference	Pages
5:6	31, 68

Obadiah

Reference	Pages
18	31, 32

Micah

Reference	Pages
2:12–13	174
4:1–8	132, 133, 137, 146

Micah (*cont.*)

4:1–3	133
4:1–2	133
4:1	146
4:3–4	133
4:4	133
4:6–7	133
4:7–8	133
4:8–13	127
4:11–13	136
5:1–5	132, 133
5:7–15	133, 136
6:8	224

Habakkuk

1:6	89, 162, 167
1:12	222

Zephaniah

1:2–3	136
1:14—2:3	137
1:14–18	134, 136
1:18	32, 67
2:1–3	134
2:4—3:8	134
3:6	136
3:8	32, 67, 134, 136
3:9–20	134, 137
3:9–10	134
3:11–13	135
3:14–19	135, 136
3:15	136
3:17	176
3:18	134, 136, 168
3:19–20	136

Haggai

2:6	67

Zechariah

2:10–11	177
2:10	180
3:10	133
12:9—13:1	237
12:10	139, 146, 196, 237
12:12	237
12:14	237
14:1–21	136
14:5	191

Malachi

4:1–3	32, 33, 208

APOCRYPHA

Sirach

1:3	167

~

NEW TESTAMENT

Matthew

3:2	139
3:7–12	139
3:8–12	35, 65, 208
3:10	36
3:11–17	140
3:11	139, 140
3:12	139
3:17	140
4:1–11	49
4:17	139
4:23–24	229
5:3–7	138
5:17–30	153
5:21–26	56, 60, 193, 197
5:21–22	36, 45, 197
5:21	36
5:22	36
5:23–26	56, 96, 149, 152, 202, 203
5:23	58
5:25–26	45
5:29–30	1, 45, 46, 197, 198
5:35	138
5:38–41	45
6:12	171
6:14–15	58
6:19–34	216
6:30	33, 38
7:1–2	58, 153
7:9–10	45
7:13–23	143
7:15–19	35
7:19	8, 37, 65, 197
7:21–27	153
8:10–11	117
8:11–12	40, 41, 197
8:11	140
8:29	194
9:18–26	140, 164, 184
9:35	229
10:7	139
10:28	1, 37, 197, 202
10:34	138
10:37–38	45
10:38–39	240
11:1–6	140
11:21–24	45, 131
11:23	53, 193, 197
11:41–42	45
12:18	138
12:21	138
12:32–37	153
12:32	141
12:41–42	150–54
12:41	151
12:42	151
13:24–30	37, 38, 197
13:24	65
13:30	142
13:31–33	143
13:36–43	37, 38, 65, 197
13:38–49	141, 142
13:38	142
13:40–43	153
13:40–42	196
13:41	39, 142
13:42	38, 52, 206
13:47–50	43, 44, 197
13:50	8, 206
15:41–42	205
16:24	161, 240
16:27	153
18:6–9	45, 197
18:7	39
18:8–9	2, 46, 96, 198, 200, 201
18:8	45, 73, 199, 205
18:9	45
18:18	200
18:21–35	57, 58, 60, 149, 193, 197, 203
18:26	82
18:34–35	202
18:34	77

Scripture Index

Matthew (cont.)

19:5	52
19:22	220
19:28–29	71
19:28	138, 172, 197, 247
22:1–14	41, 143, 197
22:13	77
22:14	165, 181
22:20–22	45
22:22–30	155
22:23–33	37
22:30–31	138
22:30	155
23:20–22	45
24–25	143
24:3	143
24:7–8	138
24:13	153
24:14	143, 229
24:21–22	51, 161
24:22	219
24:23	196
24:29–31	51, 142, 196
24:29	138
24:30	237
24:31	138
24:35	138
24:36—25:30	143
24:36–44	64
24:43–44	70
24:45–51	42, 153, 197
25	51, 53, 58, 77, 78, 193, 194
25:14–30	42, 43, 153, 197
25:28–30	43
25:31–46	47, 48, 55, 59, 60, 77, 96, 149, 153, 154, 192, 193, 197, 199, 203, 221
25:31	52, 138
25:32	51
25:34	52, 53
25:41	46–48, 51–54, 58, 64, 73, 77–79, 193, 196, 199, 200, 205
25:46	47, 48, 52–55, 58, 64, 77–79, 193, 196, 205
26:28	140
26:64	237
27:35	99
27:39	245
27:46	99
27:50–53	140, 164
27:51–53	184
27:52	138
27:53	138
28:19–20	138

Mark

1:7–11	140
1:8	140
1:11	140
1:15	139, 229
4:30–32	143
5:21–43	184
5:21–42	164
5:22–42	140
8:34	161, 240
9:4	46
9:42–50	45, 197
9:42–48	36
9:43–48	44, 46, 47, 198, 208
9:43	2
9:44	47
9:47–48	36
9:48	47, 198
10:18	200
10:22	220
10:29–30	144
11:25	58
12:18–27	37, 155
12:25–26	138
12:25	155
13	63
13:19–20	161
13:26	237
13:27	138
14:24	140
14:57	151
14:62	237
14:65	52
15:24	99
15:26	245
15:34	99

Luke

1:32	138
1:33	73
2:11	138
2:32	138
3:7–9	35, 36, 65, 139, 208
3:15–16	140
3:16–17	139
3:16	140
3:17	139
3:21–22	140
3:21	224
3:22	140
4:1–15	49
4:43	229
5:9	44
5:29–30	44
6:20–25	138
6:27–29	45
6:37	58, 153
7:11–17	140, 164, 184
7:18–23	140
8:1	229
8:31	194, 196
8:40–56	140, 164, 184
9:2	229
9:23	161, 240
9:60	229
10:11–15	197
10:11	52, 139
10:13–15	131
10:15	53, 193, 197
10:18	50
11:4	171
11:20	139
11:25–26	138
11:31–32	150–53
11:31	138
11:32	151
11:33	138
12:4–5	37, 197
12:39–40	70
12:41–46	42, 197
12:46	42
12:51	138
12:57–59	56–58, 60, 149, 152, 193, 197, 202, 203
13:18–21	143

Scripture Index

Luke (*cont.*)

13:23–30	143
13:24–28	197
13:28–30	117
13:28	19, 40
13:29	140
13:47	44
14:13–14	153
14:14	138, 155, 184, 186
14:15–24	41
14:24	41
14:27	240
15:11–32	212
15:15	52
16:19–31	52, 53, 59, 60, 143, 149, 172, 185, 193, 203
16:22–26	77
16:22–25	198
16:22–23	195
16:23	185
16:24	194, 196, 205
16:27–28	52
16:27	185
16:31	138, 185
17:1	39
17:26–28	71
17:28–30	61, 70
18:1–8	138
18:7	82
18:8–9	44
18:9–14	215
18:30	144
19:11–27	42, 197
19:11–12	139
19:24–26	43
19:27	138
20:27–40	37, 155
20:34–36	144, 155, 156, 196
20:34–35	170, 193, 196
20:34	93
20:35–36	138
20:35	155, 187, 199
20:37–38	54
20:38	156
21:11	138
21:19	81
21:24	28, 138
21:27	237
22:20	140
22:69	237
23:34	99
23:35	99
23:46	235
23:48	237

John

1:1–17	229
1:1–4	233
1:10–11	236
1:26–34	140
1:33	139
4:21	138
5:21	138, 164, 185, 186
5:22–29	153
5:24–25	185, 186
5:24	156
5:25	164, 184, 186
5:28–29	153, 164, 185–87, 202
5:29	52, 60, 138, 183
6:39–40	138, 185, 186
6:39	186
6:40	186
6:44	138, 185, 186
6:54	138, 185, 186
7:37	94, 178
9:24	78
10:16	138
11	140
11:1–45	164, 184
11:24	138, 186
11:52	138
12:25–26	153
12:47–50	187
14:18	240
14:25	240
15:6	62, 197
19:24	99
19:28	99

Acts

1:1–8	140
1:5	139
2:1–21	140
2:17	68, 69
2:30	138
2:36	138
4:21	52
4:25–28	236, 237
4:27–28	236
5:13	52
8:29	52
9:1–3	188
9:26	52
9:36–43	184
10–11	147
10:1—11:18	140
10:28	52
10:34	224
10:42	170, 171
11:18	138
17:28	212
17:31	138, 171
17:34	52
19:23–41	188
20:30–38	228
21:39	189
23:6	188
24:15	52, 60, 138, 157, 187–90
24:17	189
24:20–21	188
25:18–19	189
26:4–8	189
28:20	189
28:28	138
28:31	229
30:53	228

Romans

1:4	157
1:25	73
2:1–16	171
2:1–13	153
2:4–10	154
2:4	82
2:5	138
2:7	154
2:9	154
2:10	138
2:11–16	152
2:11	224
4:24	157
5:12—6:14	241
6:4	157
6:9	157
6:13	157

Scripture Index

Romans (cont.)

7:1–6	241
7:4	157
8:1–6	138
8:1–4	171
8:1–3	243
8:11	157
8:18–24	246, 247
8:18–23	138
8:18–22	218
8:19–23	217
8:38	49
9:5	73
9:22	82
10:7	157, 196
10:9	157
11:16	157
11:26	138
11:36	73
12:1	238
12:9	52
12:20	196
13:10	224
14:10	138
14:7–12	153
14:9–12	171
15:12	157
15:20	157
16:27	73, 145

1 Corinthians

2:6	147
2:7–8	145
2:9	81, 206, 209
3:17	222
4:4–5	153
5:5	64
6:3	49
6:16	52
10:1–12	153
10:11	145, 147
11:25	140
13:4	82
13:13	214
15	138, 208, 209
15:12	157, 158
15:20–24	157, 158
15:21–28	13
15:21–23	190
15:22–24	190
15:23	158, 186
15:24–26	183
15:24	183
15:36–38	209
15:42–43	209
15:50–55	196
15:50–53	142, 199
15:50–52	186
15:54–57	138

2 Corinthians

3:6	140
4:14	153, 190
5:7–10	153
5:8	172
5:9–10	153
5:10	171
5:14–20	241
5:21	242, 243
6:6	82
11:31	73

Galatians

1:1	157
1:4	145
1:5	73
3:10	243
3:13	243–45
3:19	228
4:25–26	138
5:14	224
5:19–21	153
5:22	82
6:7–8	153

Ephesians

1:1–2	50
1:13	140
1:20	157
1:21	145
2	140
2:11–22	138, 238
2:12–16	241
3:21	73
4:2	82
5:2	238, 242
5:14	157
6:9	224
6:12	49, 50

Philippians

3:10–11	157
3:10	240
3:11	138
3:8–20	127
3:20	145
4:3	144
4:20	73

Colossians

1:1	82
1:15–17	233
1:15	200
1:18	157
1:19–22	240, 246
1:20	138
1:21	214, 241
1:24	240
2:12	157
2:13–15	246
2:15	49, 50
3:12	82
3:25	224

1 Thessalonians

1:10	138, 157, 190
4:13—5:4	196
4:15–17	142
4:15	142
4:16	138, 190
5:1–3	64
5:2	70
5:3	64
5:4	70
5:12–18	186
5:14	82

2 Thessalonians

1:5–10	63, 138
1:6–7	62
1:6–10	138, 171
1:7–8	62
1:7–10	79
1:7	63
1:8	62
1:9	64

1 Timothy

1:17	73

1 Timothy (cont.)

3:10	82
4:10	146
6:9	64

2 Timothy

2:8	157
2:18	190
3:10	82
4:1	138, 153, 171
4:2	82
4:18	73

Titus

3:11–13	146

Hebrews

1:1–4	233
1:1–2	146
1:8	138
2:5	146
3:3–4	233
4:12	33
5:7–8	234, 235
5:7	156, 242
5:8–10	238
6:2	138, 190
6:4–8	65
6:4–6	65, 141
6:4	146
6:8–13	140
6:12	82
6:15	82
7:27	243
8:1	138
8:8–13	138
9:11–14	242
9:26	147
9:28	66, 243
10:1–22	140
10:8–10	243
10:11–22	138
10:14–16	243
10:23–31	66
10:27	66, 171, 194
10:36	81
11:19	138, 190
11:34	28
12:2–3	238
12:2	138
12:16–17	81
12:22	138
12:24	140
12:25–29	67, 208
12:26–28	67
12:27	67
13:8	73
13:11–14	162, 176
13:20	157
13:21	73
13:30	142
13:41–43	142
13:43	142

James

1:10–11	249
1:13–17	210, 211
2:1–13	224
3:1	153
3:2–6	67
3:5–6	68
3:5	68
3:6	68
4:14	249
5:1–5	68, 69, 208
5:2–3	8
5:2	69
5:3	69
5:5	69
5:7	82
5:10	82

1 Peter

1:3—2:12	140
1:3	157, 190
1:5	138
1:17	224
1:20	147
1:21	157
1:24	249
2:9–10	138
2:19–25	239
2:20	52
2:21	239
3:7–13	86
3:11–13	197
3:20	82
4:5	154, 171
4:11	73
4:12–13	240
5:8–9	50
5:11	73
5:13	83

2 Peter

1:8	71
1:19	33
2:3–12	71, 72
2:4–10	72
2:4	49, 72, 194–96
2:6	71, 95
2:9	52, 71, 194, 195
3:1–13	95
3:1–7	64
3:2–13	171
3:2	70
3:3–13	247
3:3–12	69, 70, 205
3:3	70
3:4	70
3:5–13	196
3:5–12	138
3:6–7	71
3:7	71
3:8–13	64
3:8	162
3:9	82
3:10–13	172
3:10	71
3:11–13	71
3:11	71
3:12	71
3:13	70, 138, 168, 170
3:15	82
3:16	2

1 John

1:8	201
2:15–17	214
4:7	212
4:8–10	238
4:8	210
4:16	210
4:19	212
5:18	201
5:19	221

Jude

3–4	73
5–7	72, 73, 77
5–23	95
5	73
6–7	195
6	49, 73, 77, 194, 196
7	73, 149, 194
11	95
13	73
14–15	138
14	191
20–22	73
25	73, 147

Revelation

1:1	76, 178, 195
1:5	157
1:6	73
1:7	196, 237
1:8	147, 169
1:9	81
1:10–19	76
1:16	77, 176
1:18	73, 159, 165
2:2	81
2:7	167
2:10–11	95
2:10	148
2:11	95
2:12	175
2:16	176
2:26–27	176
3:3	70, 180
3:4–5	180
3:5	144, 148
3:10	81
3:12	138, 167, 168, 179, 180
3:15–19	220
3:21	138, 175
4:2–3	174, 175
4:3	76
4:4	175
4:6–8	179
4:8	147, 169
4:9	73
4:10	73
5:1–8:5	171
5:1–10	171
5:5	76
5:6	76
5:8	76
5:9	76
5:10	168
5:13	73
6:9–11	148, 172
6:12–18	171
6:12–17	64, 138, 168, 169, 172, 178
6:12–14	80, 86
6:12	179
6:14	170
6:15–17	176
6:16	175
7:9–17	138, 175
7:12	73
7:15–17	111, 174
7:15	175
7:17	138, 180
9:1–2	196
9:3	167
10:6	73
9:14–15	49
11:2	175
11:7	167, 196, 200
11:15–19	138, 168, 170
11:15–18	147, 148, 161, 170
11:15–17	169
11:15	73, 138, 147, 168
11:18	148, 173, 176, 196, 221, 227, 247
11:19	179
12	50, 89, 90
12:1–17	116
12:1–14	50
12:3	89
12:5	176
12:6	90, 161
12:7–17	49
12:7–9	89, 196
12:7–8	160
12:9	89
12:10	50
12:12–17	89, 160
12:12	196
12:13	89
12:14	90, 161
12:17–18	89
12:17	196
13–19	160
13	79, 159
13:1–2	79
13:1	167, 200
13:3–4	83
13:3	87
13:4	87, 160
13:5–6	161
13:5	90
13:7–8	82, 158
13:7	79, 80, 83, 161
13:8–10	79
13:8	93
13:9–10	82
13:10	82
13:11–17	83
13:11	167, 200
13:14–15	87
13:15–17	79, 80
13:15	79
13:17	79
14	80
14:1–5	79
14:1	138
14:3	175
14:6–12	78–80, 203, 204
14:6–7	79
14:6	80
14:7	138
14:8–11	85
14:8	83
14:9–12	82, 149
14:9–11	79, 81, 82, 93, 94
14:10–11	79, 205
14:11–12	82, 96
14:11	73, 81, 95, 96
14:12	81, 82
14:13	81, 82, 235
15:1–5	79
15:1–4	172
15:7	73
15:15	175
16:12–16	87
16:12–14	86
16:13	79
16:15	70
16:17–21	168
16:17	175

Scripture Index

Revelation (*cont.*)
- 16:19–21   86
- 16:19   83
- 16:20   170, 179
- 17–18   221
- 17:1–18   79
- 17:3   83
- 17:5   83
- 17:7   83
- 17:8   83, 144, 167, 196, 200
- 17:12–13   86
- 17:15–16   86
- 17:16   83, 88
- 17:18   83
- 18   28, 78
- 18:2   83
- 18:5   52
- 18:7–8   85
- 18:8–21   83–85
- 18:8–10   79
- 18:8   85, 88
- 18:9   85
- 18:10   83, 85
- 18:11–17   85
- 18:14   85
- 18:17–19   85
- 18:17   85
- 18:18   85
- 18:19   85
- 18:20–21   85
- 18:21   83, 85
- 19–21   156
- 19–20   148
- 19   50, 91
- 19:1–8   88
- 19:1–3   79
- 19:1–2   176
- 19:3   73, 80, 85, 86, 88, 91, 95, 96, 149, 205
- 19:6–14   180
- 19:6–9   180
- 19:10   75
- 19:11—20:10   89, 167
- 19:11—20:6   170
- 19:11–21   138, 158, 171, 176
- 19:11–18   199
- 19:11   87, 170
- 19:13   87
- 19:15   77, 87
- 19:17—20:6   117
- 19:17–21   10
- 19:17–18   196
- 19:19–21   52, 86, 114, 158
- 19:19–20   199
- 19:19   87, 159
- 19:20   79, 86, 88, 161
- 19:21—20:6   91
- 19:21   159, 171, 173, 196, 199
- 20   3, 55, 77, 78, 127, 160, 167, 193, 195, 200, 204
- 20:1–3   49, 51, 77, 90, 110, 116, 158, 159, 196
- 20:1–15   60
- 20:1–10   73, 88, 89, 130, 159, 165, 199
- 20:2–3   89
- 20:2   89
- 20:3   162
- 20:4–6   77, 89, 91, 129, 138, 148, 160, 161, 165, 171, 172, 176, 187, 196, 197
- 20:4–10   178
- 20:4   161
- 20:5   161, 162, 173, 199
- 20:7–10   3, 49, 90, 91, 116, 117, 120, 138, 159, 162, 164, 165, 167, 168, 171, 173, 176, 181, 194, 197, 199, 205
- 20:7   89, 91, 162
- 20:8–10   90
- 20:8   90, 165, 167
- 20:9–10   89, 168
- 20:9   89–91, 166, 167, 175, 176, 181, 204
- 20:10   73, 79, 87, 91–96, 149, 167, 168, 171, 199, 203–205
- 20:11–15   89, 92, 168, 171, 172, 176, 196
- 20:11–12   177
- 20:11   170, 172, 173, 175, 176, 179
- 20:12–13   173
- 20:12   93, 144, 172, 196
- 20:13–15   52, 77, 93, 175–77, 196, 197
- 20:13   93, 165, 167, 173, 176
- 20:14   93, 159
- 20:15   144, 178
- 21:1—22:5   138, 168
- 21   168, 178
- 21:1–8   138, 172, 176–78
- 21:1–7   140, 197
- 21:1–5   64, 247
- 21:1–4   86, 138
- 21:1–3   79
- 21:1   86, 178
- 21:2–6   174
- 21:2   175
- 21:3–4   111, 180
- 21:3   76, 175
- 21:4   93
- 21:6–8   94
- 21:6–7   95
- 21:8   95
- 21:10–11   175
- 21:10   175
- 21:11   76
- 21:15–16   76
- 21:16   195
- 21:18   76
- 21:22–23   138
- 21:22   76
- 21:23   76, 175
- 21:24–27   138
- 21:24–25   112
- 21:27   144, 176
- 22   5, 168
- 22:1–5   167, 197, 247
- 22:1   174, 175
- 22:3–5   138, 168
- 22:3   175
- 22:5   73, 162, 168
- 22:8–9   75, 178
- 22:12–13   179
- 22:12   153
- 22:18   75
- 22:19   175

Other Works Cited

PSEUDEPIGRAPHA

1 Enoch
1:9 — 191

2 Baruch
29–30 — 144

4 Ezra
7:26–43 — 144
8:52–54 — 144

4 Maccabees
12:12 — 54
7:19 — 54

Life of Adam and Eve
29:7–10 — 144
48:1–3 — 144
51:1–2 — 144

TALMUD

b. Sanh. 92B — 121

CLASSICAL

Aeschylus
Prometheus Bound — 20

Hesiod
Theogony
507–616 — 20

CHRISTIAN WORKS

Didache
16:4–8 — 190, 191

Commodianus
In Favor of Christian Discipline against the Gods of the Heathens
43–46 — 190

Eusebius
Ecclesiastical History
5.29.2 — 190
5.32.1 — 190
5.35.1 — 190
5.63.3 — 190

Hippolytus of Rome
Scholion on Daniel
7:17 — 190
7:22 — 190
10:16 — 190
12:2 — 190

Hippolytus of Rome
Commentary on Daniel
4 — 190

Jerome
Commentary on Exodus
36 — 190

Lactantius
Divine Institutes
7:24–26 — 190

Milton
Paradise Lost
1 — 50

Tertullian
Against Marcion
1 — 190

Victorinus of Pettau
Commentary on Revelation
20:1–15 — 190

www.ingramcontent.com/pod-product-compliance
Lightning Source LLC
Chambersburg PA
CBHW080534170426
43195CB00016B/2556